T0255867

Springer Series on Cultural Computing

Editor-in-Chief
Ernest Edmonds, University of Technology, Sydney, Australia

Editorial Board
Frieder Nake, University of Bremen, Bremen, Germany
Nick Bryan-Kinns, Queen Mary University of London, London, UK
Linda Candy, University of Technology, Sydney, Australia
David England, Liverpool John Moores University, Liverpool, UK
Andrew Hugill, De Montfort University, Leicester, UK
Shigeki Amitani, Adobe Systems Inc., Tokyo, Japan
Doug Riecken, Columbia University, New York, USA
Jonas Lowgren, Linköping University, Norrköping, Sweden

More information about this series at http://www.springer.com/series/10481

Julianne Nyhan • Andrew Flinn

Computation and the Humanities

Towards an Oral History of Digital Humanities

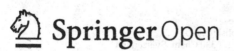

Julianne Nyhan
Department of Information Studies
University College London (UCL)
London, UK

Andrew Flinn
Department of Information Studies
University College London (UCL)
London, UK

ISSN 2195-9056   ISSN 2195-9064   (electronic)
Springer Series on Cultural Computing
ISBN 978-3-319-79297-2   ISBN 978-3-319-20170-2   (eBook)
DOI 10.1007/978-3-319-20170-2

© The Editor(s) (if applicable) and the Author(s) 2016. This book is published open access.
Softcover reprint of the hardcover 1st edition 2016
Open Access This book is distributed under the terms of the Creative Commons Attribution-Noncommercial 2.5 License (http://creativecommons.org/licenses/cc by-nc/2.5/) which permits any noncommercial use, distribution, and reproduction in any medium, provided the original author(s) and source are credited.
The images or other third party material in this book are included in the work's Creative Commons license, unless indicated otherwise in the credit line; if such material is not included in the work's Creative Commons license and the respective action is not permitted by statutory regulation, users will need to obtain permission from the license holder to duplicate, adapt or reproduce the material.
This work is subject to copyright. All commercial rights are reserved by the Publisher, whether the whole or part of the material is concerned, specifically the rights of translation, reprinting, reuse of illustrations, recitation, broadcasting, reproduction on microfilms or in any other physical way, and transmission or information storage and retrieval, electronic adaptation, computer software, or by similar or dissimilar methodology now known or hereafter developed.
The use of general descriptive names, registered names, trademarks, service marks, etc. in this publication does not imply, even in the absence of a specific statement, that such names are exempt from the relevant protective laws and regulations and therefore free for general use.
The publisher, the authors and the editors are safe to assume that the advice and information in this book are believed to be true and accurate at the date of publication. Neither the publisher nor the authors or the editors give a warranty, express or implied, with respect to the material contained herein or for any errors or omissions that may have been made.

Printed on acid-free paper

This Springer imprint is published by Springer Nature
The registered company is Springer International Publishing AG
The registered company address is: Gewerbestrasse 11, 6330 Cham, Switzerland

*I ndil-chuimhne ar Barry O Flynn
(1974–2001) agus ar Patrick Flinn
(1927–2016)*

Acknowledgements

We are grateful to the following organisations for funding the research that under-pinned this book: Das Historisch-Kulturwissenschaftliche Forschungszentrum (HKFZ), University of Trier, Germany; the European Association for Digital Humanities (EADH); the UCL Centre for Digital Humanities (UCLDH); and the Department of Information Studies, UCL.

UCL's open access office generously provided the funding that has enabled the book to be published under an open access licence.

Thank you also to Helen Desmond of Springer UK for her expertise and seem-ingly endless reserves of patience. Our Research Assistant, Jessica Salmon, made the initial transcriptions of most of the interviews included in this book. She did this with her characteristic conscientiousness, care and good humour and we are very grateful to her. When there was a short break in our funding John Nyhan was gener-ous enough to humour his daughter's selfless attempts to find him a retirement proj-ect. He valiantly transcribed two interviews before more funding, and his freedom, was restored. Thank you also to him and Eileen Nyhan for stepping in on babysit-ting duties and allowing some of the interviews that were held outside of the UK to take place.

We are grateful to the numerous members of the Digital Humanities community (writ large) who have agreed to be interviewed during the course of this research. A selection of those interviews are contained in this book; full details of all those whom we interviewed are available on our project webpages: http://hiddenhistories. omeka.net/interviews. Thank you for your time, generosity, openness and the care you showed when responding to the volley of interview transcripts that were, and in some cases continue to be, sent your way.

A number of colleagues have encouraged and supported this work in various ways. Joseph Raben, who died on 18 January 2015, aged 90, sent encouragement, documentation, comments and corrections. He made a pivotal contribution to devel-opment of Digital Humanities and it is fitting that he is so present in this book even though it was not possible for us to interview him. Roy Wisbey kindly shared other-wise inaccessible documents related to the founding of the ALLC. Helen Agüera shared useful and otherwise difficult to access documents with us. Wilhelm Ott and

Susan Hockey both allowed Nyhan to spend time perusing their personal archives and libraries. Marco Passarotti gave Nyhan much assistance during her visit to the archive of Fr Roberto Busa S.J. in Università Cattolica del Sacro Cuore, Milan. As ever, Melissa Terras has not only been a brilliant friend and colleague but also a source of much inspiration. Willard McCarty encouraged this work in all sorts of ways, from sending information about useful publications, acting as a sounding board for early plans about the shape this book might take and carrying out, on our behalf, the interview with Hugh Craig and John Burrows when we could not make it to Australia. Steve Jones has been very kind with his time and expertise and gener-ously shared drafts of work in progress. Geoffrey Rockwell shared drafts of work in progress, details of connections he has made with those who worked in DH in its earliest stages and copies of sources that are otherwise difficult, if not impossible to access. He has given tremendous and much appreciated help. Like that of Jones and McCarty, Rockwell's work on the history of DH has been crucially important for us. Thank you also to James Cronin, Claudine Moulin, Ulrich Tiedau and the many colleagues and friends with whom we have had helpful discussions about this work.

Most of all, thank you to our families without whom none of this would be pos-sible. Finally a special mention to Patrick Flinn, beloved father, who passed away just as this book was being completed.

Contents

Chapter 1
Introduction

Abstract This chapter begins with an introduction to Digital Humanities (DH) and outlines its development since c.1949. It demonstrates that the application of computing to cultural heritage has been ongoing for some 70 years yet the histories of DH have, until recently, remained mostly unwritten. After exploring some of the particular difficulties that attend any attempt to write such histories the approach that we have taken in this book is explained in detail. We close by asking why histories of DH are needed and essential to undertake.

Introduction to Digital Humanities

What is/are the Digital Humanities (DH)? This is a question of central and long standing debate between those who work within (and sometimes without) this protean and fast-moving field. Though the difficulties of defining DH will be discussed below, here we can begin by stating that it takes place at the intersection of computing and cultural heritage. It aims to transform how the artefacts (such as manuscripts) and the phenomena (such as attitudes) that the Humanities study can be encountered, transmitted, questioned, interpreted, problematized and imagined. In doing so it tends to differentiate itself from now routine uses of computing in research and teaching, for example, email and word processing.

DH is sometimes portrayed as a recent development. Kirsch, for example, admonished Humanities scholars to avoid the 'nascent' field lest they 'wake up one morning to find that they have sold their birth right for a mess of apps' (2014). However, its derivation is usually ascribed to Fr Roberto Busa S.J. (cf. Vanhoutte 2013; Rockwell 2007). Around 1949, Busa, in collaboration with IBM, began preparatory work for an *index variorum* (or concordance) of some 11 million words of medieval Latin in the works of St Thomas Aquinas and related authors (Busa 1980). In the intervening years the field has gone under many names, including Humanist Informatics, Literary and Linguistic computing and (more commonly) Humanities Computing. Its name changed to DH c.2006 (Kirschenbaum 2010) and

© The Author(s) 2016
J. Nyhan, A. Flinn, *Computation and the Humanities*, Springer Series on
Cultural Computing, DOI 10.1007/978-3-319-20170-2_1

1

it has mostly used this name since then.[1] Indeed, it is now usual to use this newer name to refer to the work of the field since c.1949 and this is a convention that will be used throughout this book. Nevertheless, distinctions between Humanities Computing (i.e. the period from c.1949 to 2006, sometimes also including an incunabular phase, 'when computing was still a curiosity and business applications didn't yet dominate the public discourse' (Rockwell et al. 2011, p. 207)) and DH (i.e. post 2006) are to be found.[2] Thus, for the purposes of giving an outline of the development of the field from its beginnings to the present day, a distinction between these two phases will now be made (and the more general term DH will then be reverted to except when a distinction between DH and Humanities Computing is necessary for clarity).

Humanities Computing (c.1949–2006)

As is the case in the wider Humanities, the principal object of Humanities Computing research was text. The disciplines that were among the earliest to take up computing included Classics, which worked with large quantities of textual information (Brunner 1993) and sub-fields like Literary Studies, which was already pursuing quantitative methods. Today, quantitative approaches to the analysis of literature are sometimes portrayed as DH-led innovations, yet Literary Studies was pursuing such approaches to problems like authorship attribution and stylistic analysis before the advent of computing (Raben 1991, p. 342). All the same, in the editorial published in the inaugural issue of *Computers and the Humanities* (CHum), the field's first journal, Raben had felt it necessary to state that 'We need never be hypnotized by the computer's capacity to count into thinking that once we have counted things we understand them. The two articles in this inaugural number concur in stressing the primacy of humanistic imagination in all our actions' (1966, p. 2).

Vanhoutte has sketched the earlier connections between Humanities Computing and Machine Translation and the seminal contributions of Andrew Booth (Vanhoutte 2013, p. 122–5). Concordances and frequency lists were typical outputs of Humanities Computing during this period and essential pillars of Machine Translation processes. 1966 brought the publication of the ALPAC report 'Languages and Machines: Computers in Translation and Linguistics', which was highly critical of research done

---

[1] Of course, the transition was not instantaneous. Rockwell and Sinclair's (forthcoming) text analysis of the Humanist corpus showed that "[w]hile we certainly found 'DH' taking off in 2004–2005, we were surprised that 'Humanities Computing' continued to be a popular phrase".

[2] For the sake of simplicity the transition from Humanities Computing to DH is here presented in chronological terms. However, factors other than chronology are relevant to a fuller discussion of this process. Svennson (2009) has explored the 'discursive shift' from Humanities Computing to DH and, in a subsequent article argued that 'the epistemic commitments and conventions of [Humanities Computing] cannot easily be subsumed in another type of digital humanities' (2010); Wang and Inaba (2009) examined the contours of DH from a bibliometric perspective, observing the shift in nomenclature from Humanities Computing and concluding that DH showed no distinct sub-fields as such and could still be viewed as an expanding discipline.

in Computational Linguistics and Machine Translation. As a result 'Computational Linguistics embraced the symbolic approach and abandoned statistical analysis which has been at the heart of Humanities Computing' (Vanhoutte 2013, p. 128).

Other typical research outputs included computer-assisted lexicographical studies and authorship and stylistic studies. At this stage, 'much attention was paid to the limitations of the technology' (Hockey 2004, p. 5). Character-set representation, for example, proved especially difficult (Ibid). Challenges related to institutional and professional acceptance arose too. When assessing the importance of CHum, Raben later recalled that 'for many individuals the mere existence of this journal has meant the difference between academic success and failure. ... Few of these articles would have been appropriate for the conventional journals of their respective disciplines' (1991, p. 341).

From the early 1960s, steps were taken that would lead to the establishment of structures that are typical of academic disciplines more generally. A number of centres (an institutional formation that DH continues to adopt to this day)[3] were founded, for example, the Centre for Literary and Linguistic Computing by Roy Wisbey in Cambridge, UK, in 1963 (Hockey 2004). In the USA, IBM funded six conferences in 1964 and 1965 that were attended by 1200 scholars (Vanhoutte 2013, p. 129); in the UK, conferences were organized by Roy Wisbey and Michael Farringdon at the University of Cambridge in 1970 and in Edinburgh in 1972 (Hockey 2004, p. 7). The field's first scholarly associations, the Association for Literary and Linguistic Computing (hereafter ALLC, founded by Joan M. Smith and Roy Wisbey in 1973) and the Association for Computing in the Humanities (hereafter ACH, founded by Joseph Raben in 1978) were formed. After 1972, conferences became regular occurrences. In the UK symposia were held in:

> Cardiff (1974), Oxford (1976), Birmingham (1978), and Cambridge (1980) ... By the mid-1970s, another series of conferences began in North America, called the International Conference on Computing in the Humanities (ICCH), and were held in odd-numbered years to alternate with the British meetings. The British conference and the ALLC annual meetings gradually began to coalesce (Hockey 2004, p. 8).

Some teaching programmes were also founded, yet in contrast with the organisational advances made during these years, Hockey argues that from the 1970s to the mid 1980s 'there was little really new or exciting in terms of methodology and there was perhaps less critical appraisal of methodologies than might be desirable' (Idem, p. 10).

The liberating effect of the personal computer, which freed Humanists to pursue their projects independently of the computer centre, and the wider take up of email were decisive developments of the mid-1980s to early 1990s (Hockey 2004, p. 10). In 1987, the electronic seminar Humanist, which remains, to this day, an active and important venue for DH researchers was founded and initially run on Listserv (Nyhan 2016). In terms of the research agenda, the achievements of the Text Encoding Initiative (TEI) guidelines for making digital texts machine readable are often emphasised. TEI

---

[3] See, for example, 'CenterNet: an international network of DH Centres' http://www.dhcenternet. org/

is endorsed by agencies such as the National Endowment for the Humanities (NEH), the Arts and Humanities Research Council (AHRC) and the EU's Expert Advisory Group for Language engineering. It has also had an impact on developments outside of the strict domain of DH, for example, on aspects of the design of the meta-markup language XML, which has become the lingua franca of data exchange.

Hockey notes that a number of new academic programmes in Humanities Computing began to be introduced from the 1990s on 'although it is perhaps interesting to note that very few of these include the words 'Humanities Computing' in the program title' (on this see especially Rockwell 1999). She further emphasises the effect of internet, which brought new opportunities for the publication and dissemination of digital projects, albeit '[t]he emphasis was, however, very much on navigation rather than on the analysis, tools and techniques that had formed the major application areas within humanities computing in the past' (Hockey, p. 14). The significance of the internet (or more specifically, the web) has also been discussed by Rockwell and Sinclair based on their text analysis of the Humanist corpus from 1987 to 2008. They detected an increase in the frequency of words related to the web from 1996 on and argue that the term DH is 'not only an administrative term but one that signals a detectable change in the way electronic texts were used' (Rockwell and Sinclair forthcoming).

DH (c.2006–Present)

As of writing, DH continues to place significant emphasis on text as an object of research. An analysis of submissions to Digital Humanities 2016 (the field's main conference) based on author-assigned labels selected from a controlled vocabulary showed that text-related topics continue to dominate the research agenda. The most common tag was 'Text Analysis' followed by 'Historical Studies'; 'Data Mining/ Text Mining'; and 'Archives, Repositories, Sustainability and Preservation' (Weingart 2015). Yet, there are indications that the emphasis on text is waning, somewhat. An analysis of 135 DH syllabi from 2005 to 2011 found that DH curricula still focus on text but increasingly also video, audio, images, games and maps (Spiro 2011); indeed, 'Visualisation' was the fifth most common tag applied to DH2016 submissions (Weingart op. cit.).

In contrast to the affinity with text that DH and mainstream Humanities share, the institutional, infrastructural and socio-cultural conditions required to carry out their respective research agenda differ. The stereotype is that Humanities research is the preserve of the lone scholar who is based in a university, academy or institute. Lone scholars feature prominently in DH too, yet, anecdotally at least, the more common mode of knowledge production involves collaboration between shifting constellations of, among others, Computer Scientists, Engineers, Library, Museum and Information professionals, DH and Humanities scholars. Furthermore, with its emphasis on crowd sourcing and public engagement (as exemplified by projects like Transcribe Bentham which invites members of the public to transcribe the

manuscripts of the philosopher Jeremy Bentham (Causer and Wallace 2012)), DH
has seen a stronger participation of the non-specialist than has recently been the
norm in the Humanities. Nevertheless, the ethics of crowd sourcing is increasingly
questioned of late (Williamson 2016). In many cases, 'doing' DH necessitates the
purchasing of equipment, the hiring of professionals skilled in programming and
computing and the paying of costs associated with the hosting and longer-term
maintenance of digital resources. Thus, it tends to cost more than mainstream
Humanities research. It can also be seen as elitist because it is more often associated
with research intensive universities that have the resources to support it (Pannapacker
2013). This can have political implications:

> Put most starkly, academics on the left blame the crisis in the humanities on the
> corporatization of the academy and the neoliberal insistence that the value of higher
> education is chiefly economic. Conversely, it is precisely because of the apparently
> instrumental or utilitarian value of the Digital Humanities that university administrators,
> foundation officers, and government agencies are so eager to fund DH projects, create DH
> undergraduate and graduate programs, and hire DH faculty (Grusin 2013).

At present, the research agenda of DH may be categorised according to three
rubrics. The first is Janus-like in scope: it looks back at questions the Humanities
have long asked and attempts to ask them in new ways. It also looks forward to
identify new questions that could not otherwise be conceived of or explored. In both
cases it incorporates new or otherwise specialized and repurposed forms of
computing. *Das Woerterbuchnetz*, a digital network of German dictionaries of the
southwest language area (which takes in the dialects of areas such as Rhineland, the
Palatinate and the euro region of Saarland) exemplifies the former. The use of
Digital Humanities methods such as TEI has allowed the multiple dictionaries
included in the network to be simultaneously consulted and interrogated in new
ways in order to answer questions that are typically asked by Historians, Linguists
and Philologists:

> As the lemmatisation and hierarchical order of the headwords have different realisations in
> the print dictionaries, the lexical matching of the different linguistic systems of these
> conjoining regions can only be examined and compared when using digital versions with
> appropriated encodings and annotation standards. Such a system then enables complex
> enquiries, such as a full-text search through all the underlaying materials or specialised
> search for specific detailed information in the dictionaries enclosed in the system (Moulin
> and Nyhan 2014, p. 50).

An example of the latter is Lancashire's computational analysis (2010) of
changes in the use of vocabulary across 14 of the works of Agatha Christie. This led
to the argument that she suffered from dementia towards the end of her life and that
this was detectable in her writing.

The second rubric can be seen as an inversion of the first in that it seeks to question 'technology' (writ large) using the methods and approaches of the Humanities.
This remains an emerging area and disquiet about DH's lackluster progress in this
regard is often voiced. Martha (2007) and McPherson (2012), among others, have
written on the absence of questions about gender, race and sexuality in the research
agenda. Liu (2012) has addressed the absence of cultural criticism:

We digital humanists develop tools, data, metadata, and archives critically; and we have
also developed critical positions on the nature of such resources (e.g., disputing whether
computational methods are best used for truth-finding or, as Lisa Samuels and Jerome
McGann put it, "deformation"). But rarely do we extend the issues involved into the register
of society, economics, politics, or culture in the vintage manner, for instance, of the
Computer Professionals for Social Responsibility ... (Liu 2012).

The third rubric has a distinct activist mission in that it looks at structures, relationships and processes that are typical of the modern university (for example, publication practices, knowledge creation and divisions between certain categories of
staff and faculty) and questions how they may be reformed, re-explored or re-con-
ceptualised. For example, much attention is given to the evaluation of digital scholarship and how evaluative criteria developed for more traditional Humanities outputs
should be extended or changed when applied to it (see below). Prominent too is the
#alt-ac (or alternative academic) movement which focuses on careers other than
tenure-track professorships that are available to those with PhDs (Nowviskie 2013).

At the outermost level the observations above will, for the most part, hold true.
However, beyond such generalisations, definitions of DH are many, varied and
disputed (see, for example, Terras et al. 2013). Space will not allow us to discuss the
literature on this topic in any sustained way (yet the oral history interviews included
in this book present a number of different perspectives on this). Rather, we will now
discuss one aspect of this wider debate, namely 'is DH a discipline?', in order
to exemplify some of the many positions on this that exist while introducing an
issue that directly informed the boundaries of the research included in this book.

Is DH a Discipline?

Is DH a discipline? This question has been asked since at least 1999 when a seminar
called 'Is Humanities Computing an Academic Discipline?' was held over the
course of that academic year at the Institute for Advanced Technology in the
Humanities at the University of Virginia. It is interesting that the wider debate about
DH's disciplinary status often seems to assume that such designations are unprob-
lematic for other fields; however, this is not universally so (Taylor 1976). The debate
is also frequently conducted without reference to the fact that the wider definition of
the term discipline is itself contested. This is clearly brought out by Gascoigne et al.:

There are a number of analytical frameworks for classifying academic disciplines. ...
Others define disciplines by their characteristics: is the area taught in formal courses at
universities? Is it defined and recognised in academic journals? Do practitioners belong to
learned societies?
    A third school considers the notion of a discipline from accreditation perspective. Does
it have a name? What are its key concepts, and what models, paradigms and perspectives
influence the field? What methods are taught, and what is the relationship between theory
(academia) and practitioner? How did the history of the area evolve? .... So, clearly different
measures can be used to determine which fields of study can be considered "a discipline" in
their own right (2010).

The pragmatic response is that DH is a discipline because it has the characteristics of one. Its scholarly societies include the European Association for Digital Humanities (which grew out of ALLC) and the Alliance of Digital Humanities Organizations (ADHO). The latter was founded c.2002 and is an umbrella organisation that includes new and more established members such as the ACH and scholarly societies that represent the interests of DH communities beyond Europe and North America, namely in Japan, Canada and Australasia. The field's first journal CHum was founded in 1966. Today, its leading international journals include *DSH: Digital Scholarship in the Humanities* (founded by the ALLC in 1986 as *Literary and Linguistic Computing*) and *Digital Humanities Quarterly*, published by ADHO and founded in 2007 by Julia Flanders. Journals with a more regional focus also exist, for example, *Digital Studies / Le champ numérique*, founded in 1992 and published by the Société canadienne des humanités numériques. Numerous monographs, edited collections and the field's first Reader (M. Terras et al. 2013) have been published on the subject in the past years. DH's first major conference is usually said to have been held in Yorktown Heights in 1964 and sponsored by IBM (see Bessinger and Parrish 1965). Today, its major conference is held annually: more than 750 delegates attended Digital Humanities 2014 in Switzerland, where the acceptance rate was approximately 30%, roughly equivalent to some leading Computer Science conferences. At present c.200 DH centres exist worldwide (according to CentreNet); as mentioned above, in 2011, 134 different academic courses worldwide offering DH were identified and anecdotally it is clear that still more have since joined those ranks. It is more common for DH teaching programmes to be embedded in existing departments, for example, in University College London the DH MA/MSc is offered by the Department of Information Studies. Yet, a few autonomous DH departments do exist, for example, at King's College London. Jockers has set out the strides that the field has especially made of late in terms of moving from the margins to the mainstream. He writes, for example, that:

Academic jobs for candidates with expertise in the intersection between the humanities and technology are becoming more and more common, and a younger constituent of digital natives is quickly overtaking the aging elders of the tribe. ... Especially impressive has been the news from Canada. Almost all of the "G10" (that is, the top thirteen research institutions of Canada) have institutionalized digital humanities activities in the form of degrees ... programs ... or through institutes ... (Jockers 2013).

Notwithstanding such factors the recognition of DH as a discipline from an institutional perspective has sometimes proved problematic. There are various reasons for this, including reservations about the integrity of typical DH modes of knowledge production and research outputs. Though a number of reports have been published on approaches to the evaluation of Digital Scholarship (MLA Task Force for Evaluating Scholarship for Tenure and Promotion 2007; Presner 2012; Rockwell 2011; Nowviskie 2011; American Historical Association 2015), a more recent article points to ongoing issues. Kaltenbrunner describes the tensions that arose in a large, transnational Literary Studies project that attempted, largely unsuccessfully, to engage senior scholars in the collaborative and digitally-mediated aspects of the research:

... an important feature of a knowledge infrastructure is what its institutions consider
legitimate forms of output. In literary studies, this has traditionally been the monograph. A
record of monograph publication(s) often is an important factor in tenure and promotion
decisions. ... Infrastructure in literary studies foresees that the primary process of producing
a monograph be the work of a single individual. A decomposition of the research process
that leads up to the publication of the monograph is not foreseen (Kaltenbrunner 2015).

Many divergent views exist in relation to the 'accreditation perspective'
(mentioned above). For example, some of the field's key concepts, such as whether
one must be able to code in order to be a Digital Humanist, remain open (Ramsay
2013a) and, as we shall show its history remains largely unwritten. So, it is not
surprising that views on its disciplinary status differ even within DH. For Flanders,
DH is 'a critical investigation and practice of the methods of humanities research in
the digital medium' for Kirschenbaum it is a 'term of tactical convenience'
(Taporwiki 2011) and for Alvarado a 'social category, not an ontological one' (2012,
p. 50). For Ramsey:

Nowadays, the term can mean anything from media studies to electronic art, from data
mining to edutech, from scholarly editing to anarchic blogging, while inviting code junkies,
digital artists, standards wonks, transhumanists, game theorists, free culture advocates,
archivists, librarians, and edupunks under its capacious canvas (2013b).

Others, such as McCarty, reject the category of discipline altogether, arguing that
it is an 'interdiscipline', and that the metaphor of the Phoenician trader can be used
to understand the experience and role of its practitioners. He draws on Galison's
anthropological metaphor of a 'trading zone' to describe their canvas of operations
as 'moving from culture to culture, bringing techniques from one very different
application to another' (1999). Later he argued that in place of the traditional
disciplinary metaphors of 'Tree, Turf and Centre', DH might be described as an
'Archipelago', its most salient characteristics being the sense of helpful distancing
that it can create and the 'core anthropological event of encounter' that it evokes
(2006).

As will be explained further below, the many disagreements that exist about
whether it is a discipline (and thus about the coordinates of its boundary lines) have
directly influenced the across-the-board approach we have taken to identifying and
interviewing those who work(ed) in DH.

The State of the Art: Histories of DH

Though the application of computing to cultural heritage has been ongoing for some
70 years the histories of DH remain mostly unwritten. Indeed, with a few exceptions
(see, for example, Burton 1981a, b, c, 1982; Raben 1991; Adamo 1994) the history
of the field was mostly ignored until McCarty included an outline of it in his
contribution to the *Encyclopedia of Library and Information Science* (2003).

In 2004, Hockey published what remains the most substantial chronological
account of the history of the field. Her approach is to emphasise 'landmarks where

significant intellectual progress has been made or where work done within humanities computing has been adopted, developed or drawn on substantially within other disciplines' (p. 3). More recent work (for example, McCarty 2011; Nyhan et al. 2015; Vanhoutte 2013) has emphasized the need for histories that can, among other things, uncover, document and analyse the social, intellectual and creative processes that helped to shape research into computing in the Humanities from the 1950s until the present day. To do so, we believe that it is necessary to acknowledge multiple and contradictory narratives of foundation and discovery and to seek to explain these contradictions in a complex and nuanced fashioned that does not simply result in a flat and simplified narrative that is linear and uncontested (Nyhan et al. 2015). As McCarty has argued 'For computing to be *of* the humanities as well as *in* them, we must get beyond catalogues, chronologies, and heroic firsts to a genuine history. There are none yet' (McCarty 2008, p. 255).

Of late, a number of publications on particular aspects of the history of DH have begun to appear.[4] As well as signalling a growing interest in the history of the field something of a 'theoretical turn' away from chronology and evolutionary accounts of progress can be noticed in them. Indeed, the fields of Media Archaeology (Zielinski 2006) and Platform Studies (see Bogost and Monfort n.d.) are emerging as formative influences on what can arguably be viewed as the emerging sub-field of the history of DH. Recent, notable contributions include Jones's study of the first decade of Busa's research (1949–1959) that seeks to 'complicate the myth [of Busa as founding father of DH] with history' (Jones 2015). Sinclair and Rockwell's study of three forgotten text analysis technologies emphasise how 'the web-based text analysis tools that we use today are very different from the first tentative technologies developed by computing humanists' (Sinclair and Rockwell 2014, p. 257).

This book complements and extends this scholarship by its incorporation of oral history and the implications of this approach will be taken up at length in Chap. 2. In the context of the emerging literature on the history of DH our research is, to the best of our knowledge, the first of its kind to incorporate oral history in this way. We will now explain the wider research context that gave rise to this research.

As mentioned above, of late, there appears to be an increasing interest in the history of DH and a number of valuable contributions on it have appeared recently. Yet, many questions remain unanswered. For example, considering the military and commercial contexts of much early computing one wonders how and why Humanities scholars decided to include computing in their research from c.1950 onwards? Why did they believe that computing would advance the Humanities given how few precedents they could reference? Through what routes did they learn about Humanities research involving computers? What did the computer symbolise

---

[4]For example, McCarty's contributions on questions such as the intellectual connections between Busa and Turing (2013) and reflections on the purpose of writing the histories of DH (2011, 2014). Rockwell et al. (2011) have examined how computing was represented during the incunabular period of DH in the major Canadian newspapers the *Globe* and *Mail*. Gouglas et al. (2013) have examined the emergence of DH scholarly associations in Canada. Vanhoutte has published on the history of electronic editions (2010) and is at work on a literary history. Earhart (2015) has published a book-length study of the history of digital literary scholarship.

for them and what did the very act of using the computer in Humanities research symbolise? How did Humanities scholars find technical colleagues to work with? How did they access training in programming and computing? What infrastructures (such as computer centres) existed in their universities and as Humanities scholars how did they justify their access to them? From where did they receive funding? How was their work perceived and judged by colleagues who did not use computing in their research? Through what routes did they enter into the emerging field (or not enter, or make a swift exit, as the case may be)? As time went on, and a field with dedicated journals, societies and conferences began to emerge what parallels and divergences in ways of working and exchange and in the expression of creativity and novelty can be identified? And how have these issues helped to shape the field of DH as it currently stands?

Indeed, our understanding of the history of the field can, at the present time, be best described as a shattered mosaic of uncertain but intricate design. Our research concerns not only the excavation and preservation of the remaining pieces but it is equally an exploration of the many ways that they can feasibly be pieced together. Indeed, the rather piecemeal state of our current knowledge raises the question of why the history of DH been neglected both by those who work in the field and by the Humanities more generally? These question will now be addressed before a more detailed overview of the approach to the work presented here is given.

Why Do We Not Have Histories of DH?

Elsewhere we have discussed some of the myriad arguments that can be put forward in response to this question (Nyhan et al. 2015, p. 74–5) These include the range of attitudes (such as uncertainty, hostility, fear and dismissal) to the computer and its place in Humanities research, and how such attitudes may have influenced decisions about what counted as 'legitimate' topics of historical study. Indeed, the Humanist archives show that that such attitudes were common even within the DH community. For example, one finds a number of exchanges on the question of whether it would be legitimate to offer a PhD in the area:

> Is it academically legitimate for a PhD student to write one of his or her exams in the general area of "Computers and blank" where 'blank' is his or her field of study? ... There are also very good arguments against allowing such an exam. The computer does function, after all, more like a "tool" than a "method," and we seldom allow exams in "tools." We would be unlikely to allow an exam in lexicons, say, or synopses of the Gospels (Humanist 1:662).

In addition to issues of 'legitimacy' we have discussed the many difficulties that attend the writing of histories of DH (Nyhan et al. 2015, p. 74–75). Given the context of this book, and especially by way of explaining the approach that we have taken here, it is important to revisit this issue.

One crucial problem is the issue of archival sources. At the present time it is difficult to both locate and access much of the field's archival documentation. Two notable exceptions exist: the first is the archive of Busa, which was formally accessioned by the Università Cattolica del Sacro Cuore, Italy, in January 2014. Contained in the archive is a wealth of material, including his personal correspondence with Thomas J. Watson, the Chairman and CEO of IBM (1914–1956), among others, and artefacts such as the punched cards that the *Index Thomisticus* was first represented on. The second is the University of Alberta's archive on the 'Histories of Humanities Computing' that includes the papers of John B. Smith and the ACH newsletter collection. However, 'most of the materials are embargoed for reasons of copyright and privacy' (Gouglas et al. 2013). Beyond these archives, we are not aware of any others that are currently accessible. Indeed, at the present time, a crucial obstacle to the writing of histories of the field is that much of DH's archival evidence has either not been preserved or is held by individuals (and so remains 'hidden' unless one can discover its existence and secure approval and the means to access it). This is brought out strongly in Gouglas et al.'s study of the emergence of Humanities Computing as a discipline in Canada:

> What remains clear in this study is the importance of unpublished administrative documents. …. If we want to be able to trace the history of computing in the humanities we need to find and archive administrative documents. … The challenge now, before the materials are lost, is to gather and properly archive such administrative documents. The *Histories and Archives Project* at the University of Alberta has begun to do that. The impetus for the project began with the discovery of boxes of documents that literally fell into our hands. In 2008, Geoffrey Rockwell rescued from the garbage boxes of materials gathered and preserved over the years by Terry Butler (Gouglas et al. 2013).

It should further be pointed out that paper (or oral) sources are but one route into the discipline's history and those who wish to study its development from a technological perspective will also require the technical skills necessary to analyse software and other computational objects as historical artefacts.

The Approach Taken in This Book

The interviews included in this book came about in the context of a project entitled 'Hidden Histories: Computing and the Humanities'. This project aimed to identify 'early adopter' scholars and practitioners in the field of DH from 1949 until c.2006 and to carry out oral history interviews with them. We selected this approach because we recognised that it could help us to fill some of the 'archival gaps' that are alluded to above. We expected that this research (which has an element of urgency due to the advancing years of many of those who were involved in the earliest stages of the field) could allow us uncover and document information not normally included in the professional literature of the field. Furthermore, such testimonies have the status of primary sources. They can be analysed in conjunction with other primary and secondary sources and reused by other researchers. In this way our research not only results in new knowledge about the field but also advances the possibilities that exist for carrying out further research into it.

With regard to sampling a purposive approach, which involves the seeking out of 'settings and individuals where … the processes being studied are most likely to occur' (Denzin and Lincoln 1994, p. 61) was adopted. Above we have reflected on the contested nature of DH. This is significant for setting the parameters of our study because questions about the constituency of the 'in-gang' cannot be definitively answered at the present time; indeed, we doubt whether it is even a helpful question to ask. Therefore, the approach we take is an inclusive one. We have conducted interviews with well- and lesser-known DH figures. Some have played a pivotal role in the development of the field. Some have been very familiar with its activities while maintaining something of an outsider's perspective (and so their reflections provide an important point of orientation and cross-reference). Our sample includes not only those who worked in academic positions in DH from the 1950s onwards but also those who worked in so-called 'service roles', for example, in computer centres. Included too are some of those who worked in the broad range of organisations outside of the university sector where DH also takes place, for example, funding bodies (e.g. NEH and Mellon), standards organisations (e.g. the World Wide Web Consortium (W3C)) and industry and consulting (e.g. Black Mesa Technologies). Interviews with those who worked in the Galleries, Libraries, Archives and Museums sector are in planning and it is hoped to include them in a subsequent publication. It should be noted that language was also a factor in our selection of interviewees. For the most part we have worked with interviewees who speak either English or German (because those are the languages that Nyhan, who has done most of the interviewing, speaks).

To date 40 interviews have been completed. Of those, five have been published elsewhere (see Siemens et al. 2012; Unsworth et al. 2012; Short et al. 2012; McCarty et al. 2012; Rockwell et al. 2012) as part of a pilot project that investigated the suitability of an oral history methodology to this research (see Nyhan et al. 2015). A further 12 interviews were carried out with those who worked on Busa's *Index Thomisticus* project and are in preparation for publication elsewhere as part of a special study on the female punched card operators who worked with Busa during the 1950s and 1960s. The interviews that could not be included in this book due to the pressures of time will be published elsewhere in due course.

The title of this book *Computation and the Humanities*: *towards an oral history of DH* has been carefully chosen to indicate that this is but one publication that has or will emanate from our research into the history of DH. It has likewise been chosen to signal that an oral history such as this will always remain incomplete because it is not possible to include all of the voices that we hoped to include. A number of those who worked in the field during its earliest stages, for example, inter alia, Roberto Busa, Antonio Zampolli, Joseph Raben and Paul Fortier were too unwell to be interviewed when we approached them or had already died. Linguistic constraints have already been mentioned. Furthermore, others whom we hoped to include either declined our invitation to be interviewed or have embargoed their interviews.

All the oral history interviews presented here were carried out in line with the premise that oral history resources are acts of co-creation between the interviewee and the interviewer. The interviews are semi-structured. Questions vary from interview to interview, depending on factors like the responses of the interviewee, but all interviews aimed to explore the following core questions:

1. Please tell me about your earliest memory of encountering computing technology
2. Did you receive formal training in programming or computing?
3. How did you first get involved in what we now refer to as DH?
4. Which people particularly influenced you and how?
5. What about scholars who were not using computers in their research? Do you have some sense of what their views were about DH?
6. What was your first engagement with the 'conference community' and how did that come about?

The recordings of the interviews are available on the website that accompanies this book (see http://hiddenhistories.omeka.net/interviews) and have not been edited except to prevent potentially sensitive or private information being revealed. An initial transcription of each interview was made from the audio file was made by the project's Research Assistant, Jessica Salmon. Nyhan then set about the editing of the interviews. This stage was most labour intensive; indeed, we radically underestimated how much work this would involve. The resulting transcripts have, in comparison with the audio files, been heavily edited to aid their readability. The editing pertained to content, for example, to remove disfluencies and infelicities of speech. It also pertained to structure, for example, to delete a repetitious section. Some interviewees were able to provide relevant supplementary information after the interview had been completed and this was added to the transcript. Where interviewees spoke English as a second language it was sometimes necessary to substantially revise the wording of the transcript to ensure that their message was intelligible. Accordingly, each of the interview transcripts went through a number of stages of editing by Nyhan and she worked closely with interviewees throughout to ensure that they agreed with the proposed changes. All interviewees received at least two (and some considerably more) versions of their transcribed interviews for comment.

The interviews were annotated, and, as far as was possible, checked and cross referenced by Nyhan. On the whole, the annotation that has been inserted references external literature, usually selected by Nyhan, which is relevant to the discussion at hand though not mentioned during the interview. Given the book's expected readership, technical references have not usually been glossed. Supplementary information about individuals mentioned in the interviews has been provided when deemed necessary, for example, when information might otherwise be difficult to find or when an explanation is necessary to the wider narrative.

This book contains one chapter of analysis on the theme of 'revolutionaries and underdogs', which occurs in many of the interviews conducted so far. A book of historical-interpretative narrative that will be based on a sustained analysis all of the interviews we have carried out is also planned.

Why Do We Need Histories of DH?

This chapter argues that the history of Digital Humanities was once neglected, is now emerging and is absolutely necessary. We have dedicated significant discussion to the lack of attention that the history of DH has hitherto received and the difficulties of researching such a history. Therefore, we will close by asking why histories of DH are needed and essential to undertake.

Perhaps the most obvious response to this question is to point out that the intersection of computing – and we use computing in the broadest possible sense to avoid the implication of either technical or social determinism or that it can be done with 'the computer' only – and the Humanities is altering not only the scope and possibilities of Humanities research (Bulger et al. 2011) but also some of the conditions under which it is carried out (Moulin et al. 2011). Of the purpose of history, Marwick has written: 'As memory is to the individual, so history is to the community or society. … It is only through a sense of history that communities establish their identity, orientate themselves, understand their relationship to the past and to other communities and societies' (1989, p. 14). Indeed, how can we understand DH's identity in any meaningful way without knowing its history? How can we trace continuities and divergences between DH and the other fields that are concerned with what it means to be Human without an adequate understanding of the multifaceted conditions that have shaped DH? As will be argued in Chap. 17, it is not uncommon for the field to communicate its contributions in a rather superficial way, for example, by reflecting on its 'revolutionary' contributions and potential. Such shallow rhetoric serves to occlude understandings of the importance of history (why consider the past when your aim is to transform the present and future?). It also casts DH adrift in the wider sea of knowledge. The History of the Humanities is a new and emerging area (viz. the recently founded University of Chicago press journal *History of the Humanities*) that complements the History of Science by studying the comparative history of the disciplines that form part of the Humanities. It seems obvious that the History of DH must be part of this wider history and that it could contribute to (and benefit from) the conversations that are ongoing there. Yet, so far, DH has engaged with this emerging field in but a limited way and this is arguably due to its underdeveloped knowledge of and attentiveness to its own history.

The last example looked out to wider developments in the Humanities but the point is no less pertinent when one looks in at DH. Indeed, we argue that the lack of such a history is hindering DH's understanding of itself and what it is that truly makes it distinctive. It is often claimed that the field's collaborative nature makes it distinct and differentiates it from mainstream Humanities. However, research that we have carried out shows that this claim is rather more problematic than it first appears. A study of one of the field's earliest projects, Busa's *Index Thomisticus*, showed that collaboration was the basis on which it was realised. Yet, it appears that some forms of collaboration were considered more worthy than others and so the contributions of the many female (and occasionally male) punch card operators who did the work of the project were not acknowledged and, until our research, their identities and the nature of their contributions had disappeared from the historical record (see Nyhan and Terras forthcoming).

So too, an unsound indicator of collaboration, namely joint-authorship, is often invoked by the DH community as evidence of its collaborative nature. Our analysis of publication patterns in two of the field's central journals: CHum (1966–2004) and *Literary and Linguistic Computing* (LLC) (1986–2011) showed that single-authorship predominated. Our control was the *Annals of the Association of American Geographers* (AAAG) (1966–2013) where we found that increases in the numbers of multi-authored papers were more wide-ranging than in either LLC or CHum (Nyhan and Duke-Williams 2014). Thus, collaboration may be portrayed as a distinctive feature of DH but, notwithstanding the small scale of the study mentioned above, it seems reasonable to question such claims further. When and how did collaboration take on this significance for the field and how is such collaboration usually signalled in DH research outputs? What is the significance of the supposed cleaving of DH from the practices of the mainstream Humanities in this regard? How deep is our understanding of the role and performance of collaboration in DH (and indeed mainstream Humanities) and how has it changed over time? Without a history of DH (that can then be set in wider contexts such as the History of the Humanities) we cannot answer such fundamental questions.

It has been argued that the absence of a history of the field is hindering the development of its future. McCarty believes that Busa's concerns, uttered in 1975, about 'why the use of the computer is… detained at some primitive and laborious stage while its services in other fields are monumental' (cited in McCarty 2011, p. 4) still hold true today. He has seized on DH's ignorance of its history as a key reason for this: 'McGann has proposed a fascinating amalgam of theoretical ideas …, but I don't think we know what to do with them because we don't know how they fit, and we don't know that because we don't know what they have to fit to. Hence the crying need for a history' (Idem, p. 6).

We hope that this book takes an important step towards meeting this need. In the next chapter we will argue why and how Oral History is an important and productive methodology for uncovering the histories of DH.

References

Adamo, G. (1994). *Bibliografia di informatica umanistica*. Rome: Bulzoni.

Alvarado, R. C. (2012). The digital humanities situation. In M. K. Gold (Ed.), *Debates in the digital humanities* (pp. 50–55). Minneapolis: University of Minnesota Press.

American Historical Association. (2015). *Draft guidelines for professional evaluation of digital scholarship in history*. Available at http://historians.org/Documents/Teaching%20and%20 Learning/Current%20Projects/Digital%20Scholarship%20Evaluation/Guidelines%20for%20 the%20Professional%20Evaluation%20of%20Digital%20Scholarship%20in%20History.pdf. Accessed 11 May 2015.

Bessinger, J. B., & Parrish, S. M. (1965). *Literary data processing conference proceedings*. White Plains: IBM.

Bogost, I., & Monfort, N. (n.d.). *Platform studies*. Available at http://platformstudies.com/. Accessed 17 Feb 2016.

Brunner, T. F. (1993). Classics and the computer: The history of a relationship. In J. Solomon (Ed.), *Accessing antiquity: The computerization of classical studies* (pp. 10–33). Tucson: University of Arizona Press.

Bulger, M., et al. (2011). *Reinventing research? Information practices in the humanities*. Research Information Network. Available at http://www.rin.ac.uk/our-work/using-and-accessing-information-resources/information-use-case-studies-humanities. Accessed 27 Apr 2011.

Burton, D. M. (1981a). Automated concordances and word indexes: The fifties. *Computers and the Humanities, 15*(1), 1–14. doi:10.1007/BF02404370.

Burton, D. M. (1981b). Automated concordances and word indexes: The early sixties and the early centers. *Computers and the Humanities, 15*(2), 83–100. doi:10.1007/BF02404202.

Burton, D. M. (1981c). Automated concordances and word indexes: The process, the programs, and the products. *Computers and the Humanities, 15*(3), 139–154. doi:10.1007/BF02404180.

Burton, D. M. (1982). Automated concordances and word-indexes: Machine decisions and editorial revisions. *Computers and the Humanities, 16*(4), 195–218. doi:10.1007/BF02263544.

Busa, R. (1980). The annals of humanities computing: The index thomisticus. *Computers and the Humanities, 14*(2), 83–90.

Causer, T., & Wallace, V. (2012). Building a volunteer community: Results and findings from transcribe Bentham. *Digital Humanities Quarterly, 6*(2). Available at http://www.digitalhumanities.org/dhq/vol/6/2/000125/000125.html. Accessed 1 Apr 2014.

Denzin, N. K., & Lincoln, Y. S. (Eds.). (1994). *Handbook of qualitative research*. Thousand Oaks/London: Sage.

Earhart, A. E. (2015). *Traces of the old, uses of the new: The emergence of digital literary studies*. Ann Arbor : The University of Michigan Press.

Gascoigne, T., et al. (2010). Is science communication its own field? *JCOM: Journal of Science Communication, 9*(3). Available at http://jcom.sissa.it/archive/09/03/Jcom0903%282010%29C01/Jcom0903%282010%29C04. Accessed 6 Jan 2016.

Gouglas, S., et al. (2013). Before the beginning: The formation of humanities computing as a discipline in Canada. *Digital Studies/Le champ numérique, 3*(1). Available at http://www.digitalstudies.org/ojs/index.php/digital_studies/article/view/214.

Grusin, R. (2013). The dark side of the digital humanities – part 2. *Thinking C21: Centre for 21st century studies*. Available at http://www.c21uwm.com/2013/01/09/dark-side-of-the-digital--humanities-part-2/. Accessed 9 Feb 2014.

Hockey, S. (2004). The history of humanities computing. In: S. Schreibman, R. Siemens, & J. Unsworth (Eds.), *Companion to digital humanities*. Blackwell companions to literature and culture (pp. 3–19). Oxford: Blackwell Publishing Professional. Available at http://www.digitalhumanities.org/companion/

Jockers, M. L. (2013). *Macroanalysis: Digital methods and literary history*. Chicago/Springfield: University of Illinois Press.

Jones, S.E. (2015). *New book forthcoming spring 2016*. Steven E. Jones. Available at http://stevenejones.org/2015/10/07/new-book-forthcoming-spring-2016/. Accessed 4 Jan 2016.

Kaltenbrunner, W. (2015). Scholarly labour and digital collaboration in literary studies. *Social Epistemology, 29*(2), 207–233.

Kirsch, A. (2014). Technology is taking over english departments. *The new republic*. Available at http://www.newrepublic.com/article/117428/limits-digital-humanities-adam-kirsch. Accessed 3 May 2014.

Kirschenbaum, M. G. (2010). What is digital humanities and what's it doing in english departments? *ADE Bulletin, 150*, 1–7.

Lancashire, I. (2010). *Forgetful muses: Reading the author in the text*. Canada: University of Toronto Press.

Liu, A. (2012). Where is cultural criticism in the digital humanities? In M. K. Gold (Ed.), *Debates in the digital humanities* (pp. 490–509). Minneapolis: University of Minnesota Press.

Martha, N. S. (2007). The human touch software of the highest order: Revisiting editing as interpretation. *Textual Cultures: Texts, Contexts, Interpretation, 2*(1), 1–15.

McCarty, W. (1999). *Humanities computing as interdiscipline.* Available at http://www.iath.virginia.edu/hcs/mccarty.html. Accessed 21 Nov 2011.

McCarty, W. (2006). Tree, turf, centre, archipelago—or wild acre? Metaphors and stories for humanities computing. *Literary and Linguistic Computing, 21*(1), 1–13.

McCarty, W. (2008). What's going on? *Literary and Linguistic Computing, 23*(3), 253–61. doi:10.1093/llc/fqn014.

McCarty, W. (2011). *Beyond chronology and profession: Discovering how to write a history of the digital humanities.* Paper given at Hidden Histories: Symposium on methodologies for the history of computing in the humanities, c.1949–1980. University College London. http://www.mccarty.org.uk/essays/McCarty%20Beyond%20chronology%20and%20profession.pdf

McCarty, W., et al. (2012). Questioning, asking and enduring curiosity: An oral history conversation between Julianne Nyhan and Willard McCarty. *Digital Humanities Quarterly, 6*(3). Available at http://www.digitalhumanities.org/dhq/vol/6/3/000134/000134.html. Accessed 11 Nov 2015.

McPherson, T. (2012). Why are the digital humanities so white? Or thinking the histories of race and computation. In M. K. Gold (Ed.), *Debates in the digital humanities* (pp. 139–160). Minneapolis: University of Minnesota Press.

MLA Task Force for Evaluating Scholarship for Tenure and Promotion. (2007). *Report on evaluating scholarship for tenure and promotion.* New York: MLA: Profession 2007. Available at http://www.mla.org/pdf/taskforcereport0608.pdf. Accessed 10 July 2009.

Moulin, C., & Nyhan, J. (2014). The dynamics of digital publications: An exploration of digital lexicography. In P. Dávidházi (Ed.), *New publication cultures in the humanities: Exploring the paradigm shift* (pp. 47–61). Amsterdam: Amsterdam University Press. Available at http://www.oapen.org/search?identifier=515678. Accessed 15 Feb 2016.

Moulin, C., et al. (2011). *Research infrastructures in the digital humanities.* Strasbourg: European Science Foundation. Available at http://www.esf.org/fileadmin/Public_documents/Publications/spb42_RI_DigitalHumanities.pdf. Accessed 7 July 2012.

Nowviskie, B. (2011). Where credit is due: Preconditions for the evaluation of collaborative digital scholarship. *Profession, 2011,* 169–181.

Nowviskie, B. (2013). Skunks in the library: A path to production for scholarly R&D. *Journal of Library Administration, 53*(1), 53–66.

Nyhan, J., & Duke-Williams, O. (2014). Joint and multi-authored publication patterns in the digital humanities. *Literary and Linguistic Computing, 29*(3), 387–399. llc.oxfordjournals.org/content/29/3/387. Accessed 21 Mar 2016.

Nyhan, J., & Terras, M. (forthcoming). Uncovering hidden histories of the index thomisticus: Busa's female punched card operators.

Nyhan, J., Flinn, A. & Welsh, A. (2015). Oral history and the hidden histories project: Towards histories of computing in the humanities. *Digital Scholarship in the Humanities, 30*(1), 71–85. Available at http://dsh.oxfordjournals.org/content/30/1/71/. First published online in *Literary and Linguistic Computing,* July 30, 2013.

Nyhan, J. (2016). In search of identities in the digital humanities: The early history of Humanist. In J. Molloy (Ed.), *Social media archaeology and poetics.* Cambridge, MA: MIT Press.

Pannapacker, W. (2013). Stop calling it "Digital humanities." *The chronicle of higher education.* Available at http://chronicle.com/article/Stop-Calling-It-Digital/137325/. Accessed 1 Apr 2014.

Presner, T. (2012). How to evaluate digital scholarship. *Journal of Digital Humanities, 1*(4). Available at http://journalofdigitalhumanities.org/1-4/how-to-evaluate-digital-scholarship-by-todd-presner/. Accessed 11 May 2015.

Raben, J. (1966). Prospect. *Computers and the Humanities, 1*(1), 1–2.

Raben, J. (1991). Humanities computing 25 years later. *Computers and the Humanities, 25*(6), 341–350.

Ramsay, S. (2013a). On building. In M. Terras, J. Nyhan, & E. Vanhoutte (Eds.), *Defining digital humanities: A reader* (pp. 243–246). Surrey/Burlington: Ashgate Publishing.

Ramsay, S. (2013b). Who's in and who's out. In M. Terras, J. Nyhan, & E. Vanhoutte (Eds.), *Defining digital humanities: A reader* (pp. 239–242). Surrey/Burlington: Ashgate Publishing.

Rockwell, G. (1999). Is humanities computing an academic discipline? Available at http://www.iath.virginia.edu/hcs/rockwell.html. Accessed 21 Nov 2011.

Rockwell, G. (2007). An alternate beginning to humanities computing? *Theoretica.ca*. Available at http://theoreti.ca/?p=1608. Accessed 1 Apr 2014.

Rockwell, G. (2011). On the evaluation of digital media as scholarship. *Profession, 2011*, 152–168.

Rockwell, G., Victoria, S., Sophia, H., Sean, G., & Harvey, Q. (2011). Computing in Canada: A history of the incunabular years. In *Digital humanities* (pp. 207–10). Stanford: Stanford University Library.

Rockwell, G., Nyhan, J., Welsh, A., & Salmon, J. (2012). Trading stories: An oral history conversation between Geoffrey Rockwell and Julianne Nyhan. *Digital Humanities Quarterly, 6*(3). Available at http://www.digitalhumanities.org/dhq/vol/6/3/000135/000135.html. Accessed 10 Mar 2015.

Rockwell, G., & Sinclair, S. (forthcoming). The swallow flies swiftly through: An analysis of humanist. In *Hermeneutica.ca*.

Short, H., et al. (2012). Collaboration must be fundamental or it's not going to work: An oral history conversation between Harold Short and Julianne Nyhan. *Digital Humanities Quarterly, 6*:3. Available at http://www.digitalhumanities.org/dhq/vol/6/3/000133/000133.html

Siemens, R., et al. (2012). Video-gaming, paradise lost and TCP/IP: An oral history conversation between Ray Siemens and Anne Welsh. *Digital Humanities Quarterly, 6*(3). Available at http://www.digitalhumanities.org/dhq/vol/6/3/000131/000131.html. Accessed 2 Nov 2015.

Sinclair, S., & Rockwell, G. (2014). *Towards an archaeology of text analysis tools*. Presented at the digital humanities, Lausanne, Switzerland. http://dh2014.org/.

Spiro, L. (2011). Knowing and doing: Understanding the digital humanities curriculum. In *Digital humanities* (pp. 232–233). Stanford: Stanford University Library.

Svensson, P. (2009). Humanities computing as digital humanities. *Digital Humanities Quarterly, 3*(3). Available at http://digitalhumanities.org/dhq/vol/3/3/000065/000065.html. Accessed 9 Feb 2010.

Svensson, P. (2010). The landscape of digital humanities. *Digital Humanities Quarterly, 4*(1). Available at http://digitalhumanities.org:8081/dhq/vol/4/1/000080/000080.html. Accessed 9 Feb 2010.

Taporwiki. (2011). How do you define humanities computing/digital humanities? Available at http://www.artsrn.ualberta.ca/taporwiki/index.php/How_do_you_define_Humanities_Computing_/_Digital_Humanities%3F. Accessed 16 Feb 2016.

Taylor, P. J. (1976). An interpretation of the quantification debate in British geography. *Transactions of the Institute of British Geographers, 1*(2), 129–142.

Terras, M., Nyhan, J., & Vanhoutte, E. (Eds.). (2013). *Defining digital humanities: A reader*. Surrey/Burlington: Ashgate Publishing.

Unsworth, J., et al. (2012). Postmodern culture and more: An oral history conversation between John Unsworth and Anne Welsh. *Digital Humanities Quarterly, 6*(3). Available at http://www.digitalhumanities.org/dhq/vol/6/3/000132/000132.html. Accessed 4 Mar 2016.

Vanhoutte, E. (2010). Defining electronic editions: A historical and functional perspective. In W. McCarty (Ed.), *Text and genre in reconstruction: Effects of digitalization [sic] on ideas, behaviours, products and institutions* (pp. 119–44). Cambridge: Open Book Publishers.

Vanhoutte, E. (2013). The gates of hell: History and definition of digital/humanities/computing. In M. Terras, J. Nyhan, & E. Vanhoutte (Eds.), *Defining digital humanities: A reader* (pp. 119–158). Surrey/Burlington: Ashgate Publishing.

Wang, X., & Inaba, M. (2009). Analyzing structures and evolution of digital humanities based on correspondence analysis and co-word analysis. *Art Research, 9*, 123–134.

Weingart, S. (2015). Submissions to DH2016 (pt. 1). *The scottbot irregular*. Available at http://www.scottbot.net/HIAL/?p=41533. Accessed 10 Feb 2016.

Williamson, V. (2016). On the ethics of crowd sourced research. *PS: Political Science & Politics, 49*(01), 77–81.

Wisbey, R. A. (Ed.). (1971). *The computer in literary and linguistic research*. Cambridge: Cambridge University Press.

Zielinski, S. (2006). *Deep time of the media: Toward an archaeology of hearing and seeing by technical means*. Cambridge, MA: MIT Press.

Open Access This chapter is distributed under the terms of the Creative Commons Attribution-Noncommercial 2.5 License (http://creativecommons.org/licenses/by-nc/2.5/) which permits any noncommercial use, distribution, and reproduction in any medium, provided the original author(s) and source are credited.

The images or other third party material in this chapter are included in the work's Creative Commons license, unless indicated otherwise in the credit line; if such material is not included in the work's Creative Commons license and the respective action is not permitted by statutory regulation, users will need to obtain permission from the license holder to duplicate, adapt or reproduce the material.

Chapter 2
Why Oral History?

Abstract This chapter begins with an overview of the histories of oral history and its use within different branches of academic and public history. Focussing next on the study of communities, it briefly explores the contested, fuzzy and fluid meaning of the term 'community' before examining the application of oral history to community histories, including academic and professional communities. It discusses some of the ethical challenges at stake in this type of historical research, including the multifaceted relationship between the interviewer and the interviewee, and the choice of which 'significant' lives are privileged to tell the story of the community (and therefore which significant lives and perspectives might be missing). Before outlining some of the issues surfaced by using oral history to document foundational stories of DH as a discipline, this chapter looks briefly at the use of oral history in some other analogous professional and academic settings. In conclusion, the chapter reflects on the suitability of oral history in telling these community stories by asking who owns these histories and how that ownership is manifested.

Introduction

The novelist David Lodge has defined history as 'the verdict of those who weren't there on those who were'. In the best dynamic of an interview, interviewees reverse the equation, trying to explain to those of us who weren't there how things really were. (Ritchie 2014, p. 56)

And the very act of the oral histories, in their long, slow, unfolding and the different qualities (long interviews, minimal interruption) enacts a different pattern of communication and exchange. (Colton and Ward 2005, p. 106)

There are many starting points to consider and questions the historian must ask when seeking to piece together the history of a community. The historian must make choices about what is his or her relationship to these histories, how these histories are to be written, what sources are to be used and to what purpose. These choices have a more profound impact on how the histories are produced than historians often like to acknowledge. This chapter will examine the nature of oral history and its suitability for recovering the histories of the use of computers and associated technologies in the Humanities, the emergence of DH as a recognised academic discipline and the development of Digital Humanists as an academic community.

© The Author(s) 2016
J. Nyhan, A. Flinn, *Computation and the Humanities*, Springer Series on
Cultural Computing, DOI 10.1007/978-3-319-20170-2_2

History is more than an account of the past 'as it happened' – the past is remembered, understood and interpreted by a number of different actors including participants, witnesses and historians. Oral history does not shy away from these differences and multiple interpretations; rather, it allows the various memories and understandings to be explored and examined in detail. This chapter (and book) argues that such an approach is appropriate and even essential to charting the often disputed and disputatious histories of the establishment of new disciplines and the development of academic and professional communities.

In demonstrating this worth, this chapter will begin with an overview of the histories of oral history and its use within different branches of academic and public history. Oral history has not been without its opponents. Criticisms of oral history approaches have included the identification of potential biases, the reliance on memory and its reliability/unreliability, and the validity of individual accounts of the past, real or socially constructed. Oral historians have responded to these criticisms both by seeking to demonstrate how oral history can be subjected to the same checks and balances as other forms of historical analysis but also, and more importantly, by arguing that some of the supposed weaknesses or 'peculiarities' of oral history are not limitations at all. Instead the differing personal narratives and varying memories offer unrivalled opportunities to explore and understand communities and their relationship to the past; something that would simply not be possible when relying on other more traditional text-based historical sources. As suggested by the quotations which introduce this chapter, oral history can be the basis for a different type of history, more dynamic, more direct and sometimes confrontational, dependent on the relationship between the interviewer, the interviewee and the past, but creating a space where in Portelli's words (1997, p. viii) history is made to listen and take account of (but not necessarily accept uncritically) the perspectives of those who were there.

Focussing next on the study of communities, this chapter will briefly explore the contested, fuzzy and fluid meaning of the term 'community' before examining the application of oral history to community histories, including academic and professional communities. The chapter will discuss some of the ethical challenges at stake in this type of historical research, including the multifaceted relationship between the interviewer and the interviewee, and the choice of which 'significant' lives are privilege to tell the story of the community (and therefore which significant lives and perspectives might be missing). Before outlining some of the issues surfaced by using oral history to document foundational stories of DH as a discipline, this chapter will look briefly at the use of oral history in some other analogous professional and academic settings. As discussed in the previous chapter, although there has been 70 or more years of using the computer and associated technologies in Humanities research inside and outside the academy, the story of that interaction has not yet been written in a comprehensive and rigorous fashion. This chapter makes the case that in these circumstances, when the histories have yet to be written, when many of the protagonists are still alive, and when the subject of those histories is memory, motivation, innovation and origins, that oral history is the perfect tool for documenting those histories, enabling those who were there to 'speak to history' and to those who were not there. Of course, history, meaning making and historical interpretation does not stop at this point. For Portelli (2013, p. 284) 'good oral history…does not end with the turning off of the recorder, with the archiving of the document, or with the writing of the book', for the interviews that is just the beginning of their lives as sources for future research. The interviews are merely one source, one version of many versions which over the years can be revisited, tested against other sources, interpreted and reinterpreted. The presentation of the interviews in this book (and on the corresponding website) reflects this approach. These first-hand accounts represent a first draft of history, vital and dynamic, drawing on the accounts of key participants, but not yet the definitive, final history.

In employing oral history techniques to examine the use of the computer in Humanities research and DH's transition from the margins towards the academic mainstream, we have sought to critically investigate shared as well as divergent foundational narratives; the significance of certain individuals as innovators, revolutionaries and boundary crossers and the personal difficulties, resistance and criticisms they faced; the discussions as to the nature of discipline; and the extent to which DH was and is as inclusive, transformatory and collaborative as is claimed and whether, for instance, it has really been able to transcend barriers around gender within the academy.

In conclusion the chapter will reflect on the suitability of oral history in telling these community stories by asking who owns these histories and how that ownership is manifested. It is impossible not to draw parallels between DH and oral history. The similarity lies not only in the relationship to technology and its transformatory role but also in a shared rhetoric which stresses notions of radical challenge to existing scholarly approaches, a commitment to participatory and collaborative practice, and an interdisciplinary approach which operates inside and outside the academy (Boyd and Larson 2014, p. 10–13). In the 1970s, Paul Thompson wrote in his seminal account *The Voice of the Past* of the potential of oral history to transform both the 'content and purpose of history' in that 'it can give back to the people who made and experienced history, through their own words, a central place' (2000, p. 3). In considering this, oral historians ask themselves whether their interviews tell us about what happened in the past, or whether they make sense of the past and subsequent lives from the vantage point of the present, and to what extent historians and researchers wish or are able to leave these interpretations in the hands of protagonists.

A Brief History of Modern Oral History

The origins of modern oral history are often traced back to the programme initiated by the North American journalist and oral historian Allen Nevins at Columbia University in 1948. Nevins' conception of oral history was in essence an archival one, aiming to record for posterity and the use of others the thoughts and memories of leading politicians, judges and businessmen, 'living Americans who have led significant lives' (Nevins quoted in Sharpless 2007, p. 11). According to Nevins (1996, p. 37) interviews should be forensic and challenging encounters carried out by 'an earnest, courageous interviewer who has mastered a background of facts and who has the nerve to press his scalpel tactfully and with some knowledge of psychology into delicate tissues and even bleeding wounds'. Although the power dynamics involved in such elite interviewing mean that is unlikely that all these interviews were as testing as Nevins advocated, the characterisation of the interview as a rigorous examination was a vital if not always attainable element of this type of oral history practice. Programmes established at other US universities and at the Presidential libraries followed a similar pattern of elite subject interviews for archives and use by future researchers.

This early emphasis on such 'elite' histories draws attention to a fault line which runs though many subsequent divergences in oral history over how 'significance' in the lives of interviewees was to be determined and where in society this 'significance' was to be located. Of course, not all oral history interviews focused on the elites. In the United States the practice of capturing the voices and life stories of the less famous and less powerful associated with the approaches of the Chicago School of Urban Sociology and the New Deal era Federal Writers' Project in the first half of the twentieth century influenced the development of a more populist form of oral history alongside the recording of the memories of the 'movers and shakers' in society (Grele 1996, p. 64–65). In the United Kingdom and elsewhere in Europe (Scandinavia in particular) oral history grew in the 1960s and 1970s from its roots in local history and folklorist studies into a practice predominantly adopted by politically engaged historians associated with new social histories, labour history, the women's movement and other civil rights movements, seeking to challenge existing dominant historical narratives and 'recover' hidden histories. Rather than elite or expert witness histories which were so prevalent in the US, the dominant approach to oral history in the UK (and reflected in the conference and journal of the Oral History Society) was one associated with histories from below, of the underpowered as opposed to the powerful, the periphery rather than the centre and of popular 'community' oral histories (Smith 2014). Ken Plummer (2001, p. 29) arguing for the return of human agency to social science research ('critical humanism') via the use of life stories and narrative approaches to research memorably likened oral history to 'a global, fragmented social movement hell bent on tracking, retrieving, recording and archiving the multiple worlds of our recent past' that might otherwise be lost.

Like many advocates for DH, oral historians have claimed that the practice of oral history could result in more democratic and transformational scholarship and histories. Reflecting the strength of this strand of oral history, Paul Thompson wrote in the preface to the first edition of *The Voice of the Past* (2000, p. vi) that 'the richest possibilities for oral history lie within the development of a more socially conscious and democratic history'. In contrast to the US, this appears to have been the dominant perspective in the UK and Europe. With the exception of academic studies of high politics, sponsored history projects instigated to celebrate institutional anniversaries and the National Life Story (NLS) projects at the British Library, much of

UK oral history practice followed Thompson's model and perhaps lacked some of the variety and heterogeneity of the US practice (Perks 2010a, b). The best of these sought to merge both approaches, interviewing individuals from all walks of life within a framework of rigorous and critical questioning.

Some projects have aimed to study professional and academic communities. Since 1987 NLS (http://www.bl.uk/projects/national-life-stories) has obtained external funding for the collecting of life histories of people working in various occupations such architects, writers, lawyers, as well as of those working at all levels in the steel, electricity, oil, water and food industries, in the City, and the post office in addition to specific firms such as Tesco and Barings (http://www.bl.uk/projects/national-life-stories). Although NLS has not yet completed a study of an academic community, the large and significant Oral History of British Science (2009–2013) captured the lives of those working in science at every level and in universities, in government research centres and in commercial environments (http://www.bl.uk/voices-of-science). Other UK collections at the British Library and elsewhere which document similar communities of practice to DH practitioners include oral histories of universities and specific departments (the Open University, Oxford University, Manchester University, the Science Studies Unit at Edinburgh, British Antarctic Survey and the British Rocketry Oral History Programme), academic and professional fields (computing pioneers), professional groups (general practitioners, geriatricians, nurses, police officers, meteorologists, archivists and museum curators), Royal Colleges and Societies (Arts, Chemistry), and campaigners (medical and political activists) in addition to the long-running oral history witness seminar programme directed by Michael Kandiah at the Institute of Contemporary British History. More such oral histories, including those sponsored by academic and professional associations or membership bodies, may exist or at least have been created in the near past but they have left very little trace (Perks 2010b, p. 219). One also wonders how many of them got much further and deeper than the celebratory and the anecdotal, and attempted the more rigorous examination advocated by Nevins.

As suggested earlier, we are consistently struck by the extent to which the experience of oral historians mirrors that of Digital Humanists. Fittingly, in the context of our study of the application of computer technologies to Humanities research, the development and growth of oral history itself is closely identified with changes and developments in technology. There is a pleasing irony that in seeking to better understand the dynamics of the application of computers to Humanities research and the growth of DH, we have chosen oral history, an approach that has been in the past, and is now again in the process of being fundamentally changed, perhaps even transformed by technology. Modern oral history developed as recording devices capable of making high quality audio recordings became easier to transport and to use (from portable reel to reel and tape cassette recorders to the mobile solid-state digital recording devices of today) and available at prices that were not prohibitive. The production of the cassette tape recorder was critical to the expansion of oral history practice in the 1960s and 1970s. The ease of achieving high quality digital recordings has been equally significant in terms of the recording process and the possibilities for dissemination and use since 2000 (Perks 2011; Thomson 2006).

For some commentators, web based access to digital (and digitised) oral histories offers the opportunity to stress the essential orality of oral history, freeing it from the tyranny of the transcript, emphasising the potentialities of aural rather than textual access to oral histories, and replacing some of the mediation ('intervention, selection, shaping, arrangement, and even manipulation') required to produce the documentary representation of the audio with a post-documentary sensibility (Frisch 2006, p. 110). There is no doubt that in the past the transcript (as in this volume) has been essential in unlocking the potential for use of oral history materials but digital formats, software developments and web based access to oral history materials do offer the opportunity to fundamentally reduce or even reverse the reliance on the transcript (Boyd and Larson 2014, p. 7–10). Others have suggested, however, that perhaps the distinctions between the transcript and the voice can be over-stated and if the social benefits of opening up the great wealth of oral history materials to the users of web are to be realised then a better understanding of how different people and cultures engage on an emotional level with audio materials, particularly voices, is required so that people accessing digital oral histories can be encouraged to listen carefully and deeply (Cohen 2013).

Challenges to Oral History: Valuing Difference

As the interviews in this volume illustrate, Digital Humanists often thought of themselves as 'explorers' and 'revolutionaries' who were upsetting and transforming traditional Humanities scholarship. Oral historians in the 1970s and 1980s expressed similar claims that their approach would open up new areas of historical study and would transform (make 'more democratic') the practice of scholarship and knowledge production itself (Thompson 2000, p. 8–9). Of course, again like the advocates of technology in the Humanities, oral history and its pioneers in the 1970s and 1980s were subjected to criticisms and condescension, especially in traditional academic circles. Beyond the primarily politically motivated criticism aimed at the focus and progressive purpose of much oral history, concerns were most frequently expressed over the reliability of the material collected by oral history interviews for use in historical research and the standard of the scholarship that the use of such material resulted in. Some critics argued that oral history resulted in the collection of trivia and others that it threatened to cause the study of history to become little more than the study of myths (Abrams 2010, p. 5–6). If oral history aimed to recover 'the past as it was', questions were asked as to whether the testimonies based upon retrospective memories of events (as opposed to documentary records produced contemporaneously and then authenticated and analysed through a professionally recognised method of 'objective' historical scholarship) could be relied on to be accurate. It was asked whether oral histories were not fatally compromised by the biases and uncertainties introduced by the interview process; and in the case of collective, community-focussed projects whether the selection of interviewees would introduce an unrepresentative or overly homogeneous data collection sample into the studies.

Some oral historians countered these arguments by seeking to demonstrate the validity of oral testimony by subjecting it to rigorous cross-checking with other sources, arguing for the general accuracy of memory and its suitability as a source for historical evidence, importing methodologies from sociology and other social sciences regarding the selection and sampling of interviewees to ensure 'representativeness', and seeking to reduce the suggestion of bias introduced by the interviewer by developing neutral questions and replicable interview schedules (Abrams 2010, p. 5; Shopes 2014, p. 258–259). In arguing for the recognition of the partial and constructed nature of all historical sources (including archival records) and the reliability of oral testimony when so tested, oral historians sought to make the case that oral history interviews could be just as trustworthy as any other traditionally valued source when subjected to proper rigorous scholarly analysis and cross-checking in writing histories of the 'past as it was' (Thompson 2000, p. 50 & 272–274).

However, from the late 1970s some oral historians, themselves critics of populist oral history approaches and the possibility of recovering the 'past as it really was', began to suggest something more radical in advancing an oral history practice which rather than seeking to account for unreliability and contingency began instead to identify subjectivity, orality and memory as critical elements of oral history as a historical source (Abrams 2010, p. 6). Michael Frisch (1979) cautioned against both the 'more history' approach (merely submitting oral testimony to historical analysis just like other sources) and the 'no history' approach of more populist approaches which saw authenticity and truth in every testimony rendering historical analysis and scholarship redundant. Luisa Passerini (1979, p. 84) influentially argued against the transformation of 'the writing of history into a form of populism – that is to replace certain of the central tenets of scholarship with facile democratisation, and an open mind to demagogy.' Both argued instead that the real critical value and strength of oral history was in its difference, not in seeking to describe the past 'as it really was' ('mere reconstruction') but in being able to open up completely different areas of historical research such as representations of culture, not just through 'literal narrations but also the dimensions of memory, ideology and subconscious desires'. Passerini's (1979, p. 104) interest in critical consciousness and how that is expressed, finds expression through the examination of oral testimony and its inconsistencies not as an unreliable source but rather a unique window on subjectivity and the inter-connection and interaction between socialised attitudes and representations, and personal self-reflection and consciousness.

In what Thomson (2006, p. 53) refers to as the second paradigm transformation in oral history ('post-positivist approaches to memory and subjectivity'), rather than being a source of unreliability and lack of credibility, over the last 30 years oral historians have identified in the dialogic nature and inter-subjectivities of the interview, in the inconsistencies of memory and in the performance of the interview not weaknesses but strengths. This is what Alessandro Portelli (1981, p. 99–100) described as 'the peculiarities of oral history' revealing 'not just what people did, but what they wanted to do, what they believed they were doing, and what they now think they did'. In particular from this perspective the inconsistencies and failures of memory become less a problem and instead the key to understanding how individuals make sense of the past in the present, and how their personal experiences and memories are constructed via the intersection and interaction with society, culture and ideology. In the context of applying oral history to the history of an emergent academic community and discipline, what oral history allows for is not just the description of individual lives working within DH but also the extent to which individuals use shared narratives to make sense of the past and their journey to the present, when these individual and collective narratives depart from each other or from what is known from other sources, and when collective narratives and memories contradict individual understanding. Questions we have explored in the interviews included here such as influences and early developments, the significance of building community, and the experience of hostility from other Humanities scholars offer an insight into individual experiences and meaning-making but also in the intra-community and cross-generational exchanges between interviewee and interviewer a strong sense of how the community understands its own memories and narratives.

Another recent criticism of oral history, its utility as an archival resource for re-use, is a subject which is of interest to all Humanities (and other) scholars who wish to use digital archives of research data for their own research. Following the 'archival turn' in their disciplines, Sociologists and other social science researchers have debated the extent to which other researchers' archived data can be useful in subsequent, possibly unrelated, research projects (Geiger et al. 2010). Unlike much social science qualitative interviewing, for instance, oral history is often archival in its nature and intention. Interviews are initially undertaken for an immediate research purpose but the recording is also being created with the aim of archiving it and making it available to others in the future. The concerns of sociologists and other social scientists over the reliability of archived qualitative data (particularly qualitative interviews) in terms of the difficulty (perhaps impossibility) of fully knowing the context and the relationship/s which frame the interview, have been extended to the consideration of oral history. The re-use of archived oral histories can throw up challenges to researchers, especially regarding issues of informed and valid consent for such use and the interpretation that is placed on those recordings. However for many, including the authors of this book, the depth and richness of historical data that would otherwise be lost makes it inconceivable not to consider utilising the archive while emphasising the importance of fully documenting and making visible to future researchers the context of the interview (Geiger et al. 2010; Bornat 2005).

With such issues in mind, in the abstract that precedes each interview we have specified the immediate context of the interview in terms of when, where and how it was conducted. Some interviewees asked for and were given the 'core questions' in advance; some did not and so answered in a more extemporaneous fashion. It is mentioned in the preamble if interviewees were given the core questions in advance of the interview. Other important contextual aspects, such as the relationship that

developed between the interviewer and interviewee during the course of the interview require a level of analysis that is not feasible to provide here (as Grele wrote,
such interactions 'require ... analysis of the social and psychological kind' (cited in
Yow 2006 p.56)). Yet, the reader will detect various differences between the interviews that arose, at least in part, through the interplay of the many contextual factors
that converged upon each interview. These range from practical issues, such as the
interviewer's ever developing expertise in and comfort with the technique of oral
history interviewing to the quality of the rapport that did or did not develop between
interviewee and interviewer. Notwithstanding the wealth of recollections contained
in the transcripts, a few interviews did intermittently display more of conversational
quality than was perhaps desirable. Equally, a few interviews seem to occasionally
suffer the lack of it. Relevant to such dynamics is the fact that the interviews included
here are intra-community interviews that were conducted between peers. We discuss both the advantages and disadvantages of such 'insider interviewing' further
below. Here, suffice it to say that in the transcripts we have done our utmost to
preserve such contextual markers not only with future researchers in mind but also
because they are important signals of the time, space and dynamic contexts that
each interview unfolded in.

Studying Communities

As has been discussed, since its post-1945 origins, modern oral history's suitability
for exploring and capturing lives of significance has been recognized. In contrast,
community oral history, the dominant form of popular oral history practice over the
last 30–40 years, has tended to look for and locate significance outside the elite sections of society typical of more conventional oral history (Thomson 2008). Although
some community histories tend to be uncritical towards their subjects, this is by no
means inevitable. Communities, whether defined by place, identity, interest, heritage, occupation, practice or some combination thereof can be well suited to a rigorous and productive application of oral history practice. A community or collective
focus allows the interviewer to explore how and why individual and collective
memories interact and to uncover what tacit knowledge underpins the community
and is understood but frequently unacknowledged by members. It also allows the
interviewer to explore how individuals and their communities share identities and
histories which bind and include as well as construct identities and memories which
restrict entry and exclude. The term 'community' is a notoriously vague and slip-
pery word. While it is generally understood to have 'warm', positive connotations,
when it is associated with marginalized and under-powered groups within society it
can function as a device for 'othering' and further marginalization, or for overlook-
ing or dismissing important differences and power relationships within social
groups or communities (Shopes 2006; Waterton and Smith 2010; Kogan 2000).

Of course there is no reason why oral history could and should not be used to
examine elite and professional communities. Although in the UK, at least, rigorous

academic oral histories of elite communities as opposed to the more common celebratory, anniversary history projects, have been comparatively rare, in the US such
studies have always represented a significant strand of oral history practice. Business
organizations and scientific or academic communities have frequently sponsored
oral history projects, sometimes out of vanity, but more significantly to raise profile
around an event or anniversary or to capture valuable corporate or disciplinary
knowledge that might otherwise be lost (Perks 2010a). In a 2003 review of oral history projects of American science, Ronald Doel outlined the breadth of projects
which represented thousands of interviews documenting, in rich and multifaceted
ways, the development of different scientific communities inside and outside the
universities (Doel 2003, p. 350). The varied approaches taken by these oral history
projects over the years reflected important developments in oral history thinking
and practice. They moved from a more limited approach (asking very focused questions, of a few key individuals, about very specific occupational and disciplinary
matters) to a more holistic process, more interested in the life stories of the interviewees and the social and cultural context to the development of scientific ideas
and discovery.

Adopting a life history approach, or at least a broader framing for community
oral history projects, means that even if there is an emphasis on a particular aspect
of the interviewee's life, occupation or academic discipline, that aspect can then be
placed and better understood within a more expansive context. According to Doel
(2003, p. 357) taking this approach to interviews with scientists results in 'important
insights about disciplines and intellectual communities, all the while focusing on
individual storytellers, their social and professional contexts and their world views'.
Hilary Young's (2011) account of an oral history project about the Open University
demonstrates how a project conceived as part of the 40th anniversary celebrations
was conducted in a fashion that undercut easy positive assumptions about the university's history and instead explored tensions around working practices, regional
identities and race. Another recent project in this vein is the NLS initiative an Oral
History of British Science (OHBS 2009–2013). Like the more contemporary projects described by Doel, OHBS seeks to place a diverse cross-section of those whose
lives are involved with science into a broader social and cultural context. In capturing 'the lives of scientists in detail alongside accounts of their work', OHBS has
been able to document step-by-step descriptions of scientific processes as well as
uncover the heavy demands of the scientific working life in the context of family
lives; it has explored the masculine cultures of British science and the experience of
women working in scientific occupations; and has provided evidence of the impact
of childhood and education on the development of an interest in science (NLS 2014;
Merchant 2013).

Although competition between academics is well established in the public mind,
it has also been noted that academic disciplines and knowledge groupings often
make for strong communities (communities of practice rather than communities of
interest) which cut across other institutional loyalties and affiliations and exhibit
solidarities and shared values in addition to criticism and competition (Kogan 2000,
p. 211–213). The necessity for these solidarities and sense of community is perhaps

even stronger amongst those working within an emergent discipline such as DH, which is challenged by and is challenging to the status quo, than it would be for better established and generally more self-confident disciplines. The interviews in the volume express this sense of solidarity very strongly, by generally affirming the significance of the community and the support it gave to individuals. Most, but not all, of the interviewees recall some antagonism or even hostility from other Humanities scholars in the early days of their careers and engagements with technology. They contrasted the collaborative and supportive ethos in the emerging Humanities Computing and latterly DH communities with the more competitive and sometimes confrontational atmosphere in other disciplines. Peer review and the conference forum is not only about being judged by colleagues, it can also be about peers supporting each other to develop and strengthen their community and the interviews seem to suggest that this was how it operated in the early years of DH.

Emergent communities can be inclusive but in their evolutionary or even revolutionary fervor they can also exclude others that express different, non-consensual views. It is important to recognize the differences expressed in these interviews and within the community broadly on the role of technology and whether DH could be considered a discipline or was more a reconfiguration aided by technology of existing disciplines. The choice of interviewees is crucial here. Rather than only interviewing those with more orthodox and conventional views within the community, care has been taken to also include the stories and thoughts of those who have different perspectives (Nyhan et al. 2015, p. 75–78). Oral history has frequently been celebrated for playing a significant role in exploring such communities, being "an experiment in releasing 'empirical knowledge'" by making visible and vividly giving voice to their inter-relationships, identifying the shared myths, foundation stories, creeds, values and sacred stories that underpin the identity of imagined communities' (Perks 2010a, p. 42–43; Colton and Ward 2005, p. 96). One of the strengths of community-based oral history in particular is the focus on the collective as well as the individual, which enables the oral historian to identify and explore the community's shared history, the tacit knowledge and understandings the group retains as well as noting the significance of individual agency and divergences. However, this is only possible if the recruitment of interviewees is broad and inclusive, reflecting critical as well as positive voices (Young 2011, p. 97–98) and the interviewer is skilled and prepared thoroughly in advance. A common criticism aimed at many community-focused or institutional anniversary projects is that they tend to approach their interviews as individual and unconnected. Whereas more thoughtful and ultimately successfully realised projects, such as the oral history of the Open University and the interviews on the history of DH, are able to analyse their interviews collectively by asking 'critical questions about broad themes of social life that cut across individuals' experience' (Shopes 2006, p. 263) in addition to capturing more personally specific memories and perspectives.

Another danger of community-focused interviews and projects is the extent to which the interviewer is an insider or an outsider and what that means for the intersubjectivities of the relationship between the interviewer and interviewee. As an outsider, the interviewer may find it difficult to be welcomed into the community, or to have the knowledge or expertise necessary to ask the right questions. However, the opposite can also be true, with narrators opening up to a trusted outsider in a way they would not do to someone from within their community (Portelli 2013, p. 278–279). An insider may have the credentials to get the interviews and to understand the situation enough to ask the right questions, but as insiders they may not acknowledge the shared tacit knowledge between them, they might avoid difficult and sensitive topics, or identify too closely with the community to present that community in anything other than the most favourable light. If there are significant cultural, socio-economic and power differences, it does not mean that the interview will not be a success but it will almost certainly impact on the dialogue in some way and that difference ought to be located and understood. An insider seeking to interview a person much senior within an organization or discipline may find it difficult to ask challenging, critical questions. The senior figure may find it equally hard not to self-censor themselves, give superficial answers or depart from their pre-prepared answers in such circumstances (Abrams 2010, p. 161–162; Young 2011, p. 104). The interviews in this volume are conducted by insiders, for the most part by the first author who is a reasonably well established member of the DH community. In one sense, therefore, these are intra-community interviews between peers but they also offer the impact of cross-generational interviewing between pioneers in the discipline and the generation that is now seeing the discipline of DH strengthen and mature.

Life history and broad contextual approaches to interviewing can be tremendously valuable in identifying special and significant events in an individual's life and placing their choices and experiences within a wider context. However, much of the interest in individual lives comes from the coherence (and dissonance) between related interviews and of the critical analysis of the life stories collectively as well as individually. Linda Shopes argues that the frequent mismatch between community history and professional history approaches leads to unsatisfying results for both sides and suggests that successful projects come from the critical engagement with the intersections of individual lives, the identification of the historical problem which defines the community and the exploration of these problems through careful and targeted questions of the individual narrators (2006, p. 268–269).

The interviews in this volume seek to follow this suggestion by asking of each of its interviewees a series of challenging questions which focus not just on their individual lives but also on cross-cutting aspects of their experiences in academia as part of the emergent discipline of DH. As outlined in the previous chapter, all the interviews take a qualitative, semi-structured approach, adhering to a common broad outline of their career and engagement with technology. The interviews seek to illuminate the journey of DH and Digital Humanists from the margins to 'respectability' by asking questions about early memories of interacting with technology, their technical and computer education, their first involvement in DH research, their influences, attitudes of other humanities scholars to their use of technology, and their first engagement with the DH community. Among the questions that this approach allow us to explore are what is DH? What are the discipline's foundation stories and origin myths? Who were the innovators and early adopters in the discipline but also what were the social, intellectual and creative contexts they operated within? We also explore, to varying degrees, the extent to which the revolutionary rhetoric of transformation and innovation, of collaborative working and inclusivity is real and to what extent this rhetoric masks deeper tensions and critical voices; and finally what, if any, were the spaces for women in these different workplaces and evolving spaces. Among the many important understandings revealed by these interviews are the multiple paths into DH that were taken and, arguably, how this is manifested in the diverse and contested understandings of the discipline that abound, even in terms of whether it is possible to characterise it as a separate discipline or subject area. Given the importance of myths and imperfect memory in modern oral history, the dissonance between many of the interviewees' memories of being 'the underdog' and struggling for recognition, with their present position as influential professors secure in their posts suggests to us that some of these shared origin stories of persecution have played a useful role as useful myths in building and sustaining the community on its journey to respectability (see Chap. 17).

In a recent volume on the subject of what the authors feel should be a fruitful and on-going relationship between oral history and DH, Doug Boyd and Mary Larson described what they feel are the similarities between the disciplines:

> To those who have long had a foot in both worlds, however, the connections are clear and abundant. In fact, three of the tenets oral historians hold most dear – collaboration, a democratic impulse, and public scholarship – are also three of the leading concerns often cited by digital humanists. Add to this the interdisciplinary (or multidisciplinary) nature of both methodologies, together with the importance of contextualization/curation, and one finds that the two camps have more in common than they would have to separate them. (Boyd and Larson 2014, p. 10)

This volume uses oral history and the interviews of the pioneers of using computers in the Humanities from around the world to explore the reality of many of these claimed tenets and disciplinary approaches within DH.

A Conclusion. Oral History and Communities: To Whom Does This History Belong?

Much oral history practice has stressed the importance, the primacy even, of the individual voice and experience. For the most part it has rejected social science norms of anonymity in favour of naming the narrator and acknowledging the interviewees' ownership and authority over their words. Under the conditions of properly negotiated informed consent, oral historians argue that the interview is jointly authored by the interviewer who has devised and asked the questions and the interviewee whose narrative we are interested in recording. The individual stories belong to their narrator and that ownership and the significance of the voice is (most often) best attested to by naming that voice, thus 'anonymity [is generally considered] antithetical to the goals of oral history' (Larson 2013, p. 38). But how is this advocacy of valid consent, shared authority and ownership squared with the oral historian's frequent practice of asking for the assignment of the interviewee's copyright over the recording and the reserving the right to quote, contextualise and interpret the words, motivations and expressions of their narrators and interviewees? Some argue that the oral historian should not only make their existence and agency transparent in the testimony (demonstrating that the words and records created are part of a dialogic exchange in which the interviewer and interviewee both have responsibility) but should also extend the process of informed consent beyond the interview and the transcript, sharing authority for those acts of selection, interpretation and publication traditionally claimed as the responsibility of the historian alone (Abrams 2010, p. 166–167). If we are to claim that these stories truly belong to their narrators as much as to their interlocutors then surely we need to think about whether asking for copyright to be assigned away is consummate with that claim, and whether the best way to present these stories is not through the selection of 'juicy quotations' and interpretation but as is done in the rest of this book, via the presentation of the interviews in their full form (Geiger et al. 2010, p. 14 & 22). Larson (2013, p. 41). Others (Dougherty and Simpson 2012) have drawn attention to these apparent contradictions and the 'distress' they can cause, suggesting exploring use of Creative Commons licences as a possible solution. The approved publication of the full transcripts in this book under an open access licence, edited into a literary style (as opposed to a more natural verbatim style) to meet the concerns of some of the interviewees, and the availability of the recordings under a creative commons licence presents these interviews and the hidden histories they relate as a jointly constructed, jointed authored project between the interviewees and the interviewers.

References

Abrams, L. (2010). *Oral history theory*. Abingdon: Routledge.

Bornat, J. (2005). Recycling the evidence: Different approaches to the reanalysis of gerontological data. *Forum Qualitative Sozialforschung/Forum: Qualitative Social Research, 6*(1), 47–53.

Boyd, A., & Larson, M. (2014). *Oral history and digital humanities. Voice, access and engagement*. Basingstoke: Palgrave Macmillan.

Cohen, S. (2013). Shifting questions: New paradigms for oral history in a digital world. *Oral History Review, 40*(1), 154–156.

Colton, S., & Ward, V. (2005). Gritty lessons and pearls of wisdom: Using oral history interviews to draw deep insights from past action, illuminate heritage and catalyse learning. *KM4D Journal, 1*(2), 95–107.

Doel, R. (2003). Oral history of American science: A forty year review. *History of Science, 41*, 349–378.

Dougherty J., & Simpson C. (2012). Who owns oral history? A creative commons solution. In: Boyd D., Cohen S., Rakerd B., Rehberger D. (Eds.), *Oral history in the digital age*. Institute of library and museum services. http://ohda.matrix.msu.edu/2012/06/a-creative-commons-solution/

Frisch, M. (1979). Oral history and hard times: A review essay. *Oral History Review, 7*, 70–79.

Frisch, M. (2006). Oral history and the digital revolution. Toward a post-documentary sensibility. In R. Perks & A. Thomson (Eds.), *The oral history reader*. Abingdon: Routledge.

Geiger, T., Moore, N., & Savage, M. (2010). *The archive in question*. (CRESC working paper series, working paper no. 81). Manchester: The University of Manchester.

Grele, R. (1996). Directions for oral history in the United States. In D. Dunaway & W. Baum (Eds.), *Oral history an interdisciplinary anthology* (2nd ed.). Walnut Creek: Alta Mira Press.

Kogan, M. (2000). Higher education communities and academic identity. *Higher Education Quarterly, 54*(3), 207–216.

Larson, M. (2013). Steering clear of the rocks: A look at the current state of oral history ethics in the digital age. *Oral History Review, 40*(1), 36–49.

Merchant, P. (2013). Scientists childhoods. *Oral History, 41*(1), 63–72.

National Life Stories (NLS). (2014). *Oral history of British science. Final report on the completion of phase one of the programme*. London: British Library.

Nevins, A. (1996). Oral history: How and why it was born. In D. Dunaway & W. Baum (Eds.), *Oral history an interdisciplinary anthology* (2nd ed.). Walnut Creek: Alta Mira Press.

Nyhan, J., Flinn, A., & Welsh, A. (2015). Oral history and the hidden histories project: Towards histories of computing in the humanities. *Digital Scholarship in the Humanities, 30*(1), 71–85. Available at http://dsh.oxfordjournals.org/content/30/1/71/. First published online in *Literary and Linguistic Computing*, July 30, 2013.

Passerini, L. (1979). Work, ideology and consensus under Italian fascism. *History Workshop, 8*, 82–108.

Perks, R. (2010a). "Corporations are people too!" Business and corporate history in Britain. *Oral History, 38*(1), 36–54.

Perks, R. (2010b). The roots of oral history: Exploring contrasting attitudes to elite, corporate and business oral history in Britain and the US. *Oral History Review, 37*(2), 215–224.

Perks, R. (2011). Messiah with the microphone? Oral historians, technology and sound archives. In D. Ritchie (Ed.), *The oxford handbook to oral history*. Oxford: Oxford University Press.

Plummer, K. (2001). *Documents of life 2 – an invitation to a critical humanism*. London: Sage.

Portelli, A. (1981). The peculiarities of oral history. *History Workshop, 12*, 96–107.

Portelli, A. (1997). *The battle of Valle Giulia: Oral history and the art of dialogue*. Madison: University of Wisconsin Press.

Portelli, A. (2013). Afterword. In A. Sheftel & S. Zembrzycki (Eds.), *Oral history off the record*. New York: Palgrave MacMillan.

Ritchie, D. (2014). Top down/bottom up: Using oral history to re-examine government institutions. *Oral History, 42*(1), 47–58.

Sharpless, R. (2007). The history of oral history. In T. Charlton, L. Myers, & R. Sharpless (Eds.), *History of oral history. Foundations and methodology*. Lanham: Alta Mira Press.

Shopes, L. (2006). Oral history and the study of communities. Problems, paradoxes and possibilities. In R. Perks & A. Thomson (Eds.), *The oral history reader*. Abingdon: Routledge.

Shopes, L. (2014). "Insights and Oversights": Reflections on the documentary tradition and the theoretical turn in oral history. *Oral History Review, 41*(2), 257–268.

Smith, G. (2014). Chairman's report annual meeting of OHS 2013. *Oral History, 42*(1), 30–33.

Thompson, P. (2000). *The voice of the past, oral history* (3rd ed.). Oxford: Oxford University Press.

Thomson, A. (2006). Four paradigm transformations in oral history. *Oral History Review, 34*(1), 49–70.

Thomson, A. (2008). Oral history and community history in Britain: Personal and critical reflections on twenty-five years of continuity and change. *Oral History, 36*, 95–104.

Waterton, E., & Smith, L. (2010). The recognition and misrecognition of community heritage. *International Journal of Heritage Studies, 16*(1–2), 4–15.

Young, H. (2011). Whose story counts? Constructing an oral history of the open university at 40. *Oral History, 39*(2), 95–106.

Yow, V. (2006). Do I like them too much? In A. Thomson (Ed.), *The oral history reader* (2nd ed., pp. 54–72). London/New York: Routledge.

Open Access This chapter is distributed under the terms of the Creative Commons Attribution-Noncommercial 2.5 License (http://creativecommons.org/licenses/by-nc/2.5/) which permits any noncommercial use, distribution, and reproduction in any medium, provided the original author(s) and source are credited.

The images or other third party material in this chapter are included in the work's Creative Commons license, unless indicated otherwise in the credit line; if such material is not included in the work's Creative Commons license and the respective action is not permitted by statutory regulation, users will need to obtain permission from the license holder to duplicate, adapt or reproduce the material.

Chapter 3
Individuation Is There in All the Different Strata: John Burrows, Hugh Craig and Willard McCarty

Abstract This oral history interview between Willard McCarty (on behalf of Julianne Nyhan), John Burrows and Hugh Craig took place on 4 June 2013 at the University of Newcastle, Australia. Harold Short (Professor of Humanities Computing at King's College London and a Visiting Professor at the University of Western Sydney in the School of Computing, Engineering and Mathematics) was also present for much of the interview. Burrows recounts that his first encounter with computing took place in the late 1970s, via John Lambert, who was then the Director of the University of Newcastle's Computing Service. Burrows had sought Lambert out when the card-indexes of common words that he had been compiling became too difficult and too numerous to manage. Craig's first contact was in the mid-1980s, after Burrows put him in charge of a project that used a Remington word processor. At many points in the interview Burrows and Craig reflect on the substantial amount of time, and, indeed, belief, that they invested not only in the preparation of texts for analysis but also in the learning and development of new processes and techniques (often drawn from disciplines outside English Literature). Much is said about the wider social contexts of such processes: Craig, for example, reflects on the sense of possibility and purposefulness that having Burrows as a colleague helped to create for him. Indeed, he wonders whether he would have had the confidence to invest the time and effort that he did had he been elsewhere. Burrows emphasises the network of formal and informal, national and international expertise that he benefitted from, for example, John Dawson in Cambridge and Susan Hockey in Oxford. So too they reflect on the positive results that the scepticism they sometimes encountered had on their work. As central as computing has been to their research lives they emphasise that their main aim was to study literature and continuing to publish in core literature journals (in addition to DH journals) has been an important aspect of this. Though they used techniques and models that are also used by Linguists and Statisticians their focus has remained on questioning rather than answering.

© The Author(s) 2016
J. Nyhan, A. Flinn, *Computation and the Humanities*, Springer Series on Cultural Computing, DOI 10.1007/978-3-319-20170-2_3

Biographies

John Burrows was born in Armidale, New South Wales, Australia, in 1928. He was Professor of English at the University of Newcastle, Australia from 1976 to 1989. Following his retirement in 1989 he became Emeritus Professor and Director (1989–2001) of the newly established Centre for Literary and Linguistic Computing (CLLC). As discussed below, his computer-assisted textual analysis research combined two previously separate approaches: counts of common words (often referred to as 'function words') and Principal Component Analysis.[1] His research is seminal and internationally recognised; his contributions are both to theory and methodology. Among his most important publications is the book *Computation into Criticism*: *A Study of Jane Austen's Novels and an Experiment in Method* (1987) and the article "'Delta': A Measure of Stylistic Difference and a Guide to Likely Authorship" (2002). In 2001 he was awarded the prestigious Busa Award for Outstanding Contributions to the field of Humanities Computing.

Hugh Craig was born in Watford, England, UK in 1952. He was appointed Professor of English at the University of Newcastle, Australia in 2004, and Director of the Centre for Literary and Linguistic Computing (CLLC) in 2001. He has also held posts as Head of the Department of English; Head of the School of Language and Media; Head of the School of Humanities and Social Science; and Deputy Head of the Faculty of Education and Arts. His internationally recognised research is on Computational Stylistics and its applications to Shakespeare and Early modern English drama. His many publications include some of the most authoritative texts on the applications of computing to literary problems, for example, his chapter on 'Stylistic Analysis and Authorship Studies' in the *Companion to Digital Humanities* (Schreibman et al. 2008). The new knowledge he has contributed to Shakespeare Studies is brought out especially in the co-edited *Shakespeare, Computers and the mystery of authorship* (Craig and Kinney 2009).

Willard McCarty is FRAI/Professor of Humanities Computing, Department of Digital Humanities, King's College London; Professor, School of Computing, Engineering and Mathematics, University of Western Sydney; Editor, *Interdisciplinary Science Reviews*; and Editor of Humanist. In 2013 he won the Roberto Busa Prize of the Alliance of Digital Humanities Organizations (ADHO). In 2006 he won the Richard W. Lyman Award from the National Humanities Center and the Rockefeller Foundation, U.S. and in 2005 he won the Award for Outstanding

---

[1] This is a statistical technique that allows single points in a dataset to be examined in terms of pattern and variation. Thus it can be used to examine trends and variations in and across large dataset(s). Oxford Index defines it as a '[m]athematical technique for condensing a metabolomic spectrum to a single point on a graph, permitting rapid comparison between different species, experimental and control groups, etc.' See http://oxfordindex.oup.com/search?q=Mathematical+te chnique+for+condensing+a+metabolomic+spectrum+to+a+single+point+on+a+graph%2C+perm itting+rapid+comparison+between+different+species%2C+experimental+and+control+groups% 2C+etc.%EF%BF%BD++

Achievement, Computing in the Arts and Humanities from the Society for Digital Humanities/Société pour l'étude des médias interactifs, Canada. His work is centred on computing across the Arts, Humanities and interpretative Social Sciences. His numerous publications include *Humanities Computing* (2005), which made a seminal contribution to the articulation and design of the intellectual foundations of DH.

Interview

Willard McCarty [WMC] I'm going to go through six questions which have been asked of everybody in this project, but unusually, because there are two of you and you've known each other for a long time, some sort of cross talk between the two of you will make this a particularly valuable record of your memories, recollections and thoughts on very long careers in DH. The first question is: what is your earliest memory of encountering computing technology and what did you think of the computing technology you encountered at the time?

John Burrows [JB] [pause … laughter… pause …]. It was 1979. I'd been card-indexing examples of tolerably common words (or frequent words) in Jane Austen's novels. My card indexing system was becoming intolerably overburdened, complicated and difficult to manage, and I went downstairs to the Director of our Computing Service, John Lambert,[2] and asked him if any of this could be computerised. He told me about COCOA (Russell 1965), the software program of the day for text management and preparation.[3] He responded with great interest and enthusiasm and we worked right on from there. So, I had the good fortune to have an early positive response from a highly competent and capable man.

Hugh Craig [HC] A Remington word processor that we had in the faculty was my first contact. There was a special room there where the word processor was sitting. Remember [to JB], you were Dean and you put me in charge of that project. Now when was that? That was in the early 1980s, so that was our first bit of word processing technology.

JB 1983.

---

[2] Lambert was first appointed to a Lectureship in Mathematics and went on to be the 'University's Foundation Director of Computing Services'. See: http://www.newcastle.edu.au/research-and-innovation/centre/education-arts/cllc/people

[3] On Tapor, COCOA I is described as 'a program and markup language for generating word counts and concordances written in FORTRAN, from the University College Cardiff and the Atlas Computer Laboratory. It produced keyword-in-context concordances and word frequency profiles for texts, and was considered to be a powerful, highly flexible program for punched card computers'. See: http://www.tapor.ca/?id=222

HC OK

JB It was known as 'the Dean's white elephant'

HC Yes it did have a few problems. I remember that the daisy wheels kept breaking on the machine.

JB It had an abominable problem. I was lucky enough to be away on sabbatical while it was being experienced and came back just after it was resolved. It had the wrong board fitted (it was a closely related but not identical model). It took about 12 months and many visits from the technicians before it was discovered that all they had to do was insert the right board. Afterwards it worked admirably, by which time nobody was interested.

HC People had spent too long battling its problems.

JB And, of course, about $20,000 of faculty money which, at that time, was a considerable sum. It just predated the vigorous growth of PCs.

HC It seemed like the solution at the time.

JB So, your experience was unluckier than mine – it's a wonder you kept going.

HC Well, that was unrelated to Computational Stylistics. I must have noted your work, particularly authorship attribution, happening here. I was working on a problem on Ben Jonson's additions to the *Spanish Tragedy* and I thought "maybe we could apply this to Computational Stylistics", as I don't think it was called then.

JB No

HC And it wasn't called Stylometrics either – what did you call it at the beginning?

JB Nothing. It was just what I was doing. An American couple, I think their name was Sedelow used the term in a book of theirs in the mid-1970s. I took it up from them about 20 years later, principally because I thought by then we were outgrowing what had always been called Stylometry because we were doing more ambitious and complex things than just one-on-one contests between two candidate authors. We were doing more than Authorship Studies and I thought a new term was needed. The old term still survives but the justification of the new one is pretty obvious.

HC The old terms come back, you see it again and again. I'm not sure why, I think because new players keep coming in and they just pick up on some of the older terminology and it comes back.

JB Yes, once again it's the dearth of the history of the field which we have talked about a number of times

HC I think that it makes a big difference if you have somebody in your own institution, or even down the corridor, doing something. I think it's in terms of the sort of confidence you can have that something can be seen through or that you'll get some payoff for your investment. I'm pretty sure that if I had been elsewhere and had just heard of John's work that I wouldn't have had the confidence to invest a lot of time. I would have thought "OK, I can spend a year doing this and get nothing out of it. I don't think I'll do that!" I had known John for a long time and I think there is something about proximity and the sense that you can observe, almost on a daily basis, that things are working out and things are progressing. It's a bit hard to define but that's why I got into it and persisted.

I know that I did my first comparison in 1988. I had maybe six Shakespeare plays and six Jonson plays and the odd thing I always say is that I prepared Hamlet for that study in 1988 and I've probably used it at least every week since then – that same text over and over again. It's a great advantage if the texts are not just a one-off; they're almost not worth it for a one-off study. There's such a big investment in the preparation of the texts in order to do it properly. I think that's true even today; you might get a database from somewhere yet you nearly always need to add something. So, it really pays off when you keep re-using your material. In my case, I've just been able to keep building it up to, I don't know, 225 plays or whatever. But the core ones are still being recycled – I won't say daily but weekly, almost. And Hamlet is still there.

JB Another piece of serendipity in my early days was my first author. As I said a while ago, I'd been doing card indexes looking at Jane Austen's language and she just absorbed this sort of punishment. She always rewarded you with an interesting answer to your question. If I'd tackled some other stylistically-duller author I'd probably have given up long before, but she just kept seducing me, which is something Ms Austen might not have wished to hear. And then, shortly after my conversation with John Lambert in August or September 1979, I went off to Cambridge for a year and had the good fortune to meet John Dawson [the Manager of Cambridge University Literary and Linguistic Computer Centre]. Through John and another man whose name escapes me at the moment, Robinson I think, I was told about Susan Hockey (see Chap. 6) and the work in Oxford University Computing Services. So, between Dawson's center in Cambridge and Hockey's center in Oxford, I was doing a lot of criss-cross travelling in the course of that year and learned a great deal and got a lot of encouragement and support to continue. I think I struck a lot of good luck, in a number of ways, early on when one might have been discouraged.

WMC Yes, stories of good luck are to be expected. The second question is – I'm not sure why it's here really – about formal and informal training. Both of you began when there was no formal training, I know I began when there was no formal training, and you've already answered more or less how you learned. But I'm wondering if you could comment a bit more on the process of picking up this set of technologies and what that was like, and your relationship to John Lambert, in particular, because you had somebody in the computing center who was sympathetic.

JB The relationship with Lambert was enormously important throughout those years. You know, by 2001 he had been retired from his post as Director of Computing Services for 6 or 8 years. To amuse himself, and to earn a bit of money on the side, he became our programmer in our center. He worked actively with us right up to the time of his death. The prototype software that he designed for us called LILAC (Literature, Language, Computing) I use every day still. It was never refined as he would wish to see it but he left us a good enough working model. Now, the essence of that part of it, I think, is how much support the Humanities person needs from the computing person, Lambert or Dawson or Hockey, while he's finding his feet. It was 15 years before I could do much work by myself, on my own, without referring to somebody else all the time. So the training was a long, long slow process. Admittedly, in my own defence, I was a busy person at the time and doing a lot of other things.

HC It's just as well we weren't Statisticians and it's just as well we weren't Linguists because we would never have started. You know, the Statisticians would have been worried about normal distribution of the data, about not having enough. I think we would have been too inhibited. If we had been Linguists we would have been interested in Chomsky and Universal Grammar and not at all interested in data, as Chomsky wasn't. We never got much buy-in from Linguists. The best buy-in was probably from Statisticians once we had accumulated quite a lot of data. I think that if we'd been trained–[to JB] I don't know what you think about it–Statisticians or Linguists, we would not have thought to do this kind of stuff because it was very exploratory, and no one would have held out much hope of finding any interesting patterns. Let's say, the less training the better.

JB I quite agree. I got a great deal of support from our Professor of Statistics, Annette Dobson, who was sympathetic to my ignorance and stupidity. I had good help from statistically-informed friends, but I agree with you here. On the whole, the more strongly expert people were statistically, the more inclined they were to want us to use methods that yielded definite answers: yes/no answers. Our interest was rather more in exploring to find out what the answers might be, and what questions they might provoke. The finality of a Linear Discriminant Analysis,[4] for example, was never really suitable to our need: it closed the question, but we didn't want it closed. We wanted to go on thinking about why it should look like that.

HC Principal Component Analysis (PCA) was just the key, wasn't it? It was a beautiful way of combining the multivariate (combining all those different variables

---

[4] According to the *Oxford Dictionary of Statistics* (2008), Discriminant Analysis is a 'procedure for the determination of the group to which an individual belongs, based on the characteristics of that individual'.

in an exploratory way) and letting the data speak for itself. PCA does this beautifully, as opposed to Discriminant, which wants a closed answer. It over trains and is
over optimistic and gives rise to all those problems. [To JB] who put you on to
PCA? That was really fortunate.

JB Nick McLaren in the Cambridge Computing Laboratory. Then friends of mine
refined the rough model that McLaren had suggested and taught me how to use it
better.

HC Nobody thought that function words would give you anything because every
one used them at the same rate and they were empty words, or stock words, you
know, classically.

JB That was me! That was just one bit of all of this. Poor judgement, good luck,
and personal friends, [laughing] and I mixed teaching with it. Unexpectedly ordi-
nary, boring, empty little words seemed to be doing a lot and that's where the card
index broke down, of course, because one can't index *and* and *of* and *the*. Once I got
it into the computer setup I was able to explore what did happen to *and* and, *of* and
the. Much to my surprise, and everybody else's I think, the result was just as interesting as the result from ostensibly more interesting words of the kind that Stylistics
has been much more focussed on. So, we got through to a layer that could not have
been seriously penetrated without the computer.

HC Yes, that part of language was waiting for the computer to arrive so that it
could become visible. Then PCA somehow went beautifully with function words;
that was John's winning hand, function words plus PCA.

JB I always expected to be completely overtaken and surpassed by some wealthy
American Institute, and it never actually happened. More luck! I seem to be in a
benevolent frame this afternoon.

HC We still come back to function words and PCA. You know, one goes down to
the more interesting words and lots of people find ways of doing that, as we have
ourselves, but then you come back to function words: they're abundant, they've got
a good distribution … they're like the very fabric of language, aren't they?

JB And they not only require a computer, they also require statistics to handle
them.

WMC People are always asking the question you've just answered, which is,
where has the computer made a real difference that no-one could have made by him
or herself – this is a very important point.

JB You can imagine a Victorian Parson mad enough to count up all the *thees* or all the *ofs* but he could never have done multivariate things with them. The first of those two steps is lunacy but the second would have been impossible.

HC And you would have probably just done Shakespeare, and never been comparative, which is the other great thing. That's why I almost challenge John about Austen – if you'd started on Dickens you might have got something of the same. If you're inside that author, you sort of feel that author is the world.

JB Austen is not alone. A comparatively small number of authors have a really strong stylistic gift but I don't think it works for the common run of writers. Nothing in my work would support the idea that it works in the commonest authors.

HC Down to the finest levels of character or progression of characters, yes.

WMC There's another important point there that I picked up on as you were talking. That is your relationship to the other disciplines that touched your intellectual lives, a glancing or peripheral relationship, which, had it been intimate, would have paralysed the work. But, starting from literature you went out and picked up things here and there where they helped the work. That would not have happened with any other kind of relationship.

HC Yes but it is very dangerous because you are working on instinct rather than training, which is risky, certainly with statistics.

WMC But it's a well-educated instinct.

JB I think we're fortunate that we never really wanted to do anything other than study literature; all of the other things were ancillary to that. That central purpose literally questioned the questions of a literary scholar. They might have been the questions of a Linguistics scholar or an Historian, or whatever, but for us they were, have been, and continue to be the questions of literary people

WMC We continue with the question of influence in your career. You spoke of one or two strong influences but who else gripped you, including those at a distance such as people whose books you read?

JB On the whole they were not in computing. As I said, I picked that up *en passant* as time went along. Background influences … let me think. I was enormously impressed by Wolfgang Clemen (1977) on Shakespeare's imagery. I took up detail of the figures and showed how they worked through the plays dramatically. In a way, I think what I am doing is something like what Clemen did except that I am doing it with words rather than with images. And I might say, by the way, looking back to an earlier answer, both Hugh and I laid some emphasis on the function words. A lot of the work was done on them early on and is still, to a very large extent, about them. But increasingly the other words have come into play. As we've developed a better understanding of what we're doing our vocabulary has spread from the bottom up, rather than the top down. So, we are enriching as we proceed, or so we like to think. So, Clemens was one.

I was also enormously impressed by Erich Auerbach's *Mimesis* (see, for example, Auerbach 2013), partly because of the way in which it was written by a refugee in Istanbul I think it was, during the war, quite without a proper library. He had just a few texts and had to simply write out of his head about what he thought of some of the books which meant most to him. A remarkable study. Those two. Then, afterwards, the New Critics generally

WMC Richards and Ogden for example?

JB Not so much the English ones – the Americans. I didn't ever warm to Richards. I didn't quite find his wavelength or he didn't quite find mine. I can see his importance but he didn't really speak to me. But some of the Americans did. Reuben Arthur Brower's *Fields of Light* (1951), was terribly important to me, you know. All in all, the main influences on me had to do with close reading: the world in a grain of sand.

HC I don't know that there's anyone very close to what we do who has been a big influence. I've lived through deconstruction and post modernism and those sort of eras but in many ways I probably define myself against some of that work. I'm very fascinated by it, it's definitely embedded in my thinking, but a lot of what I've been doing is trying to push back against that sort of work. But I was very influenced by New Historicism in our own area – that is, the renaissance area – people like Stephen Greenblatt and so-called Cultural Poetics, which is a good broadening from close reading. I don't know, a lot of that doesn't relate directly to what we actually do. We had a really nice visit from George Hunter, G. K. Hunter, who did a literary history of renaissance English, you know.

You're always looking for people who have a broader, more conspectus view, because that's, I think, what the computational stuff does well. It's extensive rather than intensive, which people, I think, have struggled with, because we're so used to the intensive. But the real gain is from the wide sweep so one looks for people there. Robert Weimann, a German scholar, latterly does that kind of thing (Weimann and Bruster 2010) and has some broad perspectives. But we're often looking for myths to bust so almost you read these people to find a reasonably categorical statement, preferably slightly quantitative, which can then be tested. So that's a strange form of influence! It's like "give me something I can disprove". I suppose I've a vaguely oppositional perspective on what would otherwise be regarded as influences.

WMC What about other people who were using computers in their research when you got started. Were there any and did you draw anything from them? Do you remember what their views were of what you were doing, or of computing generally?

JB I didn't have a lot of close contact, partly because there wasn't much else going on in Australia at that time. I just had the brief relevant periods in Cambridge, so, on the whole, not. I did learn a lot in the late 1980s and 1990s at conferences with people like Susan Hockey and Paul Fortier.[5] I heard some splendid papers here and there, at the conferences, but on the whole not much in the way of close contact because there was never anyone much close to me until Hugh came along and that made things more interesting because we began talking together and working together.

WMC How about the people here in the computing center? You mentioned Lambert, what did you think about the computing center and the relations for a person like you with the people in it.

JB Well, it was only one-on-one, Lambert and me. I'd go down and talk to him, or his deputy Paul Butler was helpful at times, but on the whole, I didn't have much connection with the center as a center or the service as a computing service. My contact was much more with the Director so that it was a personal affair rather than a departmental one.

WMC What about you, Hugh? What about the other people using computing at the time and your closeness to them or distance from them? I know that in my case I actively disliked most of the people having something to do with computing for many years!

HC I didn't have any strong feelings that way. I guess the center was already providing that sort of ambience and technical support so it was already well in train. I didn't have to do much pioneering there. We had Alexis Antonia already there as a wonderfully patient person, and a Linguist, to help with preparing texts. Certainly no negative experiences; it was fairly restricted really. There weren't a lot of competitors, not a lot of opposition, so…

JB The journals that were important were *Literary and Linguistic Computing* particularly but *Computing in the Humanities* as well. It's the only field in which I've ever worked where people really seem to read each other's articles. In English Studies, I think on the whole, this wouldn't be altogether true. A lot of people write for the standard academic necessity of writing but don't on the whole interchange ideas with each other and they don't much care what the other fellow is writing. That's putting it too strongly, but I feel there's a step difference between the inter-

---

[5] Paul Fortier (1939–2005) was University Distinguished Professor of French at the University of Manitoba, Canada. The European Association for Digital Humanities established the 'Paul Fortier Prize' in recognition of the many contributions he made to Humanities Computing. See: http://adho.org/awards/paul-fortier-prize

relationships in English Studies and those in the general area of DH where people really do seem to know what other people have said in the journals.

WMC I've heard this said before too with respect to the friendliness of the people and in the degree in which they want to relate to each other. I know that was my experience when….

JB And not too much belligerence either of the kind that's so common, for example, in Classics where so many of them hate each other. There have been some notable attacks on generally deserving objects but I don't think that there's much general belligerence at all.

HC The interesting relationship I reckon is with our English colleagues in the English department or discipline or whatever. That's been the most potent one for me, like trying to persuade them that this is a worthwhile activity, and you're actually learning something this way. I don't know if they ever quite got persuaded, but we're keeping on trying.

JB The scepticism is enormously useful!

HC Yes, so we have a number of very, very bright and learned colleagues who we found hard to persuade (but we kept on trying) and that's a very good sort of proving ground. I think some of them are half way there. They're half way to the point that they can see that there is some value in it but they wouldn't want to do it themselves, and I guess it's slightly disappointing. It would be nice to get a few more over the line and for them to say "I can see it's valuable and I'm prepared to spend the next 6 months doing it". I certainly learned a lot about trying to persuade close colleagues that I really respected that this was something worthwhile and still get the reaction that it's an awful lot of trouble to learn so little. Then you have to persuade them that it's little but at least it's something you know, if you know what I mean, whereas you can make a grand statement, as they like to on the whole, which is just worthless.

WMC It's a little bit at a time.

HC Yes, and what there is, is solid. It's not likely to be reversed in a hurry.

JB I think your father rates a mention, doesn't he, as a shrewd questioner and challenger?

HC Yes my father is a good mathematician and so I worked with him doing some PCAs. I don't think I could do it now, but, you know, diagonalising the matrix and so on was good in the early days for making sure you really understood what was happening.

Another great question came from Anne Barton (who was a very good Ben Jonson scholar) in Cambridge. Those were the very early days when I was trying to persuade her of a certain thing. She said "yes, this sounds fun but I just don't know how much faith to have in your results", which was a brilliant! "I can see technically it might be ok, but how much faith should I have in it when as a reader I might think something differently?" We've all sort of lived by that, you know.

WMC John, you used a phrase that I really liked about the mounting evidence that this multitude of weak markers is something secure, that they add up to a view of literature which is probabilistic and, well, in my words, the ground is getting more solid. The mounting evidence and the patience over time in advancing step by step (and I think it is advancing) was brought to mind by your comment about the little things versus the grand statement.

The last of the required questions is about conferences. You've mentioned a bit about conferences, I suppose that the size of this country and its distance from where most of the conference activity and literature goes on meant that there weren't a lot of them. When did the conference engagement with this kind of work begin, and what was it like?

JB Well, I gave a paper to a conference in Adelaide, the Australian branch of the MLA, AULLA in 1974, and I just talked about some word counts in Jane Austen. Someone said "have you tested this at all with anything like the chi-squared test". I said "no, I don't know anything about that, I just count on my fingers [laughing]. I used a simple word counter and here are the comparative results".

It wasn't until afterwards in Cambridge that I began to understand a bit about chi-squared and a few other things, 5 or 6 years later. Overseas conferences for me, in this field I mean, began in San Francisco in what must have been 1981 at the big ACH/ ALLC conference of that year. From then on I went to it around every second year for a dozen years or so. After I retired I eased out of them. I found them well worth doing, I enjoyed the people and the papers. It was very arduous – I was Head of Department a lot of that time, and then Dean. I'd be away for only a week in Australia or America or Europe and return to a desk full of work. Pretty sore, but it was worth it. Any particularly memorable one? Yes, Columbia, South Carolina, [to WMC] you were there with me at the time. Georgetown in 1993? You and Harold were both there.

WMC Christ Church, Oxford, in 199[2] – that's where I met you.

JB Oh yes, that's a good one too. Christ Church, that's right. We were both together at Columbia, Willard and I, but we really met in 199[2].

Harold Short [HS] New York, 2001 was memorable for lots of the rest of us, John

WMC Well, Christ Church in 199[2] was the first time I'd ever heard John talk and I went up to him afterwards and I effused in my typical fashion. We've been friends ever since [laughing].

HC It's a good beginning ...

JB How not? [laughing]

HC For me, conferences in Renaissance literature or Shakespeare, or whatever, have been just as important. And that's where I feel the work really has to be done. It's very good to learn about what other people are doing technically and so on at the DH sub-conferences. But one of the things that I think makes us distinctive is this: we made a resolution at some point that we would always try to get articles in good journals in our discipline and that those are the people we really wanted to persuade. It's still the quest! But I think we've been distinctive in always trying to keep that link with the discipline and keep persuading our colleagues. Perhaps to no avail, but ...

JB We've had a victory or two, but not a huge number, the mainstream journals are still very hard to persuade

HC Yes, but increasingly they are more open – definitely the best ones are.

JB It's beginning to be said in America that DH is the next big thing – be nice if that were true [laughing]!

WMC The last question is my own and off-piste. If you look back on what you've done and what has happened in your field since you got started, what has happened that you think is really important? Can you use that to pick out a trajectory for the field, or more than one trajectory for the field, into the future? Not in terms of predicting the future but in terms of recognising the possibilities that are now before us? What about the past really comes out to you as important, and in using that, what do you see for the future?

JB I'm not dodging it, I'm letting you go first. It is the future

HC Is it what one's self has done?

WMC Yes, start there with what you've done and what you think is important for the future of the field. Something you're proud of; something you are ashamed of [laughter]. That kind of autobiographical sorting of the past to try to pull from it something that we've learned, that makes our choices in the future more like another step in a trajectory.

HC I don't know if I can respond to that question!

WMC I'll think up another question!

JB I think that [pause] it's all empirical at present, and to my mind, that is generally speaking a very good thing. We've learned a great amount about the details of the ways in which language works. As Hugh was saying a while ago, it's becoming increasingly possible to reach out to larger and larger corpora as the capacity and speed of computers improves, so that we're able to do more with less and we know much more than we did about the intricacies of stylistic patterns.

It's never-the-less true that as Argamon (2012) says – I don't agree with his derogatory way of saying it, he says that the field is a mess – that there have been some major achievements. Now, the field is a mess, he thinks, because no-one has a deep understanding of the patterns at work and what they really mean. What that deep understanding might be, I don't really begin to understand, so for me that's a very good question for the future. I'd like to meet the person who is going to offer answers that speak to me. I don't know what form that will take.

For me, there's never been any surprise in the idea that authors should be identifiable by their style, or patterns in their language, any more than if you and Hugh and two or three people come along a corridor towards me, I don't have to stop and think, is that Willard? Is that Hugh? Is that Harold? Everything about you speaks to me: the way you move, the way you dress, the way you speak and the way you eat. We're like that. We have so much in common, we humans, but we are certainly different in so many ways. It is not in the least degree remarkable to me but people seem surprised and surprised and surprised that our own individuality should speak through and beyond and out of our community. That's the sort of big understanding that I would understand, but I don't think that's what Argamon (2012) means. I would like to know what this other deep understanding of what it is all about might look like. I don't know if that's an answer…

HC That's exactly what I think. I remember when you were working on that article and commented on how there is different individuality, that your own individuation is there in all the different strata. You said something that crystallised that whole issue of language individuation, which sort of is the answer to the idea that the author is dead, and all the rest of it! It's the empirical answer that people do in fact make their own language, or idiolect, out of languages. That gave the underpinning for a whole lot of work, not only on authorship but individuation in general. But I think we've worked through that; I mean, it's so obvious once you do it that the battle is almost won.

JB Except that people don't believe it.

HC No, I'm satisfied. I think everyone sensible is satisfied – it just makes obvious truth. I think that's a real contribution that Computational Stylistics has made: to have that broader idea and then work it through in a whole mass of different studies which show that authors can be distinguished. Linguists are still not very interested in the individuation of language; that's not what they do. They like much more general things about languages or even about sociolects or whatever. I feel we've probably done the individuation work and I don't know what the next phase is beyond that. Some people feel that the work of Computational Stylistics is to endlessly prove that authors are different and that Computational Stylistics can show that, but

I think we're sort of bored with that. That has been demonstrated, it's as rock solid as anything can be, it's no longer the mission of Computational Stylistics and it would be good if it was disassociated from it because we've got our answer.

JB Now, there's double spin here, isn't there? On the one hand, what you say in principle is absolutely true. On the other hand, for me at least, the particular problems of authorship remain fascinating, because so many of them are unresolved. So, I no longer feel that there's any need to demonstrate that it can be demonstrated, but I still passionately believe that the real interest, and the real challenge, lies in the particular problems themselves. However, it's not just authorship attribution, individuation is larger and more interesting than that. My own work will probably continue to be mostly in authorship attribution and individuation – I think the larger issues are fascinating and maybe there's room for a lot more work there

HC There is always to and fro between attribution, which is the bread and butter of Computational Stylistics and continues to ground or authenticate or validate its work. And then there's always the temptation or interest in something beyond authorship. So, I guess one continues to go back and forth between those two. And the great thing is that authorship is a very good testing ground because people are really interested in the answer and you can't muck about. You can't do too much hand-waving about very general concepts. And it's one area where people will actually go back and check your sums, people like Jackson (2002). I think that is quite unusual, certainly in our area, because most people will accept tables and numbers. That's the good thing about authorship attribution, it gets peoples' interest to a very profound degree. But, it's not the whole of the possibilities of the field.

WMC What strikes me is that it really doesn't make any sense at all. In one of his books Ian Hacking remarks that the great achievement of twentieth century physics is the realisation that nature is probabilistic. The fact that you two have shown that literary language is probabilistic means that we, as authors, are operating in the natural world as the natural world operates. And that's more of a question than an answer; I think that's a really interesting question.

JB It's a very elegant way of saying what I was fumbling with there, about the character of individuality.

WMC The fact is that we are an intimate part of the natural world and have been pretending to be separate from it for a very long time. We are an intimate part of it down to the most elusive of aspects of artistic expression – style. As you say, it's instantly recognisable when you're walking down a hallway and you don't have to pause to know who it is …

HC Yes, that concept of style, however elusive, is the other key or one of the keys, definitely.

WMC How far can we take this? How far can we take that probabilistic bond that we have with the natural world? Sociologists have been puzzling over this in large crowds of people and such for a long time. But there's a continuum here that seems to me to be a really interesting question. That is what I say is the significance of your work John, when I'm asked or when I can say it.

JB Think of those people with good musical memories – they can recognise something in a phrase or a couple of bars. Perhaps that is what style is like? But, you do it in tennis, you do it in cricket – it's circumambient. We're part of the natural world.

HS One of the things that I think of is your most significant achievement, actually you touched on it early in the interview, is that the purpose is questions and not answers. In an authorship study you are trying to establish *an* answer. The method and the results are actually about the questions. In a world that often gets far too fixated on the quantitative as a way to answer questions this keeps this work rooted in the Humanities. I think that has been incredibly valuable for the field and continues to be.

JB On Authorship again, here's an idea that has always meant a lot since it first came to me from Hugh 20 years ago. When you make a proper attribution of a poem, you're fitting it into an interpretative nexus where it makes more sense than it would if you had tried to force it into some alien nexus, and that's when it gets interesting. You get it into its proper home and then you see that the shape of the home has changed a little bit, and so you go on again. So it's not just "yes, this poem is Rochester's", it's what that means to Rochester.

HC Well, there's some connection there with computing power and speed, which is that in an older method you had to construct a sort of a test and a hypothesis and then you could painfully run that through, get an answer one way or another and then maybe try again. That was a very rigid structure. Computational power means that you can do that exploratory data analysis, change a parameter, re-do it, and then it becomes open in the way you're describing. And I think that's what people perhaps don't realise. They say "can your program tell you, or could your program tell you who wrote this book?" That shows no understanding whatsoever of the processes involved in doing a complicated authorship problem.

JB Our friend, Harold Love, used to say that after you finish the computation and calculations, and all the rest of it, that's when the brainwork begins.

HC Yeah, but then you can re-do them all.

JB One chap at one of those symposia was very distressed by the way you're talking right now. He said "how you can call it an experiment when you change your minds a dozen times in the course of a morning, and come at it from so many different angles and different ways? That's not an experiment!" [Laughter].

WMC We know now from really good work in the History of Science like David Gooding's on experiment (Gooding et al. 1989) that that's exactly how experiments are worked. That's the second thing that I think is really important about this work: it exemplifies the experimental method which is brand new to the Humanities. When I started, you planned your computer program out really, really well and did a flow chart and all that. Then you took your deck of cards down to the computing center and if you were really important like a Nobel Prize physicist, you could get your answers back in a couple of hours. Otherwise it was 2 days or a week, only to learn that you'd made some keypunch error [laughter]. It was only the hackers at MIT who had talked about the hands-on imperative who understood. They were sitting at the console, playing with the computer from midnight until eight in the morning. They understood this experimental method, which now we have because now you have these small machines. But, your point about the idea of experiment is really important.

WMC Well, thank you two very much for the interview.

References

Argamon, S. (2012). [Review of] scalability issues in authorship attribution [by] Kim Luyckx [sic]. *Literary and Linguistic Computing, 27*(1), 95–97.

Auerbach, E. (2013). Mimesis: The representation of reality in western literature (1st Princeton classics ed.). Princeton: Princeton University Press.

Brower, R. A. (1951). *The fields of light: An experiment in critical reading.* New York: Oxford University Press.

Burrows, J. (1987). *Computation into criticism: Study of Jane Austen's novels and an experiment in method.* Oxford/New York: Clarendon.

Burrows, J. (2002). "Delta": A measure of stylistic difference and a guide to likely authorship. *Literary and Linguistic Computing, 17*(3), 267–287.

Clemen, W. (1977). *Development of Shakespeare's imagery* (2nd Revised ed.). London: Routledge.

Craig, H., & Kinney, A. F. (Eds.). (2009). *Shakespeare, computers, and the mystery of authorship.* New York: Cambridge University Press.

Gooding, D., Pinch, T., & Schaffer, S. (Eds.). (1989). *The uses of experiment: Studies in the natural sciences.* New York: Cambridge University Press.

Jackson, M. D. P. (2002). Pause patterns in Shakespeare's verse: Canon and chronology. *Literary and Linguistic Computing, 17*(1), 37–46.

McCarty, W. (2005). *Humanities computing.* Basingstoke/New York: Palgrave Macmillan.

Russell, D. (1965). A word-count and concordance generator. *Atlas Computer Laboratory, Chilton: 1961–75.* Available at: http://www.chilton-computing.org.uk/acl/applications/cocoa/p001.htm. Accessed 8 June 2015.

Schreibman, S., Siemens, R., & Unsworth, J. (Eds.). (2008). *A companion to digital humanities. Blackwell companions to literature and culture.* Oxford: Blackwell Publishing Professional.

Short, H., et al. (2012). Collaboration must be fundamental or it's not going to work: An oral history conversation between Harold Short and Julianne Nyhan. *Digital Humanities Quarterly, 6,* 3. http://www.digitalhumanities.org/dhq/vol/6/3/000133/000133.html

Upton, G. J. G., & Cook, I. (2008). *A dictionary of statistics* (2nd rev ed.). Oxford/New York: Oxford University Press.

Weimann, R., & Bruster, D. (2010). *Shakespeare and the power of performance: Stage and page in the Elizabethan Theatre* (Reissue ed.). Cambridge: Cambridge University Press.

Open Access This chapter is distributed under the terms of the Creative Commons Attribution-Noncommercial 2.5 License (http://creativecommons.org/licenses/by-nc/2.5/) which permits any noncommercial use, distribution, and reproduction in any medium, provided the original author(s) and source are credited.

The images or other third party material in this chapter are included in the work's Creative Commons license, unless indicated otherwise in the credit line; if such material is not included in the work's Creative Commons license and the respective action is not permitted by statutory regulation, users will need to obtain permission from the license holder to duplicate, adapt or reproduce the material.

Chapter 4
The University Was Still Taking Account of *universitas scientiarum*: Wilhelm Ott and Julianne Nyhan

Abstract This oral history interview between Wilhelm Ott and Julianne Nyhan was carried out on 14 July 2015, shortly after 10am, in the offices of *pagina* in Tübingen, Germany. Ott was provided with the core questions in advance of the interview. He recalls that his earliest contact with computing was in 1966 when he took an introductory programming course in the *Deutsches Rechenzentrum* (German Computing Center) in Darmstadt. Having become slightly bored with the exercises that attendees of the course were asked to complete he began working on programmes to aid his metrical analysis of Latin hexameters, a project he would continue to work on for the next 19 years. After completing the course in Darmstadt he approached, among others such as IBM, the Classics Department at Tübingen University to gauge their interest in his emerging expertise. Though there was no tradition in the Department of applying computing to philological problems they quickly grasped the significance and potential of such approaches. Fortunately, this happened just when the computing center, up to then part of the Institute for Mathematics, was transformed into a central service unit for the university. Drawing on initial funding from the Physics department a position was created for Ott in the Tübingen Computing Center. His role was to pursue his Latin hexameters project and, above all, to provide specialised support for computer applications in the Humanities. In this interview Ott recalls a number of the early projects that he supported such as the concordance to the Vulgate that was undertaken by Bonifatius Fischer, along with the assistance they received from Roberto Busa when it came to lemmatisation. He also talks at length about the context in which his TUSTEP programme came about and its subsequent development. The interview strikes a slightly wistful tone as he recalls the University of Tübingen's embrace of the notion of *universitas scientiarum* in the 1960s and contrasts this with the rather more precarious position of the Humanities in many countries today.

Biography

Wilhelm Ott was born on 3 January 1938 in Gerolzhofen, Germany. From 1949 to 1957 he attended the Altes Gymnasium Würzburg. From 1957 to 1966 he read Philosophy at the Pontificia Universitas Gregoriana and Theology and Classics in

© The Author(s) 2016

J. Nyhan, A. Flinn, *Computation and the Humanities*, Springer Series on
Cultural Computing, DOI 10.1007/978-3-319-20170-2_4

the Universities of Würzburg, Tübingen and München. He was awarded a PhD in New Testament Theology by the University of Würzburg in 1965. He was a research officer (*wissenschaftlicher Angestellter*) for computer applications in the Humanities at the Computing Center of the University of Tübingen from 1966 to 2003 and, from 1970, head of the Division for Literary and Documentary Data Processing, which had been founded for this purpose and where the Tübingen System of Text Processing Programs (TUSTEP) was developed. He also had various other roles: from 1967 to 1970 he acted as the system administrator for the mainframe computer of the computing center, and from 1973 to 2003 vice-Director of the center. He was also engaged in university knowledge transfer and commercialisation from an early stage: in 1973 he was co-founder of the limited liability company *pagina*. In addition to his many other activities he was appointed honorary Professor at the Universities of Würzburg and Tübingen in 1988 and 1989 respectively. He officially retired in 2003 but continues to work in *pagina* and acts as head of the Tübingen group that is tasked with the further development of TUSTEP. In 2007 he was given the Busa award of the Alliance of Digital Humanities Organisations (ADHO) in recognition of his outstanding contributions to Humanities Computing.

Interview

JN In 1966 you had your first contact with computing as a participant of the programming course *Nichtnumerische Datenverarbeitung* (non-numeric data processing) at the *Deutsches Rechenzentrum* (German Computing Center) in Darmstadt. The question that I want to ask goes back to a little bit before then. I wondered about your earliest memory, in any context at all, of encountering computing or computing technology?

WO I do not remember too much regarding computing from this earlier period. In 1966 I noticed an announcement on a notice board at the University of Munich (where I was studying Classics) that the *Deutsches Rechenzentrum*[1] was offering programming courses that were also available to Humanities people. This interested me. I had been busy studying Theology and had completed a doctorate in it. I knew that I would not earn my living from Theology and so I had started a second study in Classics. From school times I always had a great affinity to mathematics and physics. I saw the training that was advertised as a chance to get involved in computing in the context of Humanities.

---

[1] 'In October 1961 ... the German Computing Center was founded in Rheinstraße 75 in Darmstadt. It was the first academic computing center in Germany and was one of the most important milestones in Computer Science in Germany' (translation by Nyhan). See: https://www.informatik.tu-darmstadt.de/de/aktuelles/neuigkeiten/neuigkeiten/artikel/50-jahre-deutsches-rechenzentrum-fraunhofer-sit/

JN And so you attended the course in Darmstadt essentially because you saw the notice, and thought, "that looks interesting"?

WO Yes, I thought it looked interesting and I had also some research problems which could perhaps be solved with it. In Theology I had worked on the New Testament and the differences on the teaching on prayer between the gospels (Ott 1965). In this context it was important to look for details in the speech and wording that the respective evangelist used. A lot of philological tools were available, there was special grammars and concordances for the New Testament – and I missed this in Classics. Therefore I thought that a computer could help.

When I started the programming course in the spring of 1966 it was relatively early times for Humanities Computing. The first part of the coursework was in Assembler, this means working very near to the hardware of the machine. The second part was in FORTRAN, using a set of sub-routines for character and string handling that the Darmstadt group had just developed, because FORTRAN, at that time, did not even have a CHARACTER statement. With those sub-routines one could at least get access to single characters and to strings, and one was able to move strings and to collate strings and so on. After some days I found the exercises they did a bit annoying. Therefore, since I was working on Vergil's *Aeneid*, an epic poem written in dactylic hexameters, and since I had learned from Eduard Norden's Commentary on Book VI of the Aeneid (1957) how important it was to also pay attention to the "pictorial elements" of the hexameter when interpreting the poem, I tried to design a program to automatically compile the metrical characteristics which Norden had collected in the appendix to his commentary. It worked, and it was my first experience of thinking about the application of computers to the Humanities.

When I started in Darmstadt I had just the basic tools. I had a FORTRAN compiler and I had that set of sub-routines. Later, when we moved from Darmstadt to Tübingen, it was an additional effort just to provide a set of sub-routines that were compatible with the Darmstadt ones and that would allow me to continue my work on a Control Data computer. In Darmstadt I had worked on an IBM 7090, and later a 7094.

JN What did you think about the computing that you encountered on that course? How useful or difficult was it? What is your general recollection of your feelings towards it?

WO Well, I think it was challenging and I was very curious to see if it would work. I tried hard and the courses (in assembler language and FORTRAN) lasted for a fortnight each. Of course, it worked, and it was fun, and I was happy.

JN In 1966 you became Research Officer (*Wissenschaftlicher Angestellter*) for computer applications in the Humanities in the Computing Center at the University of Tübingen. I'd especially like to hear about what your job entailed and your recollections of some of the earliest projects that you supported and worked with.

WO Well, the programmes that I wrote for analysing the hexameter were not finished by the time the training course in Darmstadt had finished. I was not able to pay for the computing time after the course. The course itself was free, but then, after a fortnight or so they said, "well, now your work is perhaps a research project and you have to pay for your computing time". Computing time then cost 230 DM per hour, and this was a bit much for a student who lived on a scholarship of 400 DM per month.

Therefore, I went to the Classics Department in Tübingen University where I continued my studies and showed them what I was working on to see whether they were interested. At the same time, the computing center had just moved out of the Mathematics Department and had become a central unit for the university, comparable to the university library. They saw the chance that in these circumstances they could also get advice for Humanities applications because I was a Humanist with a doctorate and I had proven that I had also some knowledge of computing. Therefore, they hired me, and the first thing I had to do was to continue my hexameter project but, of course, to also give advice and make it available to other interested people from the Humanities. With time those projects came.

One of the first projects that came was from outside the university. It was the concordance to the Vulgate, the Latin Bible, by Father Bonifatius Fischer (1977), a great project sponsored by the *Deutsche Forschungsgemeinschaft (DFG)*. They had heard about me via IBM Germany, whom I had also contacted in order to find out what opportunities existed for continuing my work. I had contacted Dr Hübner of IBM in Sindelfingen who had also been a member of the Classics Department in Tübingen before he went to IBM. From this contact resulted the first contact with Bonifatius Fischer, more or less a year later.

Another large project also came from outside Tübingen. Prof. Kurt Aland from the University of Münster wanted to prepare a new critical edition of the New Testament and so he wanted to determine which of the many manuscripts of the New Testament could be omitted from the apparatus. This problem required the grouping of the variant readings found by the manual collation of 98 selected passages of the Catholic letters, so as to find out the relationships between the approximately 500 manuscripts that contained the text.

Other projects came in from the University of Tübingen. In 1969, one of the larger projects was an index to 75 volumes (1895–1970) of the *Theologische Quartalschrift*.[2] Then in 1970, an index to the works of the middle-high German poet Heinrich Kaufringer was to be made by Paul Sappler of the German

---

[2] 'The *Theologische Quartalsschrift* is edited in Tübingen and is an academic journal that addresses all aspects of the discipline of Theology … it was founded in 1819' (translation by Nyhan). See: http://www.thq-online.de/wir_ueber_uns.php. For a short report on preparing the index volume, see http://www.tustep.uni-tuebingen.de:/prot/prot1.html#kustermann. The index was published in 1975 (Seckler 1975).

Department.[3] It was to be an edition plus index. He had asked for the index and I advised him to also prepare the edition itself by computerised typesetting because then the data would be error-free for the index. In the meantime the TUSTEP typesetting programme (see below) was working. It was one of the first typesetting routines that could make up whole pages on a Digiset (the first digital typesetter). And, at the same time, a further project came from the Institute of Hebrew Studies at the University of Tübingen, an edition of the *Mishna* by Michael Krupp. This meant further problems and further challenges because the Hebrew fonts needed for the Mishna edition were not available for the Digiset at that time. The right to left reading was also difficult for processing and so on, but as a former student of Theology, I knew enough about Hebrew that I could get involved with this project.[4]

JN I want to go back and ask you a little bit more about some of those projects. Can you tell me more about Bonifatius Fischer? I know you put him in contact with Busa regarding lemmatisation.

WO Well, there are many interesting aspects in this project. The first thing I told him when he asked me to work on the concordance was "well, before starting we should have an error-free, machine-readable text of the Vulgate". The edition for which the concordance was planned was the new edition which he had just finished, together with Robert Weber. Fischer told me that he was not very good at proofreading; he was much better at typing. Therefore I told him, "well, then let us transcribe this text twice and compare the two transcriptions", and so we did, and it worked out very fine. I have also published a short article about this approach (Ott 1970).

Then, in order to prepare the concordance, the word forms had to be lemmatised (which means using the word forms not as they occurred in the text but rather their dictionary forms, or *Grundformen*). And so I contacted Father Busa in Gallarate, or in Pisa, where he had just moved to, and asked him if he could give us a copy of his *Lexicon Electronicum Latinum* (LEL), as he called it.[5] I visited him in Pisa and he generously gave us his lexicon and we took it as a basis for the lemmatisation. Later he asked me to give him a list of words which occurred in the Vulgate but not in Thomas of Aquinas so as to complement it – it worked fine.

JN You showed me print outs of a lot of this material yesterday. It was fascinating for me to have the opportunity to look at your archive.

---

[3] Sappler, who died on 14 April 2010, was also active in the wider Humanities Computing community. His obituary is here: https://www.uni-tuebingen.de/en/news/newsletter-uni-tuebingen-aktuell/2010/1/leute/12.html. For a short report on the project see http://www.tustep.uni-tuebingen.de/prot/prot1.html#sappler

[4] For outline details, see http://www.tustep.uni-tuebingen.de/prot/prot2.html#krupp and http://www.tustep.uni-tuebingen.de/prot/prot12.html#krupp.

[5] Busa wrote '[f]or this, we first punched, sequenced and numbered the 90,000 lemmas in the Forcellini's *Lexicon Totius Latinitatis*' (1980, p. 86). A description of the 'LEL de Gallarate' by Busa is available at http://promethee.philo.ulg.ac.be/RISSHpdf/annee1969/02-03/RBusa.pdf.

WO   Yes. Regarding the lemmatisation itself, the first step was to isolate all the word forms that occurred in the text. A speciality of this concordance was that it included not only the words of the text but also the entries that appeared in the *apparatus criticus*. So the apparatus entries were also transcribed. The second step was to sort the word forms alphabetically. The third step was then to mix into this sorted material the entries from the Busa lexicon. For each word form of the Latin text of the Bible we got an average of two and a half lemmata, depending, of course, on the frequency of the homograph word forms in Latin. For example, *est*, 'he is' or 'it is', could not be only a form of *esse*, 'to be' but also of *edere*, 'to eat'. These are homographs. Another simple example is *facies*, which can be 'the face' or it can be a verb form of *facio*.

Then, after the lemmata had been intermixed with the sorted list of words, they were sorted back into the sequence of the text because otherwise you cannot determine which form corresponds to which lemmata in a given context. Then, a new printed list was produced again, where after each line of text all the word forms that occurred in this line were printed in separate lines along with the respective lemmata. Then the manual work that established which of the lemmata was appropriate in that place started. For this work Fischer had engaged a monastery of Benedictine nuns in Kempen on the Rhine. All of them had an *Abitur* (final secondary-school examinations) with Latin as a second language, and therefore they were very happy with this work which was of course, closely controlled or surveyed by Bonifaitus Fischer. They did work for some years on the lemmatisation.

For this step of manually controlling the word forms for which more than one lemma had been found in the lexicon, I had arranged the materials (that is the lines showing word forms plus lemma below each bible verse) so that the most probable lemma was the first one listed. For example, for *est*, the first was not *edere* but *esse*, though *edere* is, in alphabetic order, before *esse*. I tried to pay attention to the frequency in order to have the most probable solution in the first place. When, in this list, the first lemma was right, then nothing had to be done. If the second or the third lemma was the correct one then the following had simply to be typed: the number of the line and of the word which was printed in this list plus the current number of the correct lemma. Then, the material was sorted back into alphabetic order again, not according to the inflected forms but according to the lemmata. Then the material was prepared for printing using the typesetting programme that had also been developed in the course of the work on this concordance. It was from this project that I first learned that it was important to have a programme that could transport the results of philological work error-free to print. But that is a totally different theme of course!

At the time the project started, the typesetting industry was still relying on hot metal typesetting, lead typesetting. Indeed, due to a hint from Dr Hübner of IBM, the first contact that I had in this context was with the printing house of the *Mittelbayerische Zeitung* (a newspaper publisher) in Regensburg, who had a Linotype driven by paper tape. This paper tape was being prepared by a computer programme, which just provided for automatic line breaks including correct hyphenation. Well, hyphenation and line division were not important for us because the content of the Vulgate was short enough that it normally fit into a line and hyphenation for Latin was also not a problem for the concordance. The control of the typesetter itself was a problem. I had just written the first test when the notice came that the first cathode ray tube typesetter had been installed in Neu-Isenburg. Then I left the programmes that I had started for the Linotype and looked for a way to get access to the Digiset for the typesetting. Digiset was produced by the Hell company in Kiel and was the first cathode ray tube typesetter (see, for example, Sassoon 1993, p.76, 78, 88); in the States it was marketed as VideoComp by RCA Corporation. I got in contact with Lux Bildstudio in Neu-Isenburg and then I tried to prepare a programme so that this typesetter could be used for the publication of our data.

JN Yesterday you mentioned a conviction that you developed quite early on. It was that you wouldn't apply methods that you yourself didn't understand, or weren't familiar with. Would you again tell me about that and the context in which it came about?

WO Well, such concerns arose in connection with some later projects. The first projects I had supported related to Classics, a research field with which I was more or less acquainted. I knew Theology, Latin and Greek, the Bible and I also knew a bit of textual criticism from my dissertation, where it had been important to know how the text had developed over time. And I had been aware that it's a very, very sensitive field with very sensitive problems. For example, the problems of sorting. Many people do not really know how a text should be sorted. I remember many German publications from the early days where the umlauts, for example, were displaced to the end of the alphabet, after 'z'. Similar problems occur with other languages too. From observing such simple problems one concludes that some projects were overseen by a person who was not acquainted with the problems of the respective field and that the solutions that were offered were just not acceptable. Therefore, I decided to provide tools only for problems from my own field, or via a collaboration with persons who really knew their field and who were available and willing to spend some of their time on such discussions.

JN Is it correct of me to conclude that your 'philosophy' about the role of the computer was that it should support the advancement of humanistic knowledge, as opposed to being something to experiment with, and to purposely break things with …

WO No. At that time, people who decided to use a computer were people who had problems [laughs]. Sometimes I say, "well, it was the time of close reading and not the time of distant reading" [laughs]. It was not about playing with the material that was available: they had a problem and they wanted to solve it or to provide tools like dictionaries or indexes to periodical retrieval tools, and so on. Playing around was sometimes also a partial motivation, but the normal work was just helping people to solve problems.

JN You've already mentioned a number of important people in Germany and internationally. I wanted to ask about the key people who you came into contact with, how quickly you started to come into contact with them and also about processes of the transfer and discovery of knowledge.

WO In addition to the contact with the professors at Tübingen who provided that the computing center was established with a person and facilities for the Humanities, the first important contact I had was Dr Hübner of IBM. It was just 3 months after I had finished the programming course, and I wanted to ask him what facilities existed, and how one could proceed in this field. He had just written the hyphenation of German programme for the Linotype typesetter. He also had many contacts and it was due to him that the contact to Father Fischer had been established. The contact with Father Fischer also came about via the publisher Frommann-Holzboog in Stuttgart. From the course in Darmstadt and also from Hübner I got the names of some people and some projects and I tried to contact them too.

There were also some people outside of Germany. I contacted Professor Louis Delatte of the *Laboratoire d'Analyse Statistique des Langues Anciennes* in Liege[6] relatively early in July 1966. I visited him in October and reported on my approach and he found it very interesting, and gave me the hint that it should be advisable to publish or to prepare a paper on it, and to publish it in his *Revue*. So, in fact, in the last number of the *Revue* of 1966, I had the first paper on my computer-aided hexameter studies (Ott 1966). Many people worldwide, who then contacted me, found this paper interesting. One of the first was Joseph Raben from New York, who wanted a notice for CHum. I don't remember the first contact that I had with Stephen Waite (of Dartmouth College), who had been editing *Calculi*, his bi-monthly periodical for computer applications in the Classics since 1967. Father Busa, I just mentioned and reported that I contacted him in the context of the concordance to the Vulgate in April 1967. I visited him and Antonio Zampolli (his assistant at that time) in July of 1967. The contact to Kurt Aland from Münster had also been established by Bonifatius Fischer, who as an editor of Vulgate, of course, had close contacts with him.

Other international contacts came via the hexameter project. In September 1969, there was a large conference of *La Fédération internationale des associations d'études classiques* (FIEC) in Bonn.[7] It had about 800 participants, and they also asked me to give a report on my hexameter project (Ott 1969), and on this occasion,

---

[6] 'Founded at the University of Liège in November 1961, the Laboratory for the Statistical Analysis of Ancient Language (LASLA) was the first research centre to study the classical languages Greek and Latin using computational techniques' (translation by Nyhan). See http://www.cipl.ulg.ac.be/Lasla/

[7] *La Fédération internationale des associations d'études classiques* (FIEC)/The International Federation of Associations of Classical Studies (FIEC) 'is an umbrella organization that covers most associations of classical studies of national importance around the world … Every 5 years, FIEC holds an International Congress which gathers scholars from all parts of the world and from all sub-fields of classical studies'. See http://www.fiecnet.org/#!mission/ceax.

I came into contact with, for example, David Packard, who later founded the Packard Foundation.

Other contacts came too. Just about 4 years after my appointment to the Computing Center, in 1970, I heard of a conference Professor Roy Wisbey was organising in Cambridge. I wrote him a letter to ask if I was allowed to come to this conference, which seemed, at first glance, to be a national conference for England. In fact, I was the only German participant there and through it I made contacts with other important people, for example, Susan Hockey.

JN How did you find the reception, and the sense of cooperation, or not, among the participants?

WO I did not have a paper there because I noticed it relatively late and I was just in the audience. But Roy Wisbey replied and invited me and it was a very fruitful contact. I am convinced that my presence there was also important because when the ALLC was subsequently founded it was not as a national British institution but as an international one. This is also what Wisbey told me later.

JN I wanted to ask you a little bit about the founding of the ALLC, so seeing as you've mentioned it, shall we talk about that now and then I might again step back in the chronology.

WO We can, of course. There was the session in 1973, I think, when I was not present but they had asked me before then to be the German representative in the Association. I decided not to do so and I was also a bit late with my answer. So, Professor Lenders of Bonn[8] was proposed for this and they asked me to be the representative for a specialist group on textual editing techniques. I heard the details of the founding second hand because I was not present at the founding session. There was a second conference in Edinburgh in 1972, before the founding of the ALLC and after the Cambridge conference where I was also present and gave a paper (see Ott 1973).

JN So, I want to go back and ask about the metrical analysis that you published with Niemeyer, between 1970 and 1985 (see, for example, Ott 1970). Yesterday you showed me, what I might call a 'paper search engine' [both laugh] to the text made with punched cards. Will you please describe them and explain how they worked?

WO The problems that I wanted to solve (in addition to providing overviews for the hexameter poetry) I had drawn from the appendix to the commentary of Eduard Norden to the sixth book of the Aeneid (1957). He was convinced that metrics were important for interpreting a poem and had a lot of criteria that he looked for: the

---

[8] Winfried Lenders (1943–2015) was appointed Professor for 'Linguistische Datenverarbeitung' (Linguistic data processing) at the University of Bonn in 1974. A short obituary can be found here: www.gscl.org/ehrenmitglied.html.

number of words and the position of the word endings in respect to the verse structure. In the middle of a hexameter there is normally also a caesura (or a pause) and he also looked for where exactly this caesura is on average, or in most verses, and so on.

Therefore, one of the tools I provided, and which I thought it was possible to provide beyond the printed lists, was a tool to allow one to look for combinations of word endings in the verse. I thought that it could be done relatively easily using a punched card. The punched card had 80 columns, with at least 10 positions that could easily be numbered vertically. Additional rows 12 and 11, as they were called, were not used for representing the number of lines, or the number of verses. Therefore I provided 16 punched cards, one for each position in the hexameter, as the hexameter consists of 6 feet, and each foot can have either two or three syllables: two long syllables, or one long syllable and two short syllables (that makes 16 times three, or 18, but the verse end is always a word end. Therefore it can be neglected and the last foot is almost always two syllables only. That meant I had 16 positions that were interesting). And so, I provided 16 punched cards. On each card I made a hole in the respective position. Where, for example, a word ended just after the first syllable in line three of a poem, I made a hole in the first card in column zero, row three and this indicated the occurrence of a monosyllabic word at the beginning of the verse. And this I did for the 16 positions in the verse and for every line. Then, if you want to see if, for example, a verse that starts with a monosyllable, and ends with a monosyllable, you just take the first and last card and put them together, one above the other, hold them against the light, and where the holes are shining through, there you have the number of the lines of the verses which start and end with a monosyllabic word. It's as easy as this.

JN And where did the idea for this come from?

WO Well, I was accustomed to punched cards. Data entry was on punched cards and some output was on punched cards for further processing. The compiled programmes were also on punched cards. So, for a second run, if you have the same programme but different data, you could just use the binary text of the programme to produce it. I was also aware of some people's work with so called *Randlochkarten* (edge-notched cards) where one could sort the material by mechanical means.

JN *Randloch* is the hole at the side of the card?

WO It was cards where the content was written by hand. On the margin of those cards was a perforation, I think it was, and you could cut this with the help of a special scissors, so that if you got a needle or a nail or something to go through a notched hole and lifted the needle, the respective cards would fall back. This is a mechanical tool and I thought such approaches to inspection could aid this problem.

JN Wonderful. And do you know of any other Humanities Computing projects that did that?

WO No, I don't remember any at the moment.

JN In 1973 you co-founded *pagina GmbH,*[9] so I'd like to hear about how it was that the idea for a commercial company came about?

WO Well, it also has a long history. I related that I came into contact with the Digiset typesetting technique in the course of the work on the Vulgate. In fact, the first volume that I published with a programme that I wrote for the Digiset was not the Vulgate, but the first volume of my hexameter studies. One of the other earliest projects to use this typesetting program was the edition of the works of Kaufringer by Paul Sappler, which was to be published by Niemeyer. Paul Sappler asked Niemeyer if, instead of delivering a manuscript, he could just typeset it. The technical production manager of Niemeyer, Wolfgang Reiner, saw it just as he was looking for a replacement for hot metal typesetting. He got in contact with me and proposed to make this service available commercially for typesetting in publishing houses. We decided to found the firm *pagina* (*pagina* is a Latin word for the page). The programme I had made was the first programme, as far as I know, that did not only provide hyphenation and line breaks but also complete page make-up, including page numbering, running heads and so on. So we founded *pagina:* the name comes from the ready-made pages we created, and it was a typesetting firm for, more or less, publishers in the Humanities, because Niemeyer was, of course, also in this field.

JN And *pagina* is, I think, probably unusual among Humanities Computing and Humanities projects in that it is an early example of research that was done in a university and then commercialised and taken outside the university context. And so I wondered what sort of a response you got to it from your university colleagues?

WO Well, it was not very common at those times, to get a so-called *Ausgründung* (spin off), as they call it nowadays in German. Well, I, of course, made applications and it consisted more or less in the fact that I was allowed to get *Anteile* (financial shares) of a *GmBH (Gesellschaft mit beschränkter Haftung;* a limited liability company). The cooperation with *pagina* was indeed really fruitful for the university and its publishing because I was not trained in publishing or in typography and so on. I got this whole know-how from this company and from Wolfgang Reiner. Also the first description of the typesetting programme was not made by me but by Reiner as he also knew the terminology and other things that were important. So this was a really fruitful cooperation.

JN And we should make the point that *pagina* is still going strong to this day.

---

[9] See: http://www.pagina-online.de/.

WO Well, *pagina* has become an established firm in the meantime. At the moment typesetting is only a tiny part of its activities. This is another theme. The first business area of *pagina,* used as a supplement to the name of the firm, was *Elektronische Satzherstellung* (electronic typesetting) and later, in 1966, it was changed to *Gesamtherstellung Wissenschaftlicher Werke* (overall production of scholarly works).

Nowadays (and since 2011) it is "publishing technologies", including online publications and e-book publications, workflows for publishing houses, the introduction of XML technologies and so on. Typesetting is only a tiny part of it, but *pagina* in the meantime has also established an *Abteilung* (a division) called Digital Humanities, and it's also giving advice to Humanities Computing projects from transcription to collation and so on. At the moment two to three people are working there.

JN Now I want to ask you a bit about TUSTEP (*Tübinger System von Textverarbeitungs-Programmen*; a professional toolbox for the scholarly processing of textual data).[10] So, from what I've read, it was named TUSTEP in 1978, but it seems quite clear from what you've been saying, that the processes towards it were going on for some time before that. You've explained a lot of the context that TUSTEP came about in but I also want to ask about the process of identifying that TUSTEP was needed and useful and how you went about those first steps of actually setting it up?

WO As I said, I was hired by the university to give advice and support to Humanities projects. The first thing I did was to make available the tools I used (this was the set of sub-routines for character handling in FORTRAN) and to give FORTRAN courses. Paul Sappler, and Gottfried Reeg (from 1984 at FU Berlin) started with those tools and programmed by themselves. We did the programming for other people in the computing center. As the number of projects increased, it was no longer possible to continue as before. Therefore we thought of a way to make the users a bit more independent by allowing them to do much of the work for themselves. We tried to isolate the most common basic functions that were needed for Humanities Computing.[11]

One, for example, was a programme, it was indeed a separate programme in the beginning, which extracted particular sentences or records or a certain string from a file, for example. Another programme, it was also a separate programme, did search and replace functions on a file. Other basic functions related to preparing an index and allowed one to firstly break down the text into index entries, then to provide a sort key for the index, then to sort the material and then to reduce the sorted material to index entries. For example, I don't want to have 750 individual entries for the

---

[10] See: http://www.tustep.uni-tuebingen.de/tustep_eng.html.

[11] In this context it is interesting to note the later work of Unsworth (2000) on 'scholarly primitives' or methods that Humanities researchers are thought to have in common.

copula *und* (and) along with 750 individual references to it. I want the information to be summarised in one line. Neither do I want 750 references to frequent words, I only want their frequency, for example. Proceeding in such a modular way was one of the lessons I had learned through the concordance to the Vulgate.

When we started the concordance there were just two or three programmes available that produced concordances. One of them was COCOA, the word count and concordance programme provided by ATLAS in Great Britain, which later was the basis for the Oxford Concordance Program (OCP) by Susan Hockey and Ian Marriot. Susan Hockey was at Atlas before she moved to Oxford and co-developed the OCP programme. There was a further programme in Regensburg COBAPH (COBOL basic programmes for Philology), which also produced concordances, but these programs were more or less black boxes. You had some parameters that you could give along with your input text, then you got a concordance, but it was not lemmatised.

So I thought that, as problems are different in every field of the Humanities, we should provide the basic functions. I just mentioned that we included the critical apparatus in the concordance to the Vulgate. Therefore, I realised that the procedure for decomposing texts must be flexible and that it should be possible to define the details by parameters given by the user. The second step was providing the sort key. If you sort an English text or a Latin text, an ASCII key is just fine. However, when dealing with German texts, for example, you must take account of two different rules. One is for sorting lists of proper names, where you sort the umlauts as 'a + e' or 'o + e' or 'u + e', whereas you have to sort the umlauts as the basic letters without the trema or the umlaut dots in all other cases, as is done in subject indexes or in a dictionary. I think that if people from different faculties and different subject areas are to be helped, then we must provide the basic tools and the ability for them to define them according to their needs. Then the sorting (if the sort key is ok) is a purely mechanical thing. So this is also a separate module, which provides some efficiency and so on. The third step in this process of producing an index is, as I just said, to prepare the entries that have been sorted in the form required for publishing in print or on the web etc. If, like in the concordance to the Vulgate, you have a normal wordlist, it's relatively easy. If the text is indexed according to the subjects it contains, you will have a hierarchy of subjects, with a heading concept and sub-concepts and you will also want to show this. In such a case you should have also the possibility to define in detail how these records are to be built and presented.

With such elementary modules, users no longer had to care about programming in FORTRAN (or a similar language). They had those modules and they could specify input files and parameters, and they got an output file which could be used as input for the next module. Well, this is the concept we had; and in the course of time the modules turn out to be rich and sufficiently complete, so that in 1977, I think it was, I gave my last FORTRAN course. From 1977 we just instructed users on using those modules, and in 1978, when the child had some maturity, we baptised it, and called it Tübingen System of Text Processing Programmes, TUSTEP.

JN From 1973 until 2004 you organised the *Kolloquium zur Anwendung der EDV in den Geisteswisschenschaften an der Universität Tübingen.*[12] So when you look back at this very successful and, I think, symbolic symposium series, what are the real highlights for you, in terms of the papers given and those who attended?

WO We founded the colloquia to offer current users and interested guests the possibility to get together with us and with each other in order to share problems and to learn about what was happening outside of Tübingen. The colloquia started in 1973 and this was also the time when ALLC was founded. There is some correspondence in the dates because I wanted to keep in contact with international developments. In the first colloquia we had only relatively short papers that gave an overview of what was going on. Later, we tried to begin with a short overview of news followed by two papers (per colloquium) that got more into the details of the problems at hand. I invited people from outside from relatively early on. They were not using our system (TUSTEP), but other systems and this allowed me to learn what was happening elsewhere, which methods were applied in other places and so on. And so, with time, I had the chance to invite important people from the international community.

One of the most prominent speakers was Father Busa, in 1990, exactly 30 years – to the day – after he co-opened the colloquium on '*Maschinelle Methoden der literarischen Analyse und der Lexikographie*' in Tübingen in 1960. The last speaker on 5 February 2005 was John Unsworth on the 'Importance of digitisation and cyberinfrastructure in the Humanities'. Other speakers included Harold Short, on 18th of November, 2000 on 'The Role of Humanities computing: experiences and challenges'. I had planned to invite Antonio Zampolli to that colloquium, and he had just also consented to come, but then he had an accident, and could not come and Harold Short sprang in more or less immediately.

JN And when you think of the content of the papers given, is there one that really stands out in your mind as having been very exciting or one that heralded a new step forward?

WO It's difficult to say. The papers we had from the international participants were mostly overviews of what was happening. I could not say that there was one or two or three that were exceptionally important. People were coming from many projects across the whole field of Humanities Computing. This not only included texts but also archaeology, not very often, but sometimes, and so on. Well, I could not really say what was exceptionally important. Detailed reports of larger projects, for example, the Leibniz edition by Professor Schepers from Münster influenced other peo-

---

[12] See: http://www.tustep.uni-tuebingen.de/kolloq.html.

ple in their work. I'm just going reading over the list of participants. Susan Hockey was here in December 1998; David Seaman in February 1999; Michael Sperberg-McQueen in 1995; Jean-Louis Lebrave in 1986; Johann Cook from Stellenbosch in 1986; Michael Krupp from Jerusalem in 1977 …

JN You've already mentioned Eduard Norden. I wondered if there are any other people, ideas or books that influenced your approaches that you'd like to mention?

WO Eduard Norden was for the hexameter project, my own project. The other influences on the development of the software came from the particular projects. I do not remember, at the moment, a publication that had so much influence on me. Mostly the problems came from the projects, and sometimes of course, from publications I had read, but most of this was in collaboration with the project leaders. From the beginning I was also visiting the respective conferences and heard the papers that were given there. I had visited all of the early ALLC conferences and when ALLC merged with ACH I decided to go there every second year only. Much *Anregungen* (stimulation) came out of those conferences, of course. I think it was really important that for a position like the one I had, at a central institution like the computing center, that the person who is there is not only fit in Informatics (the concept of Informatics wasn't available at that time) but that they also know the methods and techniques of research in the Humanities and is at home there. I always said, when you have a technological problem it is relatively easy to get acquainted with the respective informatics methods and technology. That is much easier than it is for an Informatics scholar who must learn what Humanities problems are and the details that should be researched.

JN Yesterday I was referring to the fact that you had not one but two honorary professorships and I asked if you would have liked to have received them earlier. You said, no, because you had such freedom in your position in the computing center. Can you tell me more about that because I think it's very interesting from the international perspective?

WO Well, the first honorary professorship I got was in Würzburg, at the university, because they had established a course for Humanities Computing, and they wanted to have a Professor on their list. They selected me to be this person, and they gave me this title, and only shortly afterwards, a year or so later, the University of Tübingen gave me this title in order to give more weight to a project we had started in Tübingen. For the Universities of Baden-Württemberg there had been created *Forschungsschwerpunkte*, or centers of research expertise for a certain field. In Tübingen we were leading in *Wissenschaftliche Textdatenverarbeitung* (scholarly text data processing) and this was the context in which I got the second professorship. In Würzburg it was for the teaching aspect, but in Tübingen it was for research and responsibility for the project.

Had I been a normal professor, I would not, at least nowadays, have had the freedom that I had to develop those things. It would have entailed too much administrative work. Well, there was a lot of administrative work with the other position I had, especially since I was also the vice-Director of the computing center. All of this sometimes entailed a great deal of work, of course, especially when, in 1988, the Director changed in the middle of the year and I had the whole burden on my shoulders. But otherwise I had all the possibilities I wanted and I also had up to four collaborators who worked for my Department and I was very happy in these things.

JN You also mentioned that it was originally the Physics department that had some funds for the Computing Center?

WO When I started in Tübingen in 1966 the Professors of Classical Philology (Prof Ernst Zinn and Prof Wolfgang Schadewaldt) asked the computing center to create a post (that I would fill) in order to give support to the Humanities. The Physics Department had a post that was then free and they lent this post to the computing center for a year. It would not have been possible some years later. Well, it was in the late 1960s and I've always said that it was a time when the university was still taking account of the meaning of *universitas scientiarum* and individual disciplines had more or less equivalent weight. Well, when one sees what presently is happening to the Humanities worldwide and how they are going down in support one realises that it would not be possible today.

JN This question is probably not so relevant to you because the people who would have come to you were interested in using computers in any case. Still, I wanted to ask about your impressions of scholars who were not using computing in their research and about their evaluation of Humanities Computing research?

WO Well, I had little contact with those people. I remember one, whose name I will not mention here [laughs] because he's known, who, in a relatively important session said that the use of computers in the Humanities should be forbidden. But this statement was not very well accepted! As for myself, as I told you, I came to the Classics Department here in Tübingen, which did not use computers or even know that computers could be of help to them and I was accepted with open arms. It was seldom that I had contact with persons who were hostile to computing. There were some exceptions, of course, the one I told you about was in the context of the German Research Association.

JN Looking at the development of the field up to the present, do you have any disappointments about routes that the field took or didn't take?

WO Well, it's a question that I perhaps cannot really answer. The field that we tried to support was the field where Humanities people had problems that were not necessarily the mainstream of the field. Preparing an edition is a very laborious task and nobody becomes really known for having prepared a good edition. Indexing is also hard work and nobody becomes famous for preparing a fine index. One would perhaps say that those times and problems were connected with close reading and not with what nowadays is called big data and distant reading. Of course, the development of the web and the availability of material, and so forth, requires those questions to be asked. Yet, sometimes I have the impression that they are asked with too little real knowledge of what is being asked. You and I have spoken about the case of N-grams, where the results were not as exact as they should be because, for example, they could not consistently differentiate between the long s and f in some scanned documents. Nevertheless, big data and the availability of the data opens the possibility of asking new questions which could not otherwise be asked about the development of language, and so on. But it's another field of problems from that which we tackled.

Our TUSTEP software is more or less a set of tools for single works and it is also for development and for the analysis, editing and indexing of textual documents. It is not only for textual documents, but also for documentation. Many library catalogues have also been made with the tools we provided. At the University of Tübingen the Incunabula catalogue is still based on a TUSTEP server in the background.

JN It was really fascinating for me yesterday when you showed me so many of the beautiful editions that have been prepared with TUSTEP. It is very rare for me to see something material that has come out of these processes.

WO Well, sometimes you do not even notice that it has been prepared like this. Some people did not even mention that it had been done. This was perhaps caused by the fear that some people had in the beginning about applying computing but today it's no problem of course, no question at all.

JN Is there anything that you want to add or anything that you want to bring up?

WO Some people are supposedly against TUSTEP because it is one of the oldest programmes. So, I sometimes say, 'Well, ok, Daimler, Benz, Mercedes, they have been the first to build cars and therefore they are so antiquated!' And well, sometimes this helps as they begin to realise that TUSTEP has not been left in the state of 1966 or 1978; it has been developed. For example, the TUSTEP typesetting programme is the first one I know of that is able to typeset documents with XML encoding and to provide a stylesheet for typesetting them. There are, of course, some other reasons that TUSTEP is not very well known internationally and, perhaps also in the meantime, less accepted in the German-speaking environment. One factor is the language of documentation: it's in German only. In 1989 we had an English translation of the manual done but this is now out of date and we did not have the means to continue this work because all the funding of the *Forschungsschwerpunkt* (mentioned above) had ceased in 1989. The second factor is the command-line-based interface.

Therefore, for some years we have been working on an interface to the TUSTEP programmes in an XML environment. It's called TXSTEP, we just changed the 'u' in TUSTEP to an 'x'. In the meantime we have one user for it, working on the *Faust* edition in Frankfurt. They are using it especially for collating the sources of the *Faust* material. This XML interface for TUSTEP has the advantage that it's based on an XML schema that remains in the background but informs you about what steps are possible, what basic modules are available and so on. Annotations and instructions in pop-up windows indicate in English whether something is possible and this helps a bit to get rid of the language problem and of the necessity of studying the manual in advance. So I hope that such developments will perhaps help to make those tools a bit more attractive, also in the non-German speaking environment and in an environment where you are no longer willing to use command-line-based interfaces. Also, XML is not as 'user-friendly' as one might expect from other computing applications. But at least people who are accustomed to using computers nowadays are used to an XML environment for tools. This will also perhaps help with the switch to an application of this kind.

JN Thank you very much.

References

Busa, R. (1980). The annals of humanities computing: The index thomisticus. *Computers and the Humanities, 14*(2), 83–90.
Fischer, B. (Ed.). (1977). *Novae concordantiae Biblorum Sacrorum iuxta vulgatam versionem critice editam* (Vol. 5). Stuttgart-Bad Cannstatt: Frommann-Holzboog.
Norden, E. (1957). *P. Vergilius Maro, Aeneis Buch VI* (4th ed.). Leipzig: Teubner.
Ott, W. (1965). *Gebet und Heil. Die Bedeutung der Gebetsparänese in der lukanischen Theologie* (= Studien zum Alten und Neuen Testament, Bd. 12). München: Kösel.
Ott, W. (1966). Metrical analysis of Latin hexameter by computer. *Revue (LASLA, Liège), 4*, 7–20.
Ott, W. (1969). *Metrische Analyse lateinischer Hexameter mit Hilfe der elektronischen Datenverarbeitung*. FIEC bonn [conference presentation].
Ott, W. (1970). *Metrische Analysen zur Ars Poetica des Horaz* (= Göppinger Akademische Beiträge Nr. 6). Göppingen: Kümmerle 1970. 122 pp.
Ott, W. (1973). Computer applications in textual criticism. In A. J. Aitken et al. (Eds.), *The computer and literary studies* (pp. 199–223). Edinburgh: University of Edinburgh Press.
Sassoon, R. (1993). *Computers and typography*. Oxford: Intellect Books.

Seckler, M. (1975). *Register zur Theologischen Quartalschrift, Tübingen, 1895–1970.* Mainz: Matthias-Grünewald-Verlag.

Unsworth, J. (2000). *Scholarly primitives: What methods do humanities researchers have in common, and how might our tools reflect this?* King's College, London symposium: Humanities computing: formal methods, experimental practice. http://people.brandeis.edu/~unsworth/Kings.5-00/primitives.html

Open Access This chapter is distributed under the terms of the Creative Commons Attribution-Noncommercial 2.5 License (http://creativecommons.org/licenses/by-nc/2.5/) which permits any noncommercial use, distribution, and reproduction in any medium, provided the original author(s) and source are credited.

The images or other third party material in this chapter are included in the work's Creative Commons license, unless indicated otherwise in the credit line; if such material is not included in the work's Creative Commons license and the respective action is not permitted by statutory regulation, users will need to obtain permission from the license holder to duplicate, adapt or reproduce the material.

Chapter 5
hic Rhodus, *hic salta*: Tito Orlandi and Julianne Nyhan

Abstract This interview was carried out in Rome, Italy on 17 October 2014 at about 09:00. Orlandi recounts that his earliest memory of a computer dates to the 1950s when he saw an IBM machine in the window of an IBM shop in Milan. Around 1960, together with his PhD supervisor Ignazio Cazzaniga, he engaged in some brief exploratory work to see what role punched card technology might play in the making of a critical edition of Augustine's *City of God*. His sustained take up of computing in the 1970s arose from the practical problem of managing the wealth of information that he had amassed about Coptic manuscripts. He was aware from an early stage of the possible limitations of computational approaches: his early encounters with the work of Silvio Ceccato left him wary of approaches to cybernetics. He identifies the work of the applied mathematician Luigi Cerofolini who taught him UNIX, among other things, as having been central to his understanding of methodological issues. In relation to theory, he emphasises the impact that understanding Turing's Universal Computing Machine made on him. Indeed, his work on the significance of modelling to Humanities Computing (see, for example, the discussion in Orlandi, T. (n.d.)) preceded that of McCarty (2005). In addition to questioning inherited beliefs about the origins of DH, particularly in regard to the role of Fr Roberto Busa S.J., in this interview Orlandi argues that DH has not given sufficient attention to the fundamentals of computing theory.

Biography

Tito Orlandi was born in Cremeno (Como) on June 18, 1940. He graduated from Università degli Studi di Milano (the University of Milan) in 1963 with a dissertation in the History of Ancient Philosophy. From 1976 to 2010 he was Professor of Coptic language and literature at the Università degli Studi Roma "La Sapienza", Italy. From 1992 to 2010 he was Director of the University's Centro Interdipartimentale di Servizi per l'Automazione nelle Discipline Umanistiche

© The Author(s) 2016
J. Nyhan, A. Flinn, *Computation and the Humanities*, Springer Series on Cultural Computing, DOI 10.1007/978-3-319-20170-2_5

(CISADU, the Center of Service for Automation in the Humanities). He was also the Director (1984–1994) of 'Informatica per le Scienze Umanistiche' an early course in the area of Humanities Computing in his University in Italy. He continues to work as Director of the Corpus dei Manoscritti Copti Letterari (CMCL), an online scholarly resource that comprises a range of sources, especially in the Coptic language, for the study of Egyptian Christian culture in the first to twelfth centuries C.E. In addition to his many contributions to Coptic studies he made a pioneering and distinctive contribution to the emergence of Humanities Computing in Italy and beyond.[1] He co-authored *Computing in Humanities Education*: *A European Perspective* (de Smedt et al. 1999). A festschrift in his honour was edited by Fiormonte and Perilli (2011).

Interview

JN What is your earliest memory, in any context, of encountering computing or computing technology?

TO I saw IBM machines in the window of their shop in Milan in the 1950s and so I became aware that something like that existed. I was still at the Gymnasium [secondary school].

Then, early on in my time at the university I became acquainted with Silvio Ceccato. Does that name say anything to you? Probably not, but he was one of the first Italian intellectuals – and he was Professor at the University of Milan, of course – to become interested in the Artificial Intelligences or methods to produce artificial reasoning.[2]

I was studying Philology at the time and so my Professor of Philology and I tried to arrange a system (this was around 1960) to explore the possibilities of making a critical edition in Latin of St Augustine's *The City of God*, with the help of those card computers. I was, in a sense, the originator of the project, because I spoke with my Professor of Philology, Ignazio Cazzaniga, about it. He was curious about those things but he did not know anything about them. I also did not know anything but I had an idea of what it could be. We began to punch cards (I don't know what has become of them) and then our project finished because I had other things to do. So we tried but we gave up.

JN It was too complicated?

---

[1] The section of Orlandi's bibliography that pertains to Humanities Computing is here: http://www.cmcl.it/~orlandi/pubinf.html.

[2] Ceccato (1914–1997) was founder and director of the first Centre for Cybernetics in Milan and was 'the first in Europe to apply the cybernetic principle of self-organisation to the domains of concept formation and language' see Glasersfeld (1998).

TO No, we were distracted with other things! You know how this happens – it was just an idea. But we started to punch cards because it is easy to imagine that if you have a system that can put words into a given order and compare them you will have a critical idiom and methodology that you can start experimenting with. This is the naïve way of saying it was an idea that seemed valid in those years. So that was my first encounter with computing. But of course, the experience of the possibility remained in my mind.

By the late 1970s I had collected a great amount of information pertaining to Coptic manuscripts and other literature. It became difficult for me just to manage that information and so I thought "I must try to do this automatically." I contacted some companies like Nixdorf Computer AG,[3] and others, in order to explore the possibilities that existed then. But when I went to the *Centro di calcolo* (the Computer Centre) of the University of Rome everything really began.

JN Why did you contact companies rather than going to the computer centre in the first instance?

TO I confess that I was not very confident in the organization of the computer centre, and, most of all, I was afraid that they would not welcome a Humanities scholar. In fact, I came to realise that the personnel there who were available to help me were really good and I worked with them with much satisfaction.

JN And were others also pursuing Humanities Computing topics in the university at the time?

TO As I mentioned, Professor Ceccato, but he had also seen that those machines could, in a way, think. As a person he was very brilliant but also a bit out of reality. He was, in a sense, one of those people who is so enthusiastic that their feet scarcely touch the ground.

JN He was too enthusiastic about the technology?

TO Yes, and more than that. There is always this double side: good and bad. I mean, he had seen the relationship between pure thinking and automatic procedures. That he had seen, but then he went about it in an unrealistic way.

JN This is the story of the history of Artificial Intelligence to an extent, isn't it?

---

[3] Nixdorf Computer AG (NCAG) came about when Heinz Nixdorf, who had founded the *Labor für Impulstechnik* in Essen in 1952 bought out *Wanderer-Werke*, based in Cologne. Having originally produced products for the punched card sector, from the 1960s the company produced, among other products, stand-alone, programmable machines for small to medium sized businesses starting with the Nixdorf 820. See: 'The products of Nixdoft Computer AG' http://www.hnf.de/en/museum/nixdorf-wegbereiter-der-dezentralen-datenverarbeitung/the-products-of-nixdorf-computer-ag.html.

TO Exactly, but it has also taught me to beware of Artificial Intelligence because I don't like the uncertainty. That has to do with possibilities, another question. The man I consider my real teacher in computing and also Humanities Computing is Luigi Cerofolini. He was an applied mathematician who also studied the logical theory of numbers, and so on. He taught me very much about what is and what is not a computer and a computing system. That is what I would call the real turn in my experience with Humanities Computing. He was very realistic, very straightforward. There was no charlatanism in his approach and he hated Artificial Intelligence.

JN So when you talk about the turn in your experience, who else had you worked with before then (apart from the colleague who worked on Artificial Intelligence)?

TO Let me set the chronological development straight. In the 1950s, I had the experience with this brilliant man in Artificial Intelligence. Then a dark period! Then the experience in the seventies, first with people in the *Centro di calcolo*, the Computing Centre of the University of Rome, and they were ingenious. Mirella Schaerf, the Director, was very helpful. She was an engineer and she understood my problems and provided a Database Management System (called Omnidata), then running on the UNIVAC mainframe of the centre. She explained how it worked and gave me free access. The staff of the centre were very helpful for some practical things but not for all the rest. The methodological problems I had to try to imagine by myself.

Then I met Luigi Cerofolini and he taught me about the methodological issues and I encountered two things – that is why I speak of a "turn". First, I encountered the Turing machine and I had never heard about that before. Second, I encountered Unix. I insist, and nobody in Humanities Computing wants to acknowledge this, but I think that what is most important from the theoretical side is the Turing machine and from the practical side is the Unix system. Cerofolini taught me that Unix is not an operating system, it is an environment system. It is all the ground you have at your disposal when you work. And that is, I think, extremely important as background for this, and that was the turn.

JN I know that you've published on this (see, for example, Orlandi 2002, 2000) but would you also say a bit more about the theory of the Universal Turing machine and the impact that it had on your work?

TO Not only on my work but on my life! Well, seriously, I have understood that the Turing machine is mysterious and also, in a sense, a mystic-philosophical link between logic, reason and something that materially happens, that is the computer or whatever. You know the computer is not only what we generally call 'a computer'? It is anything that can perform automatic procedures on discreet quantities. And, in fact, it gives you the possibility to express your theoretical ideas in a way that is actionable. That is what I happened to like very much about Humanities Computing because in Humanities you can discuss everything and everybody is right. How do you check whether Virgil is a good poet or not? How do you check whether Virgil really wrote that verse or not, and so on. Those discussions have gone on for centuries and everybody is right! Well, I'm not trying to say that everything can be solved in Humanities with computers. But at least you can say *"hic Rhodus, hic salta"* to some questions. If you have an idea you formalise it and put it into something that is materially real. You could not do that before Turing. After Turing you can and this is the wonder of the Turing machine.

JN Do you think that this contribution characterises the work of Humanities Computing?

TO You know, I divide Humanities research into two sectors. One sector is governed by logic, the other sector is governed by what you might call intuition. Intuition is not manageable and you either have it or you don't. It is difficult to subject intuition to scrutiny: one can say "that is a good intuition" while another says "that is a bad intuition".

However, when one develops a historical proposition they must construct it logically. If it is not logically constructed it is intrinsically contradictory and does not stand. That part of Humanities may be automated with enormous consequences in the sense that computers (this is banal but this is where it enters) can manage quantities of memories that the human brain cannot. And so, if you can apply your method (or logic) to an enormous amount of material then you will probably be able to concretely see where it does not work.

JN When you mentioned Milan I wondered whether you also encountered Busa and the work of Busa?

TO I encountered Busa relatively late and not in Milan. Whether Father Busa is the origin of Humanities Computing is a delicate question. Here I prefer to limit myself to two observations: firstly, although his relationship with IBM (which at the time did not include real computation, like the UNIVAC, for example) is, of course, established, there is absolutely no evidence outside Busa's own recollections that he had real computation in mind. Secondly, Busa had no linguistic or semiotic background in a conventional sense and his work was placed far from ongoing computational developments.

The real beginnings of Humanities Computing can be found in some experiments, especially on artificial translation and automatic translation, which made mistakes, but never mind. Here I'm referring, of course, to the work of William Weaver, Norbert Wiener, and others. We must also look to some branches of archaeology, especially the experiments of Jean-Claude Gardin and the new archaeology, in America and beyond. There you find something really interesting. Of course, mistakes were made, it was a case of trial and error, as they say. But I don't agree that Father Busa may be mentioned among the pioneers. The position that he now has is not only wrong but misleading.

JN In the research that I've been doing on Busa, my working hypothesis at the moment is that Busa's legend is, to some extent, a useful fiction.

TO Perfectly!

JN And I don't mean to denigrate his work, but I think that his legend is something that the community has seized on as a foundation myth. He is a figure they can project things onto and organise around. But I think, exactly as you said, that the intellectual link is actually difficult to uncover in his earlier writings (though perhaps I'll be proven wrong on this as the research progresses). In any case, one of the things that I'm trying to figure out is how this 'useful fiction' came about? What were the establishment and transmission processes?

TO Busa had an enormous capacity for, if I may say so, selling himself. You know that in the modern world this is enormously important. We must also say and agree that he had a capacity for understanding what people tended to assume about the application of computers to the Humanities. He was an incredibly intelligent man, no question about that. But unfortunately he did not – this may be something to do with his being a Jesuit and that is also important – grasp the change in linguistic and mental attitudes brought about by the Turing machine. I am convinced, I don't know, perhaps I am wrong here, but in my idea Father Busa and Turing are something completely apart, one ignoring the other. So, after what I said, you understand that I do not agree that he was a pioneer. Indeed, the much more serious work done for the early Italian literary text by Mario Alinei and D'Arco Silvio Avalle does not come from Busa's group.

JN Can I ask you to name some other projects that you consider to have taken important steps forward?

TO Regarding the first critical edition, for instance, what comes to my mind is Peter Robinson's *Chaucer* (1996). But generally such projects are so open-ended. I maintain that what is important is not the fulfilment of a project but the methodological attitude that it has begun. In this regard Robinson's *Chaucer* project was very interesting. To this I would also add the work of Jean Claude Gardin (discussed below)

JN Did you at some point take formal training in computing?

TO Absolutely not. I trained myself using textbooks. The people at the University Computer Centre gave me some practical instruction and I met with Luigi Cerofolini on several occasions. We became friends; after a while, absolute friends. I remember that I went to America in about 1980 or 1981 and I went around the university bookshops to see what they had about computing and related areas. I acquired, and still have, some books about the fundamentals of computing theory and science, which today absolutely nobody in Humanities Computing mentions and it is strange how they put things.

I always studied, I try always to go deeper. What most of my colleagues in Humanities Computing don't do, one of the great things I often expose, is that they tend not to read about what they call "their subject". A worker, a mental worker in Humanities Computing, how much do they know of the bibliography on computing? From what I see, generally nothing, or almost nothing. This is the real shortcoming of the discipline of Humanities Computing; of course, you in UCL and King's College London are an exception. But generally such matters have no place in the discipline itself and of course we all weep about that. But we also have our faults!

I have, for instance, assembled a library that went from linguistics and encoding theory, for instance, to Jean Claude Gardin's *Archaeological Constructs: An Aspect of Theoretical Archaeology* (1980). Having such books ranging from the works of Gardin to treatments of the Turing machine together helps you to see their relations.

In my opinion we are still at an early stage of Humanities Computing in terms of the development of methodology. People speak about revolutions and the immediate changes that we can see on the surface of things. But deep changes require, I will not say tens of years, but hundreds. You know, Humanities Computing may be said to have existed since the late 1940s. It is almost a century old. If you go around (I don't mean in our circle) and ask people "What is Humanities Computing?" they, of course, will answer "libraries, catalogues," or "collections of texts". Well, where is the Humanities Computing in having at your disposal the pdf of this or that? This is not Humanities Computing!

JN Absolutely not. Unfortunately many people seem to think that's all it is. My impression is that this is especially the case since this move to DH, this term that's very often used now instead of Humanities Computing.

TO Yes, unfortunately people don't know what digital is! When they say "digital", they think of "electronic". What do Humanities people know about the difference between digital and analogue, for instance? They think that it's an obvious concept of which they need not to be aware. I am always against mathematics, in the sense that what you think is mathematics is really our environment, so I don't want to call that mathematics. That is logic. And "digital" is not necessarily "electronic", absolutely not.

JN You mentioned this word "revolution" and it's a word that is used an awful lot in DH and Humanities Computing circles. It's a word that puzzles me in a lot of ways, because to me, at least, a revolution involves overthrowing the corrupted past and working towards some glorious new future. So that might not necessarily be the way that it's used but would you be able to talk a little bit about encountering that term and what you understand is meant by that term within Humanities Computing?

TO I could not in the sense that when I want to describe such phenomena I find only that word. You know that computers are now very different to the "strange machines" that they were. Within the illustrious disciplines of the Humanities few conceived that an encounter between computers and Humanities could be achieved. You know very well that they said "computers are for mathematics, the Humanities is for thinking. Computers have nothing to do with languages or historical effects". All those who began to see that an encounter could be done spoke about a revolution, but not in the sense that they despised the older things. It was more so that they expected that the older habits of the Humanities would be disrupted by the new instrument. It is a revolution like what Elizabeth Eisenstein (1980) calls the printing revolution. You have nothing against manuscript, but with printing you have a revolution.

JN And why do you think the term continues to be used? I would argue that it's not so relevant anymore. It may continue to be a defining word but now it refers to circumstances that have come and gone.

TO Unfortunately, this term "revolution" has been used and continues to be used because it has taken on what I call "sociological ground". People now see that readers are not the same, libraries are not the same, archaeological excavations are not the same and so on. But just because roles have changed and instruments have changed – you do an excavation and use *telecameras*, and other wonderful things, and you have the measurements at once – they say "Ah, that is the revolution!" It's no revolution at all – it is analogous to having a microwave oven at your disposal when 50 years ago you did not. Is that a revolution? "Of course it is, it is a meaningful revolution!" Well, the food is about the same from that point of view!

JN What was your first encounter with the Humanities Computing community?

TO It's my privilege to be able to say I did not encounter it, I saw it growing. For instance I met Antonio Zampolli at the beginning of the thing. He was in Pisa at the *Istituto di Linguistica Computazionale* (Institute of Computational Linguistics) of the CNR, and so I saw how things were growing there. I met Willard McCarty here in Rome, at a meeting organised by the Canadian Embassy when he worked in Canada still. And so it was early in his career that we made our acquaintance. I think I met many of those who were present at the beginning.

I must say that Gardin is an exceptional case because he really is at the source of Humanities Computing. Gardin is another of the men (he died just recently) for whom I really feel a deep sentiment of respect. He was reflecting on the possibilities of computing in the 1950s, but nobody knew. He was a very reserved man; his story is rather unknown. And so I was not aware of his work until I read his book on archaeological constructs. I met him, not at the beginning, but when Humanities Computing was growing in France. In Germany I met Manfred Thaller (see Chap.

13) who is one of the other men who really knows things. He did not have much luck, of course, just because he is a good theoretician, and this happens.

JN What do you mean when you say that Thaller didn't have much luck?

TO To become a professor Thaller had to *"venire a patti"*, to compromise. He produced the collection of reproductions of manuscripts in Cologne, which is wonderful (see Chap. 13). I like it. Is it Humanities Computing? No, or yes with many reservations.

JN In some ways that interconnects with another question I had about your perception of how those who were not doing Humanities Computing reacted to and evaluated that work?

TO With scepticism, or even a range that went from *negazione* (denial) and *rifiuto* (refusal) to scepticism. I would say "rightly so" because unfortunately the enterprises in Humanities Computing were generally not sound enough to meet the attention of Humanities scholars who were not computing. Of course, the production of concordances, or things like that met with their approval at once. Such tools were very important but there is nothing theoretical about them. The Oxford Text Archive[4] is a wonderful thing and, then, after that, came Google. You see, everything that is practically useful is appreciated but such examples have nothing to do with the methodology and the study of the individual Humanities scholar.

The advancements in linguistic theory that emerged from the unfortunate experiments in artificial translation are very important (see Hutchins 2000). In this context I'm not only referring to experiments here in Italy. Geoffrey Sampson and the British National Corpus[5] and a lot of those enterprises are important too because they went together with Sampson's insights on two things. The first is syntactical linguistics and the polemic (Sampson 2005) he wrote against Chomsky (who, on the other hand, is a good example of the real interaction between computing principles and languages. Unfortunately I maintain that he was not philosophically sound enough, he took historical languages as something given by nature. Nevertheless, he was very interesting in this regard). That book is wonderful. The second is encoding principles, which is joined to alphabet theory. Sampson has written a wonderful book about alphabets (Sampson 2015), strange for one who creates the British National Corpus, you see, but this is just what I say. Advancements in Humanities

---

[4] 'The University of Oxford Text Archive develops, collects, catalogues and preserves electronic literary and linguistic resources for use in Higher Education, in research, teaching and learning'. See: http://ota.ox.ac.uk/.

[5] 'The British National Corpus (BNC) is a 100 million word collection of samples of written and spoken language from a wide range of sources, designed to represent a wide cross-section of British English, both spoken and written, from the late twentieth century.' See: http://www.natcorp.ox.ac.uk/.

may be obtained through reflection on computer applications and this book is a wonderful example of that.

JN Regarding the projects that were not accepted, is it your interpretation that they were not accepted because their applications were not so clear to the Humanities?

TO I think that they were not accepted because of a phenomenon that I will submit to you with much regret. When you begin to work seriously with automation (computers, but in the sense of automation) in the Humanities, you almost at once realise that in Humanities you don't know exactly what you do, and this is very hard to accept. This is my personal experience: how can I tell the colleague in, for example, Italian literature that he does not really know the texts he studies? How can I tell him that he does not understand what a text is and in which sense we can say that this text is by Dante or not? Or, even more, what is the meaning of orthography in this and that manuscript? What is the difference between the actual material design of a letter and the idea of a grapheme as part of the graphic and the spoken apparatus of one language?

The colleague would tell me that I am completely crazy and that these are not problems and in any case he does not want to study them. This is probably because they are intuitive problems. However, when you have to teach a machine how to manage such data, you must tell the machine exactly what everything is and you realise that you don't know the answers to the questions I just asked! Here is where the normal Humanities scholar keeps back because he cannot accept all that. It is a long process and in due course the normal Humanities scholars may come to accept such issues about the difficulties of formally defining such phenomena. And this is "*la scommessa*", the bet for the future, because from one side everything will be computerised. Whether we want that or not is not the problem – it will happen. And if so, the way that all the data of our disciplines will be computerised, the correctness of that depends on the generations from now on. And this is why I am very much, I will not say preoccupied, but why I try to think about this crucial problem.

You know, the trend now is infrastructures. The European community recommends the building of infrastructures for many domains but they will go by themselves. What is the idea of convening meetings on how to organise Humanities Computing infrastructures? Of course it takes money but they will have to build them in any case, with or without European money. Universities will have to build them at some point, and in any case it will cost them less and less. I don't see any research problems in the area of infrastructures, on the contrary. You will have huge amounts of data, of course, and bless it. But how will that data be put in digital form? That depends on a very delicate attitude and few people will understand that. Willard McCarty, Geoffrey Rockwell and Manfred Thaller will understand that, one, two, three and yet the phenomenon is spreading around the world. But we must not be pessimistic, of course! In any case we must realise that this is the great challenge of the next years. Let's try to sell that to responsible people even though it is not easy.

JN A lot of those I've interviewed have reflected to me that when they went to their first Humanities Computing conferences they often found that people were very friendly or that sometimes their experience was that the community was much friendlier than their home Humanities disciplines. I just want to ask how you respond to that?

TO Yes, I would agree. There was a great deal of *cameratismo* (comradery). This was a custom, just as it was in the wider computing environment. It was not so in Humanities. For instance, when the Oxford Patristic Conference[6] started it was not as huge as it is now, it was just held in a meeting room. In any case, everybody has his school. I think that now it is different in Humanities too because they have acquired that sense of comradery that was not present at the time.

JN You've already mentioned a couple of people who especially influenced you. Is there anybody else that you'd like to add, just to finish off?

TO No, I think one always forgets somebody on such occasions but I have mentioned most of them already.

References

de Smedt, K., et al. (1999). *Computing in humanities education: A European perspective*. Bergen: University of Bergen. http://gandalf.aksis.uib.no/AcoHum/book/
Eisenstein, E. L. (1980). *The printing press as an agent of change: Communications and cultural transformations in early-modern Europe*. Cambridge/New York: Cambridge University Press.
Fiormonte, D. & Perilli, L.(Eds.). (2011). *La macchina nel tempo: Studi di informatica umanistica in onore di Tito Orlandi*. Firenze: Le lettere.
Gardin, J. C. (1980). *Archaeological constructs: An aspect of theoretical archaeology*. Cambridge/New York: Cambridge University Press.
Glasersfeld, E. (1998). Obituary: Silvio Ceccato (1914–1997). *Cybernetics and Systems, 29*(3), 213–214. doi:10.1080/019697298125687.
Hutchins, W. J. (Ed.). (2000). *Early years in machine translation. Memoirs and biographies of pioneers. Studies in the history of the language sciences* (Vol. 97). Amsterdam: John Benjamins Publishing Company.
McCarty, W. (2005). *Humanities computing*. Basingstoke/New York: Palgrave Macmillan.
Orlandi, T. (2000). *Ideas for a theoretical foundation of humanities computing*. London Seminar, King's College London: Unpublished. http://www.cmcl.it/~orlandi/pubbli/saggiomio.pdf
Orlandi, T. (2002). Is humanities computing a discipline? In G. Braungart, K. Eibl, & F. Jannidis (Eds.), *Jahrbuch Für Computerphilologie* (Vol. 4, pp. 51–58). Paderborn: Mentis. http://computerphilologie.uni-muenchen.de/jg02/orlandi.html
Orlandi, T. (n. d.). A reaction on Willard McCarty's talk on the computational transformation of the humanities. *Home Page: Prof Tito Orlandi*. http://www.cmcl.it/~orlandi/mccarty1.html

---

[6] Founded in 1951, this is one of the leading conferences for those who study Patristics. See: http://www.oxfordpatristics.com/#!conferenc/c1jxp.

Robinson, P. (Ed.). (1996). *Geoffrey Chaucer, the wife of Bath's prologue on CD-ROM*. Cambridge/
    New York: Cambridge University Press.
Sampson, G. (2005). *The "Language Instinct" debate: Revised edition* (2nd ed.). London/New
    York: Continnuum-3PL.
Sampson, G. (2015). *Writing systems*. 2nd Revised ed. Sheffield/Bristol: Equinox Publishing Ltd.

Open Access This chapter is distributed under the terms of the Creative Commons Attribution-
Noncommercial 2.5 License (http://creativecommons.org/licenses/by-nc/2.5/) which permits any
noncommercial use, distribution, and reproduction in any medium, provided the original author(s)
and source are credited.

The images or other third party material in this chapter are included in the work's Creative
Commons license, unless indicated otherwise in the credit line; if such material is not included
in the work's Creative Commons license and the respective action is not permitted by statutory
regulation, users will need to obtain permission from the license holder to duplicate, adapt or
reproduce the material.

Chapter 6
They Took a Chance: Susan Hockey and Julianne Nyhan

Abstract This interview was carried out via Skype on 21 June 2013. Hockey was provided with the core questions in advance of the interview. Here she recalls how her interest in Humanities Computing was piqued by the articles that Andrew Morton published in the *Observer* in the 1960s about his work on the authorship of the Pauline Epistles. She went on to secure a position in the Atlas Computer Laboratory where she was an advisor on COCOA version 2 and wrote software for the electronic display of Arabic and other non-ASCII characters. The Atlas Computer Laboratory was funded by the Science Research Council and provided computing support for universities and researchers across the UK. While there she benefitted from access to the journal CHum and built connections with the emerging Humanities Computing community through events she attended starting with the 'Symposium on Uses of the Computer in Literary Research' organised by Roy Wisbey in Cambridge in 1970 (probably the earliest such meeting in the UK). Indeed, she emphasises the importance that such gatherings played in the formation of the discipline. As well as discussing her contribution to organisations like ALLC and TEI she recalls those who particularly influenced her such as, *inter alia*, Roberto Busa and Antonio Zampolli.

Biography

Susan Hockey was born in Halifax, UK. She has been Emeritus Professor of Library and Information Studies at University College London (UCL) since 2004; she is also Emeritus Fellow of St Cross College, Oxford. She graduated from Oxford in 1969 having studied Classics and then Final Honours in Oriental Studies (Egyptian with Akkadian). From 1969 to 1975 she was Assistant Research Officer at the Atlas Computer Laboratory, Chilton, Oxfordshire; she spent 1975–1991 at Oxford University Computing Services and was a Fellow of St Cross College 1979–1991. From 1991 to 1997 she was the first Director of the Center for Electronic Texts in the Humanities (CETH) at Rutgers and Princeton Universities, where together with Willard McCarty, she founded the CETH Summer Seminar on Methods and Tools for Electronic Texts in the Humanities. She also held a full professorship in the Faculty of Arts at the University of Alberta 1997–1999 and was a co-Investigator of the Orlando Project. She made major contributions to the founda-

© The Author(s) 2016

J. Nyhan, A. Flinn, *Computation and the Humanities*, Springer Series on Cultural Computing, DOI 10.1007/978-3-319-20170-2_6

tion and establishment of numerous DH activities. For example, she was a founder member of both ALLC and ACH; Editor of the ALLC Bulletin, and, as Chair of ALLC from 1984 to 1997, she oversaw the startup of *Literary and Linguistic Computing* with Oxford University Press. She is the author of *Electronic Texts in the Humanities: Principles and Practice* (2000), *SNOBOL Programming for the Humanities* (1986) and *A Guide to Computer Applications in the Humanities* (1980) as well as numerous articles on text analysis, encoding issues and digital libraries for the Humanities. Her pioneering contributions to DH have been honoured in various ways: in 2004 she was awarded the Busa Prize "for her contribution to the establishment of the field of Humanities Computing, and for her work on computers and text".[1] The field's first named lecture series (the Susan Hockey Lecture in Digital Humanities) was established at UCL in 2015.[2]

Interview

JN Please reflect on your earliest memories of encountering a computer or computing technologies.

SH Well, I'll tell you how I got started. I was an undergraduate in the late 1960s. I did Classics at Oxford and then did my final degree in Egyptian with Akkadian. I was always interested in language things, and I think it was in about 1967 that I remembered reading those articles in the *Observer* from Andrew Morton (see, for example, Morton 1963), who'd been doing this text analysis study of the Pauline Epistles with a computer (Morton 1965). It sounded really interesting and I thought I'd like to work in something like that. So, I checked how I could do this. I met one of the lecturers in Arabic, called Alan Jones, and found out that he was already doing some computing things (see Jones 1971). I think my tutor told me about him and I met him and found out that he was doing some text analysis work on the Koran. Because technology within the universities at that time was quite small, and very much focussed on Sciences, he was doing his work at an organisation called the Atlas Computer Laboratory,[3] which was funded by what was then called the Science Research Council to provide computing support for universities – the things that the universities couldn't have the technologies to do themselves.

---

[1] See: http://eadh.org/awards/busa-award/busa-award-winners

[2] See: https://www.ucl.ac.uk/dh/events/SusanHockeyLecture

[3] The Atlas Computer Laboratory was operational from 1961 to 1975. It was set up by the British government and was a national center that served universities and research councils. Government and treasury-supported officials could also avail of it. The lab was first set up around the Ferranti-ICL Atlas computer and it 'soon became clear that the Laboratory was meeting a very real need, and within a very short time of starting up it was giving computational support to research workers in every field of science (including the biological and human sciences as well as the physical) and in every British university' See: http://www.chilton-computing.org.uk/acl/about-us.htm

I applied for a job there, having no qualifications in computing, and my only mathematical expertise was up to O level, and they hired me. They took a chance, which was very, very nice, because I had no qualifications and, in fact, they had to create a special job title for me because I didn't fit in with the requirements for the Science Research Council. They wanted someone who could be a focal point for these kinds of activities at the Atlas Computer Laboratory. It's been merged into many other things since then and is on the Harwell site at Chilton. When I started they already had a concordance program called COCOA, which was running on the Atlas, which was the first ever paged memory computing machine. It filled the whole room. It was a British machine – I think they only built three of them – but they had several people using this COCOA concordance program, which I think was written in the Atlas machine language. It had a somewhat difficult user interface and you've got to remember that this was in the days when you put things into the computer on punch cards or paper tapes and that was it. They wanted something that would have a slightly better user interface, and something that would outlive Atlas, so they started a project to re-write it in FORTRAN. I didn't actually do the coding. I was an adviser on that project. They also wanted a means of generating output, not in Latin characters, this was the days when you put uppercase letters into the computer and nothing else. So I wrote some programs to display Alan Jones's Arabic concordances on a graph plotter, which is a really ancient device. It was the latest technology then and the only way of doing graphs. So I got interested in doing that kind of thing.

Several other people were using the Atlas facility including, in fact, Andrew Morton who's a terrific character and very entertaining to me. So that's how I got started. As you could only really put capital letters and numbers into a computer it was more text analysis or number crunching. The other thing was that there was so little disk storage. Anything more than a very small file was stored on a magnetic tape which you could only access serially. So, what you actually did with your data was rather dependant on that. You couldn't jump around in it is what I'm trying to say, the tape had to wind backwards and forwards. There was very little remote access to computers; basically, you turned up with your deck of punch cards.

I stayed there until early 1975 when Oxford University decided they wanted to do something more on Computing in the Arts, as it was called then, and they started looking for someone who could get people interested. So I applied for that job and got it and it was first of all described as Teaching Officer for Computing in the Arts. I started giving courses there and then we started developing more in different facilities. I don't know how much more you want there – I was there from 1975 until I went to America in 1991.

JN What did you know about computing before you read the articles by Andrew Morton in the *Observer*?

SH Well, I'd heard of computers and was interested but I didn't know anything about them. There wasn't a lot of computing going on before then; just a few businesses had taken it up. I had read a few things about IBM, who were, in the main, manufacturing systems in business computing, but I wasn't really interested in the business world.

JN Would you have heard of Busa, for example?

SH I wanted to talk about Busa. I don't think I'd heard of him until I started doing work in this area and had started to dig around quite a bit. The Atlas Computer Laboratory was generously funded and they had a good library which included CHum right back to when it started in 1966. So I spent quite a bit of time when I first got there looking around in the library and I found out about Busa then and started following up about what he was doing. I can't remember when I first met him. It must have been about 10 years later, I'm not sure. I remember him coming to Oxford and then coming to my office in Oxford but that was probably in the late 1970s. I think he'd asked to come and see me – he'd obviously heard about what we were doing. He spoke so many languages. Most of his operations were actually in Italian, but his English was pretty good. You know, he wrote the introduction to his Thomas Aquinas thing [*Index Thomisticus*] in Latin, so that it could be read by a lot of different people. But, I don't remember in detail. I know I read a lot about what was going on, and I went to the first conference in this country [the UK] in 1970 on what was called Literary and Linguistic Computing. I know Busa wasn't there but that is where I met Antonio Zampolli, who was there, as were quite a lot of other people. You know, Antonio Zampolli started as Busa's research assistant.

JN Were you quite unusual among your classmates and other people in Oxford when you became interested in computing, having just finished a degree in Oriental Studies?

SH To some extent. Quite a few of my friends went into teaching or did a variety of things. I remember going to the Careers Service in Oxford, which was nothing like the kind of thing it is now, and they were suggesting that everybody should apply to the Civil Service or GCHQ [the UK Government Communications Headquarters], or something like that. But they couldn't help me when I said what I was interested in doing computing. People went to all kinds of jobs so I don't think it was particularly unusual. I'm sure some of my contemporaries went to work in computing, almost certainly in places like IBM and big computer companies. Some of them then ended up in university computing but probably later on after that.

JN I wanted to ask you about the special job which was created for you in Atlas Computer Laboratory and I think you said it was there on the job that you were trained up in programming.

SH Well, they created the job and hired me. I'm not certain that it was created for me but I was appointed to it. I was given some books and they said "read and get on with it. You need to learn FORTRAN and if you need any help come and ask", and that's how I learned. They were very, very helpful and I think I had one or two little tutorials with the head of one of the programming groups there. But basically somebody explained to me how I got my punch cards done – probably by doing them myself – and what I had to do to hand in my punch cards to get my programs to run, and I learned like that. I still like playing around with computers quite a bit. I'm actually a great believer in reading book manuals to get going. If you have a good overview of what's happening and then understand what you can and can't do – I've always almost entirely learned that way. I think the first time I went to a computer course was when I was giving it. I think it depended on the atmosphere I was in. I don't think I could have learned like that, you see, if I was out on my own with a group of people who were not interested in it or who were not doing it. But, there were lots of people around and if you were stuck and asked for help they would help you. That's really how I learned.

JN The first programming language you learned was FORTRAN?

SH And I learned some ALGOL, a little bit of Atlas machine code, and I started seriously doing SNOBOL when I wanted to give a programming course in Oxford and it seemed the obvious thing for text handling. I think I looked at that a bit when I was at the Atlas Computer Laboratory but they didn't really have a proper compiler for it there. FORTRAN was the thing that everybody used for almost all the applications in the Atlas Computer Laboratory.

JN When you started essentially teaching yourself FORTRAN how did it compare with 4 years learning Akkadian and other ancient languages?

SH Well, I'm not the only person who said computer programming is not dissimilar from Latin and languages like that. When I first got started doing this I met a lot of people who'd got into it from Classics, or who were Classicists and took to programming very easily. So, I think there is this kind of mental approach which makes the two somewhat similar. I was always interested in the linguistic and the symbolic side of the languages that I studied.

JN And this was another language....

SH Another language, yes, and you couldn't break the rules in it

JN I had a question about how you first got involved in the Humanities Computing community, but that was essentially through the Atlas Computer Laboratory?

SH Yes, not my immediate boss, but the person that I did quite a bit of work for when there was called Bob Churchhouse,[4] who left to take up a chair at Cardiff. He and I went to what I think was the first Literary Linguistic and Computing confer-

---

[4]Church house was the first head of Programming at the Atlas Computer Laboratory and left in 1971 to take up a chair in Computing Mechanics at University College, Cardiff. His inaugural address 'Computer Applications in the Arts and Sciences' is available here: http://www.chilton-computing.org.uk/acl/literature/reports/p016.htm

ence in the UK, in Cambridge in 1970, and we gave a preliminary talk on what we were planning to do with all this non-standard character output (published as Church house and Hockey 1971).

There were about 70 or 80 people there and that's when I first met people who subsequently became quite well known worldwide in the field. I met Joseph Raben, for example, and Bob and Joe got on very well, so we kept in touch a lot. There was no email then, so you had to rely on things such as putting a letter in the post or meeting people again at conferences. These conferences were such a success that another one was organised in Edinburgh 2 years later and I think they carried on every 2 years for about 10 or 12 years and more people kept coming. The proceedings were published in real books and so people got to find out quite a lot more about what was going on because of these books. Mostly they were published by well-known publishers. I think Roy Wisbey edited the first one (1971), which was published by Cambridge. So, there was a core of people that came every time. That core was probably between, I don't know, 50 and 70 people, and others sort of dipped in and out.

But that's how I got involved more with this field. I'm just trying to remember what happened. That was before the ALLC was founded: there was a lady called Joan Smith, who was in Manchester then, and she was energetic and felt it would be a good idea to form a society to support all of this. She persuaded Roy Wisbey to take on doing this. And there was a meeting at King's College in London in 1973 when it was formed. Of course I was there with a number of other people from the Atlas Computer Laboratory. The Society ran its own bulletin and journal for quite some time. Quite a few people came from outside the UK for that meeting. You must know Wilhelm Ott (see Chap. 4), who started computing quite a bit before I did, and I first met him at the conference at Cambridge. He was there, Antonio Zampolli was there, and a number of other people, and I don't know what happened to it but ALLC had a book that used to go round for everyone to sign at general meetings and that started at that conference. I had it for a long time but I passed it on to somebody else. I think Harold Short might have it. …

Yes, I think I ended up on the committee of the ALLC fairly early on, and then I was editing the *ALLC Bulletin*, and then I got elected to be the Chair, which I actually did for quite a long time, and by then various other international things had got going, like the TEI, and more conferences and things like that.

JN You were also very involved in TEI.

SH Yes. The obvious reason why people were interested in it is because people were fed up of not being able to use somebody else's text in a different application and they were fed up of not being able to encode complicated things very well.

TEI started with a meeting organized at Vassar College Poughkeepsie in 1987, November, I think, and that was invitational. There were about 20 people there. It tried to get some idea of whether there was enough willingness among the community to do something about that, and how such a project might be organized. I think it was at that meeting that it was decided to organise it with two representatives of the three societies that were involved with it. There was the ALLC, ACH and the Association for Computational Linguistics, whose long term Secretary Don Walker had also realised that this was something important. I was one of the two ALLC representatives on the Steering Committee. The other was Antonio Zampolli. We got some money from the NEH to get started and Antonio was instrumental in getting some money from a European Commission stream (I don't remember exactly what). There were six of us, I suppose, who organized it. We took it in turns to chair the Steering Committee and when it was the ALLC turn it was me. So, we basically planned out how we were going to do this work and found some people to do some work and found some money to get it done. We did get it done and I know there is still a lot of interest in it but the real issue later on was how to keep it funded. I remember now, at the Vassar meeting it finished up with a sort of discussion about the basic principles for doing this project. Nancy Ide asked me to lead that discussion and it was one of the earliest instances where I saw something projected up from a computer screen onto a big screen. We sat for an afternoon and defined these things which became known as the Poughkeepsie principles (TEI 1988). You can find all that in the TEI archives.

JN That was really cutting edge at that point?

SH Yes, there was quite a lot of cutting edge about a lot of things that were going on. I think that we were all feeling our way and we had some intellectual goals that we wanted to meet and it seemed that the obvious thing was to use the technologies to get there. We said in the TEI right from the beginning that anybody who wanted to do any work for it had to do it by email. It was not long after international email started but we could see that was the only way we could get any work done. But we soon discovered how difficult it is to get closure on an email discussion and we did have funding to have face to face meetings, which really were very productive.

JN I served on the TEI council a few years ago and email is still certainly at the heart of all of it. Something that I wondered about, looking at all of the chronologies, is that I noticed that the ACH, which I think you were also a founding member of, was set up a couple of years after the ALLC?

SH I think it was later than that. I think it was perhaps 4 or 5 years after the ALLC. I can't remember the details about the founding of ACH, but Joseph Raben was interested in having some kind of society to support CHum, which had been round various publishers. And I think also the Americans had sort of looked a little bit at what was going on in Britain and they'd started a series of conferences in the alternate years and the [third] one of those was at the University of Waterloo in 1977 (Lusignan and North 1977). I remember that because it was the first time I ever went to North America. That was similar in some ways and different in others because there was a lot of interest in North America at that time about using computing to support all those courses they give to teach students how to write. Of course, we didn't have any of that in Britain. About half the papers there were about computing in composition – I can't remember exactly what they called it – but they started a series of conferences in odd-numbered years to correspond with those European ones which went on in even-numbered years. They were organized in a slightly different way because conferences in America tend to be more condensed – more papers happening at the same time and fewer days. I did go to quite a number of those as well. I was a member of the ACH for quite some time but I don't really remember exactly what happened about the organization of that. It was run in a slightly different way, you know. Learned Societies operate in a different way in the UK certainly, I don't know about the rest of Europe, than they do in America. It was run in a more American style.

JN What about the people who influenced you and how and why they influenced you?

SH I made some notes about this. Busa because I think it is amazing that you start talking about the potential and the future of multimedia when you're nearly 90 (Busa 1999) and also going back to what he did when he first started. You know, in the 1950s he wanted to have a completely lemmatized version of his text and we still can't really do that automatically now, though things are a lot better than they used to be, I think. What I learned from him was to keep looking ahead. You know, he's been an enormous influence on all of us.

Another one was Antonio Zampolli because he also was thinking all the time about how we can do this better. Not just to do this particular project but to think about how we can make it better and what better tools we can make for it. He was very, very keen on linking up literary computing (as it used to be called) with research that was going on in Computational Linguistics, and there still aren't all that many people looking at that now. I'm not really up to date on what's going on now, there are probably still some others as well, but Antonio was really keen, even in the 1980s to do work, to try and apply the tools and techniques they'd developed for Computational Linguistics to see how well they worked with literary texts like Dante and other works of Italian literature. One other thing I learned from him was how to think about turning an idea of something you want to do into something that would be a project that was fundable. As you know, there is a difference there. You can obviously have grand ideas but if you want some money to do something you've got to think about what's practical, what bits of it can be done and how you're going get the next bit of money to carry on after that.

Two people who helped me a lot when I started were Bob Churchhouse and Alan Jones – I've already mentioned them. I've a couple of others which are a little bit different again. David Barnard who was involved in the TEI quite a bit when he was Professor of Computer Science at Queens University, in Canada. He's now the President at the University of Manitoba. He taught me how to run a meeting and how to get things done. He ran the best meetings I've ever been in by a long way.

There's one other person I wanted to mention and this is a little bit different again. There's always been a very, very friendly atmosphere amongst DH, or whatever you want to say. That goes back, I'm pretty certain, to the late Paul Fortier whom I remember talking to when he was at a conference in Edinburgh in 1972. He was in French Studies and he said that nobody spoke to him at the first conference he went to in French Studies and he vowed it would never happen in this field. He made a point of making sure that everybody spoke to new people and got them involved in the discussions and the social events. I think that is one of the main reasons, why there's always such a friendly atmosphere. That's a different thing again, but I think that started from Bob Churchhouse, who was very sociable. It helps a lot, you know, because new people come to a conference to learn and they don't want to feel that they're just looking up to other people. I think it's nice to think that they feel on equal terms in many ways.

JN Do you think the field is somewhat unusual in terms of the social cohesion and kinship that exists in it, in addition to its shared intellectual goals and interests?

SH I don't know, I've never really been involved in other fields. Another thing I wanted to say in relation to your question about what other Humanities people think about it – for a very long time I never came across them. I worked in the computing center and so I only met people who were interested. I know we've always tried to be a sort of friendly and sociable group, and I think things have changed generally since the 1970s, but I think also in computing you can realize that a lot of the good work comes from the young people. You only have to look at what's happening in the world of business computing and things like Facebook and Google and whatever, so I think it is important to give them a chance to talk about whatever they are doing.

JN Can we talk a small bit more about what other scholars who were not using computing views may have been of the field?

SH Well, I think I was lucky that I didn't encounter it for a very, very long time because at the Atlas Computer Laboratory we only met people who were interested in using the computer. I was 16 years in the Computing Center in Oxford. A good deal of that was before people had their own PCs, so they came to the computing center if they wanted to do something because Humanities, at that time in Oxford, except for Oriental Studies, had no departmental facilities. You spoke to people who were in your College more than anything. I was elected to a fellowship of St Cross College in 1979, which was one of the new young graduate colleges and I met a lot of people from other disciplines there, but actually they were predominantly Scientists and Social Scientists. There were very few Humanities people there. But St Cross was also very forward looking and it was actually the first college to have a computer in Oxford, so I didn't really have any way of meeting people who weren't interested in computing because of where I was based and what I was doing.

Occasionally I got invited to dinner in some other colleges by some of our computing users and got to talk to a few other people then but I think people who weren't interested just basically ignored it. I benefited, and I think a lot of those who worked in Humanities Computing at an early stage benefitted from the interest of well-known scholars. I was reading your other interviews, I think Harold Short mentioned that as well (Short et al. 2012), particularly Anthony Kenny, the well-known Philosopher, who did various computer-based stylistic studies based on concordances. I got to know him very well. I did quite a bit of work with Kenneth Dover as well, a very well-known classicist. So, I didn't really encounter that.

My next job in New Jersey was based in a library and that had a different atmosphere. As I had never worked in a library in the UK I didn't really know what the atmosphere was going to be, but I think it was still a time when electronic resources were rather strange things in libraries and they tended to be treated as if they were another kind of book. You know, you make a catalogue record for it and stick it there for somebody to use rather than thinking "this is a very different kind of object and what are we going to do about it?" It was very, very early days for computing and electronic resources in libraries anyway – they were almost all CD-ROMs. So, there was quite a lot of interest there but more in the way of how to treat this as something that librarians needed to deal with. That's still the case now, but I think it's rather different from when your electronic resources are just a lot of CD-ROMs and its quite difficult for anybody to be able to support them because it takes so long to find out what you can actually do with them.

So because I wasn't ever in a Humanities department until I got to Alberta where there was a very stimulating intellectual atmosphere, I didn't really have much cause to be around people who weren't computing. I think the same was true in Alberta where there was a very big project which I was extremely interested in, and I did quite a bit of work with, the Orlando project, and that was really pushing the boundaries of what you can do.[5] It generated, I think, quite a lot of intellectual discussion and it got down to the bottom line, which is how do you represent interpretation. I think that was really the nuts and bolts of what was going on and that generated a lot of interesting discussion

JN My final question is about the participation of women in the field?

SH I didn't feel any problem at being a woman and there were quite a number of women. I wouldn't say we were a majority but it didn't seem to me to be a problem. I think one of the real things, certainly in the early days of Humanities Computing, was that everybody treated everybody else as equals because they were interested in what each other was doing and needed to learn something from them. So, I didn't find any problem in that, and I think there has always been quite a lot of women in computing right from the beginning. I think there is now a bit more of an issue regarding people who get into certain management positions in universities and

---

[5] The Orlando project is 'an ongoing collaborative experiment in the use of computers to engage in women's literary history.' See http://www.artsrn.ualberta.ca/orlando/

certain disciplines. I never noticed it, shall I put it that way? Certainly when I got to work in libraries there was a predominance of women and it was very obvious when I went to some library conferences in America that women were a big majority.

JN Thanks a million – that was really fascinating

References

Busa, R. (1999). Picture a man … Busa award lecture, Debrecen, Hungary, 6 July 1998. *Literary and Linguistic Computing, 14*(1), 5–9.

Churchhouse, R. F., & Hockey, S. (1971). The use of an SC4020 for output of a concordance program. In R. A. Wisbey (Ed.), *The computer in literary and linguistic research* (pp. 221–231). Cambridge: Cambridge University Press.

Hockey, S. M. (1980). *A guide to computer applications in the humanities*. London/Duckworth/ Baltimore: Johns Hopkins.

Hockey, S. M. (1986). *SNOBOL programming for the humanities*. Oxford: Clarendon Press.

Hockey, S. M. (2000). *Electronic texts in the humanities: Principles and practice*. Oxford/New York: Oxford University Press.

Jones, A. (1971). Some oxford projects in oriental languages. In R. A. Wisbey (Ed.), *The computer in literary and linguistic research* (pp. 191–197). Cambridge: Cambridge University Press.

Lusignan, S., & North, J. S. (Eds.). (1977). *Computing in the humanities: Proceedings of the third international conference on computing in the humanities*. Waterloo: University of Waterloo Press.

Morton, A. (1963). A computer challenges the church. *The Observer,* p. 21.

Morton, A. (1965). *The authorship of Pauline epistles: A scientific solution*. Saskatoon: University of Saskatchewan.

Short, H., et al. (2012). Collaboration must be fundamental or it's not going to work: An oral history conversation between Harold Short and Julianne Nyhan. *Digital Humanities Quarterly, 6,* 3. Available at: http://www.digitalhumanities.org/dhq/vol/6/3/000133/000133.html.

TEI. (1988). Design principles for text encoding guidelines. *TEI Vault*. Available at: http://www. tei-c.org/Vault/ED/edp01.htm. Accessed 4 Aug 2015.

Wisbey, R. A. (Ed.). (1971). *The computer in literary and linguistic research. Papers from a Cambridge symposium*. Cambridge: Cambridge University Press.

Open Access This chapter is distributed under the terms of the Creative Commons Attribution-Noncommercial 2.5 License (http://creativecommons.org/licenses/by-nc/2.5/) which permits any noncommercial use, distribution, and reproduction in any medium, provided the original author(s) and source are credited.

The images or other third party material in this chapter are included in the work's Creative Commons license, unless indicated otherwise in the credit line; if such material is not included in the work's Creative Commons license and the respective action is not permitted by statutory regulation, users will need to obtain permission from the license holder to duplicate, adapt or reproduce the material.

Chapter 7
The Influence of Algorithmic Thinking: Judy Malloy and Julianne Nyhan

Abstract This interview was carried out via skype on 11 August 2015 at 20:30 GMT. Malloy was provided with the core interview questions in advance. Here she recalls that after graduating from university she took a job as a searcher/editor for the National Union Catalog of the Library of Congress. About a year after she arrived Henriette D. Avram began work on the process of devising a way to make the library's cataloguing information machine readable (work that would ultimately lead to the development of the MARC format (Schudel 2006)). Malloy recalls this wider context as her first encounter, of sorts, with computing technology: though she did not participate in that work it made a clear impression on her. She had learned to programme in FORTRAN in the 1960s when working as a technical librarian at the Ball Brothers Research Corporation. She had also held other technical roles at Electromagnetic Research Corp and with a contractor for the Goddard Space Flight Center, which was computerising its library around the time she worked there. She recalls that she did not use computers in her artistic work until the 1980s (when she bought an Apple II for her son). However, she had been working in an interactive, multimedia and associative mode for some time before then, as evidenced by the card catalog poetry and electronic books that she created in the 1970s and early 1980s. In this interview she traces the importance of card catalogs, Systems Analysis and algorithmic thinking to many aspects of her work. She also reflects on why it was that the idea of combining computing and literature did not occur to her (and also was not practically feasible) until a later stage in her career. Among other topics, she reflects on the kinds of computing and computing environments that she encountered, from the reactions in the 1960s of some male engineers to the presence of a female technical librarian in the mainframe room to the thrill of discovering the community that was connected via the Whole Earth 'Lectronic Link (The WELL).

Biography

Judy Malloy (née Powers) was born in Boston, MA in 1942. In 1964 she graduated with a degree in English and a minor concentration in Art from Middlebury College. Over the next years she held Information Science positions such as National

© The Author(s) 2016
J. Nyhan, A. Flinn, *Computation and the Humanities*, Springer Series on
Cultural Computing, DOI 10.1007/978-3-319-20170-2_7

Union Catalog searcher/editor for the Library of Congress (c.1964); cataloger for J. Walter Thompson (c.1967 on a contract for the Goddard Space Flight Center Library's computer catalog) and Technical Librarian for Ball Brothers Research Corporation in Boulder, Colorado, where she designed and worked as a programmer for an innovative computer catalog of the library's holdings (c.1969). Hired in 1988 as coordinating Editor for *Leonardo*'s fledgling electronic publications, she moved from Information Science to electronic publishing in the Arts. She worked in the ensuing years as a Contributing Writer in new media for Microtimes; artist in residence and consultant in the document of the future at Xerox PARC; consultant for the *Internet Yellow Pages*, and from 1993 to 2004 for Arts Wire, an Internet-based program of the New York Foundation for the Arts, where she was at various times, Content Coordinator, Network Coordinator, and Editor of Arts Wire Current/ NYFA Current.

As a poet, writer and researcher, from the early 1970s on she created a number of artist's books, in addition to installations and performances. In 1986 she published *Uncle Roger*, the first online hyperfiction (Malloy 1986). It was published as a serial "narrabase" and as an interactive database on Art Com Electronic Network on The WELL. Her hyperfiction *its name was Penelope* was included in the exhibition *Revealing Conversations* at the Richmond Art Center in 1989 and published by Eastgate in 1993 (see Malloy 1993). As an artist-in-residence at Xerox PARC in Palo Alto she developed *Brown House Kitchen*[1] and she and then PARC researcher, Cathy Marshall, wrote *Forward Anywhere* (Eastgate 1995; see also Malloy and Marshall 2000). She has recently completed work on an electronic manuscript, *From Ireland with Letters*.[2] Her work has appeared in numerous international exhibitions. She is editor of *Social Media Archaeology and Poetics* (2016b) and *Women, Art and Technology* (2003) and author of number of non-fiction publications too. She has taught and lectured widely, most recently as Visiting Lecturer in Electronic Literature, and Social Media History and Poetics at Princeton University in 2013–14. Her papers are archived as 'The Judy Malloy Papers' at the David M. Rubenstein Rare Book and Manuscript Library at Duke University.

Interview

JN What is your earliest memory of encountering computing technology?

JM I'm going to start with a pre-encountering of computer technology because I think it's important to my story. My first job, after I graduated with a degree in English with a minor concentration in Art, was at the Library of Congress in Washington DC, where I worked as a searcher/editor for the Union Catalog. Now,

---

[1] See: http://www.well.com/user/jmalloy/kitchen.html. See also Malloy (2000).

[2] See: http://www.well.com/user/jmalloy/from_Ireland/opening_page.html

the Union Catalog is the Library of Congress' huge catalog that includes every book that it holds.[3] It contains millions and millions of records, and at that time in 1964, it wasn't computerised. It was a year later that they hired Henriette D. Avram to come and begin computerising the library[4] (see, for example, Avram et al. 1967). I think that this was important to me because I certainly saw the need for it. The catalog was in this huge room in the Navy Yard Annex and not in the Library of Congress building itself. It was a huge, huge warehouse, full of card catalogs. And to work on the cards, we rolled around on chairs. It's important to me because card catalogs have pervaded my life and my work to a certain extent, not only due to the experience of seeing so many cards, but also due to knowing that the need to automate them was of interest.

JN Whether in descriptions of preparing punched cards or of manually manipulating card catalogs and other earlier technologies it is the physicality of the operation that always strikes me. That is something we have lost.

JM Indeed, we have lost that. A few years later, following an interval of camping around Europe and doing some writing, I went to work for, I think it was, the J. Walter Thompson Company, who had a contract with the Goddard Space Flight Center. It was around 1967 and the Goddard Space Flight Center was computerising their library. It was one of the earlier efforts to computerise libraries on a large scale. My job there was to catalog the documents and books that were in their collection, and then, sometimes, I'd key punch them in myself or sometimes a key puncher offered to do that.

I never saw the computer at the Goddard Space Center. When we were finished creating the records for the computer we took them and put them in the slot. Now, I used to think that the slot accessed some long tunnel to the Goddard Space Flight Center, but when I was looking at the map I saw that the Space Center was actually not that close to where I was working. They must have gone to a truck or something. I remember very clearly punching the cards, or taking the punched cards from someone who punched them, and putting them in the slot, and then they went off to the computer. But I'm not sure that this was a standard key punch card operation or precisely what the output was. It may have been an interim step in the process because I don't think the output was the standard IBM keypunch card.

The other thing I remember clearly is problems with the machines. Has operating key punch machines and how finicky they were come up in some of your other work with key punch people?

JN Yes and no because everybody tends to have a different focus.

[3] 'The National Union Catalog (NUC) is a record of publications held in more than 1100 libraries in the United States and Canada, including the Library of Congress'. See: http://www.loc.gov/rr/main/inforeas/union.html
[4] On Avram's early work in this area see, for example, Avram et al. 1967.

JM The machines tended to break a lot, and it turned out that the best way to fix them was to sort of hit them. It was actually a known technique – just gently slap them! [Both laugh]. It was something I would get very good at, some people would call me and say, "would you come and do whatever it is you do to make this thing work?" And, so I remember struggling with that technology.

I always enjoyed cataloguing – it was a relaxing kind of job. So, after that, my boyfriend got drafted, and he was sent to Germany. I went to Germany and we got married there after much paperwork. I worked in the Special Library System in Furth, and I lived in *Dürer Platz* in the old walled City of Nurnberg and bicycled to work.[5] Then, we came back to America, and when we got to Boulder, in Colorado, we decided that we'd like to stay there. We were camping in the mountains, so I remember putting on a suit very clearly. In those days, fairly often as a woman, you could not go into a company wearing pants. I went down to this huge aerospace company called the Ball Brothers Research Corporation (BBRC; now called Ball Aerospace), where a position was advertised. I applied for the position of technical librarian and got it. Actually, that was a bit of a surprise for me and so all of a sudden I was the head of a large technical library for a big aerospace company. They made the orbiting solar observatory. It was an incredibly beautiful piece of hardware, it got mounted on rockets and then launched with a mission of solar observation.

So, the library was quite large. You could not take things out of the company because you had to have a clearance to work there. It wasn't military, but some of the technology was top secret. I dealt with the documents and I'm not sure exactly how it occurred that I began to computerise the library. I think part of the idea may have come from me, because I had been interested in that since seeing how Goddard was doing it. It was a fairly sizeable library of documents and the computer room was fairly close to where I was working. So I undertook the job to computerise the library. Now, at that time, there were not a lot of known ways to do this. Not like now. There was no applications software; there were very few documents that told you how to do this. Essentially I was working with a computer that I had to programme in FORTRAN and so I learnt to programme in FORTRAN.

This was not the era of big Computer Science departments, it was 1969, and not all engineers and scientists knew how to programme. BBRC at that time, like many other corporations, went on a campaign against what they called the 'slide rule engineers', who were still there then. You know, they walked around the company with slide rules in their pockets. BBRC decided that engineers needed to use the computer, and luckily for me, since I needed instructions in how to do this, they gave classes. So I joined the slide rule engineers and scientists, and took classes in FORTRAN from Dan Anderson. He ran the computer room and also taught the classes. Then I still had some questions about how to do it, so I took a summer institute at the University of Denver's Graduate School of Librarianship on Library Systems Analysis, I think it was. That was possibly the most important thing I ever did as far as my later career of writing electronic literature was concerned. It was so

---

[5] This experience is captured in a lexia of l0ve0ne. See: http://www.eastgate.com/malloy/love2.html

important to me to learn that way of thinking. It's not just programming, it's also a way of thinking when you have a problem.

The problem that faced me was actually not that difficult, and I had staff. I had a woman who worked with me, Jo Sanford, who was also learning to programme. So we worked on this together; occasionally Dan Anderson helped us when we ran into blocks. The most important thing was not the act of the programming but the Systems Analysis, the act of analysing how we were going to do this. I like to tell electronic literature students, "step back". Nowadays people are using applications and they don't always think this through. Step back, and even if you use the old-fashioned flowchart, think about exactly what you want to do. Think about the algorithms you are going to use. I don't want to scare them too much, so I always use this book, *The Art of Asking your Boss for a Raise*, I don't know if you've ever seen this?

JN [laughs] No.

JM It's by Georges Perec (2011), who was a member of the Oulipo,[6] and the 2011 English edition was translated by David Bellos. Essentially, Perec was asked to write a book using computer processes. So, he simply rambles on and on about this poor fellow who was trying to get a raise, and walks into his boss' office, "is the boss there?", "yes", "is the boss there?", "no", "is the boss in a good mood?", "is the boss in a bad mood".[7] Somebody actually computerised this[8] and I show it to students so they can see how flowcharts work. It's a wonderful example because it's entertaining and uses different ways of thinking about how to create a work. Perec was a fairly well known experimental author. I mean, somebody might say "huh?" but creating a library catalog where you enter information in order to make it searchable and retrievable, for instance, is not so different from writing hypertext. Actually, if you look in *Uncle Roger*, you can see that I played off the programme I wrote for BBRC. For instance, I used the Boolean operator "and" to allow readers to combine words and phrases such as "uncle Roger" and "men in tan suits".

JN I picked up on two comments in the Pathfinders interview[9] that I'd like to ask you more about. Firstly, when you were discussing the period that we have just been

---

[6] 'OULIPO is the Ouvroir de Littérature Potentielle, or Workshop of Potential Literature, a group of writers and mathematicians. Members include Raymond Queneau, François Le Lionnais, Claude Berge, Georges Perec, and Italo Calvino'. See: http://www.nous.org.uk/oulipo.html

[7] Or, more precisely in Perec's words: '…so you go to see mr x its one or t'other either mr x is at his desk or mr x is not at his desk if mr x is at his desk it will be quite straightforward but obviously mr x is not at his desk…' 2011, p. 3.

[8] See http://www.theartofaskingyourbossforaraise.com/

[9] The Pathfinders project is 'a digital preservation project that captures an important moment in literary history: the development of early digital literature' see http://dtc-wsuv.org/wp/pathfinders/description/. Judy Malloy was one of five authors interviewed for the project. The videos of her interviews are available on the project's vimeo channel: https://vimeo.com/search?q=Judy+Malloy+AND+Grigar

discussing, you mentioned that the idea of using computers in your artistic work had not yet occurred to you. So how did those two things come together?

JM I had no intention of that at all, it was two separate lives. In fact, I think I told you in an email, that my immediate boss at BBRC, and this is kind of interesting, was José Antonio Villarreal, who was a pioneer Chicano writer. The company hired writers and artists, which I thought was kind of wonderful. José, quite shortly after that, was able to get a university teaching job based on his work as a writer. Neither of us had graduate degrees and we had to make a living. At the time he was writing *The Fifth Horseman*, which was a story of the Mexican Revolution. His father actually fought with Pancho Villa. One of the best experiences working for BBRC was when José used to come up and sometimes talk with me about what he was working on.

At that time I was working on things like a hand-made map that I made a few years later on rice paper[10] and then I made versions on Xerox that I sold, not a lot, but a few copies. This is a colour Xerox copy of a map that I made on rice paper [she holds the map up to the webcam], and a portion of these maps were narrative and under the category of what you would call 'Artists' Books'. But there was certainly no intention at all of using computers in my artistic work. One thing you didn't have access to in those days was personal computers, all you had was a large, scary computer.

JN That was actually my second question. In the Pathfinders interview you said something like "you have no idea of what a different experience it was using computers then, compared to what it is now" but the conversation went in a different direction and you didn't get a chance to develop that idea. Would you say something about it now?

JM Develop that idea? I think the Pathfinders interviewers weren't so interested in that aspect. Also, I don't talk about it too often, because in some ways it's so removed from where I work, and what I do. I think I used a mainframe, I've been trying to research what computer I used. I'm not positive it was a mainframe, I'm pretty sure it was an IBM. I thought it was an IBM 1130 but those are smaller in the pictures from what I recollect. My recollection is of a room, about the size of a smallish bedroom, in which the whole wall was covered with a computer. Then there was a large, noisy printer. That was all you got, and there was no monitor – this is important. That there was no monitor is one reason that many people didn't think of using the computer to make interactive art or literature. Of course, some people did (see, for example, Higgins and Kahn 2012), but I certainly didn't think of using it to create my work. (Oh, we have a thunderstorm, can you hear it? JN: Oh, yeah!)

Data retrieval was inelegant. If I wanted to do a search on the system with the application I was creating, I first of all had to load the programme on punched cards.

---

[10]*Map*, circa 1976, Judy Malloy Papers, David M. Rubenstein Rare Book & Manuscript Library, Duke University.

Every time you ran the programme you took the stack of punched cards into the computer room and put them on this conveyor belt, which ran across the room and took them into the computer. If you did not have the correct start card on your stack of punched cards, you were in trouble as it wouldn't run. Otherwise it ran the programme and printed out the results. So, if somebody wanted to search for something (satellite guidance systems were the kind of things they looked for) they would give me what they wanted, I would have to create a punched card for that, and then I would integrate that punched card into the entire programme and feed it into the computer. We would come out with a print out of the documents in the library on satellite guidance systems.

So, this was not an easy way to work; in fact, it is not my recollection that the database systems that we were creating were used a lot by the engineers. They were still happier to come in and say "can you just find this for us?" It was not like now, when you can sit at your desk in your office or at home and search a library catalog – it wasn't wired for one thing. 1969 was the beginning of ARPANET (Naughton 2000) and this technology was not accessible. A few people were connected, MIT's *Compatible Time-Sharing System* (CTSS) used MAIL to coordinate their research and exchange information, for instance. But BBRC was not connected, as far as I know. So, essentially the access was very different, the process was very different and it was finicky to a certain extent. I told a story about this in the Pathfinders interview, but I can tell it again here if you'd like?

JN Yes, because it's lovely. Well, it is lovely now, but it probably wasn't so lovely then!

JM This was a terrible moment. I had the programme we created on a big stack of punched cards. This was not a small stack of punched cards and they all had to be kept in order. If you dropped them it was very bad, and putting them in order was not easy. So, I took the punched cards in over lunch hour. You had to sign up for access to the computer, and I had to use it over lunch hour so as not to interfere with important engineer tasks. I took the card stack in and put it on the conveyor belt. I'm standing there, and all of a sudden, all the cards fly into the air. How this happened, I don't know, but when I was telling the story to Stuart Moulthrop[11] during the Pathfinders interview, he told me the same thing had happened to Nancy Kaplan,[12] who's his wife. So I had to go find Dan Anderson (who ran the computer room), and tell him what happened and all those cards had to be put back in order. It was not fun and it was also horrendously embarrassing because it was important to look professional when you were going into the computer room because not everybody was hugely in favour of somebody who wasn't a regular engineer using the equipment.

---

[11] Moulthrop is Professor of English at the University of Wisconsin-Milwaukee and author of numerous hypertexts, see https://pantherfile.uwm.edu/moulthro/index.htm

[12] Until her retirement Kaplan was Professor and Director of the School of Information Arts and Technologies at the University of Baltimore.

For years I didn't like to tell people that I had worked for BBRC, because they would go, "you what?" I didn't like to talk about that although it was germane. I don't mind it now, because I'm going over an age hump and I've realised this was important. The companies in that era (Bell Labs in New Jersey was like that also) were very open to whom they were hiring. They didn't hesitate at BBRC to hire artists and writers, they didn't hesitate to hire someone who had just been bumming around Europe for a year. Nowadays, that would never happen.

JN Many other people I've interviewed have mentioned to me that they also worked in commercial companies. You can read more about that when the other interviews are published.

JM I'm really looking forward to that because I feel like I'm less out on a limb hearing that. And I think there is some credit due to those companies. I think their willingness was also related to the post-World War II context; what women did during World War II was still remembered. Companies thought that, as a woman, you had some skills, and you could come in and do that.

JN So, in asking this, I'm probably jumping forward in the timeline a bit, but how did the ideas of technology and artist books start intertwining?

JM OK, this was a bit of a longish process. I was creating various kinds of artist's books. After my son was born, and this is something that you will know as a parent of a young child, it became difficult to create something like this (though I think this is a good story and it's always good to have a positive story of how children influence your life). It became difficult to stretch large sheets of paper out across a drawing board – sometimes children like to play on your drawing board! I was creating connected texts and drawings on large sheets of paper. Some were on rice paper, so they were very fragile. Because I was working for months on one sheet of paper that couldn't easily be corrected the process was not conducive to good interactive parenting. A lot of times I was working during naps, or didn't have that much time to work, or I was working in short bursts. It started by just thinking "how can I do this?" It happened that catalog cards were accessible to me, and I thought, "why don't I try drawing on catalog cards?"

I started drawing on the catalog cards without the vision of how I was going to use them eventually. I started using text and I started using photographs, and I began to have this vision that I could create a non-sequential narrative using catalog cards.[13] I had no access to a computer – it was 1976 when I started doing this. So I thought "well I generally show my work in exhibitions", but there weren't a lot of

---

[13] An image of 'The Woodpile' (card catalog), 1979 is available here: http://www.judymalloy.net/ artistsbooks/artbooks2.html. A number of slides and photographs of the card catalogs and exemplars such as 'The TV blew up', 1980, 'made from 50 3×5 photos, drawings, and text and filed in a plexiglass box; it can be read sequentially or hypertextually' were accessioned in the Judy Malloy Papers, David M. Rubenstein Rare Book & Manuscript Library, Duke University.

people using computers in exhibitions, although there were a few. So I began making what were essentially small, metal card catalog trays. I used cards that had writing, photographs and drawings on them. I categorised them with text but it was somewhat poetic text. So, if I was telling a story I would write a line of poetry (sometimes I used an image) and put that on a divider on the top, like the old card catalogs were sometimes indexed. Then, behind the line of poetry, the narrative would be told by images, texts and photographs. Essentially, it was early multimedia and not so different from what you might see people working on today as they create narratives with images and all kinds of media.

I became almost obsessed with this for a few years, to the point where I began thinking "what the heck am I doing?" I thought it was fascinating, it was a wonderful training for becoming an electronic literature writer. I spent hours trying to make certain that the narrative worked exactly right. But when I showed these works, people generally just pulled the cards out and looked at occasional cards. I let them do that, and they usually didn't experience the narrative the way I had intended them to experience it. At that point I began to stop and think, "Well, I'm enjoying doing this, I think this is great, but I can only make one copy, and I'm not sure I'm reaching the reader with these works".

I then made a small switch to trying to use electromechanical books. I think I started doing that in 1981. In those days, Radio Shack made these electromechanical address books (this was in the days before personal computers were widely available, although they were being used at that point). So, I would purchase these houses for electromechanical address books from Radio Shack, open them up and take out the scrolls (on which you were supposed to put addresses). Instead of the addresses I would put images and text, and these books had little buttons on the front, so you could press the buttons and make them spin around.[14] Once again, it's a protogenic hypertext structure.

They had another kind of address book – if you look at the start of the pathfinder interviews, you'll see I'm holding one up, although you can't tell what it is. Essentially, it looked like a small TV. I painted it blue-green. I'd been to the bleachers of a baseball game, and taken pictures of mostly men and a few women. They were all very entertaining (by which I mean that the men and women I photographed played to the camera). And so I took the photographs, colour Xeroxed them, opened the address book, took out the scroll that was in it, and substituted my own scroll of the pictures of the bleachers. So, when you pushed the button you could scan across the bleachers, like a contemporary scrolling web narrative. I don't know if you've seen any? JR Carpenter's *City Fish*, for instance,[15] is kind of wonderful. The scroll books I made with Radio Shack address books were big hits in exhibitions because they were fun to use. So, I'm still not using computers, but I'm essentially simulating computer technology. To tell you the truth, I hadn't thought of using computers.

---

[14] Images of some electromechanical books from the period 1982–1991 are here: http://www.judy-malloy.net/artistsbooks/artbooks2.html. See also Judy Malloy Papers, David M. Rubenstein Rare Book & Manuscript Library, Duke University.

[15] See: http://luckysoap.com/cityfish/

Why? I don't know. I was using a sculptural object process, partially because I was working with my hands, but it was proto-computer-mediated, and here we go back again to the influence of algorithmic thinking and how that had pervaded my own work without using the technology itself.

I started using a computer when my son wanted one. We didn't have a lot of money, but we went and bought a used Apple II, and he brought in Infocom games (interactive fiction; the kids traded the disks) and all kinds of things. At the time, I was doing another kind of work, but I won't spend too much time on that, and I also made works of information art. The works collected information, and then organised it in order to look at the culture of technology and what is conveyed about technology in advertisements. So, I had a project where I was collecting advertisements for computers, it was something I was interested in. I took the slogans off them and created a database. This one I didn't initially programme myself, I used the early Apple II programme called Visidex. But I quickly realised that if I wanted to distribute this I had to write my own programme. So this was the first time I used computers since I left BBRC in 1969, and it was 1986.

JN When you were telling the anecdote about the punched cards you mentioned how embarrassed you were because you were aware that you were supposed to act in a way that was considered professional. Quite aside from your artistic vision, and quite aside from the resources and facilities that were available to you, I wonder, did those attitudes (those of the engineers and others) towards the computer, and the things that were done around the computer, feed into your thoughts? Did you wonder whether computers could even be used in the artistic context?

JM Well, I'm coming to your question from reading Willard McCarty's interview (McCarty et al. 2012). I was so interested in his attitude to the computer and that of doing computer programming and the men in suits.[16] I don't know if you've seen the man in suits in Uncle Roger? When I read Willard's interview I thought "oh no, the man in tan suits". His attitude is was reminiscent of the narrator of *Uncle Roger*'s attitude to the ubiquitous "men in tan suits". My attitude was a little different than that of Jenny (the narrator of *Uncle Roger*), I was really interested in working with information systems, and I learned a lot from that experience. I didn't mention that the Professor of the Systems Analysis course I took was Richard M Dougherty, who went on to be the Head Librarian at UC Berkeley and worked on computerising that catalog. He also went to the University of Michigan and worked on computerising that catalog, again as Head of the Library System. He was very good at showing the thinking, but I've gone off on a bit of a tangent here, a common Irish quality!

---

[16] There McCarty discusses his earlier dislike for the computer and computer programmers: '... the society of people [that] formed around the computer ... were, in the academic world, a servant class, a lot of them came from business and had a scientific background of some sort. The IBM people and the CDC people all dressed alike and all looked alike, they looked like they were made in the same mould, they all had the same kind of clothing. ... it wasn't what I wanted to do – I didn't want to be a slave in a society that had really no respect for the workers who did the work for them' (McCarty et al. 2012).

JN It's good because you're making clear the many ways that you encountered the technologies and the many attitudes that existed towards it. You're also making clear that it shouldn't only be seen in the context of sterile professionalism …

JM Well, I think that helps me answer your question a little bit. Yes, there was a complete gap between my work as an artist and writer, and my work with information. I noticed the same thing with José Antonio Villarreal. I don't think he talked to too many people in the company about what he was doing, except maybe me. He may have but I'm not sure the researchers would have known what José was writing because it was not what you were expected to convey on the surface. For instance, if you were a woman you couldn't wear pants into the company and you couldn't have long hair at that time. I had to buy a wig! I had long hair, this was the late sixties, and you couldn't wear short skirts, you couldn't even wear your hair in a pony-tail. You could have a bun, but that's too library!

Initially, we were commuting from a tent (I say we because my then husband was also working in a technology company) and we had to get dressed and look professional. The tent was up sort of about 5,000 ft in the Rocky Mountains. There was a long drive down, so you'd have to take a shower at the camp-site, which was not a very convenient shower. This illustrates the contrast and the two lives that I led. And I don't think it's totally uncommon, I mean reading what Willard said in his interview (see McCarty et al. 2012), I could see that contrast again. It's interesting that he picked that up pretty quickly and used it in his own work.

But yes, I think what you are saying is actually a part of why I didn't connect the technology with my work. I connected the thinking with my work, I learned a lot from the thinking. I was interested in information. But in the idea of actually using computers some of that attitude may have lingered. Using computers meant I had to go into a big room with a huge computer, I had better look nice and if all the cards go into the air …. This was, perhaps, a gender issue. My colleague, Jo Sanford and I were the only women using the computer room. In some corners, we weren't completely welcome, and that was just the kind of thing that would happen to us. So that was part of it.

The other part was access, I didn't have access to a large computer system. It's not totally true that I wasn't thinking about my work in that way, because what I had learned about organising information systems and my focus on how information describes technology came from that experience (see Malloy 2014). But no, it wasn't until we got the old Apple II running in my home that I touched a computer. Occasionally in the 1970s and early 1980s I ran computer searches for companies that I was working for, so this is true only of my own creative work.

JN So, you had formal training at BBRC and in systems analysis at the University of Denver. When you were learning FORTRAN, for example, what were your impressions of it, what did you think of it?

JM It was hard. I was very good at systems analysis, although in my recollection, not to the liking completely of Professor Dougherty, who had his own ideas. But for my own way of thinking, I was very good at systems analysis and I was very interested in it. The FORTRAN itself I found difficult and occasionally I would get stuck on the programming. I would go to Dan Anderson, and if he was in a mood to help, he would. He was actually very helpful, but he had a lot of other, more important things to do. I think he was the only computer guy in this whole huge company.

Occasionally, my colleague Jo Sanford was able to solve things I couldn't. My impression was that she was a better hands-on programmer, but I was good at creating the algorithms and setting up the systems, so we worked pretty well together. But I'll tell you, there's another issue here, I realised that one of the other problems was that there were no manuals at BBRC. I think there was one FORTRAN manual. Nowadays, if you want to learn a programming language, you can get a whole shelf of books that will help you. There are people you can ask who will help you. My recollection is that there was one FORTRAN manual and that was it! There were none of these 'FORTRAN for Dummies' or 'Here's how I did this in FORTRAN' books. When I started using BASIC, which was hugely easier to use, and BASIC is actually not that different from FORTRAN, I had access to the University of California's libraries. When I got stuck, I would go down to the basement and there was an entire bank of at least 40 books on BASIC. I would go over them one at a time until I found out how to do what I wanted to do. You couldn't just go to Google to search online then. Although actually I could have done computer searches because I did have access to that but engineering databases weren't oriented towards fixing your sink or how to do something in BASIC.

I also programmed Uncle Roger in Unix Shell scripts (see Malloy 1991), and there the community on the Whole Earth 'Lectronic Link (see, for example, Rheingold 2000; Turner 2010) was very helpful. The people I was working with weren't that knowledgeable at BASIC, so I had to use the books. But once again, this was not available when I was first learning to programme. So what happened was, I was OK on how to write the programme, but I would get stuck on how to do certain things, the way we all do. I'm sure you've encountered that?

JN Yes, absolutely. So, what did you do? Did you hit dead-ends?

JM I also wasn't familiar with ways of testing to find the bug. And testing to find the bug on a punched-card system is not as easy as on the kind of systems we use nowadays. At that time, if you couldn't find it by your eye you could start running portions of the programme until you found out which portion didn't work. But you didn't have that much access to the room. It was more difficult.

JN When you bought the Apple for your son about 15 years later you must have been struck by how much easier it seemed.

JM I was struck, I was thrilled. I mean this was 1986, when this all came together for me. I was thrilled by how easy it was, and by how I already had those skills. I knew how to think about the algorithms, I knew how to do the basic programming, and I knew the programming structures. I was finding it hugely easier than I did working at BBRC. Some of that may have been the corporate situation and some of it may have been that it wasn't my own work. Although I was interested in it I was not excited about it; those are two different things. As I noticed also in Willard's interview, I was not financially able not to have a job, in my case because I didn't make that much money as an artist. So, all of a sudden, all these things came together and it wasn't that difficult. I realised that I could do what I'd been trying to do with the card catalogs. You see, I'd started working on the card catalogs in 1976, about 10 years previously. I started working on them before I could actually make the vision I had for the kind of literature they were meant to be into something real by using the Apple II. It was sitting on the desk in our house, you know, it was right there.

On top of that, I had the enormous good fortune of having a very good friend, my old friend Carl Loeffler, who made an alternative arts space in San Francisco (see Malloy 2013). Early on, in 1979 I think, he worked on an early communications project, a satellite, using NASA technology. So he had some computer background – he was the founding director of Art Com/La Mamelle and then of Art Com Electronic Network (ACEN) and he also did a fair amount of publishing. But they were always underfunded; like any alternative press and they didn't have large amounts of money. He came up with the idea of taking his whole gallery online. This was in 1986, and he turned that into a place (ACEN) where he could not only communicate with people, but also publish art and get an audience.

So he called me up around April or March of 1986, and said he knew I was working with computers because he had seen the database I was making (Bad Information Base no 1). I didn't even know what he was talking about by "going online", but he was very persuasive. So, I went out and bought a modem (you had to buy a modem in those days). I got online and when I got there, it was such an extraordinary experience. I mean nowadays we all grow up with this but to actually be able – even though it was slow – to log on to a computer, and suddenly talk to people in Canada, talk to spoken word poet Fortner Anderson in Canada, to Jim Rosenberg in Pennsylvania, Fred Truck in Iowa! And there was a conferencing system (the WELL used the conferencing software PicoSpan) and we could talk about what we were doing.

But on top of that, I discovered that you could co-opt the conferencing system into a place for additive storytelling. It was how I first published *Uncle Roger*; I told people to use their own database software, because most people in that community had something like dBase at that time. So I published each lexia (a hypertext node or block of text) with the keywords, and said to the community, it was a fairly computer literate community, "I'm gonna put out a lexia every day, like a serial. Pull it into your database, use the keywords that I've given you, and you can make this work on your home computer". This was in 1986, it was pretty interesting.

To add to this, Carl Loeffler initiated and Fred Truck programmed a system and menu where the works could actually be published. The WELL gave ACEN direct access to the server which even nowadays is not easy to get. So basically there was a top menu that accessed the works, which is what I'm talking about here. The works themselves, and in my case the programs I wrote that ran them, were housed in The WELL's VAX. So if you chose *Uncle Roger* from the menu, my program (written in Unix shell scripts) that ran *Uncle Roger* was set in motion and the program and data were interactive in response to user commands. This was incredible for 1987!

Moreover, we had an audience, and this was part of what Carl was looking for. He had the idea that if you work in the conceptual, performance or video art field that your audience is pretty much limited to the other artists working in the field. That's who goes to openings; that's who looks at work. He thought the work was good enough that it should go to a wider audience and all of a sudden we had an audience too. All this came together at once and it was probably one of the most exciting years of my life. Therefore, I made a shift in my work, I was so thrilled by how I saw that words could be used and how words could be manipulated by the computer, that I thought, "OK, I can't use images here, but, you know, images, to a certain extent add a different dimension. I'm going to start just working with words".

JN As you were talking I was trying to think through the various strands of this. What about those colliding points, those points where ideas collide with technology? What you were saying about words seems to be going very much in that direction now.

JM Yes, in looking at some of the chapters in the book I just finished, this issue of the technology colliding with what you want to do comes up fairly often. Many people wanted to use images. There was also the amount of time to get online, a lag, as they called it at that time. It was frustrating and it was expensive too.

JN I don't really mean that. I mean, did the computer also become a sort of – going back to Willard McCarty – an exploratory tool?

JM Yes, but maybe I was coming at it a little differently because I already knew what I wanted to do, to a certain extent, because I'd been working with these card catalogs for so many years. It was exploratory, so I had to find out how to make it work on the system. But maybe I was in a slightly different position than other people coming to look at technology with the idea of making art. I had a certain advantage of knowing what I was going to do and I also could put it into practice very quickly. Essentially I was using the computer to fulfil a vision I already had. Now I don't know…that's a little different than the way other people approached it I think.

JN Yes and no. I always think that this is something that's very important to bring out in these interviews, because sometimes it's said, whether of digital artists or digital humanists or whoever, that the technology drives what they're doing. But as you've been so carefully explaining, no, that wasn't always the case at all and the ideas were there and being developed well before the means through which you could computerise them became available.

JM I see what you're saying. Also, I'm comparing my approach to the approach of other artists, but in DH you are probably more likely to work the way I do and less likely to just play with the technology.

In my case, I might also say that this may go back to the beginning of working with systems analysis. In the case of the BBRC library, I already had the problem – there were so many documents and books in the library and I wanted the engineers and scientists in this country [the USA] to be able to access them. That was the problem and I did not start out by playing with the technology, I started out solving a problem, and in most of my work I do that, even now. In other words, when I start a new work, I know this is the narrative I'm going to do: I start with content. Then I design the authoring software; I don't use a lot of application software. If you use application software, you're limited to a certain extent by what it can do. I also don't use a lot of multimedia. I work with words, but I start with what I want to do. I'm generally not using a programme, other than that I'm using HTML or JavaScript, or in the early days, I used BASIC or Unix shell scripts. Then I try to fit the authoring system to the work itself.

Now, there's no doubt there are times I get stuck, and recently I've been stuck in a few places trying to force JavaScript to do what I want; I have various ways of doing that. Sometimes I'll bang my head against the wall until it works, or nowadays, instead of having to go to the basement of Berkeley library, you can go to Google and search. Other times, I'll think, well, there must be some other way to do that. I mean this is a little difference again between how I and some digital artists work and how Computer Scientists might work. I'm not sitting there thinking, "I have to write a perfect programme". That is not my aim (although I do like elegant code). My aim is to write a programme that displays what I want it to display, or does what I want it to do. If I need a hack to get that happening, I'm not concerned. So yes, I've run up against snags, some recently, and sooner or later I've managed to solve them. Sometimes they can take a long time.

This is an issue that always comes up with students of electronic literature. You have to be aware that you can't always take your idea and put it into practice in, you know, 2 days. If you have a final project, you might be lucky and it might work, but it might not, and particularly at this stage in the field, where we are still exploring and experimenting, we're kind of like musicians in the Middle Ages, when music composition theory and practice was developed. We are still developing those things. So, we can't necessarily expect that something is going to happen and that we're going to get what we want overnight. If we're using an application (Storyspace,[17] for example, was a wonderful application) we still, to a certain extent, have to work within the application. It's always been my contention that if you do that the person who designed the application is, to a certain extent, a co-author, because you are working within that system. But I don't actually object to that at all.

---

[17] Storyspace is 'a hypertext writing environment that is especially well suited to large, complex, and challenging hypertexts'. See http://www.eastgate.com/storyspace/index.html

I think a good application, like Inform 7[18] or Storyspace is really at the heart of the field. It's just that for the work I want to do I generally prefer to come up with my own authoring systems.

JN OK, so my next question would have been how you first got involved in what we now refer to as DH. I think you've probably covered a lot of that. Is there anything that you want to add?

JM Well, here we have the issue, and it is something you're much more knowledgeable about than I am, of what DH means? Is there a place for electronic literature in DH or not? This is a question that I don't think there's one answer to…

JN Not so long ago, my colleagues and I published a book called *Defining Digital Humanities: a Reader* (Terras et al. 2013). It includes a couple of new chapters and otherwise is mostly reprints of some of the most highly-cited articles on this question. Anyway, it comes as no great surprise that we concluded the book by writing that there is no one definition, and probably we shouldn't even have a definition, or that at this stage, a definition isn't useful. So, another question that I was going to ask, related to that, is maybe equally impossible to answer – I wondered what you thought of the Humanities Computing/DH work that you encountered? Did you think it was interesting?

JM I found it very interesting. One area that deserves more attention is systems for creating DH databases, the kinds of things you've worked on. More attention should be given to how that software works; how it might be applied to creating electronic literature; how, in some ways, electronic literature is reversing the process (for instance, by teasing literary meaning out of vast databases; so, perhaps co-opting the process is a better way of putting it) and what the contingencies are. I don't think enough has been enough done in that field. I would like to spend more time looking at DH processes. And so, it's on my list, and I actually have thought it quite wonderful that in some places, or at some conferences, electronic literature has been shown in conjunction with DH work. I think we in electronic literature should be looking more closely at what you're doing also.

JN The next question is about scholars who were not using computers in their research? Do you have some sense of their views about Humanities Computing? But again, I'm asking that in a very broad sense.

JM I looked at that question with interest. Well, I don't want to go into this too much, and I'm sure you've encountered this too, the Humanities scholars occasional cold shouldering. I had a couple of stories I thought I'd tell in response to that.

---

[18] Inform 7 is 'is a design system for interactive fiction based on natural language'. See: http://inform7.com/

Sticking somewhat with the Arts community, and the writers' community, the first story concerns John Cage, who, in 1986 or 1987, I'm not sure which, published a work on Art Com, called the *First Meeting of the Satie Society* (see Malloy 2016a and Couey 1991). Fred formatted it, and it was available on the ACEN menu, and so we had a big party and Art Com invited John and he came. I'd never met him before, and I started talking to him and we were talking about just this subject, you know, what is going to be the reaction?

He told me that in about 1952, when he had done *Silence* (officially called *4'33"*, a work in which the musicians did not play and sometimes actually put down their instruments and did not play. The whole work was about trying to hear the sound in the area) that many people did not speak to him for years. And I thought that was really surprising because *4'33"* is now a very famous work. Yes, it's challenging what music is, and yes, he asked musicians to put down their instruments. When he was telling this to me, I began to see what he was saying. I think what he was saying to me was to expect trouble. It's always easier to think that artists are famous all their lives. They aren't. They run into a lot of problems. I didn't believe that there was that reaction to Silence, because it's such a celebrated work. I actually went and looked later and there was (see, for example, Kostelanetz 1988, pp. 65–68). So what Cage said stuck in my mind for years.

There's been a bit of a larger problem in the Literary Arts with electronic literature, but this is a difficult subject. When I was talking to Stuart Moulthrop at the Pathfinders interview about the role of electronic literature in the literary community, I said that I thought it was so helpful when Robert Coover (1992) wrote a series of articles for the *New York Times* because they really brought a lot of attention to electronic literature. It was reviewed in the *Washington Post Book World* and in a lot of places.[19] Stuart said "no, that's when we attracted the attention of the police". That's when critics stepped in and said "no, no, this is not good". I didn't argue with him but I said "OK, I know what you're saying". There are so many good poets, not just in this country, everywhere, who spend their lives writing poetry and they are not getting a whole page in the *New York Times* book review. All of a sudden electronic literature is getting all of the attention and it's not so much that they don't like electronic literature. It's that the community gets so little coverage anyhow, and this is true of any art form, so there's bound to be hostility if electronic literature attracts a lot of attention and is the new deal.

And there are some other issues also. I think this issue hasn't been addressed enough. Personally, I think electronic literature and print literature are both literature, and eventually we will consider both to be literature. I do not want to lose print literature; the book is a wonderful interface but it's a different interface. So, I've always wanted what I do to be considered as literature. But that may be somewhat frightening to print writers. I don't think it should be because they do something different. Yes, there's a certain set of skills involved in writing electronic literature that not everyone has. I mean, I think the best comparison to that is music composi-

---

[19] See: http://www.well.com/user/jmalloy/reviews.html

tion, in other words, not everyone can compose music. It requires a certain set of skills.

JN Could you briefly outline what you think those skills are?

JM That's a difficult question. To begin with, for me composing electronic literature is like the Middle Ages when there were theory composers who wrote lengthy treatises on composing music. Contemporary notation had not yet arrived, and there was a certain beauty in that you could compose in any way you wanted and score in any way you wanted. But, returning to the basic question you were asking, I say you don't have to code and you can use an application. It is still a different skill than writing poetry and print fiction. I don't think it's necessarily an issue of difficulty. You know, as children we grow up reading print literature. If you step back and look at poetry, the novel and print literature, these are all constraint-based art forms to a certain extent but they are art forms that we are familiar with. Now, at this point in time (this may change) to write electronic literature it is helpful to have writing skills and code skills and the ability to manipulate the words in the same way a composer manipulates notes. I should also say that I'm talking here about hyperfiction, interactive fiction and generative poetry. And they are not the only ways to write electronic literature.

JN It's something that's incredibly difficult to answer anyhow, isn't it?

JM Yes. I think it's also because everyone in the field at the moment approaches it differently and I think that's good. I don't like to see us in the electronic literature field saying that everything should be created with Twine[20] or Inform 7 or that everything should be created in Processing; these are different authoring systems. I like to urge students to step back from the process. I tend to say to them "what is your vision and what do you want to create? *Your* vision – not where the software's going to take you". Then we can see whether there is an application to do that, or, if not, how to do it. Some students can become very excited by that; others can say, "you know, I don't think so".

JN Next I want to ask you for your impression of the conference community and the type of conference communities you encountered?

JM Coming from an art background, I couldn't understand why anyone would want to go to a conference. We went to openings that were free and you were never asked to pay a conference fee to talk. It was either free or you were paid for being on a panel. Also, I couldn't see why you would want to sit around a room, who would want to do that? The first minute I went to a conference I completely changed my mind. The first conference I went to was in 1989 and it was the NCGA Conference that took place in San Jose State University. It was a conference on

---

[20] Twine is 'an open-source tool for telling interactive, nonlinear stories'. See: http://twinery.org/

Computer Art and was hosted by the Computers in Art and Design, Research and Education Institute (CADRE) at San Jose State. I was invited to be on the Art and Telecommunications panel, organized by Carl Loeffler, and including various other people connected with ACEN. Let's see, there was Robert Edgar, Anna Couey, Jeanelle Hurst (from Australia) and, I think, Howard Besser was there also and he is actually connected more with the Museum Computer Network. So it was a mix of people; I was amazed at the interaction, it was very different from going to an art opening or a reading, in that, you know, you're meeting people from all over the word, and there's a lot of very targeted information exchanged. It was exciting, so I changed my mind about conferences. But I was run down in 1994, and I've been on crutches ever since, so unless they are in my area I don't go to a lot of conferences any more, which I miss.

JN I want to ask you about who particularly influenced you, and how. And they can be from any sphere whatsoever.

JM OK, I want to start with the librarians who worked in the early days with early library retrieval systems, because I think they aren't given enough attention. There was Ralph H. Parker and Richard M. Dougherty, from whom I was lucky to take a systems analysis class, and women such as Henriette D Avram. If you look at what they were doing, Ted Nelson (see, for example, Barnet 2013) essentially took it, romanticised it, and has gotten all the credit. Now, I think he deserves a lot of credit. At the same time, when you're looking at hidden histories, and particularly since there are quite a few women involved … It's not my subject, so I haven't been following the scholarship in this field, but it doesn't come up in newspaper articles and the kinds of literature that everybody reads. It's an area that deserves more attention and what I mean is that I want to credit all those unsung librarians, who developed computational ways to automate libraries and retrieval, because that's deeply important to the culture, our culture, which runs beneath hypertextual systems. There's not much difference between a keyword and a link, if you look at it in that way. So I think that's important.

I've already talked about John Cage. His work lies beneath everybody's work in experimental literature, I think. Many of the works he's done have been influential on my work, I'm thinking of his *Interdeterminacy*.[21] But he created this work years ago. Cage gave a lot of talks in interesting ways, and I think it happened that David Tudor suggested that he try just telling stories. So he started telling very short stories, the way lexias look. He numbered them and told them in different orders and they were all about his life and the people he worked with. He and David Tudor created a work where Cage read those stories in one room, and in another room Tudor played one of Cage's piano concertos. They did not hear each other, so Cage had to time his stories. A recording was made by putting the two streams together, and this was the kind of thing that Cage did. He did lectures where he created con-

---

[21] See: http://media.smithsonianfolkways.org/liner_notes/smithsonian_folkways/SFW40804.pdf

centric circles and he put words in them. So many of the things he did – we call them constraints in the electronic literature community – are so embedded in what we do nowadays and I think he's very important. Also, important, of course, are Virginia Woolf, James Joyce and Dorothy Richardson, the three writers who tried to break the conventional narrative. Personally, I also love Jane Austen. And so once again, it's like looking at electronic literature and literature as parallel streams. And different kinds of writing flow in each of these streams.

On a personal level, my friend of 35 years, Sonya Rapoport (1923–2015), who just died this June inspired me and many others.

JN Oh, I'm sorry

JM She was a visual artist who used information in her work (Rapoport et al. 1995). She created scrolls and integrated computers into her work. The first time I met her was, I think, in 1980 or 1981, when I went to an installation at 80 Langton Street called 'Objects on my Dresser'. She had created a work where she had taken the objects on her dresser, I think, and written texts about each object. Then, on the floor she had this huge plot called a netweb, this was basically a web, where the writing and the work she did with a psychiatrist were all laid out like a piece of information. Then she did another work called *Shoe Field*, where she asked people to come in, take off their shoes, and input what they thought about their shoes to a computer. She didn't programme, she worked with a programmer who created a programme to make an array out of each person's statement. So you would take off your shoes, you would put in the information, and you would get a print out back, the kind of print out that people in your field make nowadays, these beautiful graphs. And so we talked.

We had working with information in common. We weren't in direct competition, which I think is helpful. I worked more with narrative and she worked more with images, and for over 35 years, we used to talk all the time. We would call each other up. I still think, almost every week, "I've got to talk to Sonya about that". You know, I'm working on this problem, I need to talk to Sonya. I can't call her and it makes me so upset. But she was 20 years older than me, more than that actually, a fair amount older than me. She was kind of like an art mother. I think everybody needs an art mother, so she was influential in my life.

We've already talked about Carl Loeffler. I'd like to say a few words about Mark Bernstein (chief Scientist at Eastgate, one of the leading publishers of hypertext) because he's so important in the hypertext community. He did something incredible. He was working with the hypertext community, not the literary community. He said people were asking "where are the hypertexts?" So, he answered that question by publishing hypertext literature. You know, it's rare to have such an innovative publisher to work with. He put out, oh, I don't know how many titles, but over 30 or 60.[22] I took a look recently when we were talking about representation of women

---

[22] Eastgate publishes 'serious, interactive writing'. See http://www.eastgate.com/ http://www.east-gate.com/catalog/Fiction.html

and half of them were by women. He worked with writers as people and was very good at seeing things in our works. He picked up Storyspace from Michael Joyce, and the other people who worked on it, and made it publicly available. He managed to attract attention. I still think the works that came out of Eastgate, which is his company, are certainly among the best in the field. So, I like to give Mark a lot of credit. I'm sure I've left off a lot of people but that's a start. People ask me this question, and sometimes I say something completely different because someone's work is on my mind.

JN Do you regret that you didn't get a full professorial post?

JM I would love be a full professor. I would love to continue teaching. I just had a wonderful 2 year visiting lecturer job at Princeton. When I was younger, I actually accepted the dual-career situation with some happiness. Plenty have done that. TS Eliot, worked at a bank, Nathaniel Hawthorne worked at a customs house.

JN Philip Larkin worked in a library, didn't he?

JM Yes, I think so. These are good jobs for poets and writers. Libraries, particularly, are lovely, they are quiet and the work is interesting, I was not unhappy with that at all, you know, when I was in midcareer stage. Although occasionally, as a single parent, I was juggling an awful lot between two careers, and being a parent. Also, it wasn't until recently that I thought, and I think this is partially an age thing, "I have so much to pass on to students, and I'm so thrilled to be working with students". I love the work they do and want to see it continue.

Now I feel that maybe I only have so many years left, and it's important to me to work with students, to essentially pass the small torch – we all have different torches in electronic literature – to pass on the knowledge that I have about how to make it work. I think people with the knowledge of the history of the field that I have should teach. We won't be around forever, and what we know is very valuable.

JN The final question that I want to ask is whether you feel any disappointments about, about routes that electronic literature didn't take (whether social, cultural, intellectual, technological or whatever)?

JM Well, I don't put it quite that way. I still think of this as an incredibly open field. I mean, when I started using a computer to do my work in 1986, part of the excitement was the many ways to manipulate words. There are thousands of things we can do. I wonder about recent moves to take electronic literature into the field of multimedia because that's a different field. I see people who work with words leaving words, and I want to ask "why are you doing this?" They are doing it partially because that is more encouraged. I mean someone implied to me that one reason why the electronic literature community is going in that direction is hostility from the literary community. A digital writer perceived far less hostility if less words and more images were used. By the way, I think a lot of the works created with images and sound and video are very good. I just want people to also see that there are ways to work with words that are incredible and that we haven't yet explored.

References

Avram, H. D., Guiles, K. D., & Meade, G. T. (1967). Fields of information on library of congress catalog cards: Analysis of a random sample, 1950–1964. *The Library Quarterly: Information, Community, Policy, 37*(2), 180–192.

Barnet, B. (2013). *Memory machines: The evolution of hypertext.* London/New York: Anthem Press.

Coover, R. (1992). The end of books. *The New York Times.* Available at http://www.nytimes.com/books/98/09/27/specials/coover-end.html?scp=1&sq=robert%20coover%20the%20end%20of%20books&st=cse. Accessed 29 May 2013.

Couey, A. (1991). Art works as organic communication systems. *Connectivity: Art and Interactive Telecommunications, a special issue of Leonardo, 24*(2). Available at http://www.well.com/~couey/artcom/leonardo91.html. Accessed 12 Nov 2015.

Higgins, H. B., & Kahn, D. (Eds.). (2012). *Mainframe experimentalism: Early computing and the foundations of the digital arts.* Berkeley: University of California Press.

Kostelanetz, R. (1988). *Conversing with cage.* New York: Limelight.

Malloy, J. (1986). *Uncle Roger.* Available at:http://www.well.com/user/jmalloy/uncleroger/party-top.html. Accessed 5 Apr 2016.

Malloy, J. (1991). Uncle Roger, an online narrabase. In: R. Ascott, & C. Loeffler (Eds.), *Connectivity: Art and interactive telecommunications, Leonardo 24*(2) pp. 195–202.

Malloy, J. (1993). *Its name was Penelope.* Eastgate systems. See http://www.eastgate.com/catalog/Penelope.html

Malloy, J. (2000). Public literature: Narrative structures in LambdaMOO. In C. Harris (Ed.), *In search of innovation – the Xerox PARC PAIR experiment* (pp. 102–117). Cambridge, MA: MIT Press.

Malloy, J. (2003). *Women, art and technology.* Cambridge, MA: MIT Press.

Malloy, J. (2013). Memories of art com and La Mamelle. *Judy Malloy.* Available at http://www.well.com/user/jmalloy/artcom.html. Accessed 11 Nov 2015.

Malloy, J. (2014). OK research/OK genetic engineering/bad information, information art defines technology. In A. Bureaud, R. Malina, & L. Whiteley (Eds.), *META-LIFE.* Cambridge, MA: MIT Press (originally published in *Leonardo*).

Malloy, J. (2016a). Art com electronic network: A conversation with Fred Truck and Anna Couey. In: J. Malloy (Ed.), *Social media archeology and poetics.* Cambridge, MA: MIT Press.

Malloy, J. (Ed.). (2016b). *Social media archaeology and poetics.* Cambridge, MA: MIT Press.

Malloy, J., & Marshall, C. (1995). *Forward anywhere.* Eastgate Systems. See http://www.eastgate.com/catalog/ForwardAnywhere.html

Malloy, J., & Marshall, C. (2000). Forward anywhere: Notes on an exchange between intersecting lives. In C. Harris (Ed.), *In search of innovation – the Xerox PARC PAIR experiment* (pp. 118–143). Cambridge, MA: MIT Press.

McCarty, W., et al. (2012). Questioning, asking and enduring curiosity: An oral history conversation between Julianne Nyhan and Willard McCarty, *Digital Humanities Quarterly, 6*(3). Available at http://www.digitalhumanities.org/dhq/vol/6/3/000134/000134.html. Accessed 11 Nov 2015.

Naughton, J. (2000). *A brief history of the future: Origins of the internet.* London: Phoenix.

Perec, G. (2011). *The art of asking your boss for a raise.* London/New York: Verso.

Rapoport, S., Couey, A., Malloy, J. (1995). *A conversation with Sonya Rapoport: On the interactive art conference on arts wire.* Available at http://www.well.com/~couey/interactive/rapoport/sonya.html. Accessed 12 Nov 2015.

Rheingold, H. (2000). *The virtual community: Homesteading on the electronic frontier*. Cambridge, MA/London: MIT Press.

Schudel, M. (2006). Henriette Avram, "Mother of MARC," dies. *Library of Congress Information Bulletin, 65*(5). Available at https://www.loc.gov/loc/lcib/0605/avram.html. Accessed 1 Feb 2016.

Terras, M. M., Nyhan, J., & Vanhoutte, E. (Eds.). (2013). *Defining digital humanities: A reader*. Surrey/Burlington: Ashgate Publishing.

Turner, F. (2010). *From counterculture to cyberculture: Stewart brand, the whole earth network, and the rise of digital utopianism*. Chicago: University of Chicago Press.

Open Access This chapter is distributed under the terms of the Creative Commons Attribution-Noncommercial 2.5 License (http://creativecommons.org/licenses/by-nc/2.5/) which permits any noncommercial use, distribution, and reproduction in any medium, provided the original author(s) and source are credited.

The images or other third party material in this chapter are included in the work's Creative Commons license, unless indicated otherwise in the credit line; if such material is not included in the work's Creative Commons license and the respective action is not permitted by statutory regulation, users will need to obtain permission from the license holder to duplicate, adapt or reproduce the material.

Chapter 8
I Would Think of Myself as Sitting Inside the Computer: Mary Dee Harris and Julianne Nyhan

Abstract This oral history interview was conducted on 3 June 2015 via Skype. Harris was provided with the interview questions in advance. Here she recalls her early encounters with computing, including her work at the Jet Propulsion Lab in Pasadena, California. Despite these early encounters with computing she had planned to leave it behind when she returned to graduate school to pursue a PhD; however, the discovery of c.200 pages of a Dylan Thomas manuscript prompted her to rethink this. Her graduate study was based in the English Department of the University of Texas at Austin, which did not have an account with the computer centre, and so it was necessary for her to apply for a graduate student grant in order to buy computer time. Her PhD studies convinced her of the merits of using computers in literary research and she hoped to convince her colleagues of this too. However, her applications for academic jobs were not initially successful. After working in Industry for a time she went on to secure academic positions in Computer Science at various universities. During her career she also held a number of posts in Industry and as a Consultant. In these roles she worked on a wide range of Artificial Intelligence and especially Natural Language Processing projects. Her interview is a wide-ranging one. She reflects on topics like the peripheral position of a number of those who worked in Humanities Computing in the 1970s and her personal reactions to some of the computing systems she used, for example, the IBM 360. She also recalls how she, as a woman, was sometimes treated in what tended to be a male-dominated sector, for example, the Physics Professor who asked "So are you going to be my little girl?"

Biography

Mary Dee Harris was born in 1942 in Houston, Texas. She completed a Bachelor of Arts in Mathematics at Texas Tech University in 1964, followed by a Master of Arts in English Literature there in 1965. She was a diagnostic programmer for IBM in Los Angeles, 1965–1966, then a Systems Engineer in Austin, Texas, 1967–1968. She received her PhD, which combined English and Computer Science, in 1975 from the University of Texas at Austin. As discussed below, she held posts at various universities and was a Professor in the Department of Mathematical Sciences in Loyola

© The Author(s) 2016
J. Nyhan, A. Flinn, *Computation and the Humanities*, Springer Series on Cultural Computing, DOI 10.1007/978-3-319-20170-2_8

123

University in New Orleans from 1979 to 1986. In 1989 she became an independent consultant; her company 'Language Technology' specialised in Natural Language Processing (NLP) and Artificial Intelligence. She also held a number of roles in Industry, for example, she worked on natural language generation problems in medical applications from 2002 to 2010 in a small start-up company in Texas called 'Catalis'. Her publications include *Introduction to Natural Language Processing* (1985) and 'Poetry vs the computer' (1987). She also published on the integration of Computer Science and Natural Language Processing in the Undergraduate curriculum (Harris Fosberg 1981, 1982). In addition to this she served as President of ACH (1981–1985) and was Software Editor of CHum (1977–1982).

Interview

JN What is your earliest memory, in any context whatsoever, of encountering computing or computing technology?

MDH Well, I go way back. I was in college in the early 1960s and I majored in Math. My mother at one point said, "I guess you're going to be a Math teacher?" meaning in high school. I said, "No, I don't think so" and she said, "Well, what are you going to do?" I didn't have a good idea. So, I went to my adviser at the College and she gave me some books about careers in Mathematics and one of the things in one of the books was about computer programming. I didn't really know what that was. I'd heard of computers but didn't know anything about them.

Like I said, I was majoring in Math and the university where I was had no computer courses at all until my senior year. A friend of mine, who was in the Graduate School of Engineering, told me that there was a 1 hour course in FORTRAN 2 and because I was a senior I could take the graduate course. I signed up for that but didn't learn anything about the computer. All I knew was that you put cards in one side of this machine and you pushed a button and some more cards came out the other side of the machine. You ran them through another device to get the print out to see what had happened, and then you fixed the errors and went through that whole process again. But it was fascinating to me! I thought programming was kind of like playing a game or solving a puzzle, so I was excited about it.

At the end of my senior year I decided to go on to graduate school and get my masters in English Literature. With those tremendous credentials I got a job [1965–1966] working for IBM at the Jet Propulsion Lab (JPL) in Pasadena, California. I was trained for 6 weeks. The people they hired were smart, had logical ability and passed the programming aptitude test but none of them had any background in Computer Science because it wasn't taught anywhere. About 20 of us were in the class and we were then assigned to different places. I worked as an assembly language programmer out at the Jet Propulsion Lab on one of the early unmanned space shots to the moon.

JN Wow!

MDH [Laughs] My background is a little different from most people in DH.

MDH Well, after I'd worked for IBM for a while, my husband and I moved to Austin so he could go to graduate school. I continued to work for IBM for 1 year and then I went back to graduate school in English. I had had some uncomfortable experiences at IBM and I sort of swore to myself that "I'm never going to have anything to do with computers again".

JN Will you say a little bit more about these bad experiences?

MDH At IBM I worked as a Systems Engineer helping clients set up and maintain the software systems on their IBM computers. After a while, though, management wanted me to only teach classes, which I did. I would teach 6 week sessions starting with an Introduction to Computers, then Assembly Language Programming and finally Systems Programming. It wasn't anything terrible but it was not what I was interested in doing. It's kind of ironic that I ended up teaching Computer Science at the academic level, but that's very different from 6 hours a day for 6 weeks straight. Sometimes I would teach Computer Operations as well. I wasn't happy teaching and asked for more client work. My request wasn't granted so I decided to go back to graduate school.

I went straight into an English Literature programme at the University of Texas at Austin (UT Austin) and concentrated on bibliographical methodology, among other things. My adviser took me over to the Humanities Research Center and we found about 200 pages of one of Dylan Thomas' manuscripts. The first thing that came to my mind after several years of saying I wasn't going to have anything to do with computers was "if I put this on the computer, I can get it all sorted out". So that turned into my dissertation, *Computer Collation of Manuscript Poetry: Dylan Thomas' 'Poem on his Birthday'* (Harris Fosberg 1975). I got a lot of flack from the Department about my work. One of the graduate advisers swore that I was trying to destroy literature by using the computer.

JN I found a note from you on Humanist (Harris 1990) where you discussed UT Austin and mentioned that you had taken a course there called 'Computers in the Humanities' led by Nell Dale.[1] You mentioned that the English Department had no account with the computer centre and that you had to secure an additional grant to buy computing time. How do you think it came about that this class 'Computers in the Humanities' was taught in the Computer Science Department with no input from the English Department?

---

[1] Nell Dale was faculty in Computer Science at the UT Austin from 1975 to her retirement in 1994. See: http://www.cs.utexas.edu/~ndale/

MDH I found out about the Computing in the Humanities class as I was working on my dissertation and trying to find out more about how to use the computer for this work. Nell Dale taught the class and became a lifelong friend. At that time she was in the Computer Science Department and working on her dissertation as a Computer Science graduate student. I don't remember the details of her dissertation but it had something to do with taking a text and trying to find the words that showed emotions of different sorts. In the class We used the SNOBOL language to do some programming. We learned about various things that were going on in Humanities Computing. Nell put me in touch with the field, and it gave me some confidence in what I was doing, that I wasn't the only person in the whole wide world who was trying to use a computer in literature.

Regarding what I said about having trouble getting access to the computer, I ended up having to apply for a graduate student grant in order to get an account set up with the computer centre, because in those days the English Department had no account. I never knew why there was no contact between the English Department and the Computer Science Department back then. It had never occurred to any of them to think about using computers on campus. I'm not even sure they used computers for keeping student rolls. So, I got a small grant that gave me enough money for the computer time (which was fairly minimal) and the computer paper. It all had to be charged to something, so that was how I handled that.

Later, when I taught in Computer Science at UT Austin, the English Department had a program for combining English and Computer Science, but, of course, that was 30 years later.

JN And I noted you ended up paying for some of it out of your own pocket as well?

MDH I don't remember really, did I say that on Humanist?

JN Yes, you wrote, "Later when I'd left Austin and continued my work long distance from New Orleans, I had to haul two boxes of punch cards back to Austin, beg and borrow computer time from friends and acquaintances and then the final processing was accomplished by using some of the funding set aside for the computer processing of DH Lawrence and I later paid back the HRC out of my own pocket." (Harris 1990)

MDH I had forgotten about that. I think one of my advisers had a student who was working on the DH Lawrence manuscripts and had set up a fund after the initial grant that I had, we're talking a couple of years later. We had an interesting conversation about the fact that DH Lawrence gladly loans Dylan Thomas some computer funds, or something like that! It was all very scholarly but informal, I mean, it wasn't like anything was written down, I just remember the phrase. I don't think I was required to pay back the money that I'd spent (it wasn't very much, probably wasn't more than $20) but I did just as a gesture of thanks for the help and because it had eliminated one more hurdle.

As I went along my goal became to change the world of Literary Analysis and research by showing people how to use the computer. Well, I got a lot of flak when I started publicising that. When I applied for jobs, I got mostly "no". A couple of people said, "That's kind of interesting but we don't have a place for you". Now, you have to remember this was the early 1970s.

JN And when you talk about applying for jobs, do you mean academic jobs?

MDH Academic jobs, yes, like as a professor of English Literature somewhere. But that didn't work out. In the meantime, while I was trying to finish my dissertation, I went to work for a small computer company in Massachusetts. I was living in New Orleans at the time. When I finally got my degree, in 1975, I got a job teaching Computer Science at a University in Oklahoma, so I was in Oklahoma for 4 years and then I moved back to New Orleans and most of my academic career was at Loyola University in New Orleans. That was when I did most of my publishing and made a name for myself. In Oklahoma (I was in the Department of Mathematics, Computer Science and Statistics) I discovered the journal CHum and then Joseph Raben and the Computers and the Humanities group.

JN Is it fair for me to say that the opposition that you met with when you started applying for jobs was from Humanities departments rather than Computer Science departments?

MDH Well, I really got it from both sides and that continued throughout my career, for various reasons. If I applied for a job as a Computer Scientist a lot of people along the way assumed that because my PhD is in English Literature that I must not know much about Computer Science. But then, if they looked deeper, they saw that I was trained at IBM and had worked there and that I had taught practically every course on the Computer Science curriculum so I had a pretty strong background.

Looking back to when I was still at work on my PhD (in Austin before I moved to New Orleans), I had to get approval for my two foreign languages and I had a minor in German as an undergraduate. I had to get the graduate adviser to sign a form that said, "Yes, this document shows that she passed the German exam", that's all I needed, for him to certify that I had passed the German exam. But he started asking me questions about what I was working on. I told him about the work I was doing with the manuscripts and putting it on the computer. I remember very clearly he sat there behind his desk and just glared at me. Then he said, "Young lady, you're trying to destroy literature". He used very dramatic terms and I was flabbergasted because I had no intention of doing that and thought that I was doing a great service for the field. Some of the other things were more subtle.

My direct advisers were very enthusiastic about the idea and were quite helpful in terms of working things out.

JN I also want to ask about the training that you got in IBM, what it was that you did and the perspectives that it gave you because at that time you would have been,

I think, even in the context of Humanities Computing, still quite unusual in that you had formal training and formal experience of computing.

MDH Right, it was unusual that I ended up in the Literature field and the Humanities field at all. Even though I was teaching Computer Science, my research focused on the Humanities initially and eventually I shifted into Natural Language Processing (NLP) and never really got back to the Humanities directly for various reasons.

The training I got was for what we called second generation IBM computers. The third generation at IBM was the 360, which was the basic architecture that is still the foundation for mainframe IBM computers now, after all these years. That was when they switched from octal to hexadecimal; in other words, they developed the 8-bit byte and combined bytes for various data structures. So I learned that a little later. I was initially trained on the IBM 7000 series, mainly. The system I ended up working on was a 7094 with 7040 and 7044 systems attached. Anyway, we were trained in assembly language because in those days if you didn't know the machine-level language, they just assumed you didn't know anything. The 1 hour course in FORTRAN from college was helpful but not of any use to what I was going to be doing. In the 6 week training class we learned from the very bottom. I remember that when I started actually programming at JPL they had several different computer systems on different floors. These were duplicates of the systems described above – I think there were six systems all together. The production system had its backup system and there were two development systems with their own backups.

I'm sure along the way you've seen the big room where everybody's sitting at a device and something great happens and they all stand up and cheer? That was the main production area; we were not allowed in there. Only the JPL scientists worked in there. Our job was to develop diagnostic software that would essentially exercise the hardware and investigate whether or not it was functioning the way it was supposed to. This was very different from today where the hardware tests itself. Back then we actually felt that software was more reliable than hardware. Everything in the computer was wired together by hand and you could get a loose wire that would make everything go haywire. So, it was a very different world. I would think of myself as sitting inside the computer and moving things around in order to accomplish whatever the goal of my programming was. In those days, the computer had a great big front with lights blinking and you could actually set switches to change the value of a word in the computer memory and then restart your program with new values. That's how you could debug – I mean we're talking way back! But it was really interesting and a great background for teaching Computer Science. I've never figured out for sure how it influenced my use of computers in the Humanities. But I'm sure it did give me a very different perspective, particularly from people who were coming from the Humanities and then later learning computing.

JN And in your career you also have this movement from industry to academia and then you also did consultancy for a time?

MDH Yes, I mentioned that I first taught Computer Science in Oklahoma. It really was a hard position because I taught so many different courses. But I taught everything so I learned a whole lot. Then I went to Loyola in New Orleans. I wrote several papers about some of the things that we did there to change the curriculum to fit a small liberal arts college while still teaching everything that a Computer Science student should know (See, for example Harris Fosberg 1981, 1982). I also wrote papers on teaching NLP at the undergraduate level. Based on that I wrote a book, the *Introduction to Natural Language Processing* (1985), which was the first college text book in the field. Other books had come out but they were mostly compilations of papers from various conference. I had already taught the NLP course so I thought, "Well! You know what? I can do this!" My book didn't stay in publication for very long, but I think it inspired some other people to write books in the field and I can always say mine was first.

Based on that book, I was contacted by a company in the Washington DC area, SRA, which is now SRA International. They were setting up a Department of Artificial Intelligence and wanted to talk to me about going to work for them. I flew up there to talk to them about what they were doing and to meet the people they'd already hired. I moved from New Orleans up to Washington DC in 1986, and I worked for that company for about 3 years. We did a variety of projects, mostly related to NLP. One was a project for the Air Force. The back end of it was an expert system that was related to flying sorties over Europe and the front end of it was a natural language interface so a person could ask questions about flying sorties by typing questions in English. It would output answers mostly in a kind of canned text. Although the Air Force never did anything with that project it actually was fairly successful in terms of what we were able to understand. There wasn't a lot of work available related to NLP at that point so the company kept trying to move me into different areas.

I decided after 3 years that I would go to work for myself. I worked as an independent consultant for about 10 years and called my little venture 'Language Technology'. I worked for almost 6 years with the Educational Testing Service (ETS), the GRE SAT[2] folks here in the US, and did a variety of projects for them including a project to automatically score essays that were part of the SATs or other exams. A computer and a human would score an essay. Then, if they didn't match, they would have a second human look at it, so the system wasn't totally dependent on the computer. It saved them a lot of money because they didn't have to pay two humans to mark all the essays.

In the meantime, I had moved back to Austin in 1997, and was finishing up one project with ETS when UT Austin contacted me about teaching for them. There was another computer boom shortly before Y2K when everybody was trying to hire programmers to fix things so they needed more faculty. I taught there for about 5

---

[2] The GRE and SAT are tests that are required for admission into university programmes in the USA.

years, until 2002. I initially taught a course called 'Contemporary Issues in Computer Science', kind of like a 'Computers in Society' course but focused on the Computer Science part of it. I suggested teaching a NLP course since that was what I loved and ended up teaching that four or five times. I also worked with undergraduates doing research on a project with the AI Laboratory. I had a number of students who went on to do graduate work in NLP, based on the work we had done, so that was very rewarding. To add the final bit to it before we move off to something else, the last semester I was there, I knew I wasn't going to be teaching at UT anymore and wasn't sure what I would be doing. I found out from one of the professors in the Computer Science Department that there was a small start-up company looking for somebody to do natural language generation work for their system. It was an electronic medical records system that needed to produce a narrative based on the data that the doctor had input about the patient. I ended up working for them for 9 years and then I retired from there in 2010. And that's my career.

JN It's really a fascinating trajectory. Tell me about how it was that you met Joseph Raben and went on to become president of ACH?

MDH Although I was teaching Computer Science in Oklahoma I was still interested in English Literature. I had attended the Modern Language Association (MLA) conference in New York City in 1977 or 1978 and met Joe there.[3] He had organized a session at MLA that was related to computers in the Humanities. He had already established the newsletter and founded the journal CHum [in 1966]. I initially worked with Joe and helped him to edit articles and I did book reviews of computer-related books. I was Software Editor. A year or so after I made that contact Joe organised a meeting of people who were interested in the field and formed the ACH. Joe was elected the first President and I was elected to the Executive Board. He was President for a 2 year term [1979–1980] and decided that we needed a different president. Everybody knew me, and I kind of volunteered to be the next President. Everybody thought that was a good idea and I was elected. When would that have been?

JN According to the ACH website that was from 1981 to 1985?

MDH OK, 81–85, that sounds good. That's a lot of water under the bridge! Anyway, that was very interesting and having been the President for 4 years, I decided it was time to switch and that's when Nancy Ide took over. I first met her when she was still a graduate student trying to find a job teaching English, without much luck. She had the same kind of degree I did, a background in English Literature and academic training in Computer Science. I suggested to her that she try to get a job in a Computer Science programme. That's when she took the job at Vassar

[3]The MLA was held in New York in 1978, see https://www.mla.org/Convention/Convention-History/MLA-Convention-Statistics

where she has been since. It was just a conversation that she and I had saying, "why don't you try this?" and it really worked out well for her.

JN I was reading the early newsletters of the ACH and some of the editorials that you wrote when you were president. In some of them you were talking about how you felt that the tide was turning, that the opposition to computing that had been encountered at an earlier stage was abating and that you really noticed an upsurge of interest in and acceptance of the subject (Harris 1984). I was wondering whether you would reflect on that development as you saw it over those years?

MDH I'll have to think back. I think I was referring to what I felt was making a difference. There was beginning to be a little bit of publicity about some of the projects that were coming out of the field. Some of the early projects were very time consuming. It was really tedious to deal with punch cards and magnetic tape and that level of technology and lots of the language work was restricted because of the limitations of computer speed and computer memory sizes. But a lot of us really hard-headed people who wanted to do computing on Humanities subjects just kept at it. Gradually the disciplines of Literature and History began to see areas where the computer could actually help research and that it wasn't going to destroy literature. It could help sort things out and help find patterns in novels or in plays and so on. It was very gradual and had a lot to do with the technology improving.

Also, those of us in Humanities Computing were learning more and more from each other as we organised and spread the word. There was still a fair amount of reluctance about people in say Computer Science teaching if their work was primarily in the Humanities and vice versa. I think that continued for a long time when people tried to get jobs. In fact, that may still be the case in some places, but the direct opposition became less over the years. One thing that would have made me write that was my change in jobs. In the position I had in Oklahoma, they were not at all helpful. When I moved to Loyola in New Orleans, they were very helpful and very encouraging. I was given a lot of financial support to do research and to travel to conferences and just publicise the field in general, so from my personal perspective, I think that helped.

JN Maybe this question is slightly naïve but I'm very often struck by how brave and how determined people were who worked in the field at this earlier stage, not only in terms of the difficulties of finding acceptance and jobs but also in terms of the difficulties of just doing the work. What I sometimes wonder about is how the conviction came about, or where it came from, that the computer really would allow something new to be achieved within the context of, let's say, literature. Where do you think that belief came from? Was it based on observations of successes in other domains that were then transferred to the Humanities? What do you think about the roots of it?

MDH I think there were a lot of different paths to the conclusion and the conviction that it was possible and that each individual should be the one doing it. It was a struggle, and it was a struggle for most of us, I think that was why we were so happy to form the ACH and to find people in other parts of the country who were working on similar problems and had the same kinds of struggles.

And why? I was such an exceptional person for my generation because I knew I wanted to go into Science and Math from an early age. That was usual for a woman back then. I've always said I wasn't very well socialised because I don't remember anybody telling me that girls don't do Math and Science! I mean nobody told me I couldn't until I actually got into college! Then some people discouraged me. They weren't saying I couldn't but, for example, a Physics professor patted me on the knee and said, "So, are you going to be my little girl?" This was my freshman year in college and I thought "No, that's not the way this is supposed to work". So there were obstacles.

I had always intended to have a career. Most of my school friends and family got college degrees, they got a job, met somebody and got married. They worked until they had children and then stayed home with the children. I didn't stay home, even after my son was born. I always felt that if I had stayed home with my son, we both would have been crazy! I mean it was obvious to me that I needed to be working, so if I was going to be working then I needed to be doing something that I really enjoyed. I could never see any reason not to combine the fields. And like I said, when I saw those manuscripts, I mean 200 pages of handwritten manuscripts is lot of material and what would you do? Write it out on index cards and try to sort it that way? That was basically the way people had been doing things. That was the option!

So the idea of putting it on the computer, of typing in all the words and all the lines from the written manuscripts and seeing how they would work together just seemed logical to me. Why wouldn't you do it? I think because I had training in more than one field that I could make those connections, that synergy that comes from seeing how things work in more than one field of study. Over the years, I have found many, many people who were interested in more than one thing. Maybe they were attracted to me because of my background, but I used to say to my undergraduate Computer Science students, "If you're interested in Journalism as well as Computer Science, take some courses; there's going to be a need for people in Journalism (or in History etc.) who know computers". Back then it was unusual to combine fields but I think there's been more acceptance of interdisciplinary studies over the years. And I think some of the studies of creativity have really backed up the notion that when you've been trained to think in more than one way you have more than just that combination. It is that whole idea of synergy, that one plus one makes more than two, if you will.

JN People often remark to me that when they got involved with the Humanities Computing community that they found it to be very welcoming and open; indeed, some found it more welcoming than the other disciplines they worked in. Do you agree with that?

MDH Oh, absolutely. When I first met the group who knew Joseph Raben and attended the various meetings at the MLA it felt like we were all old friends because we had been doing these oddball projects off on our own, for the most part. Here I was, in Oklahoma of all places; there wasn't another person in the whole state who was doing anything similar. But gradually, as more and more people discovered us, it got better. I think we were all very encouraging to anybody new because we felt like we just wanted to increase our ranks so that we wouldn't be quite as alone. I remember some of the early meetings. I can't remember everybody's name but a good friend was Donald Ross, at the University of Minnesota and there was a fellow Jim Joyce out in San Francisco. Also Jeffrey Huntsman at Indiana. And other people from across the country who were mostly working independently and had come together. It was sort of like if you're shipwrecked and you find one more person who's shipwrecked, you say "here, come join the club!"

JN I found references to papers you gave at the Humanities Computing Conferences up to at least the 1990s. Did you move away from the field after that point?

MDH Well, as long as I was in the academic world, I had financial support to attend conferences. After I went out on my own, it was harder. But the biggest problem was that I got sick in 1993. I came down with Chronic Fatigue Syndrome (CFS), which in Europe is called Myalgic Encephalomyelitis (ME) and was quite ill for several years. I was basically bed-ridden for a couple of years, and then housebound for a couple more and that's the reason I moved back to Texas. The cold weather in Washington DC was very hard on my health and gradually I have been able to recover more of my ability and energy here in the warmer climate. But that really slowed me down and I never really got back into doing research or making contacts. I didn't totally lose contact with people, but since I wasn't attending conferences and got out of the loop, I just wasn't able to keep up with it.

JN Regarding this really fascinating trajectory that you were on that involved moving between all these different areas, did it make you quite unusual among your Humanities Computing colleagues?

MDH Because I started in computing? Is that what you mean?

JN I think also because you were moving between Academia, Industry and Consulting. Of course, the thing about Humanities Computing is that it can be done in Industry, it can be done in Academia, and it can be done in, say, heritage contexts like museums and libraries. But what I often see is that many people seem to follow one path through. I'd love to get a better handle on how common it is for people to move seamlessly, it seems, between these different spheres but I don't really have a sense of that. I was wondering if maybe you do?

MDH You know, I'm not sure. A lot of it happened to me – it wasn't always my choice to move from one place to another when I was married. I've been married twice. The first was a fairly traditional marriage, and my husband expected me to go where he was, which I did. That's the way we did things then. There was not the agreement of "we are in this together". Even at one point, when I had a very strong opportunity and he didn't have a job at all, he didn't want to go because it was my opportunity and not his, so we didn't.

When I was married the second time, it was kind of the opposite. I basically told him from the beginning, "I have a career and I intend to keep working at it and if you are willing to come along with me we can work this out" and that worked. But part of the reason for moving around so much was because I was in this oddball field and having trouble finding an academic job. When I was trying to finish my dissertation, I did a number of things just to support myself. I worked as a typist for about 6 months and then I got a job working in New Orleans for a little computer company in Massachusetts (early telecommuting). Later I took a job as a bartender in the French quarter for about a year just to pay the bills while I finished my dissertation. Then I taught at Loyola in the Computer Science Department where I later came back in a tenure track position. It wasn't a straight path.

If you get a job straight out of getting your PhD, you may stay in that job forever. But since we didn't have easy access to academic positions I think that some of us moved around. Not everybody, I mean a lot of people stayed in the same field. My split field was a positive in many ways because of the work I did but it was a negative in terms of what people thought of me and thought of my ability, without looking at what I had done. I can't say I ever got used to it, but I certainly got to the point where I wasn't surprised by it. Even in the last job I had, people would say, "Oh, I know you know about language," but they just assumed I didn't know anything about computers and it's sort of like, "How do you think I got here if I didn't know anything about computers?"

JN The other question that I want to ask you is about the people, from any sphere (it doesn't necessarily have to be DH) or the books or ideas that particularly inspired you?

MDH Well, obviously one of the people who inspired me was Nell Dale. She got me started, even though she didn't continue in the field. And there was another woman called Patricia K. Galloway. She's teaching in the School of Information at UT Austin now but she was in Mississippi for quite a while in the Department of Archives and History. She was the person who put me in touch with NLP and showed me where to look things up and who were the people that were working in that field and so on. Those were pivotal points.

I had a couple of Professors, the two thesis advisers here at UT, Warner Barnes and William B. Todd, who supported me emotionally, if you will, as well as academically and intellectually, in terms of following up on this idea because it just was so off the wall. To get back to your previous question on that, one of the things that

I found when I came back to graduate school after having worked at IBM in the computer industry, was that I felt kind of like a fish out of water because most of the other graduate students had always been in school. You know, they might have had a summer job or worked at a camp somewhere or have done something to support themselves, but they had never been in the business world for any length of time. I remember in one of the poetry classes, we were analysing some poem by Wallace Stevens and the images that I came up with were so off the wall compared to these other students. I remember finding out later that he was an insurance agent who wrote poetry on the side, so I was possibly closer in terms of seeing the world the way that he did than these people with all their academic experience in literature. I think moving back and forth like that did give me a different perspective at each point.

JN I must ask you when you look back at when you were president of ACH, what's the action you are most proud of or that sticks out the most in your mind?

MDH I think the fact that we opened the field up. One of the things I really tried to concentrate on was broadening and expanding the definition of Humanities. So, we accepted any comers in those days whether you would officially be defined as in the Humanities or not. Initially the group was almost entirely literature and then we started expanding into History and Archaeology and various other non-technical fields. I think that was one thing that made a difference. Because of the academic support that I got from Loyola, I was able to travel and really make connections. Of course, at that point the ALLC and Susan Hockey (see Chap. 6) and her colleagues were doing quite well in Europe. But bridging that gap was another part of it, I think, and one of the contributions that I started and that Nancy Ide certainly continued.

This has been very entertaining to me because I don't spend a lot of time thinking back on those days. Most of the people I know nowadays have only a vague idea that I did something in the computer field and they don't have a clue about the details of what I did. So, talking about my personal history and how we got that whole thing going, I think, has been very entertaining to me, so I thank you.

JN And thanks so much for giving me so much of your time and for such a fascinating interview.

References

Harris, M. D. (1984) Observations on computers and poetry. *ACH Newletter*, 6(4), 1, 6.

Harris, M. D. (1985). *Introduction to natural language processing*. Reston: R.J. Brady, U.S.

Harris, M. D. (1987). Poetry vs the computer. In Zampolli, A., et al. (Eds.), *Linguistica Computazionale: Studies in honour of Roberto Busa, S. J.* (Vols. IV/V). Pisa: Giardini.

Harris, M. D. (1990). Humanist archives (vol. 3) : 3.929 support of humanities computing (53). *Humanist Discussion Group (archives)*. Available at http://dhhumanist.org/Archives/Virginia/v03/0923.html. Accessed 9 Jul 2015.

Harris Fosberg, M. D. (1975). *Computer collation of manuscript poetry Dylan Thomas' poem on his birthday*. Austin. PhD thesis.

Harris Fosberg, M. D. (1981). Natural language processing in the undergraduate curriculum. In: *Proceedings of the twelfth SIGCSE technical symposium on computer science education* (pp. 196–203). SIGCSE'81. New York: ACM. Available at http://doi.acm.org/10.1145/800037.800988. Accessed 11 Aug 2015.

Harris Fosberg, M. D. (1982). Adapting curriculum 78 to a small university environment. In *Proceedings of the thirteenth SIGCSE technical symposium on computer science education* (pp. 179–183). SIGCSE'82. New York: ACM. Available at http://doi.acm.org/10.1145/800066.801364. Accessed 11 Aug 2015.

Open Access This chapter is distributed under the terms of the Creative Commons Attribution-Noncommercial 2.5 License (http://creativecommons.org/licenses/by-nc/2.5/) which permits any noncommercial use, distribution, and reproduction in any medium, provided the original author(s) and source are credited.

The images or other third party material in this chapter are included in the work's Creative Commons license, unless indicated otherwise in the credit line; if such material is not included in the work's Creative Commons license and the respective action is not permitted by statutory regulation, users will need to obtain permission from the license holder to duplicate, adapt or reproduce the material.

Chapter 9
There Had to Be a Better Way: John Nitti and Julianne Nyhan

Abstract This oral history conversation was carried out via Skype on 17 October 2013 at 18:00 GMT. Nitti was provided with the core questions in advance of the interview. He recalls that his first encounter with computing came about when a fellow PhD student asked him to visit the campus computing facility of the University of Wisconsin-Madison, where a new concordancing programme had recently been made available via the campus mainframe, the UNIVAC. He found the computing that he encountered there rather primitive: input was in uppercase letters only and via a keypunch machine. Nevertheless, the possibility of using computing in research stuck with him and when his mentor Professor Lloyd Kasten agreed that the Old Spanish Dictionary project should be computerised, Nitti set to work. He won his first significant NEH grant c.1972; up to that point (and, where necessary, continuing for some years after) Kasten cheerfully financed out of his own pocket some of the technology that Nitti adapted to the project. In this interview Nitti gives a fascinating insight into his dissatisfaction with both the state and provision of the computing that he encountered, especially during the 1970s and early 1980s. He describes how he circumvented such problems not only via his innovative use of technology but also through the many collaborations he developed with the commercial and professional sectors. As well as describing how he and Kasten set up the Hispanic Seminary of Medieval Studies he also mentions less formal processes of knowledge dissemination, for example, his so-called lecture 'roadshow' in the USA and Canada where he demonstrated the technologies used on the dictionary project to colleagues in other universities.

Biography

John Nitti was born in 1943 in Yonkers, NY. He has been Emeritus Professor of Spanish and Portuguese at the University of Wisconsin-Madison since 2001. His PhD thesis was based on the Aragonese Book of Marco Polo and his degree was awarded by the University of Wisconsin-Madison in 1972. Shortly thereafter he took up the post of Assistant Professor of Spanish and Portuguese and became full Professor in 1985. In the early 1970s, Nitti, with the support of his mentor Professor Lloyd Kasten, began to explore the application of computing to Old Spanish lexicography. He subsequently won major funding from bodies such as the NEH and, in

© The Author(s) 2016
J. Nyhan, A. Flinn, *Computation and the Humanities*, Springer Series on
Cultural Computing, DOI 10.1007/978-3-319-20170-2_9

later years, the government of Spain. Such grants allowed him to devise innovative ways to bring computing to bear on the Old Spanish Dictionary project, which the Wisconsin Seminary of Medieval Spanish Studies had been at work on since the 1930s. In addition to his Directorship of the Old Spanish Dictionary project (1975–2001), in 1975 he and Kasten founded the Hispanic Seminary of Medieval Studies (HSMS), initially to disseminate the large numbers of transcripts and other materials that the dictionary project was producing. Today, this not-for-profit organisation (now based at the Hispanic Society of America in New York) has become an important publisher of texts in Hispanomedievalism and related fields. His many publications include (together with Lloyd Kasten) *The Electronic Texts and Concordances of Medieval Navarro-Aragonese Manuscripts* (1997) and *Diccionario de la prosa castellana del Rey Alfonso X* (2002)

Interview

JN My first question is: what are your earliest memories of encountering computing technology?

John It is a very vivid memory because it really was the pivotal point in my approaching lexicography using as much information technology as possible and, of course, we're talking about a long time ago. We're talking about the very late 1960s and early 1970s. My first significant grant was, if I remember correctly, for $242,000, from the NEH. I was still a graduate student at the time I developed that proposal. But prior to that time – it's an odd sort of a thing because I know one of your questions here is "which people particularly influenced you and how" (with regard to the technology aspect, obviously not Medieval Hispanism, which is my field) and the two are linked – my first contact with computer technology, with an eye toward employing it and applying it to my research, occurred via one of my fellow graduate students. Actually, he was not one of our best graduate students, but I owe him this. One day he said to me "you know I'm looking for a thesis topic? What I really want to do is to generate a concordance of a large Medieval Spanish text, based on a transcription that I'll do." At the time, our campus academic computing facility was mainframe-based, as most if not all were. We had mini-computers, of course, but there were no microcomputers at that time. He said "I heard that our campus computing facility bought a concordancing programme and brought it up on the UNIVAC (which was the big campus mainframe at the University of Wisconsin at the time). You're interested in things technical, would you do me a favour and check it out?" I said "OK".

So I went over to the computer centre and started talking to the people and they gave me a few dollars' worth of credit so I could actually run a sample concordance. Now we're talking really primitive stuff, I mean it printed the concordance but these were the days when you were lucky if your campus had an IBM system for academic research, because then you could use extended ASCII and you could get upper and lowercase characters. But if you didn't, you were simply lost because all it could produce and print were uppercase characters and, of course, the input device, was a big disappointment to me as well. The University of Wisconsin-Madison had a very large campus computing facility. It is a campus of some size, we have traditionally had 40,000–45,000 students at this campus from year to year and the University of Wisconsin-Madison is, in fact, the flagship campus of the University of Wisconsin University system. Well, the input device that they pointed to was a keypunch machine, and I'm thinking "What? I have to use punch cards to do this stuff?" Of course they only had uppercase letters. That was it, so you had to punch all these cards and transcribe all these texts in uppercase. Well, I took my colleague (who I mentioned above) over there and I got him started. Eventually he did produce a concordance and he submitted that with an introduction as his doctoral dissertation (we were both working on our dissertations simultaneously).

But at the time I was doing other stuff. I was already working as a graduate assistant for my mentor Professor Lloyd Kasten (see, for example, Jover 2002) while completing my doctoral dissertation. Mr Kasten and I forged a partnership which lasted until his death at the age of 94, though, it is important to note that he was still going strong and still working on the *Dictionary of the Old Spanish Language* (hereafter DOSL) with me 3 months prior to his death. I remember well that when I first proposed computerising DOSL, he took to the idea right up front. At that time he was already in his late 70s and he said "Let's do this. Wouldn't you like to get into this computer thing more deeply and see if we can't computerise the Old Spanish Dictionary project?" I said "I sure would, except we don't have any money to do it!" He said "Well, we'll start out with some."

He was a very frugal man, a single man. He had a sizable savings account so he was totally willing to put up what for an individual were quite large sums of money so that I could start playing around with computers. So it was probably Mr Kasten who was more influential in giving me an opportunity to get my feet wet, or get both our feet wet, as it turned out. But I have to give credit to that one graduate student. That poor guy died young, he became a professor at the University of Wisconsin, Steven's Point, a smaller campus, and he died in his 40s, which was a tragedy. But in any case that's how I got started in all of this.

JN When you headed over to the computer centre and got some credit, were you one of the few Humanities people who had turned up there?

John There was a Professor of English who in fact went before me in this historical sequence and I can't remember his name. Quite frankly, he and I didn't have much contact at all. He was involved with the computational aspects of the *Dictionary of Old English* project under the directorship of Professor Angus Cameron at the University of Toronto, and was therefore into the application of computer technology to humanistic research, such as it was, sooner and more deeply than me. He eventually left the University of Wisconsin for another position and we had no further contact.

As the years passed I got interested not only in developing ad hoc software to do what I wanted for the creation of DOSL but, more importantly, to develop, believe this or not, novel hardware applications. Not ourselves physically, although I did end up doing some microcomputer kit building. These were the early years before there was much in the way of microcomputers: Radio Shack had not yet released the TRS-80, Apple was on the verge of releasing its first Apple, which wasn't very powerful at all and couldn't even do what I wanted to do and IBM had not yet released its PC. In any case, I started looking right from the very outset.

We were obliged to use the campus mainframe because it was in the university's interests since they were renting it from UNIVAC at great expense. They wanted to generate as many users as possible and, up to that point, and even afterwards, the lion's share of users were Scientific as opposed to Humanities people. Things changed a little bit as the years went on. But what happened with the DOSL project was once we got some substantive funding – although Mr Kasten continued to contribute out of his own pocket so that I could indulge my whims testing out devices and I'll mention some to you in a bit – it became patently clear to me that our having to use the campus UNIVAC of the University of Wisconsin for our processing was in fact what we call today 'a rip off'. It was outrageously priced. I'll give you an example. A project such as ours, which presupposed that we were going to be transcribing from the original manuscripts (or photographic reproductions of the original manuscripts), required a number of things. Number one was that I develop a manual of transcription for the *Dictionary of the Old Spanish Language*, an encoding text, if you will. I was given to understand that I was one of the earliest ones around to actually develop such a thing.

In order to publish it, and anticipating the publication of large quantities of data, Mr Kasten and I created a non-profit publishing house called the Hispanic Seminary of Medieval Studies.[1] Here I'll mention John O'Neill, my Irish student. The then Director of the Hispanic Society of America, Theodore S. Beardsley (who had held that post for some 40 years), was a very close personal friend of mine and he asked me "have you got a good PhD who could be my replacement as departing Curator of Rare Books and Manuscripts?" I said "I sure do, he's an Irish man, if you don't discriminate against the Irish!" Ted just chuckled (parenthetically, Ted just died a few months ago). He said "well, I'm coming to Madison". He wanted to meet this Irish boy. He came and met him and liked him as much as I liked him, so he hired him on the spot to be the Curator of Rare Books and Manuscripts. This was some 15 years ago and John O'Neill is still there as Curator but they've made him, in addition to the Curator of Manuscripts and Rare Books, also the Head Librarian of the Hispanic Society of America.

Mr Kasten and I decided that we wanted to begin publishing as soon as possible, even in intermediate forms, the large numbers of texts that we were transcribing from the original manuscripts or from photocopies of the originals. We wanted to distribute them to the world. So, we looked around for another technology: what would it be that we could marry to the fact that we were capturing all these key-

---

[1] See http://www.hispanicseminary.org/index-en.htm

strokes in a computer-readable form? The technology for mass dissemination of data was – there weren't any DVDs or CDs then – 'computer output on microform' (or microfiche in this case). We miniaturised all these thousands of pages of transcription and/or concordances that we were generating because we weren't going to be able to publish this stuff, which was fairly esoteric, in standard book form. There are relatively few people in the world who are interested and willing to pay the fortune you're going to have to charge just to recoup the expenses of all this material. So we said we had to distribute this in a medium that we could afford to distribute for pennies, literally, pennies on a dollar. And what was that medium? It was computer-output on microfiche. So we worked a contract with a commercial service bureau in Minneapolis, Minnesota, and I went up there a number of times and we got it all coordinated and going.

For years we published and disseminated the data that we were generating, both textual transcriptions and corresponding concordances with frequency counts and all that typical stuff that you get with concordancing schemes. And we were able to sell it through this new publishing house we created, the Hispanic Seminary of Medieval Studies. You may want to go online to the Hispanic Seminary of Medieval Studies. John O'Neill in New York has created its website and he actually sells the publications out of that website. John has kept the Hispanic Seminary going.

The medieval seal on the website was drawn freehand by my sister. It's inspired by seals of the thirteenth century for the Kingdom of Alfonso the Wise, who is, in fact, the King for whose original manuscripts we generated the largest database. Many of those manuscripts that Alfonso had produced for him, and that we assume he held in his own hands have survived, believe it or not. And we were able to use photostatic reproductions or microfilm of those manuscripts to create the *Dictionary of the Castilian Prose of Alfonso X*. John O'Neill is keeping that publishing operation going on his own time, he operates it out of the Hispanic Society of America now. When I retired I had it all legally transferred to him and the Society, knowing that he would keep it going.

JN Do I understand correctly that it was the time you spent in the computer centre that inspired you to involve computational technology in your research?

John Yes, but I quickly learned that the state of that technology as applicable to our research was deplorable; quite frankly, it was primitive. I thought "God, we have to print anything we publish out in uppercase letters? That's ridiculous!" All they had were these high speed chain printers (the 15 in. wide paper with the perforations on the side) that fed the paper through these machines at breakneck speed. It was just crap and if they hadn't changed the ribbon, you were bound to get something that could barely be read.

JN And how, despite those limitations, were you able to foresee ...?

John Well, here's how. Initially, I was working hot and heavy on trying to find a data input mechanism – this is hardware we're talking about now – that would have upper and lowercase letters from the get-go. On the mainframe computer in those days the typical editor you had was referred to as a 'line editor'. Imagine this: you're working with a terminal, not with a CRT terminal but with some sort of a teletype terminal, printing out this junk at ten characters per second, or whatever it was that they eventually cranked it up to, it wasn't much. What you had to do was locate the line that you wanted to edit, bring it up and print it out. Then you'd have to use search and replace algorithms with the editor (I'm talking about an online editor to the mainframe. To make a change you had to go "find this, change to that"). Now imagine how you do that a zillion times to correct the transcriptions which were input. That's another very important point with my research, the need to get a much better method for inputting data or capturing keystrokes, as we used to say.

I decided early on that I wanted to get away from the keypunch as soon as I could. So, I used as a pilot, basically, the transcription of the very first manuscript of Alfonso the Wise, which was a very large manuscript. We used the keypunch for that and we managed to produce the entire transcription all in lower and uppercase, but we were flagging. I decided we would flag the uppercase letters with an extra symbol so that we'd at least be able to convert all those when we got better technology. In fact this did take place but there was a disaster. We had something like 15 boxes of keypunch cards, in long-ish boxes as they had in those days. We were trying to transport them to the computer centre so we got one of these wheeled carts and stacked all these boxes up on it and wheeled it across various intersections in the city to get to the computer centre. Well, wouldn't you know it, the darn thing, we were trying to get up a curb and the thing spilled over and it took us a week to reassemble all the damn cards in the proper order. I said after that "we are going to change this thing".

I was absolutely convinced that there had to be a better way. I got this brilliant idea, or an idea that I thought was brilliant about computer-based hardware, not just computers but what they used to refer to as 'peripherals', basically. You had mainframe computers and then you had these peripheral devices that were hooked up to them to do one thing or another. They were referred to as monitors and terminals because they weren't really very capable devices, they were basically slave devices hooked to the mainframe. Anyway, I wasn't happy with that, I wanted an offline device because – and this is the other sort of scary thought in this day of dirt cheap, hard disk, Winchester-based technology – the campus computer facility was charging us, you ready for this? Almost $17,000 a year to rent 20 MB of disk storage on the mainframe!

JN That seems incredible!

John $17,000 a year! But, of course, that implied that they had the liability of backing it up and being sure that it was safely stored on tape copies, typically on the big 8-track tapes.

Anyway, I said "that's ludicrous", so what happened? Round about the time that we finished the transcription of that first keypunch card text, I started going to these computer hardware shows. I found two different companies, they were both start-up companies. I don't know if they even exist any longer but at the time they were these young geniuses who were working with microcomputer-based devices. They were incorporating that early microcomputer technology, those early Intel chips, the 8080, the 8-bit system and subsequently the 16-bit 8086 etc., to make these devices intelligent and programmable.

So what was the first thing that I found? I found terminals! They were intelligent terminals. Now, you have to remember that memory circuit chips and microdevices were very expensive at this time. But these intelligent terminals that I was looking at had built-in editing capability and button editing capability. The buttons were actually labelled 'insert character', 'delete character' and all that sort of thing, right on the keyboard. You could do that one 1024-character page at a time. It had enough memory to do what was more or less equivalent to one page of single spaced text, you could hold it in memory, bring it on the screen and edit everything locally.

Then I said "Well, now we need to transmit it somewhere. I don't want to transmit it directly to the mainframe computer because they're charging me by the second of online computer usage at an outrageous fee". So, lo and behold, at the very same hardware show I found a booth where they were selling a low cost magnetic tape cartridge, these were digital grade Philips cassette tapes and it had a dual tape deck. Philips, one of the few we still have around, right? It wasn't cheap, it was five grand for that particular device. But it would be cost effective for us over the long haul to enter our data and edit it offline of the mainframe UNIVAC computer.

Then, of course, I had to bring pressure to bear on the moguls who ran the campus computer system to develop spooling software that would enable us to spool the data off of these cassette tapes, in a batch mode, into the campus mainframe for processing. Now this is all before I was able to get us off the mainframe computer anyway, but in any case, I'm trying to be as chronologically correct as possible. What I managed to do was to convince these two companies (since they were small and flexible) to interface and to write the microcode which would tell the other company's tape drive to open up and receive the data that was being transmitted. That is a page of edited data and we'd just concatenate it, ok? And they were willing to do it! I think back and think that today these people would tell me to get out of their sight. You know, you ask them to do something that's going to sell five units or whatever but they were anxious enough to be willing to do it and they did.

Now, why did I do that? Well, there was an alternative device, it was called the IBM Magnetic Tape Selectric Typewriter (MTST) as it was dubbed by IBM, which interfaced its own tape drive. There was nothing else like it, it was IBM and it was not compatible with anything, obviously, nor would ever be compatible with anything. It was built into this box and connected to an IBM Selectric Typewriter with the little bouncing ball on it. They were leasing that device for about $15,000 a year. I needed five of them as data entry stations and I had the first pilot grant from the NEH at this point and so I was able to hire staff.

Now you have to understand that my data entry problem was nothing like most of the other Humanists who were getting started in the field. Many of them actually would send their books to Hong Kong and there were these data entry services that would simply sit there and type. All these people being paid peanuts to bash away the stuff they were seeing on these printed texts. Well, we couldn't do that because you had to be a trained palaeographer to be able to read our input and work directly with original thirteenth century manuscripts (and later ones after we completed the Alfonsine Corpus).

So I was fortunate, quite frankly. I finished my dissertation and graduated and they decided to keep me on as an assistant Professor. Someone jokingly said that the Dean kept me on because he knew that I had a quarter of a million dollar federal grant and they wanted to get their 45 cents on the dollar. That wasn't true, I actually asked the Dean myself personally and he laughed and said "no that wasn't true". They kept me on because they thought I was worthwhile; it was quite straightforward.

JN The first NEH grant was awarded around 1972?

John I can't remember the exact date, I remember drafting the proposal in '71. It might have been granted in '72, it's a lengthy process of passing through.

JN And what was your PhD thesis about?

John While working on my PhD thesis I did use much of the computer technology that we had developed up to that point. Now remember that we were doing data entry using intelligent editing CRT terminals with their own internal editing capability and interfaced to a standalone system, those dual tape drive affairs that I referred to as storage media. That duo, made by two different companies, replaced what would have been this outrageous rental from IBM for their Magnetic Tape Selectric Typewriter. Moreover, we didn't have to print out the lines when we wanted to edit, do you follow? We could do all of our editing right on this very fast CRT and when the page was edited we pushed a button and it was transferred over to tape two (the unedited version was on tape one on this dual tape drive). So, we could transfer the newly edited version to drive B and then we ended up with an edited version of the data. In any case, this was available to us when I published a version of my dissertation years later. Can you see? [He holds a book up to the webcam].

JN Yes I can: *El Libro de Marco Polo* (see Nitti 1980).

John Yes, my dissertation wasn't even on a Castilian Spanish text, it was the editing of the only extant medieval manuscript translation of the Book of Marco Polo in an Ibero-Romance tongue (Nitti 1972). It was translated into fourteenth century Aragonese and fortunately the manuscript itself still exists at the Escorial Library in Spain. I got a grant to go there and work with the original manuscript. It's a beautiful thing, it's huge, about 3 ft tall, open it's about 2 and a half ft wide and the letters are a good ½ to ¾ in. high. It was all done by hand, of course, on parchment with fancy illuminations and miniatures and what not. Just beautiful – that really got me going. I was at the Escorial for a month working with that. I had done the rough transcription here in Madison from a black and white microfilm copy and then I took it there and actually had to make changes to the rough transcription. I can tell you right now, very often what happens is there will be secret little notes or changes that are written in the folds of the parchment and concealed by the binding. If you open it up and photograph it you have to spread the sheets apart to be able to see the notes. I found many of those, where they were actually making corrections to the text in the margins.

In any case, how do we get the edition to print in a beautiful, professionally-done typeface? Well, I'll tell you what we did. The only true typesetting was, in fact, commercially available because then typesetting devices were quite expensive. So I struck up a deal with a company based in Milwaukee, Wisconsin called Color Corp and they basically had a contract with one of those big chain stores to do all of their printing of ads and that kind of stuff. And so I said "when your machine is fallow wouldn't you like to make some money?" And they said "Sure".

So, the typesetting was very cheap, we were able to get professionally-done typesetting for probably less than a third of the cost that it would have been if we'd gone specifically to a typesetting service. These guys were doing it during fallow time. So, this book, my edition of Marco Polo was done using professional typesetting. Now, I prepared all the data input from this end and they gave me a copy of their typesetting language, that is, their mark-up language and I put the codes into the magnetic file myself, bold face, italic and whatever, point size changes and everything. It's difficult for me to talk about this sequentially Julianne because all this stuff was coming in tangentially. The technology I'm talking about was coming in tangentially and we were looking around and grabbing at whatever was available and affordable and that we figured could make it easier for us.

Now, when you look back you might say "ha ha, they did that? Who cares?" I remember that CHum asked me to write a piece and at the time I had just discovered, at another one of these hardware shows, a new device that had dual 8-inch floppy disks. Imagine that, each one of those disks would hold a quarter of a million bytes, this is nothing, right? But dual because you could edit, then go from one to the other and that device actually had a built in version of the BASIC programming language. I looked back at this article that I had written years ago and I thought "what?" I wrote this "it even has built in BASIC programming in this device and firmware!" And I even put a big exclamation mark at the end![2] I had to laugh afterwards, 15 years later, I'm thinking "who cares about that?" It's that sort of a thing! When you look back on this early technology, even some of the then more sophisticated stuff, it all becomes a historical curiosity, which I assume is what you are really all about here in this thing!

---

[2] The article stated: 'One such floppy can be purchased with options such as extended core memory, or the BASIC programming language, in addition to a million characters of disk storage!' (Nitti 1978, p.46).

JN Exactly and what also fascinates me is the process of how people encountered the computing of that time and thought "I can apply this to my research", especially considering how few Humanists used computing then.

John Well, there were many such eureka moments for me and most of it came from going to these computer hardware shows. In May of 1981 I took a show on the road for publicity purposes and was asked to give lectures about our work and the technology we used. I must have gone to 20 different American Universities, I was even invited by the University of Montreal in Canada. I went there, and I had a sort of a roadshow; my friends jokingly referred to it as 'Nitti's dog and pony show'. I would actually lug some of this computer equipment that we had put together, which was innovative at the time, and take it there and show how it worked. I haven't told you yet about the other little piece of technology that I was able to work into this and that was Optical Character Recognition (OCR) at a time when the Kurzweil Scanner was very new. It cost more than $80,000 and we couldn't afford it.

In fact, I discovered at that time there was only one Kurzweil true OCR device in the entire state of Wisconsin. It happened to be here in the city of Madison and it was owned by a wealthy attorney who had set about to scan retrospectively all of the law statutes for the state of Wisconsin from the printed books. So I worked up a deal with him that I could use his Kurzweil and get my staff to go in during the graveyard shift when he wasn't using it. So I hired graduate students to go there late at night and we trained them on the Kurzweil device.

I was already thinking about how we were going to create a body of word definitions in Spanish for the purposes of the *Dictionary of the Old Spanish Language*, right? It's a different issue. We were simultaneously developing software to bring together all of the lexicon that we were compiling in the *Dictionary of the Old Spanish Language*. The first phase was to be the *Dictionary of Alfonsine Prose*, that's the thirteenth century corpus, and so what do we do? Well, I figured, if we scan and get into machine readable form what was in the public domain, which was the then last edition of the Royal Spanish Academy's *Dictionary of the Spanish Language*, a monolingual dictionary, then we could modify it to our liking and it would be our definitional canon, in effect. While it's a contemporary dictionary of Spanish the first editions of it were created in the late eighteenth century, you know, the Century of Lights, and so it contained retrospectively huge quantities of the word forms that we were finding in these medieval texts. And so I said "Ok, let's do that". Well, we did manage to get the whole thing scanned and one of the big shots in the Real Academia Española was a buddy of mine, a senior Professor. In fact, I had brought one of his sons, who was and is still a scholar of Medieval Spanish, here with NEH money that I had to help me work on the *Dictionary of Old Spanish*. We were working on it, and his father liked that obviously.

When we finished scanning the 1992 edition of the Royal Spanish Academy's dictionary I sent his father, who was one of the top two people in the Academy at the time, a copy of the machine-readable text of their dictionary. Obviously a political stunt but anyway it worked so they never frowned upon our using that text and creating a definitional database in effect out of their dictionary. Obviously, it didn't look anything like their dictionary when we were done with it. It existed only in machine-readable form because all we needed was to be able to develop a software that would go in and grab the appropriate definitions out of the dictionary and pull them into our growing *Dictionary of Alfonsine Prose*.

JN So did you have some formal training in computer programming?

John Two programmes existed on the campus mainframe and both of them were uppercase-only type things. One was the concordancing programme I mentioned and the other was a bibliographic management programme, as they called it. This basically enabled you to create bibliographic records and sort them and index them and that kind of thing, which was handy but once again in uppercase. In fact, I used it because in addition to creating the *Dictionary of Old Spanish* ourselves, I had to create and establish a canon of the known Old Spanish manuscripts and early printed texts.

Old Spanish is considered up until the year 1501 or the beginning of the sixteenth century. So, obviously, early printed books had already begun thanks to Gutenberg in the last half of the fifteenth century and a number of printed texts were included in the corpus of Old Spanish texts. I created what we called the Bibliography of Old Spanish Texts (BOOST). So we started there and, of course, it was printed out using the yucky chain printers, all uppercase, on the campus mainframe. But the thing started to grow and it assumed a life of its own until finally I turned the whole bibliographic arm of the thing over to a famous Professor at the University of California-Berkeley, he recently retired, his name's Charles Faulhaber. One of his interests was bibliographies, so I turned it over to him, and he's turned it into a completely different thing. His much expanded work is called PhiloBiblon,[3] and I guess it's still available online.

You know the other thing that I didn't really emphasise and it must not be lost sight of is that the DOSL project required first-hand knowledge and training of Medieval Spanish palaeography. Fortunately, I was teaching at the time, and continued to teach right up until my retirement, courses in Old Spanish palaeography and a surprising number of graduate students would enrol in those courses, especially given the sort of esoteric nature of them. It was from those classes that I was able to recruit many of my workers, my student help. We would have to adjust and fiddle the schedules and the like but many of them wanted to pick up some extra money in the summer months because they were Teaching Assistants, let's say, in Spanish at the University of Wisconsin during the school year but they didn't have any income in the summer. So the NEH grants provided me an opportunity to pay them a salary for the summer months. They knew that I could only hire them once they had taken

---

[3] PhiloBiblon is 'a free internet-based bio-bibliographical database of texts written in the various Romance vernaculars of the Iberian Peninsula during the Middle Ages and the early Renaissance'. See http://bancroft.berkeley.edu/philobiblon/

my course and therefore knew how to transcribe Old Spanish texts from the photo-graphic reproductions of the originals.

From the very outset of the project I thought "is this going to be too much? How can I manage to input 11 million words of text from the original manuscripts unless I have a small army of people who are trained to do it?" But I came up with another solution which also involves technology and it has to do with the OCR. The true OCR is the only way we could scan the Royal Academy's Dictionary because of the complexity of the typography.

But when we were doing the transcription directly from a photographic repro-duction of a medieval manuscript, I thought to myself "now there are a number of professors out there and I know most of who would be likely to participate". Assistant professors largely were the ones who were hungry and wanted something to do but some senior people also got involved in it. I found, in another one of these computer equipment shows, a standalone textual scanning device, except it wasn't true OCR. Since it wasn't true OCR it wasn't bothering to read the letters and there-fore it wasn't going to cost $100,000, right? It was a device made by a start-up company in Miami, Florida. I became good friends with the sales rep at the show, I mean, literally, we became good friends and he managed to convince his bosses to sell us one of these devices (which list priced for $20,000) at cost price, about $10,000.

So we bought one of these devices on the promise that I had to take it on my 'dog and pony show' and show it off as I went to these various campuses. This device used, are you ready? IBM Selectric Typewriter technology with the little golf ball, except they manufactured special little golf balls that had, under each of the letters, a miniaturised barcode. So, when you typed the text it would come out in alphabetic words and beneath each of the letters was a miniaturised barcode. That enabled this device, which had an automatic page feeder and everything, to scan the sheets. You could put 100 sheets in the hopper and it would scan them and create the digital images of the characters, the underlying ASCII code for the letters. I managed to convince the company to programme the device to transmit to those Philips cassette tape recorders that we had interfaced to what we were using at the time to do the data entry and editing. So the company that produced this scanning device, I call it that because it wasn't true OCR, it was reading the barcodes and outputting text which I was receiving from my colleagues at various universities who were trained palaeographers in their own right. They would sit at home and I would provide them with the typewriter element, the ball, right? They would get their Deans to buy them an IBM Selectric Typewriter if they didn't happen to have one already, you know, which is low-tech really and then they'd prepare transcriptions.

And what could I give them in return for this? The promise that our publishing house, the Hispanic Seminary of Medieval Studies, would publish, at least in micro-fiche form (because we were now creating microfiche as a publication medium which enabled us to publish hundreds of thousands of pages of information). We are still selling those microfiche packets where we've got the medieval text transcribed and its concordance printed out on microfiche. We sell them for $10 apiece. In some cases, 10,000 pages of information for 10 bucks. Because it was so cheap for us to produce microfiche we could afford to sell those packets for 10 bucks and we were making probably, I don't know, 75 % profit or something to feed back into the thing.

JN This is almost a prototypical scholarly crowdsourcing approach. Maybe crowd isn't the right word, more learned community…

John Exactly. We didn't have personal contact with these people. There would be long intervals of months, in some cases years, and then suddenly a stack of these specially typewritten, barcode-type texts would appear on my doorstep for scanning. So, I'd go out there myself, feed them into the hopper and dump them onto these Philips tapes and then I'd print it out. By that time we had our own high speed upper and lower case printing device, which cost us about $5000. It was a standalone device which I interfaced to the tape drive. I'd play out these tapes on this printer and mail back a printed copy of what got scanned to the individual who had submitted the typed pages. Then it was their responsibility to go through and markup those pages for errors of theirs and for any possible scanning errors. And then they'd send them back to us with red correction marks on them and I had my grad student staff sit down and interactively, using the devices I told you about (the intelligent CRT terminal interfaced with the tape drives) make the corrections for the transcript.

I never finished the question you asked me about computer programming. I took a course in BASIC and I said to myself "this is silly, I'm going to try to get money from the government or wherever I can get it from." In fact, Mr Kasten put up some seed money out of his own pocket to hire our first computer programmer. By the way, all of my salaried programmers for the entire duration of this project, nearly 20 years, were women. And I'll tell you why. I discovered that young male computer programmers did not possess one quality, many of them were brilliant and excellent programmers, but that quality was constancy. I knew that with these gals, and I hired females from age 22 to 56, that they were there today and I could count on them being there tomorrow.

I haven't even talked to you about the programming we did to create a dictionary from what we'd come to refer to as citation slips. We modelled this thing, in broad terms, after the *Oxford English Dictionary*, so that our dictionary has, for instance, dated citations (bits of snippets of text out of a manuscript with the date of the manuscript associated with the snippet). In that sense it's not only a period medieval dictionary but it's historical, within that period. And that was all done through the programming that we developed ourselves, our own ad hoc software.

JN You developed a whole intellectual, technical and social infrastructure that supported the project. Did the OED's use of 'crowdsourcing' also inspire you?

John I still think OED is the best dictionary there is! I had been impressed with it from the very outset and I remember having read and seen stories about how the conception of OED came about and the idea that they actually had a bunch of non-technical people sitting at home and writing down what they found. Their job was to read text and pull out words that they thought were neat and hadn't yet been documented, or whatever, and then they had to write them on snippets of paper. That intrigued me. I said "well, let's see, how we can do that and go one step further. We can capture their keystrokes instead of having them send us a bunch of snippets of paper, right? We can actually have them send us machine-readable pieces of paper." That's what inspired me, the analogue in a technologically more sophisticated and facilitating manner.

JN Can you please reflect a little more on the whole process of how you conceptualised, designed and implemented this whole infrastructure?

John Well, it started out sort of helter skelter. I was learning as I went along, basically. This is going to sound terribly immodest, I don't mean it to be, it just happens to be true. I didn't at any point say "I can see that computers can create a concordance from this albeit primitive looking machine." I didn't have that capability. No, I said "is there computer technology available, both hardware and software, that can do what I really want to do … my dream world, what's my dream world?" I was driven, and I think that's the proper word, I was driven by this notion that there had to be a better way. So, every time in the process of integrating all these things, people and equipment, I felt as though it could be done a better way, whatever particular aspect it was I was dealing with. I would set about to try to see if there was a different, better and improved way to do it. Of course, I was fortunate that during the course of this 20-odd year odyssey, technology itself was not static, obviously, so there were new devices coming on the market, there were even new software packages.

I haven't told you yet about the software that we wrote. I should have gone back because mixed in with all this stuff was John Nitti assembling PCs before there were PCs. There were kit computers coming out in California, these garage built kit computers and they would send you the components. The first one I built was driven by a little 8-bit, Intel 8080 chip and it started with 64 K of RAM, which cost a lot of money. It came in what looked like a mahogany window box, something you'd plant flowers in. It was about a yard long and quite narrow because at the end of it you had two of these 8-in. floppy disk drives. Those were the days when the floppy disk actually did flop. I built the damn kit computer and I actually started to try to offload some of the sorting procedures that we did in organising words. Believe it or not, and it was a pain in the tail because the storage capacity was limited to these two quarter of a million byte floppy disks. One floppy disk you'd stick in there with text and you'd sort the stuff you wanted to sort and it would write the output to the other. We developed our own little sort algorithm to run on that early microcomputer. This is before IBM PCs and TRS-80s and that sort of thing. That was my favourite old thing, I should have kept that.

Then I connected with another outfit in California. You're too young to remember the battle between the two big microcomputer operating systems, the CP/M

('Control Program for Microcomputers'; see Kildall 1982) and MS-DOS. Why, Gates was very lucky because when IBM was planning to release its 16-bit PC and were looking for an operating system they chose Bill Gates' MS-DOS. As a result, everything was modelled after that operating system and then Gates and the Microsoft Corporation, of course, started producing subsequent iterations of that plus Windows. In any case, in the early days you bought the components and you had to build the computer yourself. Because there initially was no multi-user operating system, I later migrated to MP/M, the true multi-user, multi-tasking version of CP/M. In fact, the MS-DOS notion in IBM was basically about networks, so you would network a series of PCs attached to some central PC, right? Well, during all of this, I build an eight-user multi-user system, a true multi-user system where there were eight terminals. We used it for years. These were just dumb terminals interfaced to the computer I had built that was running the multi-user version of CP/M, called MP/M. Now people say "What? What's that?" Most people don't even know what that is because it didn't happen to be chosen by IBM as their favourite operating system. So, in any case, we used that system as a subsequent data editing station. I had 8 students simultaneously entering data to a kind of a hard disk device, early Winchester technology. I concatenated four, are you ready for this? Four 80 MB (that was a lot then) disks drives together in one enclosure and interfaced it to this multi-user computer. So we actually had a sizeable chunk of hard disk. Now remember, I was no longer paying the $17,000 a year to the campus mainframe people for 20 MB of hard disk.

JN You just mentioned your vision, as it were, of your perfect world. It just occurred to me that I didn't actually ask you to describe that.

John My perfect world was also dynamic because I went about it in the following way. I said "OK, there are particular tasks that this project of ours needs to be able to do, using computing technology and computer-related technology". They included, of course, computer-based typesetting. I went with that and had the sub-contract early on with this company I told you about. But I wasn't content; I wanted to be able to do our own typesetting, in house. We finally had some sophisticated output printing devices coming on the market. Now, of course, I did buy a Lexmark all-in-one multi-purpose printer for $50, which is as much as the inkjet cartridges for it cost. Of course, it produced good typographical quality stuff, not necessarily the finest typographical but certainly suitable for reproducing and publishing in books.

So we then went to "how are we going to be able to do the typography ourselves on a microcomputer?" Well, it turned out that Donald Knuth had invented and wrote for Unix mainframes the TeX typesetting language (Knuth 1979). He turned it over to public domain and as soon as he did little companies started producing, in this case early on, MS-DOS-based versions of TeX for 200 bucks. I bought the complete typesetting capability, with more sophistication than I ever, ever, ever imagined we could use, because it could also typeset sophisticated mathematical formulae and that sort of thing (in fact Knuth had designed it for that purpose originally). So then

I said "now we've got the core software" and we actually bought the source code of that package. And my programmers, the different ladies I was referring to earlier, could in fact develop and interact with that typesetting language in such a way as we could create our own output in electronic form: typeset pages including the changing of the running heads with the alternating pagination. We were controlling the typesetting software itself. We were sticking our noses into that typesetting software and saying "this is what we want you to do, dammit!" And it did!

In fact, I typeset the *Dictionary of Castilian Prose of King Alfonso X* right here at my home in Madison in 2002. I printed the entire dictionary on a low-cost, high quality laser printer which cost under $1000. I had already transferred the Hispanic Seminary (the publishing house) to John O'Neill in New York, right? I sent him the camera ready copy and he negotiated a contract with a printing outfit and that's how we were able to sell this.

Well, I think as a result of all this, whether correctly or not, I guess I got the reputation of doing what I did best and knowing what I was doing. So Helen Agüera at the NEH (see Chap. 10) and I used to go on site visits a lot. We'd meet and say "we're going to Yale this time" and we'd convene there for a site visit of a humanistic project that wanted to employ computer technology, especially research tools projects, which was Helen's area. We had great fun! Stuffy Ivy League professors weren't necessarily happy to get my advice, but they got it anyway!

JN So this brings us back to the question about scholars who were not using computers in their research and the sense you might have of their views on Humanities Computing?

John I'm glad you made the link, it's a good one. Basically, I have to start out by underscoring the fact that some 3 months before his death at age 94, my mentor, Mr Kasten, was still working with me on a daily basis on completing the *Dictionary of Alfonsine Prose*. We were sitting side by side, with me at the computer terminal and Mr Kasten working through the proofed copy of the dictionary pages, effecting the corrections he had found. I would make the electronic change and go on to the next page. Mr Kasten was an incredible fellow, he didn't know anything about computer technology, nothing! Zero! He knew less than I knew at the beginning. But I was able to start the computer experimentation, thanks to Mr Kasten because he was bankrolling me, particularly before we got anything from the NEH pot. In total, the largest funding we got was from NEH but we also got $300,000 worth of matching money from the Spanish Government. I was in fact named as a visiting Fulbright scholar to the University of Salamanca, which is important for this purpose, not because of me but because I went there after we had developed all the microcomputer-based lexicographic software.

I installed all the software gratis on the computers of my colleagues in Medieval Spanish at the University of Salamanca, which is one of the oldest universities in Europe. I was there for 3 months to teach them how to use our software, which I installed on three PCs they purchased for the purpose. They were three ladies, two professors and the wife of a Spanish professor of English, and I jokingly referred to them as *mis tres Marias*, 'my three Marys', because Spanish Catholic ladies names frequently start with "Mary". We had a heck of a good time there and I taught them all how to use the stuff and they, in their own right, created two separate dictionaries, big monster dictionaries. The more important of the two was a *Dictionary of Medieval Spanish Medical Texts*. So the people who didn't use computers, right? These three ladies had never looked a computer in the eye. I mean their campus was bringing in PCs for the offices and what not so they probably were writing letters or something. But they got into this with both feet. As a matter of fact, in terms of the chronology of the publications, their medical dictionary actually came out before ours did. I did all the typesetting and everything here, again, in my house. I typeset that dictionary and they paid for a courier to hand deliver the typeset pages to them in Salamanca.

So I had two long-term experiences with older people, in this case, scholars, researchers and professors. You might expect some resistance, you know. I guess that's why you raise that question and the answer is yes and no. The people here at the University of Wisconsin, the older people were delighted with this stuff. As soon as I was using PC-based technology Mr Kasten said "buy me one of those things, I want to take it to my house". He was, by the way, a fantastic typist (I'm talking about conventional, manual typewriters), even as an old man. So I got one for him and sat him down with it, taught him how to use it, the word processor and all that stuff. He was actually typing in his bibliography, his own library collection actually, typing and entering. So it was a delight to see him with absolutely no hesitation or no griping about this technology stuff.

Another one I think you'll get a kick out of, which is very important, was a delightful and brilliant scholar by the name of Frederic Cassidy. Professor Cassidy was Mr Kasten's contemporary and also died in his 90s. He was the founder and the editor of the *Dictionary of Regional American English*. I was talking to him one day and he had invited me to serve on that dictionary's Board of Advisors (it wasn't that we met all the time, but he happened to stop by to see Professor Kasten). When I showed him what we were doing with the computers in terms of data entry in particular (you remember I mentioned to you those intelligent terminals and the tape drives that we had interfaced at that point?) He said "I want those". So, he incorporated that same hardware technology and even hired away one of my female computer programmers to work for him programming the *Dictionary of American Regional English*. She was on top of everything we had been doing. His dictionary was considerably different in its nature and scope obviously, so there wasn't any software transfer. But the hardware, of course, needed to be able to handle these great gobs of data and somehow capture the keystrokes instead of being fleeced by the campus computing facility for the online services.

I then started to give lectures on our computer-based techniques at various universities. I would meet people who would come up afterwards to talk and there were some instances of people who were Humanists. Though I don't think it was simply an age proposition, quite frankly, the youngest ones were on board from the get go. They saw it was not only the future, it was the present, so they wanted to know. The International Congress on Medieval Studies held annually at Kalamazoo, Michigan is the biggy of international Medieval Studies. I don't know how, but Professor Otto Gründler, who ran it for some 34 years, until his death in 2004, had gotten a hold of my number or something and called me and said "would you like to chair an ongoing session on computers in the Humanities here at the Kalamazoo conference every year?" I said "I suppose so". I signed up to that and I did it for some 5 years, and I was told, though I don't know if this is true or not, that it was the most heavily attended session at the conference, which seemed a bit much to me.[4] But you can see it spanned all the fields so somebody who wasn't interested in Chaucer or Alfonso the Wise but was interested in the application of technology to their own research would attend.

It went on until the fifth year when we had PCs hitting the market, the Apples and the TRS-80s and that sort of thing. I sort of got this sinking feeling that many of the people were attending not because they were interested in learning anything new, but because they wanted me to confirm that they had made the right choice in buying their PC. You know, it got to be brand specific, shall we say. I figured this session had outlived its usefulness now so I stepped down.

By the way, I found this little card right here [holds card up to web cam]. John Nitti, Professor of University of Wisconsin is on it, and it is an admissions card to the 1981 National Computer Conference, which was the big conference for computer types, not for Humanists. This was 1981, it was being held in Chicago and I was invited to present what I was told was the first talk offered by a Humanist at the National Computer Conference. I can't swear to that, that's what I was told by the people who invited me to do it. I gave a presentation and what excited these people, I think, was the fact that I was incorporating all sorts of computational and related hardware that demonstrated how this technology, in particular the hardware, could be applied to humanistic research. My session was well attended. I was surprised, since I figured there'd be four or five people sitting there, you know, out of thousands of people but I was in disbelief! You know, who cares about this? Particularly among computer types, you see.

JN You already anticipated the issue of resistance. So did you encounter any significant resistance?

John I'm a very pragmatic person and stubborn as hell. I went into the thing saying "I know what the devil I want to do and so the only thing that's going to impede me from doing this is money. The moment the money valve is shut off I can't do anything more". I'm not independently wealthy so I couldn't do it myself. Fortunately, I had that angel in Mr Kasten, who was willing to put up tens of thousands of dollars. He was an elderly man already and he was at times as giddy as a kid when I introduced him to a new gizmo.

---

[4] The International Congress of Medieval Studies 'Archive of Congress programmes' lists Nitti as having participated in three such sessions at the 16th, 17th and 18th Congresses, from 1981 to 1983. See http://scholarworks.wmich.edu/medieval_cong_archive/

There is stuff I haven't even told you about. Another gizmo I interfaced into all this was a product that was initially made to order for the United States Patent Office. It was a computer-driven microfiche retrieval and display play unit that had a carousel in there. This was the time when we were doing microfiche output. You could load it up with microfiche and each frame had its own address and you could build an address table for everything that was in there.

We would bring up, in one second, a photographic colour reproduction of a manuscript page (that corresponded to a page of transcription that we had just done) to do final checking against the original manuscript. "You see", I'd say to Mr Kasten "I want this machine". He'd say "well, what does it do?" and I'd explain it to him and he'd say "ok, how much do you need." I'd say "$10,000" and he'd say "ok" and write me a cheque. This was very important because with NEH funding you have to have pre-budgeted everything. So if there was a new gizmo and I liked it and wanted it because there was a place for it in the project I couldn't go and rob the NEH grant that I had because everything had already been allocated. So I'd go to Mr Kasten and he'd provide me with the money to do it. I had great fun doing it, as a matter of fact, as you can well imagine.

JN You've already mentioned a couple of things relevant to this question but I wanted to ask about your encounters with the Humanities Computing community or conference scene

John It is funny because when the whole thing started, I was, I guess, one of a handful of pioneers. I hate to use that word as it sounds self-serving but other people use that in my connection. In fact, instead of having existing bodies and groups that met on a consistent basis that I could go to, I was throwing parties, as it were, for Principal Investigators in projects that were purporting to use or were using computer technology. They would come to Madison, to the Seminary of Medieval Studies where I hung out, and where we basically owned three quarters of the 11th floor of our tower building. We paid for every square foot, by the way, as the Dean kept reminding me in the indirect cost that they would rake off the top of the NEH fund.

I think we had at least three such events and they were not terribly formal. I just contacted them and said "why don't we have a brainstorming session? Come to Madison and I'll arrange for your hotel room". It was always six, at the most, seven Principal Investigators from various projects around the country; they came from as far away as California. When I finally got everything established I knew exactly where I was going with the project. This, again, is going to sound terribly self-serving on my part … let's put it this way, my need to communicate to other people was being ratified by various universities where I talked about the project. Then the fun part was not me giving the talk, the fun part was afterwards. I'd hang around and people would come up in great droves with all sorts of interesting questions. I don't know if I answered them all successfully but it was fun.

In fact, there was a sort of a clique-ish group of us, perhaps that's not the right word, there was a group of Principal Investigators, myself included, in the early days of the NEH's first willingness to offer funds for incorporating computer technology into Humanistic research. That group of guys, it was all guys at that point, were all asked by the Endowment to draft the first guidelines for Principal Investigators in the Humanities seeking to incorporate computer technology into their research. It's been redone countless times, I'm sure, since then.

JN Many thanks indeed for your time and this fascinating interview

References

Jover, F. G. (Ed.). (2002). *Two generations: A tribute to Lloyd A. Kasten (1905–1999)*. New York: Hispanic Seminary of Medieval Studies.

Kasten, L. A., & Nitti, J. J. (Eds.). (2002). *Diccionario de la prosa castellana del Rey Alfonso X*. New York: Hispanic Seminary of Medieval Studies.

Kildall, G. (1982). CP/M: A family of 8- and 16-bit computer operating systems. *Education, 102*(3), 211–219.

Knuth, D. E. (1979). *TEX and METAFONT: New directions in typeseting*. Bedford: Digital Pr. and American Mathematical Society.

Nitti, J. J. (1972). An edition, study and vocabulary of the unique Aragonese book of Marco Polo translated by Juan Fernández de Heredia. PhD thesis. University of Wisconsin-Maddison.

Nitti, J. J. (1978). Computers and the old Spanish dictionary. *Computers and the Humanities 12*(1–2): 43–52: 46.

Nitti, J. J. (1980). *Libro de Marco Polo. Aragonese versión*. Madison: Hispanic Seminary of Medieval Studies.

Nitti, J. J., & Kasten, L. L. (Eds.). (1997). *The electronic texts and concordances of medieval Navarro-Aragonese manuscripts*. Madison: Hispanic Seminary of Medieval Studies.

Open Access This chapter is distributed under the terms of the Creative Commons Attribution-Noncommercial 2.5 License (http://creativecommons.org/licenses/by-nc/2.5/) which permits any noncommercial use, distribution, and reproduction in any medium, provided the original author(s) and source are credited.

The images or other third party material in this chapter are included in the work's Creative Commons license, unless indicated otherwise in the credit line; if such material is not included in the work's Creative Commons license and the respective action is not permitted by statutory regulation, users will need to obtain permission from the license holder to duplicate, adapt or reproduce the material.

Chapter 10
It's a Little Mind-Boggling: Helen Agüera and Julianne Nyhan

Abstract This interview was carried out between London and Washington via skype on 18 September 2013, beginning at 17:05 GMT. Agüera was provided with the core questions in advance of the interview. She recalls that her first encounters with computing and DH came about through her post in National Endowment for the Humanities (NEH), where she had joined a division that funded the preparation of research tools, reference works and scholarly editions. Thus, she administered grants to a large number of projects that worked, at a relatively early stage, at the interface of Humanities and Computing, for example, *Thesaurus Linguae Graecae*. In this interview she recalls some of the changes that the division where she worked made to its operating procedures in order to incorporate digital projects. For example, in 1979, a section that was added to application materials asking relevant projects to provide a rationale for their proposed use of computing or word processing. She also discusses issues like sustainability that became apparent over the longer term and reflects on some of the wider trends she saw during her career. Computing was initially taken up by fields like Classics and lexicography that needed to manage and interrogate masses of data and thus had a clear application for it. She contrasts this with the more experimental and exploratory use of computing that characterises much of DH today.

Biography

Helen Agüera was born in San Juan in Puerto Rico. She joined the NEH in 1979 in the role of program officer. At the time of her retirement in 2014 she was Senior Program Officer in the Division of Preservation and Access. During her tenure at NEH, she was involved in the development of several programs related to DH, including the National Digital Newspaper Program, Preservation and Access Research and Development Grants, the JISC/NEH Transatlantic Digitization Collaboration Grants, and the NSF/NEH Documenting Endangered Languages Program. She also played a major role in NEH's funding and support of the Text Encoding Initiative.

© The Author(s) 2016
J. Nyhan, A. Flinn, *Computation and the Humanities*, Springer Series on Cultural Computing, DOI 10.1007/978-3-319-20170-2_10

157

Interview

JN The first question that I would like to ask is about your earliest memories of encountering computing technology?

HA Well, when I joined the NEH in 1979 I had no personal experience with computing technology. I came as a Humanist myself to work at NEH, someone who had done work in Spanish literature and language actually and had never even used any computer-based projects of any kind, or done any kind of that work. At that time computers were large hardware units that were used primarily by businesses for administrative purposes. At the NEH I was introduced to a database of evaluators that the agency was beginning to compile. It was intended to help the programme officers with the reviewers and panellists who assessed NEH applications. And then, shortly after that, the Endowment got its first word processing system to help us create grant documents that had very similar text because changing the address on the letters and other types of documents was repetitious. My only other personal experience in the early 1980s was when IBM PCs became available and I pretty much just did word processing. My first real encounter with the application of digital technology to the Humanities was through the projects that NEH supported.

You know, I started working in a programme in the "Division of Research" that supported the preparation of research tools, reference works and scholarly editions. These projects were the ones that were using digital technology at the time. The NEH had been funding some of these projects since the 1970s, primarily, one large text corpus, the *Thesaurus Linguae Graecae* (TLG),[1] which began getting funding in the early 1970s. Other projects were using computer technology to generate a print product, and that included dictionaries. We supported many of the dictionaries. But even concordances to texts – of course, now it is almost unthinkable to think of this as a separate tool – were considered separate tools at that time. We funded a project to do concordances to the works of Darwin and to the works of William Faulkner, for instance, and then from the output of the computer they created print products.[2]

JN I understand that you can't speak in detail about the evaluation of individual projects, but I just wondered, in an overall sense, whether the digital components of

---

[1] The goal of TLG is to 'create a comprehensive digital library of Greek literature from antiquity to the present era'. It was founded in 1972 and is based at the University of California, Irvine. See: https://stephanus.tlg.uci.edu/index.prev.php

[2] Documents shared with us by Agüera show that the first NEH Programme Information guidelines from 1967 (the year that the first NEH Fellowships and Summer Stipends were awarded) include the possibility of funding for 'Grants for development of humanistically oriented computer research, and for training programs in data processing techniques for humanistic studies' (NEH 1967). A further document entitled 'Reference Materials Program Tool Funded Projects 1967–1991' shows that a project that used computational methods was also awarded in that same year to 'Stephen M. Parrish, Cornell University, Computer Concordance to four English poets: Jonson, Marvell, Pope and Swift (1967–69)' (NEH n.d.).

TLG, for example, would have been "noticeable" at that time? Or, how were digital projects received and discussed as far as evaluation was concerned?

HA Well, in this programme in particular there was a very positive reaction to the use of the computer because it was seen as a tool that would help expedite the work of creating the research tool or reference work. The TLG was a little bit different because it was the only one that really was intended to be used electronically rather than as a printed work that anyone could use in a library, or wherever. So, the TLG as a pure database was obviously was a little different, but, because it had the support of the entire field at the time (it was always well-received) we made many awards to it.

Now, I believe it was probably in 1979, just shortly after I joined NEH, that the programme introduced a separate set of guidelines for projects that involved the use of computers. This had to be a separate statement within the proposal that addressed a number of issues about the use of the computer. The very first question was a justification for using computers; it was so rare, obviously, to use the computer within other fields of the Humanities that you needed to justify why a computer was necessary for the work that you were proposing.[3]

JN How did it come about that the NEH started funding those projects at what was still a reasonably early stage?

HA It was an early stage and I think it's really because NEH has always responded to the field. So, you know, we have open calls. For Classics at that time being able to query the whole corpus of Greek was such an important part of the scholarly work they did. People were doing it manually, so the very thought of being able to query the corpus of all those texts, and being able to come out with instances where a word was used was just a tremendous opportunity in the eyes of people from the field (see, for example, Crane 2004). I think every time we've seen a project that is essential to the scholarly work of the field there has been an impetus from the field to come and request funding and the evaluators have always responded extremely positively.

JN When did you start becoming active in the conference community?

HA At the time the main organisation that was having conferences, at least here in the United States, was the ACH. They were having meetings in the early 1980s. I went to an early 1980s conference, but my first recollection of going to a meeting was in 1987 at South Carolina. I remember that because it's where I met Nancy Ide

---

[3] In addition to a section on the 'Rationale for using the Computer or Word Processor', the document 'Computer and Word-processing Guidelines' (NEH 1979) also listed the following topics for applicants to address: 'Computer Hardware; Computing Software; Input; Output of Final Product for Distribution (where it is asked "If software is unavailable, please simulate sample output with a typewriter"); Costs; Data Base [sic] management; Non-exclusive License'.

and Michael Sperberg-McQueen (see Chap. 12) and that made me aware of the importance of coming up with encoding guidelines. That started the opportunity for the Text Encoding Initiative (TEI) to apply to NEH for support and we funded the first planning grant to them. That planning grant was for TEI to hold an international meeting. They brought together 30 people who had been doing work in computing to discuss the possibility of collaboratively developing guidelines for encoding text in the humanities.

JN How easy or difficult was it to making the case for the necessity of funding standards-based work (such as TEI)?

HA That was a little bit different than the TLG, which the whole field was really interested in doing. Regarding TEI, there was an awareness on our part that there were lots of people and lots of projects (and the case for this was made in the application) that were creating their own encoding standards and formats. A lot of work was expended doing that yet texts could not be exchanged and reused. So, for the purposes of the review process, that was what persuaded the evaluators at the NEH to go ahead with that kind of support. That was a little bit less tangible to support; after all, you could always think of querying a database and getting results out and that seemed pretty tangible. The development of standards was a little bit outside of the realm of what we normally did. But the Endowment always thought it was important to support tools that were going to facilitate research in the Humanities. In fact, we even did so before computers. An example is the development of a typewriter element for Coptic because there was no way for people to use existing typewriters to create that, so we supported that. That was just an example of things that would seem outside of research tools per se, but they were the tools for the field.

JN So there's definitely a longer history of supporting tools irrespective of whether they happen to be digital or not.

HA Primarily research tools, obviously, and this has been the case since very early on in the history of the Endowment and before there were separate programmes. Eventually separate programmes were created to support and focus on different types of activities. The "Research Materials" programme supported all the various tools, scholarly editions, and so forth.

JN Can I ask about those who have been quite good at canvassing and advocacy work or communicating with the Endowment about DH research trends and what might be considered for funding at a later stage?

HA Well, there have been some pioneers in different areas and fields. I already mentioned the TLG. Ted Brunner[4] was the lead person on this in the 1970s and

---

[4] Ted F. Brunner (1934–2007) was Chair of Classics at the University of California and, among other roles, was the founding Director of TLG. See: https://www.tlg.uci.edu/about/ted.brunner.php

1980s and he was very outspoken on the use of computer technology for his field. Greg Crane is well known for his promotion of computing technology, first for Classics, but really for the Humanities largely. Early on in the field of lexicography there were some people who promoted use of the technology.

I remember John Nitti who worked on the *Dictionary of the Old Spanish Language* (see Chap. 9), and he was involved with computer scientists and actually doing the programming. They had to do everything from scratch because mainframes were more in use at the time. Eventually they moved everything to other computers.

In the context of text encoding I remember Nancy Ide, Susan Hockey (see Chap. 6) and Michael Sperberg-McQueen (see Chap. 12). They were very outspoken in terms of the need to come up with guidelines for encoding text and for ways of archiving material so that it can be reusable.

I also worked a little bit with people in scholarly editions like Peter Shillingsburg and David Chesnutt[5] who were creating scholarly editions in History and in literature. They were working at a time when the use of computers for scholarly editions was not really the main mode of doing editions. They were working with the field and trying to persuade it that there were some things computers could do for scholarly editing. That took a little bit more, I would say, persuasion than in other areas where tool development was an easy sell.

JN I think that nicely interconnects with another question I had about scholars who were not using computers in their research and the views they may have had about aspects of Humanities Computing (or DH)?

HA The scholarly editors, in general, initially saw some value in working with the word processor but nothing else. I think there was a somewhat slower trajectory for scholarly editing until people could understand how some types of editions could be rendered electronically. Critical editions and things that involve a lot of collation and the generating of different views of the text seemed a bit harder to do with the tools that were available in earlier years.

JN Do you think the objection, or lack of attention, was due as much to not seeing the possibilities as the difficulties of implementing the computational work? Or do you think other factors were also involved?

HA I think it was primarily due to the challenges of using the technology for what they wanted to do. The only other issue that occurred across all the projects was the question of rights to use the material. In the case of scholarly editions, they was a contract with a publisher and so the publisher's point of view on how the content might be made accessible was a factor in perhaps not making the editions available online right away because at that point there wasn't the subscription mode possibil-

---

[5] David R. Chesnutt (1940–2014) was Research Professor in the History Department at the University of South Carolina. See: http://www.documentaryediting.org/wordpress/?p=1975

ity that could be as fully used as now, for instance. I think it was technological issues and also questions of how valuable the technology was for what they needed to do. They were collating multiple texts and they had to put all these versions of multiple texts together – was that easier than actually doing this by hand?

JN There are myths about time saving and productivity!

HA For the other things, you know, they were compiling information from many different sources to create one new item or new entries. That's a different use.

JN Did you ever encounter cultural or social factors that questioned whether the computer actually had a place in Humanities research, whether it was just a tool and perhaps not something with which Humanities people should concern themselves? Or had that already abated by the late 1970s?

HA I think there was a difference between the people who were developing the reference works and research tools (the people we were working with) and people who were working in other areas. Historians, Literary scholars or Philosophers at that point had much less need to use computers other than for word processing. Or maybe, as some of the online bibliographies and catalogues and so forth started coming out, they did see value in using computers for doing their research and for creating their monographs and articles. But as something that would be useful in any other way … I think that took a long time. The mind-set that you see now, "let's see how the computer can actually allow us to question or visualize some areas of interest for us that we can then do research on" wasn't there at all. There was a sense that the computer was not teaching them anything, it was primarily a tool at that point.

JN What about the sustainability of the projects that NEH has funded?

HA Well, that's a big issue, and it has been for a long time. It is particularly so for the long-term projects that have received multiple awards from the NEH. We have been working with that issue for many years as we understood that at some point we could not continue to support all of the existing projects in addition to new projects. Accordingly, we started to urge the long-term projects to find ways of sustaining themselves.

Some projects created endowments that would help them meet part of the costs of continually updating. Initially everybody was so excited because you could update this resource easily. But then it became a big burden because you never finish this work, right? At least with a print work, you printed it and were done with the work. In this domain you must continue to update that resource all the time; that requires support and not only in terms of people (the most costly part of it) but also equipment and resources. We managed to urge people; we'd work with them, we'd visit them and we'd talk about some of the funding strategies they could develop to become self-sustaining and not depend on NEH funding forever because it would not be possible for the agency to continue to fund their project in perpetuity. We had to give a clear message. For instance, we worked with the classical bibliography, *L'Année Philologique*[6] for many years to make them understand the need to be self-sustaining. Not only did they have a lot of bibliographic work to do, and we helped support that, but every year they had new work to do, as new publications came out.

JN If you think back on the portfolio of NEH projects – I know that just because of lifecycles that some wouldn't tend to be sustainable in any case – in general, have projects been able to make that shift?

HA Well, they have to a great extent. Some of the early ones have done that. The TLG is a good example. I think they're in existence for over 40 years now and they have received institutional support, support from the field, an endowment plus a subscription that I think they still have for part of their database. That has helped them maintain themselves over many years. With other projects the institutions have taken that responsibility, and often it's an international effort as well, but it is a struggle for some projects. It means that someone needs to be constantly, not only fundraising, but thinking of new ways of doing things more efficiently, or partnering with other people. And we encourage them to do all of that because it's always good to have projects that have a track record of being useful to the field.

And I must say that I have a list of projects that we have supported since 1967 and another list of databases and other computer tools that we supported from 1967 to 1990. I was pleasantly surprised to look at these lists and check these projects on the web to see whether some are still around. They are, for the most part! In some cases they just resulted in print works but some of these databases are actually still accessible. They have migrated and continue to be accessible. Actually this was an interesting thing for me, because you would think that after so many years some of these projects would have disappeared. Actually, what's interesting about it is that we see a range of the old technologies (obsolete now obviously) that were used at the time to create these databases.

JN Did people whose work was funded tend to stay in the field? Or, did you see, because of the nature of project funding, people being quite active in the 1970s, for example, and then maybe 'disappear' (from academia) or go to industry?

HA Well, there is some of that, some people moved into working in industry. But in general I would say that they stayed in academia, or in education for the most part, even though they may not be working on that particular project any longer. They may have moved to other positions in academic libraries or in archives. I see less movement from academia to the business world, for instance. Some, but not everyone who worked on these projects moved on to something else. They continue

[6] See: http://www.annee-philologique.com/index.php?do=&lang=en

to have an interest, maybe not directly in the project they started with, but in other related projects or enterprises that have to do with research and innovation.

JN What about the participation of women in the field over the time?

HA Well, it's interesting. Initially there were some women in the ACH: I mentioned Nancy Ide and Susan Hockey. But overall, it was a smaller number of women. If you compare that situation with now, or if you go to DH meetings now, you do see a large number of young women involved in these projects. I don't know whether that had to do with the fact that in the initial days it was such a challenge to do any work with computing. The people who knew how to work with computers were mostly Computer Scientists and they did work with mainframes and then minicomputers. Maybe there was more of an influx of women to the field when the microrevolution came in, and then the personal computer.

Among scholarly editors there were more women, but then again, they were not really using the computer in advanced ways, with some exceptions, and people who were doing some indexing. I don't want to suggest that there were not people who were ahead of others, it's just as a group I'm talking.

More women were involved in bibliography systems for libraries, which are very natural places for computers to help with this mass of work that you would have never been able to do without the help of the computer. On the issue of the take up of computing across the disciplines, Lexicography was also a natural fit, you can think of all the manual work that was required for the Oxford English Dictionary or just to collect all those individual cards [slips] and try to compile a dictionary out of that. We had a project, the Assyrian Dictionary at the University of Chicago that did everything manually. It started in 1923, and it finished everything manually, well not manually, at the end it was working with computers a lot. But the actual card index was done manually and it had two million little cards.

JN Yes, part of my PhD was on historical lexicography. The *Dictionary of the Irish Language* took over a hundred years.

HA Correct! I think it's really in those areas where the task was so large that the computer was really a blessing. That's the only way to describe it. Or, in the case of Classics, it was important because the field had, I think, that tradition of philology, or enquiry into specific use of words and phrases within the entire corpus.

JN It's interesting, isn't it? With Classics and lexicography the application was very apparent.

HA Yes and I think it was a good match for the needs of those fields. While for Historians, who were building arguments and looking at many different things, it wasn't clear how the computer was going to be a useful tool.

JN We have really seen a tipping point since the publication of *The Companion to Digital Humanities* (Schreibman et al. 2008). Do you remember seeing that critical mass build up in terms of more and more fields saying "ah yes, now I get it!"?

HA I do. Looking, for instance, at Philosophy, first it was bibliographic controls, then the *Encyclopaedia of Philosophy* was the first fully online encyclopaedia. But more and more, once it became clear that these different resources could be connected together to create something new, I think people saw the value of doing it for their field. Now everybody wants to digitise, in part because they feel that if it's not online, its non-existent. So, from small institutions (that perhaps have unique resources) to very large institutions (that have huge bodies of information and artefacts) it isn't any more a question of making accessible the key things in a field, but all extant evidence. It's a little mind-boggling actually.

JN Yes, as are the dangers of whole swathes of things just "disappearing" because for some reason they are not on the web and so people don't access them. Is there anything else that I haven't mentioned that you would like to discuss?

HA Obviously, I think the Endowment has managed over time to work with the field and to address the needs as they arise. Now I'm pleased that there's the Office of Digital Humanities[7] that is looking at those other questions from how technology affects our lives and the way we do research on what should be the cutting edge of the use of computers in the Humanities. So it has been an interesting trajectory for me to watch from just being at the part where the main focus was on developing resources, because there were so few. Now that we have this large amount of information the focus is on how we are going to use it. How can we actually focus on materials to make better use of them?

JN Many thanks for your time

References

Crane, G. (2004). Classics and the computer: An end of the history. In S. Schreibman, R. Siemens, & J. Unsworth (Eds.), *Companion to digital humanities*. Blackwell companions to literature and culture (pp. 46–55). Oxford: Blackwell Publishing Professional. Available at http://www.digitalhumanities.org/companion/
NEH. (1967). *Programme information 1967*. Washington, DC.
NEH. (1979). *Computer and word-processing guidelines*. Washington, DC.

---

[7] The NEH Office of Digital Humanities 'works closely with the scholarly community and with other funding agencies in the United States and abroad, to encourage collaboration across national and disciplinary boundaries'. See: http://www.neh.gov/divisions/odh/about

NEH. (n.d.). *Reference materials program tool funded projects 1967–1991*. Washington, DC.
Schreibman, S., Siemens, R., & Unsworth, J. (Eds.). (2008). *A companion to digital humanities*
(Blackwell companions to literature and culture). Oxford: Blackwell Publishing Professional.

Open Access   This chapter is distributed under the terms of the Creative Commons Attribution-
Noncommercial 2.5 License (http://creativecommons.org/licenses/by-nc/2.5/) which permits any
noncommercial use, distribution, and reproduction in any medium, provided the original author(s)
and source are credited.

The images or other third party material in this chapter are included in the work's Creative
Commons license, unless indicated otherwise in the credit line; if such material is not included
in the work's Creative Commons license and the respective action is not permitted by statutory
regulation, users will need to obtain permission from the license holder to duplicate, adapt or
reproduce the material.

Chapter 11
I Heard About the Arrival of the Computer: Hans Rutimann and Julianne Nyhan

Abstract This oral history interview was conducted between Hans Rutimann and Julianne Nyhan via Skype on 15 November 2012. Rutimann was provided with the core questions in advance of the interview. Here he recalls that his first encounter with computing was at the Modern Languages Association (MLA), c.1968/9. Following a minor scandal at the organisation, which resulted in the dismissal of staff connected with the newly arrived IBM 360/20, Rutimann was persuaded to take on some of their duties. After training with IBM in operating and programming he set about transferring the membership list (about 30,000 contact details) from an addressograph machine to punched cards. After the computer's early use to support such administrative tasks the MLA began investigating the feasibility of making the research tool called the *MLA International Bibliography* (information about accessing the present-day version of the bibliography is available here: https://www.mla. org/bib_electronic) remotely accessible. Rutimann worked with Lockheed to achieve this. It was in Lockheed's information retrieval lab that the system known as Dialog, an online information retrieval system was developed (see Summit 1967). He vividly recalls how he travelled the 3000 miles to San Francisco to deliver the magnetic tape to Lockheed so that they could make the database available online. He "jumped for joy" when, once back in New York, the data was available to him via the newly acquired terminal of the MLA. While making clear that his roles in MLA, Mellon and the Engineering Information Foundation have primarily been enabling ones (and to this we can add advocacy, strategy and foresight) he also recalls the strong influence that Joseph Raben had on him and mentions some of the projects and conferences that he found particularly memorable.

Biography

Hans Rutimann was born in in Zurich, Switzerland, in 1939. He graduated from the Handelsschule KV, Zurich with a degree in *Germanistik* (German language and literatures). He is the Senior Advisor to the Scholarly Information and Information Technology Program of the Andrew W. Mellon Foundation and President of the Engineering Information Foundation (EIF). He was formerly International Program

© The Author(s) 2016
J. Nyhan, A. Flinn, *Computation and the Humanities*, Springer Series on Cultural Computing, DOI 10.1007/978-3-319-20170-2_11

Officer, Commission on Preservation and Access and Council on Library and Information Resources (1988–1999) and Deputy Executive Director of the MLA (1965–1987).

Interview

Julianne Nyhan (JN) What is your earliest memory of encountering computing technology?

Hans Rutimann (HR) It's a complex story and I'll try to make it very brief. It was about 1968 or 1969 and I was at the Modern Languages Association (MLA) in New York. The MLA at that time was in the process of introducing a computer, mainly to help with administrative tasks.[1] I was a research assistant at the organisation, having come from Switzerland just a year or two before, and I heard about the arrival of the computer and a whole staff was hired: an Operator, Punched Card Operators, Programmers etc. I had nothing to do with it, I was doing a study on the teaching of German in high schools. But then the computer arrived, it was a 360/20, which is the smallest in that famous 360 line and the preparations were on-going. In spite of its size, the 360/20 had a memory of only 12 K, later augmented to 16 K. A programmer in those days spent more time sub-dividing programs than writing whole programs.

Then there was small scandal at the organisation when the Head of Computing, as we called it then, had a romantic liaison with the woman who was hired to be the Operator. The Executive Director of the MLA was very offended by that, he was the son of a missionary, and he fired everybody connected with the computer. It just came to a standstill and he called me up and said "I saw in your resumé that you worked in a Swiss bank, so you're probably good with numbers. Would you like to make a go of it and try to help us with this new computer?"

The computer was huge, at that time it filled a room that had a double floor and extra air conditioning. I said I would think about it, thought about it and I said "yes" and went to training classes. But that's really leading into your second question, "did you receive formal training in programming and computing?" At that time the IBM customer service was excellent and I took courses in operating and programming. Regarding the work, the first task was to convert the membership list, an address list of about 30,000 members, which at that time were still on metal plates

---

[1] It seems likely that MLA had already been interested in computing for some time. Photographs held in the Busa archive in Milan, dated to 27 June 1952 were taken at IBM's headquarters in New York. They include images of Prof. William R Parker, then 'Secretary of the American Modern Language Association of New York City' attending a demonstration given by Busa and others of IBM Card Punch Machines. He also attended the subsequent luncheon given by IBM in Busa's honour later that day.

on what we called an addressograph machine.[2] Those were all punched on cards. So that was my beginning.

JN Did you go somewhere to take the training?

HR Yes, IBM had a classroom building in Manhattan and I took courses, first in operating and then in programming. Usually we were a group of about 15–20. I took the courses and we successfully converted the membership list and went on to other administrative tasks. Within a year or so we had it up and running.

JN What did you think of the computing that you encountered on that training course?

HR I found it very interesting and not boring at all. It was all new to me, and obviously not my field, so I felt I was getting a valuable additional education through the courses. It was splendid and didn't cost us a thing!

JN And was it difficult?

HR Yes, I found it challenging because of the amount of precision that you had to work with. I remember the frustration I felt when I used a colon instead of a semi-colon; in programming that is, of course, deadly. I could never quite get used to the fact that you had to be very, very precise.

JN And what about the other people who were on the course with you?

HR They were from businesses all over New York that had ordered IBM equipment recently, or at that point, and needed to programme. So, it was a real cross-section of individuals, including people like me who were drafted in to do that. It was a new activity for most companies, and we were all in the same boat.

I remember another frustration was that they only had one mainframe available. So, when you finished your programme you had to line up and sort of sign up for your programme to be evaluated. At that time you had to run it against a compiler, which was about 1000 cards, to turn the programme that you have written into what we called the project deck. And that was another 2000 cards, so it took time. And every time you had to line up or sign up for your evaluation to realise that you'd made another mistake …

JN Yes, so then it was back to fix the semi-colon again!

HR Yes, so I started going on weekends because that mainframe was less busy then … I'm talking about a long time ago in the early 1960s.

---

[2]The most helpful description of an addressograph that I could find is that given in Wikipedia: https://en.wikipedia.org/w/index.php?title=Addressograph&oldid=677429610

JN What was the gender breakdown of students and instructors on the course?

HR As I recall it was practically 50/50. It was pretty balanced.

JN And the courses were in operating and programming?

HR It was billed as operation (which required a different set of skills to make those huge monsters run) and programming (the programming was, at that time, nothing very complex but we had to do something.)

JN And how long did it last for?

HR Those courses, on average, I would say about 5 months, 6 months.

JN Were you going every day or was it part time?

HR No, it was sort of twice or three times a week.

JN And later in your time at MLA you also worked on electronic reference tools?

HR Yes, well that was a parallel development. As we worked on converting all the administrative tasks (accounting, budgeting, membership services etc.) so that they could be done with computing, we also had an outside firm compose the *MLA International Bibliography* (MLA IB). By 'composing' I mean that we would prepare a tape with all the typesetting codes and they would then set the type from this tape. We did that for a few years, I'm now moving through the 1970s and we produced the MLA IB, which was at that time the largest reference work for English, Foreign Languages, Folklore and Linguistics. Then, I'm skipping a few years now, we also looked into the possibility of making this available 'online' and that leads to another anecdote!

We worked at that time with a company called Lockheed, the airplane manufacturer in California. They made databases available for online searching. The MLA was the first organisation to make a reference work in the Humanities available online. I remember very well, we produced a tape and stripped it of all phototypesetting composition codes. It was one of the large tapes, you know, the old tapes, I don't know if you recall those? [JN: No] They were quite large, about 15 inches in diameter. They were called the seven-track tapes. I had one under my arm and I took a plane from New York to Palo Alto, San Francisco. I drove to Lockheed and gave them the tape and they made it available online as the first international database in the Humanities.

And I remember so well, I flew back to New York and we bought one of those early online terminals. It was not really a terminal, it was a telephone with two rubber receptacles: you dialled the number, and you put the receiver in those rubber receptacles and then you typed in your search query. I remember I jumped with joy when the first results came in and I marvelled aloud that this was from 3000 miles away and I got the answers that I requested. Of course the searching was nowhere near the sophistication of today but it worked and proved to be very successful. I then negotiated, now we're moving into the late 1970s or early 1980s, with the Wilson Company in New York, a publisher of articles and books for the library world. The *Wilson Quarterly* also had an online service. We produced the first CD of the MLA IB to be made available through Wilson. So that was all very exciting for our membership and the usage increased, we got royalties, and it was a success, as I recall.

JN What was the reason for selecting Lockheed?

HR Well, basically it was the only name in town. Lockheed, as I understand it, at that time got into computing and machine readable this and machine readable that and saw a need to host databases from all over. There was no such thing at that time but they, in fact, became the host. I couldn't go elsewhere and then Lockheed spun off that service and called it DIALOG.

JN Was it very expensive to work with them?

HR No, as I recall, it didn't cost a thing. I mean, they put it up online and the terms of the fee structure was that they somehow got a part of the hourly usage from each user. So, Lockheed got a cut too and they got their money in the end that way.

JN I wondered whether you were aware of any other projects in the area of Humanities who would have been working with Lockheed around that time?

HR No, later we prided ourselves on having been the only one at that time. The MLA IB was our most extensive work and it was, at that time, the only exclusively Humanities database. We prided ourselves on being the first from the Humanities because all the others that came before us were in Science, Social Science or other fields.

JN I know that we agreed the questions in advance but can I ask you one that just occurred to me? You mentioned that the first computer that arrived in the MLA c.1968 was procured for administrative purposes. Over time there was obviously a shift to include research-oriented ends. Would you reflect on that shift and on whether you were aware of a wider context to it?

HR It was really through the reactions of the membership that I became aware of a lot of work being done with the aid of computers, for example, word concordances, frequency studies and authorship tracking. We began to dabble in all of this but not very seriously because most of that work was done at universities. I saw my role as an enabler and that goes on to another question. Very early on, there was a very active group of people in the MLA, dealing with computers and the Humanities.

That was also the time that the journal CHum came out, and we organised an Association of Computers and the Humanities. I was on the board and they were looking at first for an opportunity to meet and to talk about issues and to plan the next steps. I made the conference room of the MLA available to a small group and that turned out to be the founding, not the founding meeting, but the beginning of the Text Encoding Initiative. And so the early beginnings of TEI were really at the MLA in a conference room that I made available to that group, just an aside.[3]

And you have a question "which people particularly influenced you and how?" I would like to mention Joseph Raben. I think he's retired by now. He was the person who influenced me greatly, he was a professor at Queen's College. He founded the journal CHum; he was also very active in the ACH. He and I worked very closely in those years on another aspect that I think I should mention. The MLA has an annual meeting, a fairly large gathering of its members, it usually draws about 10,000 members. Parallel to the convention we had book publishers organize a huge exhibit of scholarly books. Early on, Joseph Raben and I felt that it would be very interesting to have some computer-related activities at that exhibit. At that time there was a lot of talk about computer-assisted education, computer-assisted teaching, computer-aided teaching, it went by all kinds of names. We invited hardware manufacturers, software publishers and related industries to exhibit at the convention. At that point I visualised that this would be so successful that in the next couple of decades the computer-related exhibitors would outnumber the traditional book publishers. Well, it didn't quite happen that quickly. At that time we had maybe three or four, I remember Apple was one of the first to agree to come. Now, when I look at the convention programme some 30 to 40 years later, I notice that there are quite a few more. They're still not in the majority but getting there. Joseph Raben and I worked on that very intensively and he was a huge help because of his contacts and his knowledge.

JN You've mentioned about the TEI and your earliest engagements with the conference community, does a particular event stand out? Perhaps one where you had a sense that a community was being formed?

HR Yes, indeed, that was just a hard-core group of around 10 people and that of course grew over time. My real involvement with the conference community was, I think, later. We're talking now about the 1990s, and later, when I became a Senior Advisor to the Mellon Foundation. That was (or is, I'm still doing that) in the Scholarly Communication and the Technology Information pro-

---

[3] TEI keeps documents about the early years of its existence (from 1987 on) at the TEI Vault. See: http://projects.oucs.ox.ac.uk/teiweb/Vault/.

gramme.[4] That's where I really became involved in all kinds of projects in this country and also abroad. They included the sophisticated digitisation of medieval manuscript collections, infrastructure problems and projects like Bamboo (see, for example, Dombrowski 2014). But while I was at the MLA I just had peripheral contact with the group that was involved with Computing and the Humanities.

Can I just go forward on your list because you're asking a very interesting question? One of the questions is "what about scholars who were not using computers in their research? Do you have a sense of what their views on Humanities Computing were?" Yes, indeed I do, on many levels. First of all, I experienced a lot of hostility early on, in the late 1960s and early 1970s. I heard comments along the lines of "computers have no business in Humanities disciplines, computing is a scientific instrument and we don't want to have anything to do with it". And that, of course, changed over time with more and more people getting involved in computing and research. But the interesting thing was that at that time it was very difficult to get any kind of recognition for computing work in the scholarly community (and I think that's still a sore point today). So any kind of work, be that research with the help of a computer, or the creation of software, or anything related to computing, at that time anyway, got very little recognition. The desire of the Humanities Computing community was to get the same kind of recognition that you would get by having an article published in a peer-reviewed journal but that was not the case. But then slowly it began to change. I think today you get a little more recognition but from reading the literature, I realise that we're not quite there in terms of equivalency with a peer-reviewed article. That was my experience; the hostility against computing early on in the 1960s was profound.

JN Why do you think that started to reduce? Why do you think the hostility became less as time went on?

HR I think by sheer force of the evidence and the growth of the industry and the fact that you couldn't argue with it anymore and that it proved that it can be a very useful tool. The field of computer-aided instruction really missed the boat because at that time it announced itself as something totally new that would replace the teacher. You had to be with it or you would be out of it. That proved to be absolutely not the case because the teachers were as important as they always were and the computer was just a help in the teaching. Of course, now things have developed in so many other ways and the field as such really ceased to exist.

---

[4] For the Scholarly Communications Programme see https://mellon.org/programs/scholarly-communications/.

JN Something else occurred to me after I sent list of questions. I read about your work with the Engineering Information Foundation (EIF) and I noticed that part of its mission is in terms of the recruitment of women. I was wondering if you might say a little about that and whether you have some reflections on the role of women in Humanities Computing?

HR Women can be as effective as men, if not more effective, in computing in the Humanities. In my work at the EIF we have an explicit mission to support women, I mean, girls really, in 11th and 12th grade, to choose an engineering career because of the dismal rate of women in Engineering. It's lower than 20 % and it was recognised by many studies that this had something to do with the environment. There was a bias against women in engineering and that was exemplified by comments from teachers, other students and a not-very-welcoming atmosphere. That's one of the things they're trying to change. So, we're giving grants to the so-called STEM programmes – Science, Technology, Engineering, Mathematics – to change the environment in the classroom and also to do much more work on the equally important issue of how to retain women once they have started on their engineering career. So far we have been reasonably successful, the topic is being discussed and recognised. Large organisations have taken up the cause and we continue giving grants to organisations that have innovative programmes in helping to attract and retain women in Engineering. So my regard for women's work in Engineering, Computing, Mathematics is extremely high. I'm the President of the foundation so I think my views are well known.

JN How does DH fair in terms of attracting and retaining women?

HR I think very well. What I'm saying now is more anecdotal than documented. I work with a lot of groups here and abroad in digital projects (and I also worked with earlier projects that dealt with what we used to call library automation, where card catalogues were being converted to digital form or to computer-readable form). In those groups, I think the majority of the people that I met were women who showed an enormous capability and interest in the work they were doing. When I think of the DH projects that I've had to deal with, they really did not have the preponderance of men that you would expect in a scientific environment. The majority were women and very effective women.

It is extremely different than the traditional Engineering field, there we have slow-going change in the atmosphere and climate. In DH we didn't fall into the trap in the first place. We managed to stay out of it, luckily. I hadn't thought about that but that seems to be true.

JN Is there anything else that you would like to add to the interview?

HR I'm glad to still be involved in what I would call the advancement of computing in the Humanities.

References

Dombrowski, Q. (2014). What ever happened to project bamboo? *Literary and Linguistic Computing, 29*(3), 326–339.

Summit, R. K. (1967). *DIALOG: An operational on-line reference retrieval system.* In Proceedings of the 1967 22nd national conference. ACM'67. New York: ACM, pp. 51–56. Available at: http://doi.acm.org/10.1145/800196.805974. Accessed 23 July 2015.

Open Access This chapter is distributed under the terms of the Creative Commons Attribution-Noncommercial 2.5 License (http://creativecommons.org/licenses/by-nc/2.5/) which permits any noncommercial use, distribution, and reproduction in any medium, provided the original author(s) and source are credited.

The images or other third party material in this chapter are included in the work's Creative Commons license, unless indicated otherwise in the credit line; if such material is not included in the work's Creative Commons license and the respective action is not permitted by statutory regulation, users will need to obtain permission from the license holder to duplicate, adapt or reproduce the material.

Chapter 12
I Mourned the University for a Long Time: Michael Sperberg-McQueen and Julianne Nyhan

Abstract This interview took place on 9 July 2014 at dh2014, the Digital Humanities Conference that was held in Lausanne, Switzerland that year. In it Sperberg-McQueen recalls having had some exposure to programming in 1967, as a 13 year-old. His next notable encounter with computing was as a graduate student when he set about using computers to make a bibliography of secondary literature on the Elder Edda. His earliest encounters with Humanities Computing were via books, and he mentions the proceedings of the 'Concordances and the Dictionary of Old English' conference and a book by Susan Hockey (see below) as especially influential on him. In 1985 a position in the Princeton University Computer Center that required an advanced degree in Humanities and knowledge of computing became available; he took on the post while finishing his PhD dissertation and continuing to apply for tenure-track positions. Around this time he also began attending the 'International Conference on Computers and the Humanities' series and in this interview he describes some of the encounters that took place at those conferences and contributed to the formation of projects like TEI. As well as reflecting on his role in TEI he also compares and contrasts this experience with his work in W3C. On the whole, a somewhat ambivalent attitude towards his career emerges from the interview: he evokes Dorothy Sayers to communicate how the application of computers to the Humanities 'overmastered' him. Yet, he poignantly recalls how his first love was German Medieval languages and literature and the profound sense of loss he felt at not securing an academic post related to this.

Biography

Michael Sperberg McQueen was born in 1954 in Borger, northern Texas. At present he is Principal of Black Mesa Technologies, a limited liability company that specialises in XML and other descriptive markup technologies. His PhD (1985) from Stanford University is in Comparative Literature. From 1988 to 2000 he was the Editor in Chief of the TEI; from 1996 to 1998 he served as co-Editor of the Extensible Markup Language (XML) 1.0 specification. He was also a member of the technical staff of the World Wide Web Consortium (W3C) from 1998 to 2009 and performed various functions in this role including staff contact of the W3C XML Schema Working Group and co-editor of the XSD 1.1 specification. He has

© The Author(s) 2016
J. Nyhan, A. Flinn, *Computation and the Humanities*, Springer Series on
Cultural Computing, DOI 10.1007/978-3-319-20170-2_12

been a visiting researcher at the University of Bergen and, more recently, a visiting Professor in the Program in DH, Dept. of Linguistics and Literary Studies, Technical University of Darmstadt (*Institut für Sprach- und Literaturwissenschaft, Technische Universität Darmstadt*). As well as his internationally acknowledged work on XML (which has become the lingua franca of data structure and exchange in very many domains) his scholarship on knowledge formalisation is of seminal importance to DH where the TEI has become the de facto standard for making Humanities texts machine readable.

Interview

JN My first question is about your earliest memory, in any context at all, of encountering computing or computing technology?

MSMQ My first direct encounter with computing technology was in the Summer of 1967. I think I must have been 13, and some programme in the public schools offered, I think, a programming course. It was offered through some programme that I was involved with and a friend of mine and I said "ok, we'll go to this programming course". I went for a couple of weeks but then my friend didn't want to go anymore and I couldn't get a ride so I stopped. But I had 2 weeks of exposure to FORTRAN and they started by giving a test to distinguish people who had already learned a bit of programming from people who didn't.

They obviously hadn't instrumented it very well because they asked questions about what parenthesised expressions would mean, and whether in a+b*x the multiplication or the addition would bind more tightly. I'd had no computing experience at all but just the sense of the expression was obvious and they said "oh, you must have had programming". So they put me in the advanced class and I couldn't figure out anything because I didn't know anything about computers or FORTRAN.

After that, as they say "*lange Zeit gar nichts*" [nothing for a long time]. The next contact would have been as a graduate student. Well, sorry, occasional things, computing, punch cards. One had periodically at that point in the 1960s, 1970s and 1980s, during my school and university time, encounters with organisations that used punch cards and so forth for organisation.

JN Why did you want to take the course in programming? That first course?

MSMQ It sounded intellectually challenging, I think. I don't remember more than that.

JN That's very impressive for a 13 year old!

MSMQ I think I was in seventh or eighth grade. The next time I remember thinking at all seriously about computing was, I believe, as a graduate student. I was a Medievalist and I ran across a collection of essays, actually it was the Proceedings of a small conference held at the University of Toronto called 'Concordances and the Dictionary of Old English'. It was a planning conference that the *Dictionary of Old English* (DOE) people had organised to talk about how computers might help them write a new DOE (see Cameron et al. 1970). As a Medievalist I had spent a lot of time, as everyone I knew in Medieval Studies or Classics did, transcribing glossary entries on to index cards and transcribing locations of occurrences of words on to index cards so I could sort them and re-sort them and analyse them and think "what's the meaning of this word as opposed to that word? How many different words are used for 'King' in Beowulf? What are the nuances of the different words? What's their etymology? And so forth".

So you spent a lot of time leafing through Klaeber's glossary (1936) and the idea that you could generate a concordance automatically seemed like magic. I remember talking to other people about it and mentioning it to my advisers. One adviser said, "I wouldn't get involved with that if I were you" and I said, "why not? It seems like the obvious thing to do, it seems like the way to build better tools for Medieval Studies". He said, "yeah, but everybody who gets involved in computers are pretty soon spending all their time doing computer stuff and not Philology". I always thought that in later years he must have told his students the same thing and pointed to me as an awful example: "he's never gotten a job in Philology", as indeed was the case. The other adviser, on the other hand, handed me a shoe box and said "this is the bibliography of the Elder Edda [Old Norse poems that are primary sources for Scandinavian mythology and heroic legend] since 1953. The goal of this project is to computerise it and your job is to figure out what that would mean and then do it". I learned a lot, I made a lot of stupid, ignorant mistakes and I learned a lot from my stupid, ignorant mistakes.

JN Did you have some access to formal training by that point?

MSMQ When he handed me that shoe box I went down to the computer center and signed up for their 'Introduction to the Computer Center' course and all the other courses that seemed relevant. Of course, as you go through one course you learn about other things that are relevant and so I had the kind of short course training (3 or 4 hours), that was offered by computer centers at that point. It may still be offered by some computer centers somewhere, although probably not so much anymore. But I have never had any formal academic training in computing.

JN And have you been for the most part self-taught? What sort of strategies did you use?

MSMQ As a beginning user, first at Stanford, where I was at graduate school, and then at Johns Hopkins University, where my wife got a job and I had access to computing, I was still finishing my dissertation. I was using mainframes and because we didn't own a terminal or a modem, using a mainframe meant that you had to go to a terminal room on campus. And if you go to a terminal room often enough you see who's there all the time and you can get some notion, just by glancing at their screens as you walk past them to a free space, what kind of thing they're doing. And you overhear people talking and so forth and eventually you get some notion in a completely informal way of people who are sharp and who may help. And if you walk past somebody and they do something clever with the system editor, you can say, "wait, how did you do that?" They're often happy to show you. So, in fact, a lot of the practical interaction with computing seemed to me to be conveyed through a kind of oral tradition. You could learn parts of it by reading documentation but I spent a lot of time studying documentation and I found a lot of it completely impenetrable because it was not in my vocabulary. So I learned a lot by looking at other people and from that sort of informal helping. I often have wondered, how do people learn that kind of thing now, when they don't have to go to a terminal room? In some universities, I guess, PC pools still exist and presumably still have similar social effects but I don't know.

JN I think it's an interesting question. I wonder, especially as DH gets more established and formalised, about the types of differences in modes of learning that will follow, and the implications of this.

MSMQ Of course, at some point I did set out to teach myself computing more seriously, in particular, in 1985 when I got my first job at the Princeton University Computing Service. I said "oh my God, I'm in a computer center, I've got to learn about computers, I'm responsible for advising Humanists on the use of computers, I have to understand this." So I spent a lot of time going to the library and reading about databases and compilers and so forth. And compilers always seemed interesting, partly because they were magic and partly because they involved something called parsing and that sounded like language processing and that sounded interesting. So I have, I believe, many of the odd unevennesses in my knowledge that you find with some autodidacts because they go very deep in some areas and they are completely ignorant about some other things.

JN So, you seem to indicate that you didn't get a job in Philology because you had pursued computing to the extent that you did. Is that interpretation correct?

MSMQ The causality could be, is probably, a far step. But it is true that, as I normally put it to myself, I never got a job. Certainly as I conceived of the world as a graduate student, no job I've ever had has counted as a job. I never had a teaching job.

JN Because you were forced on this professional route?

MSMQ Yes, yes, the only reason to study Old Norse as far as I could tell was to become a professor of Old Norse.

JN Will you talk a little bit about the process of looking for 'the job', so to speak, and how it was that you ended up in the Computer Center and your emotions and thoughts about that?

MSMQ Sure. I was finishing my dissertation and starting to look for jobs. At the time I was finishing my dissertation or doing my dissertation universities in the US and Canada were producing probably, judging from *Dissertation Abstracts*, I think there were on average 10 Medieval Germanists a year, give or take, including Old Norse. And there were maybe two or three tenure track jobs that mentioned Medieval German as a potential area of specialisation. So I had friends in graduate school who applied to every position in English or the language that could possibly fit for them and they were sending out 200 applications. None of the Germanists could find 200 institutions to write to, so the chances were very great that the large majority of people getting PhDs in the kind of field that I was in were not going to get academic jobs.

Of course, I always expected to be the exception. I was finishing working on my dissertation and a friend of ours who had done her degree at Johns Hopkins, where my wife was teaching, phoned us one Sunday. She said "have you read the *New York Times* today? Have you looked at the Education Supplement?" And we said "no, we haven't got it today" and she said, "stop what you're doing, go out and get the *Times*, get the Education Supplement and turn to page 13. There is a job there with your name on it." I said "ok." We went out and got a copy of the *New York Times* and the Education Supplement had an ad from Princeton University Computer Center looking for a Humanist, someone with an advanced degree in the Humanities and knowledge of computing, and it did certainly sound interesting, so I applied (in the summer of 1984, I believe).

I felt a little guilty about applying because I was very close to finishing my degree and I was applying for academic jobs. I knew that if they hired me and I started there at the computer center and then one of my academic jobs came through I would be there for 6 months and then I would leave. I felt a little bit guilty about that but I said if they ask me, maybe I'll tell them and maybe I won't, but if they don't ask I'm not going to tell them. So I applied and got the job; they may have assumed more computing knowledge than I had, or I may have talked a good game, or they may have been perfectly clear that what they needed was somebody with an advanced degree in the Humanities who was willing to tolerate learning about computers and that they certainly found in me. I felt they were taking a risk but I was very grateful to them. And then, of course, the academic jobs didn't come through. I don't know who those people hired but that is probably just as well so I don't resent person X or person Y!

So I found myself at the Princeton Computing Service, actually when the woman who became my boss called to offer me the job she said, "so you're finishing your dissertation, how close are you? How long is it going to take for you to finish if you don't come here?" I estimated a time and she said, "fine, we'll start you after that. It's important for me to get this decision made but it's not important that you start next week, you should finish before you come." She had long experience with people being almost done. Of course, I missed my self-imposed deadline. I was probably 2 weeks away from finishing my dissertation when, in fact, the time came for me to start work and so it took 6 months because I was starting a new job and I could only work nights and I was distracted. And, of course, I thought it was 2 weeks and it was probably a little more like a month. But I finished my degree.

Then I applied for more jobs, feeling again a little guilty, but at some point your degree is old enough that the first question any research committee is going to ask (or at least this is what I thought) is "wait, he got his degree this many years ago, he's never had an academic job, there must be something wrong with him". You begin to look like damaged goods. So at some point I stopped applying for teaching jobs and I made my career in computing. Of course, in 1985 and 1986, the years that I was at Princeton, I attended the predecessor of the DH conference, it was the International Conference on Computers and the Humanities, it wasn't even called ACH/ALLC yet.

JN Was that the first conference that you attended in this field?

MSMQ The first that I attended was in 1985 in Provo, Utah. I heard a talk from the President of the ACH, Nancy Ide, who I think talked about teaching programming to Humanists. Since I was trying to learn programming that sounded like an interesting topic. She said she was writing a textbook and I asked if I could see the draft of the textbook. She said "sure, on one condition"; I said, "what's the condition?" She said "you must send me comments on every chapter that you read" and I promised to send her comments. In her book *PASCAL for the Humanities* (Ide 1987) she teaches students how to write PASCAL and the ongoing example is essentially an interactive concordance programme. And at some point she says "now, when you display the 'hits', the occurrences of a given word to the user, you probably want to tell them what chapter it's in, so you need some way to tell when a new chapter starts so that you can keep your counter". And I wrote in my comments "is there a standard way to do that because if there is you should probably mention it" (I had the importance of standardisation hammered into me at my job) "if there's not a standard way, then isn't this one of the things that you were asking about in the ACH General Meeting? You said "if there was anything the Association should be doing and we're not let me know"- if there's not a standard way for people to keep track of where chapters begin then isn't that the kind of thing ACH should be doing?" She wrote back and said, "you know, you're right, it is, and in fact there's a small group of us that's working towards some sort of text encoding format or guidelines. Would you like to be involved?" And she and I started talking about this; I never saw any of these other alleged people. I don't think they were a fiction but I think they weren't actually getting any forwarder, whereas Nancy Ide and I, somehow we clicked. And so, beginning in 1987, we were working on the TEI and that essentially became my career.

JN Before I ask you about TEI, I want to ask you for your impressions of that first DH conference that you attended. People often say that the field was remarkably open and that there was very little animosity. Is that what you found?

MSMQ Yes, and in fact, by and large, that was mostly my impression and I remember other people saying that as well. In fact, I remember thinking, being a little alarmed at how effusive the welcome from some people was at that conference in Provo. I remember thinking, this field must be very small if someone who's here for the very first time can seem so important or impressive; is there something wrong here? Of course, looking back, I realise it wasn't me that was impressive, it was having someone there from Princeton that was impressive, because they were mostly fanatics or people who felt that they had been through a long trip in the desert. Here was someone from Princeton interested in computing in the Humanities. I suspected that felt very good.

So it was, in fact, an open and welcoming community (the excessive level of interest and enthusiasm was from a few people who were clearly looking for people to later serve on the ACH Executive Committee and stuff like that, fill bureaucratic slots.) In general there were a lot of interesting people, there were a lot of helpful people and there was a lot less of the competitiveness that I was familiar with from the MLA and a great deal less of the kind of competitiveness and aggressiveness that I'm familiar with from conferences in other fields like Computer Science or Linguistics. So, yes, I found it a very friendly, welcoming field. The fact that the President of the Association, Nancy Ide, was willing to talk to me as a complete stranger and to take my suggestions and comments on her book seriously, and to involve me in the planning for this idea that later became TEI: she was a very strong embodiment of that openness.

JN Given that we're at DH 2014, I should ask whether you think more competitiveness and 'typical conference behaviour', so to speak, is beginning to enter these meetings.

MSMQ I don't know. I hope not because I always liked the way the community interacted. It is true that at the final banquet of a conference, I guess it was a couple of years ago, I was in a small group and there was a sort of stranger there and it was her first DH and we said "oh how did you like it?" She said, "actually I hated it, I couldn't find anybody to talk to the entire time, I felt completely isolated." We felt stricken, but one of the things that can happen is, people who have been here for a long time have people that they only see at these and so it's easy for either cliqueishness or the appearance of cliqueishness to develop. If we care about making it not happen it's something that one has to watch out for. As regards professional competitiveness, I don't know. I haven't seen anything that looks like strong signs of that but I might not notice because of my professional situation. Some of the things that people compete for are not things I compete for so I wouldn't notice some forms of competitiveness.

JN Let's go back to the beginnings of TEI. How did you set about this?

MSMQ Well, of course, any project as big and complicated as the TEI has many roots. I know some of them, I know the ones that I was involved with and I've heard about a few others. I talked with Nancy Ide a little bit after that meeting in Provo in 1985, I guess, in possibly 1985 or 1986[1] when the MLA was in Chicago and she came in to give a talk. I remember going downtown and listening to her talk and then chatting with her a bit before she headed for the airport and talking about how this should be done. She said "oh there should be some sort of advisory committee and then somebody should write up some guidelines, as a sort of style book or something". I don't remember exactly how she put it, but she had some notion of a project to produce some suitable result.

Then in 1987, when I had just left Princeton and my wife and I were living in Chicago, I went to the ICCH Conference in Columbia, South Carolina as a sort of independent. Two things happened: I gave a talk (Sperberg-McQueen 1987) about support for Humanities Computing from central computer centers, because that was my experience and some group of people, Willard McCarty at its centre, organised an evening get-together for people in positions like the ones Willard and I were in, in some sort of centre supporting Humanists who wanted to use computers. It was out of those discussions that the idea of a mailing list and Humanist came (see Nyhan 2016), and one of the people who came to listen to that discussion was Helen Agüera, the Programme Officer from NEH (see Chap. 10). As the discussion and as the evening wore on, and the discussion continued, at some point she got up to leave and she walked out. I ran out after her and I tapped her on the shoulder and said, "I'm sorry, I know this must happen to you all the time but I have to say you guys made a terrible mistake when you rejected so and so's project to catalogue machine-readable datasets in the Humanities". Helen, god bless her heart, was calm and polite and accepted the comment and didn't react as she would have had every right to react. That was my first encounter with Helen Agüera.

There were several people from NEH there [in Columbia], and the next day or the day after, I fell into conversation with one of them during a coffee break. He said, as a way of making conversation "so, what are the important things that need to happen next in computing in the Humanities?" And I said, "well, for example, I think that there needs to be a standard way to represent text because so much of the work that people are doing is, in fact, textual analysis or involves electronic text. There is no standard way so you can't reuse texts and there are various problems". He seemed interested so we continued talking and the bell rang and the sessions began and I said "excuse me, please wait here for just a minute." I ran and I found Nancy Ide and I tapped her on the shoulder and I said, "I don't care what you're doing, I don't care who you're talking to, you must come here now!" And she came and we talked to this guy from NEH and developed the idea of actually moving

---

[1] The MLA was held Chicago in 1985. See: https://www.mla.org/conv_stats

forward an idea that had been kind of vague and nebulous before. On the way back, on the flight out of South Carolina, Nancy was seated next to Helen Agüera and continued the conversation.

When we got back to our respective institutions I found an email for me from Nancy saying "get out your pen, we have an application to write". Helen had said "well, the next application deadline is the fall but we have a sort of special fund for emergency short-term situations that shouldn't wait, so make an application for that." So we wrote a quick application to fund a planning meeting and involved Lou Burnard and David Barnard[2] and Nancy Ide and me. I think those were the four authors. And we made this off-cycle NEH application and NEH came through with funding to host a meeting in Poughkeepsie, at Vassar (where Nancy Ide was and still is) to plan the idea for some sort of text encoding standard. That was the beginning, in some sense, of the TEI (see N. M. Ide and Sperberg-McQueen 1995).

JN How much of your time did TEI take up? Did you have any problems with release from your job? How did the logistics of it work?

MSMQ During that planning phase, it was work that I snuck in, in the corners. After the planning meeting the idea took hold that ACH, ALLC and the Association for Computational Linguistics (ACL) should jointly co-sponsor this effort. We formed a Steering Committee with two people from each of the organisations. One of debts I owe to Paul Fortier is that although he was the vice-President of ACH and Nancy Ide was the President and they had seniority and I was firmly expecting that the two ACH representatives to the Steering Committee would be Nancy and Paul. Paul said, "no, I think you've done the work, you should be the second representative." Later, at the first TEI Steering Committee meeting in Pisa in December 1987, we realized we were going to need somebody to edit the material and it would take some time. Nancy said, "I'm coming up for tenure, I can't do this, how about you?" And Susan Hockey said, "how about you?"

So, after the meeting in Pisa, I went back to my Computer Center and I told the Associate Director "there's a group putting together a grant proposal; if it's funded they are going to want to buy half of my time to do work on this grant project". He said "you know, you're responsible for maintaining the library information system, so from my point your job is to keep the library happy. If you think you can do that in 20 hours a week and use the rest of your time for this grant project, that's fine with me. If you can keep the library happy in 6 hours a week and use the rest for this grant project, that's fine with me too. And if you can keep the library happy by working 80 hours a week, and spend the rest of your time on this grant project, I'm ok with that too. But the moment I get a call from the library, I'm not ok. If they're not happy, I'm not happy. If they're happy, I'm happy, I don't care how you manage your time." So on paper it was half-half and then as the time went on and went on

---

[2]David Barnard is a Canadian Computer Scientist. In 1987 he was at Queen's University in Canada; he later moved to the University of Regina and is now President and vice-Chancellor of the University of Manitoba. See http://umanitoba.ca/admin/president/president_cv.html

and went on, at some point the TEI Steering Committee said "no, let's buy 100% of your time", so for a while I was full time on the TEI, in the quixotic belief that that would make it go faster! One of the reasons that I ended up as the American Editor[3] was that it was easier to buy my time because I was in a staff position and staff positions are, from an administrative point of view, fungible in that way. Faculty positions are much harder to handle that way, so it would have been harder from an administrative point of view for Nancy to do it, for example. So by not having a 'real' job, I managed to make myself available for what became my real job for 10–12 years of my life.

JN Do you have regrets that you didn't get this so-called real job?

MSMQ Sometimes, sometimes. My wife was appalled when she realised that as late as 10–12 years after I got my degree it still bothered me. She said, "you gotta let it go" and I said, "if someone loses their leg do you expect them to forget that they ever had a left foot?" It doesn't bother me all the time, but I remember telling her at the time, this was probably the mid-1990s, "no, there's not a day that I don't think about it".

An interesting thing happened in the early 1990s though, so it's no longer true that there's not a day but the thought crosses my mind that I would rather have had an academic job. Sometime in the early 1990s I taught a number of workshops in Tübingen with Winfried Bader, who worked for Wilhelm Ott (see Chap. 4) in the computer center there. Winfried had studied Theology, he did his doctorate and he was working at the computer center while looking for a real job or something. When his time at the computer center ended (he had the sort of time-bounded position that one sometimes ends up with) there were no academic jobs to be had. He ended up going to the German Bible Society, where he ran their electronic publishing programme for a time. And we were chatting, together with his successor in Ott's organisation, and she asked how it was going and he said "oh, you know, for a long time I was in mourning for my academic career but I'm getting over that." His way of formulating it was "*langezeit habe ich der Universität nachgetrauert*" [I mourned the university for a long time]. This comment managed to click something in my mind and I recognised that the concept of mourning was a useful way to organise that part of my psychic experience, and, having identified it as mourning, it became easier to deal with. So I have had greater acceptance of the loss of that academic career.

JN I don't want labour this point too much but I'm just really interested to know what exactly it is that you feel that you lost by not having this academic position? You've made a seminal contribution to DH. So by doing that what have you lost that was equivalent to losing a leg, a part of you?

---

[3] A version for public distribution of the 1988 proposal to NEH to fund an 'An Initiative to Formulate Guidelines for the Encoding and Interchange of Machine-Readable Texts' is available here: http://www.tei-c.org/Vault/SC/scg02.html

MSMQ My ambition, as a student of German Medieval languages and literatures, was to be a great Medievalist. And the shortest, punchiest formulation of it that I can think of, the kind of thing I used to tell myself, half as a joke but half in seriousness, is that my goal was to make the world forget about Andreas Heusler or Karl Lachmann, the way a student of Mathematics might have the goal of making the world forget about Galois. No one's going to make the world forget about Galois, even a new Galois will just be a second Galois. And no one is going to make the world forget about Karl Lachmann or Andreas Heusler, but the ambition to have that kind of position in the field and achieve that kind of work, to be able to do the kind of work on German verse history that Heusler did, or the kind of editions that Lachmann did.

So one concrete thing that I lost, that I have lost, yes, I guess that's the right tense, is the ability to devote my professional life to the problems that I spent those years preparing myself to work on. Of course, in many ways, it was a better than even trade because, as I say, no one is going to make the world forget about Andreas Heusler. You can be extremely good, and the times are not the same, so it's not really an option, because you can't now have the same influence on German Medieval Studies as Heusler once did. DH is young, you can have that kind of influence. It's a smaller field but the ability to be here as close to the beginning as I was (not at the beginning, the beginning was long before, but as close to the beginning as I was), the ability to serve in the TEI, in the development of XML, those are opportunities that were, well as I say I was lucky, they came to me in large part by accident. I was the one whose day job counted for least so it was easiest for me to do the editorial work that happened on the TEI.

It happened again on XML; the reason Tim Bray and I were the lead Editors on the XML Working Group was that he was a consultant and I was working in a Computer Center and both of us were willing to neglect our day jobs. There too, I had a different manager but we had an equally memorable conversation about this activity. I went to my manager and said, "oh, they're starting a Working Group at W3C and they've asked me to participate, may I say yes?" and he said "how much time will that take?" I said, "well, there's supposed to be a one hour call once a week and then there'd be some email" and he said, "ok". Now I know all that he said was ok because I remember thinking hard about it later. He didn't say "ok, if it's only 3 hours a week you can do it". He didn't say "ok, you can spend so and so many hours a week on it". He said "ok, you can do it". Of course, the little bit of email turned into something like 40 hours a week of reading and writing email in the development of XML.[4] I fulfilled my obligations to the Computer Center, I keep detailed time logs and I know what time I spent on the university projects and I didn't cheat the university. But a lot of my colleagues were fairly unhappy with the amount of time I was spending on that project.

---

[4] The mail archives of those discussion are public at http://lists.w3.org/Archives/Public/w3c-sgml-wg/.

JN What were the main differences between working with the W3C on XML and working with the Humanities Computing community on TEI, even if that's probably an artificial distinction that I'm making.

MSMQ Sure, they were two projects that absorbed a lot of my effort and attention for a long time so it's a good question. As a project the TEI worked hard to draw in as many people, as many stakeholders as possible. We had a fairly broad Advisory Committee and fairly large Working Groups in the initial phase of the TEI to try and get as many different voices as possible and people to feel responsible for it. I think that helped a great deal with uptake, but one of the consequences of having so many different people from so many different directions involved, and so many of them being academics, was that it took quite a long time. I think we expected it to take 3 years and it was, in fact, seven before TEI P3 (Sperberg-McQueen and Burnard 1994) came out.

The XML work was much less exploratory, much less new, in some sense, and the group was much smaller and more cohesive. The chair of the XML Working Group, Jon Bosak, had had extensive experience in standardisation and he had developed a set of rules of procedure that had a number of unusual properties. One was that membership is limited, there will be 12 members of this Working Group and no more. Strictly speaking, for bureaucratic reasons within the W3C, the group of 12 was not the Working Group, it was the Editoral Review Council. Working Group membership was open to any member of the W3C but the Working Group was a much larger and very important discussion body. But the decisions were made by the Editorial Review Board. Membership of this was essentially controlled by Jon with the proviso in writing that any member of the Editorial Review Board could be removed by the unanimous vote of everyone else, the point being, as Jon put it more than once, that the reason to have such a clause was so that you don't need it. The interesting thing is that if you talk to people who were involved in some of the same earlier standardisation efforts as Jon, and you mention that clause, they'll say "oh that's the blank clause" and they fill in a name and they all know who that was aimed at. And if you talk about that clause to later people who were in the XML Schema Working Group, which I co-chaired, they will say, "oh, that would be a clause to take care of blank" and they will all name the same name. Interestingly enough, having that clause in the XML Working Group meant no one became so obstreperous as to unite everyone else against them.

So it was a very small group, it was very coherent, all of the people had years of experience using SGML and the whole goal was to make a sub-set of SGML that was small enough that anybody could implement. Anyone with a degree in Computer Science could write a parser in a week. And it would capture all of the stuff that we really cared about in SGML.

It was extremely difficult work but it was extremely compressed. We started our discussions at the beginning of September in 1996 and somewhere along the way we said "oh, you know what would be really nice? We should present the first draft of this at the big winter SGML conference, SGML '96 in Boston, which is at the end of November". Well, if we wanted to have 500 copies to distribute at SGML '96 in late November that meant we had to have the text locked by mid-November so that it could go to the printer. Boy does this feel dated now! John needed a couple of days to adjust the styling, so we had a date of mid-November. We started making actual design decisions around the first of October, and the first design had to be finished by the middle of November, so we had essentially 6 weeks and we went through the entire design space at a furious rate.

We started with a group of 6, later I think 7 and 8 different proposals to simplify SGML. Various people had said "SGML is really complicated but if I define this subset it becomes easier to process." So we said "oh, ok, all of these people have essentially done first drafts of the kind of thing we want to do". I prepared for the discussions by comparing them and said "oh, some of them get rid of feature X, some of them keep it, some of them modify it in this way, some of them get rid of this". So every point at which those 6, later 8, proposals differed from each other and from the SGML spec was a design issue, and my idea was "you answer all those questions, you say what decision to make on all of these things and you have a design" and that's the way we did XML. And so the design felt essentially complete within 6 weeks, which was much, much faster than the TEI. And then it took a year and a half to do the last 10%. It was a well-spent year and a half, there were some things that were very useful and important that came out of it, including the xml:lang attribute [which indicates the natural language of the text it encodes] and case folding [unlike SGML, XML does not perform case folding on element names], and we cleaned up some other problems and so forth, but the speed dropped tremendously after those first 6 weeks. So, it was much more intensive work with a small group of people compared with a much larger group of people and somewhat slower work. But my relations with Tim Bray were in their way very similar to my relations with Lou Burnard. At the SGML '96 conference they were both there. We all three saw each other at the opening reception or something and I think I was standing talking with Tim and Lou came over and Tim said, "oh so this is the other editor you've been spending your time with!"

JN What about your relationship with TEI nowadays?

MSMQ I look on benevolently. When we first started the idea was this is a project, we'll produce it but then everybody goes home. And my mental model, at least, was very, very strongly influenced by the development of the Anglo American Cataloguing Rules (AACR).[5] I knew about this because I hang around a lot with librarians, because I hang around in libraries whenever I get the chance, although I am not a librarian, I have no library training and so forth. But the first stage of the Anglo American Cataloging Rules were in use for a number of years and after a few years they did a revision project. I figured "oh, TEI could be something like that project, to make a version and then we'll use it for some years and at some point

---

[5] The AACR 'are designed for use in the construction of catalogues and other lists in general libraries of all sizes. The rules cover the description of, and the provision of access points for, all library materials commonly collected at the present time'. See http://www.aacr2.org/about.html

there'll need to be another one". As we were nearing completion of the original project plan with the publication of TEI P3 we had guidelines that were as good as we thought we could get them. Various people said "no, it needs to be an ongoing institution" and, to make a long story short, I thought "the one thing an ongoing institution has to do is survive the departure of the founding generation. If this is going to work, it can't be because Lou and I are working on forever to carry it." So I left, I thought that was the best thing I could do for the TEI. Partly purely organ-isational, the new consortium needed to be responsible, and as long as the guys who did the first edition were hanging around saying "well this is the way we did it in my day," the transfer of responsibility wasn't going to work. And in some ways whose details I no longer remember for sure, I remember thinking and saying when I announced to the Steering Committee that I was going to leave, "I need something else to do, and the TEI needs somebody else to do what I've been doing." And since the TEI is still alive, I think that it may have worked. At least I hope.

JN Is there any other influences (people or systems) that you would care to mention?

MSMQ Influences on me? Oh gosh. Well, in my work in DH, the biggest influ-ences, the influences that come to mind are first of all the various people I worked with in the TEI: Lou Burnard, Nancy Ide, Susan Hockey and I haven't mentioned Don Walker but they were extremely influential in their ways. Hockey because it was from her book (1980) that I got the idea that there was a field of activity here, so I found her tremendously intimidating.

JN You would say Hockey's book was your first encounter with the field?

MSMQ Yes. I remember encountering that book and reading it. I was in Baltimore in the basement of Johns Hopkins, the Eisenhower Library at Johns Hopkins, so that was after the encounter with the Toronto volume. But having gotten involved with computers I began to think, "well, okay, this is alright. I'm learning to use the text editor, I'm learning to use the computer in some sense for this bibliography of the Elder Edda. But in a sense all I'm doing is using it as a typewriter. There has to be a way to apply it to more central notions of research that will make it a more inter-esting thing – because an electronic typewriter, well yeah, it's an improvement on an electric typewriter but at some level it's no big deal." So I read Susan Hockey's book as one of the many ways I used to avoid working on my dissertation. And then to be working with her I did find very intimidating. Exacerbated, I guess, by the dif-ference in interactional style between Susan's rather reserved British – let's say English – personal style, and what I was used to. So that was an interesting chal-lenge. But I owe Susan and Don a great deal. And of course as soon as we turn the tape off other names will come to me. Those will do for now!

JN You now have your own company, Black Mesa Technologies Ltd, so you've worked in many different domains. I wondered, is it common for people of your generation in Humanities Computing to also have made the jump from the work that we do in Humanities Computing to the commercial sector.

MSMQ There are at least some. Two examples come to mind that are probably worth mentioning for a Hidden Histories kind of project.

There was a man I never knew, named James Joyce. Not that James Joyce but another James Joyce, who I believe began as a teacher of English, and got involved with computers and ended up leaving the academic world. I believe he was doing Unix utilities of some sort. I heard about him and I learned about him because he died young and unexpectedly and I remember being at one of the conferences when Nancy Ide got word that he had died, and we sat and she talked about him. And he obviously had made the jump.

I said there were two but more are coming to me as I go. The second example is John B Smith, who was Nancy Ide's, I believe he was her doctoral advisor, certainly one of her instructors. He was a Joyce specialist and he wrote a book on *The Portrait of the Artist as a Young Man* and in particular the thematic structure of *The Portrait of the Artist as a Young Man* (Smith 1980). In order to do the kind of close stylistic analysis that he wanted he wrote essentially an interactive concordance system called ARRAS (Archive Retrieval and Analysis System) (Smith 1984, 1985). One of the things Nancy Ide did as a graduate student was work on ARRAS, which was one of the ways she learned computing and programming. And ARRAS did the kinds of things you expect from an interactive concordance system. It was a main-frame system, command line driven and so forth, and it had a user interface that not many people would like today but it had some great facilities. Once ARRAS had parsed a text you could say "I'd like to see all the occurrences of the word fire with one sentence of context. Okay, now let's try the word fire with the sentence in which it occurs and two sentences following. Or one paragraph of context, or three words of context, or one word before and seven words after." So you could specify the context for display and for searching: "I'd like the word fire within two sentences of the word water, or within one sentence of the word ice and within two sentences of the word water". You could build up very complicated conceptual categories. Fire, flame hot, fiery, burning – all the things that appear that mark the occurrence of the theme you're interested in. And then you could say, "now show me the distribution of that over the text," and it would draw a little plot, a little ASCII art plot with pluses and dots, and segmenting the text into 2 % chunks because it had to fit on an 80-line terminal screen. By the time I met him, John B Smith had moved to the University of North Carolina, to the Computer Science Department, and had a sort of dual academic career from then on. He had a spin-off that did software development and ARRAS was commercialised, not terribly successfully, but we bought a copy at Princeton (it was the first time I ever said we should buy a piece of software and somebody actually laid out money based on my say-so.)

And another example is an Anglo-Saxonist, I think of him as an Anglo-Saxonist, named David Megginson. That is to say, a man who did his doctoral work on Anglo-Saxon and has, I think, never worked academically since. He's been an XML consultant. Does a lot of work with newspapers and newspaper mark-up. I'm not sure that's a majority, but it's a recognisable pattern.

Fourth example, again, someone I've never known personally, but I encountered their work in the course of my own work. I believe he was a Slavicist at Cornell, or he did his dissertation at Cornell, and he, like me, was interested in the oral formulaic theory. And he, unlike me, was a computer programmer, or before me anyway. He wrote software to analyse Serbo-Croatian texts for formula content and estimate the formulaic density, which was a kind of study that A.B. Lord and Milman Parry had pioneered in the thirties through the sixties and so forth. They had applied this approach to a number of texts and used it as an argument that this or that text is transcribed from oral tradition. And this fellow, Rudy Spraycar, used computers to make an argument in that field. I think his argument was they're using the wrong measure, you know, "if you define formulas that way, I can get a formulaic content of thus and such a percentage in something that we know was first written in writing [i.e., that we know is an instance of literate, not oral, composition]." It was part of the long argument about whether the degree to which the presence of formulae indicate oral composition. An interesting technical topic but maybe I'll not go further into it now. But he left academic work and the last I heard of him he was working in an insurance company writing software for them. I'm not sure, I never encountered him at one of these conferences, but the kind of work he was doing was certainly the kind of work that I would count as Computing and the Humanities or what we now call the DH.

So yes, a recognisable pattern. Some people managed, a minority in my experience, but some of the people who got involved with computers as graduate students managed to get jobs and go on and get tenure. Or people who got interested as assistant professors managed to get tenure. For a long time I had the impression that that didn't happen. For a long time my mental model was "gee, there are two kinds of people here. There are people with tenure, all of whom got involved with computers after they had tenure, and there are people who don't have tenure." And after a while I began to think "and nobody ever moves from one to the other because all the people who are here and have tenure had tenure before they got involved with computers."

I think that's changing. I think that started changing some years ago when departments first started hiring people for their expertise in DH. But for a long time I had the impression that, I think the analysis is "oh, we've got 200 applications, this person will be able to get a job outside of academia, so we don't have to feel guilty if we turn them away." And for that reason, if for no other, and of course there may have been others, like "computers don't belong in our discipline," I always thought a visible affinity with computers was probably a kiss of death on a job application. I'm glad to think that that is no longer the case necessarily, although I'm still a little worried about the old mainline Humanities departments. It troubles me that all the people with computing expertise are in specially labelled DH programs. I think they ought to be in standard English and French and German departments too.

JN There is also the issue that you find people on very short-term contracts. I did this for a couple of years. It is really stressful and you start panicking already at 3 months in to the work and thinking "will I be able to pay for food, will I be able to pay my rent in a few months?"

MSMQ That was one of the things that worried me when the TEI Steering Committee said "no, the TEI should be ongoing". That was one of the reasons that I said "if the TEI is going to be ongoing, there will have to be a consortium to support it, because we can't live exclusively on grants forever, that's just not going to happen. Even if you write good grants, eventually the reviewers say 'they've had their share, stop giving it to them.'" So I pushed for the formation of a consortium within the organisation.

JN Okay, very final question. So had you secured this academic post, would you have used computing in your research?

MSMQ I believe so. But it's clear that I would not have been able to learn as much about computing. I would not have been able to use computers the way I now think they should be used, because I would have been too busy teaching my field. The huge luxury I had in my first job at Princeton was that I was at a computer center full of extremely bright, extremely knowledgeable people. They all loved to talk about what they did and how they did it. None of them took it amiss that I was such an ignorant git and they were all eager to help me learn and some of them flattered that I should be interested. So I was able to spend a lot of time reading about database theory and parsing and so forth and that's time that I would not have had as an assistant professor of German at any of the institutions that I applied for. So I think I would have been able to use computers with some effectiveness, but I don't see how I would have been able to learn as much as I have been able to learn, because eventually I realised that the application of computers to Humanistic research was the topic that had come and tapped me on the shoulder and said "you, pay attention to me."

   Dorothy Sayers has a couple of her characters (Harriet Vane and Miss de Vine in *Gaudy Night*) have a conversation about recognising things that are of overmastering importance, that are of extreme importance, and have to be done right. And one of them says "yes, but how do you know that something is of overmastering importance?" And the other says, "That, I'm afraid, is something you often know only when it has overmastered you." And Computers and the Humanities overmastered me.

JN Okay, well I think that's a lovely point to end it on, unless there's anything that you want to add.

MSMQ Thank you very, very much

JN Thank you.

References

Cameron, A., Frank, R., & Leyerle, J. (Eds.). (1970). *Computers and Old English concordances*. Toronto: Published in association with the Centre for Medieval Studies, University of Toronto, by University of Toronto Press.

Hockey, S. M. (1980). *A guide to computer applications in the Humanities*. Baltimore: John Hopkins University Press.

Ide, N. (1987). *PASCAL for the Humanities*. Philadelphia: University of Pennsylvania Press.

Ide, N. M., & Sperberg-McQueen, C. M. (1995). The TEI: History, goals, and future. *Computers and the Humanities, 29*(1), 5–15. doi:10.1007/BF01830313.

Klaeber, Fr. (Ed.). (1922). *Beowulf and the fight at Finnsburg*. 2nd ed. 1928; 3rd ed. 1936 and frequently reprinted. London: Heath.

Nyhan, J. (2016). In search of identities in the digital humanities: The early history of HUMANIST. In J. Malloy (Ed.), *Social media archaeology and poetics*. Cambridge, MA: MIT Press.

Smith, J. B. (1980). *Imagery and the mind of Stephen Dedalus: A computer-assisted study of Joyce's a portrait of the artist as a young man*. Lewisburg: Bucknell University Press.

Smith, J. B. (1984). A new environment for literary analysis. *Perspectives in Computing: Applications in the Academic and Scientific Community* 4.2–3 (Sum-Fall): 20–31.

Smith, J. B. (1985). *ARRAS user's manual*. Technical report 85-036. Chapel Hill: University of North Carolina at Chapel Hill, Department of Computer Science. Available at http://www.cs.unc.edu/techreports/85-036.pdf. Accessed 11 Nov 2015.

Sperberg-McQueen, M. (1987). Providing centralized support for Humanities Computing. In R. L. Oakman (Ed.), *Proceedings of the eighth international conference on computers and the humanities*. Dordrecht: Kluwer.

Sperberg-McQueen, M., & Burnard, L. (Eds.). (1994). *Guidelines for electronic text encoding and interchange (TEI P3)*. Chicago/Oxford: Text Encoding Initiative.

Open Access This chapter is distributed under the terms of the Creative Commons Attribution-Noncommercial 2.5 License (http://creativecommons.org/licenses/by-nc/2.5/) which permits any noncommercial use, distribution, and reproduction in any medium, provided the original author(s) and source are credited.

The images or other third party material in this chapter are included in the work's Creative Commons license, unless indicated otherwise in the credit line; if such material is not included in the work's Creative Commons license and the respective action is not permitted by statutory regulation, users will need to obtain permission from the license holder to duplicate, adapt or reproduce the material.

Chapter 13
It's Probably the only Modestly Widely Used System with a Command Language in Latin: Manfred Thaller and Julianne Nyhan

Abstract This interview took place on 9 July 2014 at dh2014, the Digital Humanities Conference that was held in Lausanne, Switzerland that year. In it Thaller recalls that his earliest memory of encountering computing in the Humanities dates to c. 1973 when he attended a presentation on the use of computational techniques to map the spatial distribution of medieval coins. The difficulties of handling large, paper-based datasets was impressed upon him as he compiled some 32,000 index cards of excerpts for use in his PhD thesis. When he later encountered statistical standard software at the Institute for Advanced Studies in Vienna he found that such software could not be beneficially applied to historical data without first transforming in some way the historical data under study (indeed, the formalisation of historical and cultural heritage data is an issue that reoccurs in this interview, much as it did in Thaller's research). In light of his experience of the problems of using such software 'out of the box' to work with historical data he went on to teach himself the programming language SNOBOL. Within a few weeks he had joined a project on daily life in the middle ages and was building software to manage the descriptions of images that the project compiled and stored on punched cards. Having contributed to various other projects with computational elements, in 1978 he took up a post at the Max Planck Institut for History in Göttingen. As well as discussing the research he carried out there, for example, CLIO/κλειω a databased programming system for History with a command language in Latin, he discusses the immense freedom and access to resources that he benefitted from. He also goes on to discuss some of the later projects he worked on, including those in the wider context of digital libraries, infrastructure and cultural heritage.

Biography

Manfred Thaller was born in Feldbach, Austria in 1950. His PhD, from the University of Graz, Austria, is in modern History and was awarded in 1975. Following this he held a post-doctoral fellowship in empirical Sociology at the Institute for Advanced Studies, Vienna. From 1978 to 1997 he worked at the Max Planck Institut for History in Göttingen and he held visiting Professorships at uni-

© The Author(s) 2016
J. Nyhan, A. Flinn, *Computation and the Humanities*, Springer Series on Cultural Computing, DOI 10.1007/978-3-319-20170-2_13

versities in Jerusalem, London and Firenze. From 1995 until 2000 he was also Professor of Historical Computer Science and Director of the 'Humanities Information Technology Research Program' at the University of Bergen, Norway. In 2000 he became Professor of *Historisch Kulturwissenschaftliche Informationsverarbeitung* (Humanities Computer Science) at the University of Cologne, Germany and retired from this post in 2015. Among other things he was also President of the International Association for History and Computing from 1991 to 1994 and a member of the Library Committee of the German National Research Association (DFG) from 2002 to 2008. His many contributions to Humanities Computing include software, the digitisation of cultural heritage and the development of research infrastructure along with critical investigations. For example, the software CLIO/κλειω that he developed was widely used by Historians in the German speaking world and later released as an English version too.[1] Meanwhile, the ideas that Thaller began developing in the 1970s and that CLIO embodies (see below) which question the suitability of using commercially developed software to model and interrogate historical source materials has much resonance with present-day DH. His questioning of the role of, and assumptions embedded in, commercially-developed relational database systems provides a discipline-specific context for some of the most pressing concerns of present-day DH, namely, its lack of Cultural Criticism (Liu 2012) and the necessity for it to engage in 'interrogations of structures of power' (Prosner 2015).

Interview

JN What is your earliest memory, in any context at all, of encountering computing or computing technology?

MT I assume you are referring to computer technology within the Humanities. Well, in approximately my third or fourth year at the university, which must have been something like 1973 or so, we had a working group of students who invited people outside of the normal context to present what then was considered innovative approaches to History. We had a presentation from somebody who used a pre-runner of what would later be called a database to map the spatial distribution of medieval coins

JN Did you find it interesting?

MT Oh yes, it was definitely interesting but I didn't have any immediate application for it in the kind of work I made.

---

[1] A discussion of the English version is here: http://dhhumanist.org/Archives/Virginia/v07/0346.html

JN And was this seen as an unusual type of presentation or would it have been par for the course at that stage?

MT No that was definitely highly unusual at the time, and it was also in no way covered by what you would have heard at a university regularly. That really was just a presentation to people who had shown unusual interest in History in general, not in this specific topic.

JN What was your first engagement with the Humanities Computing community of the time?

MT Well, how far a Humanities Computing community existed in 1976, when my active work in the area started, is a bit doubtful, particularly in Austria. My first professional contact was to a Historian of the family, not in the sense of Genealogy but the development of structures of family, like the Cambridge Group did in England (see, for example, Laslett and Wall 1972). That was in Vienna in early 1977, where I was immediately hired because a professor had approached me as he had heard that I was doing some computer work for other historical projects.

JN And what kind of research did you do on the project?

MT That was standard statistical calculations of demographic behaviour.

JN Tell me about when you started leading your own research projects, and the factors that led you to include the computer in that or to theorise about the role of the computer in that research.

MT Well, that's a different story. My own doctoral thesis dealt with roughly the History of Mentality, or more properly, how opinions would be created out of information available at the time. For that purpose, between 1973 and 1975 I filled roughly 32,000 index cards with excerpts from approximately 500 years of newspapers, which certainly was impressive but impressed upon me that it was not very simple to handle such stuff. And after finishing my doctorate (Thaller 1975) I had the possibility to get a scholarship for 2 years of post-doctoral training at the Institute for Advanced Studies in Vienna, which offered courses in empirical Social Science even to people who had no formal training in Social Science. There I encountered statistical standard software and found that while this was interesting, their statistical paradigms could not be applied sensibly to historical data without these data undergoing certain transformations from the stage in which the stuff was kept in the sources.

This led me to the decision to do, besides the application of statistical software, some programming exercises in SNOBOL. This led very, very early (actually, something like 4 weeks after I started programming) into an involvement with a project on the daily life of the middle ages at a research institute where one of my friends worked. This project had started to create a collection of all the surviving medieval images in the area roughly coincident with today's Austria and some of the neighbouring countries. The project had started approximately 1 or 2 years earlier. The idea was to create a database which would use those images not as Art Historians use them, but for historical purposes, that is, for the study of material aspects of daily life. This meant that you had to represent the content of these images (it was still the time of punched cards) because digitising them was completely out of the question, at least with equipment we had available at that time. And my first exercise in applied programming was to build software to administer the descriptions of images. It was controlled by a command language that was supposed to be sufficiently far from a computer that the people working at that research institute actually could use it themselves. Of course, one has to say that in 1976 the visibility requirements (by which I mean the expectation to see a medieval painting on a computer screen) were slightly lower than they are now!

JN Am I right in saying that at the Institute for Advanced Studies, you had access to formal training in programming?

MT No. We had formal training in statistics and some in Mathematics, but formal training in computer usage simply consisted of how to use SPSS. What went beyond that was based on the advice that SNOBOL, which nobody else at the Institute had ever used in practice, was suspected to be particularly useful for what I had in mind. And then I simply had to learn the language myself.

JN Will you please reflect on that process of self-teaching: how you went about it, what it entailed and whether there was, at times, a social element to it?

MT Well, people learn in different ways. I remember that a few years later when I went to the place where I later had my first long-term permanent job I was basically reading a description of the programming language PL/1 and I simply started thinking how nice it would be to realise certain things with that. And I really think that how you learn things is very, very, very much a personal matter, which is the reason why until today I am a bit suspect of didactics. Some people like very much to learn programming by trying things out themselves, other people need a group of three or four reference persons with whom they can talk about it. This is the reason why when I formally teach computing and programming I try not to impress a model of how people have to learn (any more than is absolutely necessary to keep classes consistent).

JN What was the first Humanities Computing conference that you attended?

MT The first ALLC conference that I attended was in Pisa in 1982. The first conference that I attended which dealt with computing in parts of the Humanities was in Cologne in 1977, where there was a conference of what is still called Quantum (Association for Quantification and Methods in Historical and Social Research – *Arbeitsgemeinschaft für Quantifizierung und Methoden in der historisch-sozialwissenschaftlichen Forschung e.V*), which is a membership-driven group which at that time was working very intensively with quantitative methods in

History. The reason why my voice became slightly slow when I said membership organisation is simply that after the very few first years it basically evolved into a group of people who still publish a journal (*Historical Social Research*) in the field but there's not very much happening beyond that. In those years they organised summer schools themselves in which I, of course, was heavily involved.

JN People frequently comment to me that when they attended Humanities Computing (and Digital History and so on – labels are always so difficult in this context) conferences that the community was always very open and welcoming. They say that the type of spats and arguments that one may see in more established disciplines didn't tend to be as apparent. I wondered whether you agree or disagree with that interpretation?

MT Oh yes, I totally agree with that. Not all of the people were young in that group, but the mean age was probably something like 30, possibly even below. It was very clear that the people at these conferences considered themselves, well, if not as a group of elite at least as a group of revolutionaries who grumbled against the conservative people trying to keep away from their inter-disciplinary work, which at that time was rather innovative in many Humanities disciplines.

JN Did you present your DH research also at "pure" History conferences?

MT Oh yes. Still linking back to Austria, I was part of an Austrian-based group who organised a series of summer schools in Austria that ran between 1978 until the early 1990s. This group also organised regular workshops or sections at the annual Historians' conference in Austria. This I remember rather clearly because it was a whole series of events and we were present at each of the Historians' conferences. From something like 1978 onwards, I also quite frequently presented the work I did at all sorts of Historians' conferences, but there were too many of them for me to have a very clear memory of when I presented what.

JN And what kind of reception did you receive, especially from those who were not using computing in their research?

MT Well, I would say about a third of the people saw this as a positive develop-ment, though there was a slight reserve about the feasibility of it all. Roughly a third of the Historians more or less did not indicate any interest. And there was a hard core of Historians who, at that time, considered computation as a kind of vulnera-tion against the principles established by Ranke. But that is a very mixed matter because in the early days of quantitative History the assumption was not so much one of usability of computers or of publishing something. The assumption by the avowed quantifiers was that you could produce better historical results with statisti-cal efforts. In this way the usage of a computer was only a secondary aspect. So, the *Poverty of Historicism* (Popper 1957) was frequently quoted by the quantifiers and, as a side-effect, there were Historians who were clearly against quantitative work because they saw it as a conscientious attack upon proper historical methodology.

But on the other hand, one also should not say that this describes the frontline completely. Since this first wave of quantitative work there have been a couple of research projects in History that used decidedly non-quantitative approaches, like for example, trying to identify the agreement between witness lists of medieval charters (see, for example, Schmid 1978), which were implemented by some of the more, if not most, methodologically conservative medievalists in Germany. They did not see any problem with it as long as it was clear that the methodological and conceptual framework of their work would not be endangered.

JN As you look back on your career do you view the process of using the computer in History as one that moved from the margins towards the mainstream, or how would you characterise that process?

MT Well, it's really a kind of circular process. We had a couple of very important events. For example, the advent of easily available quantitative methods with the arrival of SPSS and similar programs; the arrival of easily usable databases together with PCs; and the arrival of easily usable web publication possibilities or web services in something like 1995. And there have been similar indications of a new wave in the last 5 to 7 years, where it is not yet so clear what the primary type of application will be.

At the stage of each of these introductions of a new method two things happened which ran a little bit against each other. On the one hand, at each of these stages, the number of computer applications in History increased by about one order of magnitude. On the other hand, the methodological conceptual refinement dropped sharply. That can be very simply described when we talk about the advent of the personal computer. Before 1985, quantitative studies usually meant that you would have to do a statistics course and then you would apply statistical software, which created tables, co-efficients and other things that you would have to interpret in order to get any insight. Relatively many Historians were very, very sceptical of whether these figures could actually show something. There are some very good reasons to be doubtful about quantitative studies in History, there are other reasons which are not so good. But there was certainly a scepticism among many Historians.

The interesting thing that happened when the PC was invented is that there came with it some very simple-minded statistical programs that offered the possibility of very easily creating graphical representations of statistical data. The first 3 years of the introduction of PCs in to History departments produced a flood of totally unrefined pie charts. Some of them did show absurd things because the data that had gone into them were beyond recovery as they never had been clarified. But they suddenly made pie charts very, very popular. Well, after people had played with PCs for something like 3 to 5 years, it turned out that things were not quite as simple as they had seemed in the meantime. The methodological refinement increased again because people accepted that even if you had the computer on your desk, you needed more than a passing acquaintance with what happened in the software if you actually wanted to use it.

And if one would go into detail you could show exactly the same thing with the first web projects. You had an explosion of people using the computer, but it's rather good for everybody's reputation that some of the webpages that were created at that time haven't been preserved so well!

JN Both a loss and a gain! Who influenced you? This can be as much in terms of traditional Historians as Humanities Computing people.

MT It's a shame, but it's relatively hard to remember the names. Unfortunately I have a very bad memory for names, so I would have to look up some of the books that I vaguely remember.[2] I'm afraid I can't point to any specific name. What influenced me very much was *Historical Methods,* a journal which had its heyday from the 1970s until the 1980s. It published very much about the usage of computers and particularly the usage of computers for non-quantitative purposes in History. I'm not quite sure if that journal still exists. I haven't looked for it recently because after the end of the 1980s it turned its focus mainly towards Anthropology and interpretative inter disciplinarity rather than the formal methods. But that's probably the one thing that influenced me most directly.

What influenced me more systematically was simply the working conditions I found at the place where I had my first long-term work in the Max Planck Institute for History in Göttingen. There I was originally hired for a rather specific project that was supposed to be a complex Social History analysis based on things called family reconstitutions or extended family reconstitutions, for specific types of Economic and Social History. Now, a Max Planck Institute is a pure research institute, which is actually not connected to a university, and the Director of that institute at that time, Mr Vierhaus, let his people have great leeway. So the assumption was basically that you were supposed to be visible worldwide and be on the same level as your competition (or whoever is best in this discipline). Otherwise you can do more or less what you want. Fortunately this approach was backed up by resources which meant that in the late 1970s and early 1980s I had the possibility to buy, relatively systematically, all the literature which was available at that time. Now, in pre-Amazon times, all the literature that was available probably wasn't very much more than something like 50 titles or so. But I had access to all the conference volumes published since the early 1960s about the early stages of Humanities Computing all over the field.

---

[2] After the interview Thaller recalled the following books: Hymes, D., ed. 1965. *The Use of Computers in Anthropology.* The Hague: Mouton; Bowles, E.A., ed. 1967. *Computers in Humanistic Research.* Englewood Cliffs, NJ: Prentice-Hall; n.A. 1972. *La Demographie Médiévale. Sources et Methodés.* Actes du Congrè de l'Association des Historiens Médiévistes de l'Enseignment Public (Nice, 15–16 mai 1970) (= Annales de la faculté des lettres et sciences humanines de Nice, 17). Paris: Les belles lettres; Wrigley, T., 1973. *Identifying people in the past.* London: Arnold.

The other big thing that influenced me is also immaterial: the Max Planck is an institution which has Humanities institutes but which is primarily shaped by hard Science institutes. It's really not an institute but a collection of something like 80 institutes which run joint infrastructures. And these infrastructures assumed that people should have the computing capacities and devices they needed quite irrespective of which institute they came from. Why this is important I can describe by telling you an anecdote which at that time left me in deep shock. In the early 1980s our work on social and economic History had led to databases of roughly about 200 MB, which now seems relatively trivial, but at that time, as will become clear in a moment, was rather large. And I could do that as somebody who had just finished his thirtieth year because I belonged to an institute which was supposed to be entitled to use computing resources, period.

When my position became permanent I went to the US on a 3 week journey. I basically went to a dozen or 14 people at universities all over the US, including Harvard. In Harvard at that time there was an extremely prominent social or economic Historian named David Herlihy who had done one of the very first studies of Italian censuses. He was truly famous for the first fully quantitative study of the Tuscan or Pisan census, one of the first censuses of their first years. So, I entered the holy halls of Harvard, met one of the great men of the field, and wanted to talk to him about what he thought of computer technology. He became very, very enthusiastic because Harvard had just made extraordinary capabilities available to him, more precisely a 10 MB hard disc and he would only have to find the money for a programmer so he could actually use it! So this is a bit unfair, but the possibility to have access to all the resources I could dream up has probably influenced me much, much more than any specific article or paper I've read.

JN In a way that doesn't surprise me, it sounds like a truly amazing, dream-like scenario.

MT It may be a dream scenario for people in the Humanities nowadays, but if you look at the capabilities at research institutes in Computer Science it is actually a well-tried principle: make resources available for people, force them to produce results, but don't hinder them by counting bytes or bandwidth or other nice things.

JN Were other Humanities people also working at the Max Planck Institute in Göttingen?

MT Yes, there were people who were working on something called proto-industrialisation. Proto-industrialisation is defined as the phase when artisanry in agricultural areas was, by various economic constructions, converted into a system where a relatively large portion of available income was also produced by the systematic production of items, particularly in the textile pre-industry or proto-industry. And there are all sorts of theories about how that was connected with social behaviour and similar things. Now my task, and that was exactly the job I was hired for, was to create a computer system able to take the marriage registers of a village, find out which children belonged to which marriage, which death record belonged to which individual (which is called family reconstitution) and then to augment that with just about any conceivable source that contained names, lists of taxation, property lists and various other stuff.

In this context David Sabean [Distinguished Professor of History & Henry J. Bruman Endowed Chair in German History, UCLA] who in the meantime, I think, has retired, indirectly influenced me very much, though not in detail, because he was not following things up very much himself. But he most certainly had very visionary ideas about the necessity of connecting every conceivable source to the kind of system that was being developed. This forced me, at an early stage, to think relatively generally, because it was not a limited set of sources to be processed but every conceivable source which might exist. And, my experience from Vienna of building systems which, at least in theory, should be used by the researchers themselves, let me then invent the programming system CLIO (Thaller 1987a), which some people still remember because it's probably the only modestly widely used system with a command language in Latin, which in any case was rather general and could be used for, theoretically, all types of historical sources.[3]

Then something happened which was relatively typical for that type of project. While the data arrived and while everybody was very happy that his data would be processed, people actually finished other books or wrote other articles and more or less postponed the analysis of the data which we had prepared for them. And at that time I somehow decided that if this were so, and if it would be supported by Mr Vierhaus, the Director of the Institute at that time, then I would simply ask people at other institutes whether it would not be possible to use some of their data to test out the features we had implemented. I have to admit again here that the possibility to use what, for all practical purposes, were unlimited computing resources helped. This meant that within a relatively short period of something like 5 years, what originally had clearly been a supportive function for a specific number of research projects gained the status of an abstract research project on its own, simply geared towards building a general software system for historical purposes, for which I invented the term "source-oriented data processing" (see Thaller 1987b, 1988, 1991). Behind that term was the assumption that previous software, like, for example, SPSS, was focused on making a specific canon of methods (quantitative methods or analytical quantitative methods to be precise) available more or less to the researcher him or herself. Source-oriented databases, as I understood them, or source-oriented data processing as I understood it, meant that you would try to take historical sources and try to convert "everything" (I hope you heard the quotes) that a source possibly contains into a form which then could be analysed for various purposes.

That was going on for something like 5 years. At the end of which this research project had emancipated itself to such an extent that I got a grant from the

---

[3] A web-based version of CLIO that contains some additional features and links to older copies of documentation is available: http://www.hki.uni-koeln.de/kleio/

Volkswagenstiftung funding agency. This allowed me to start a new implementation of that software that was not implemented in PL/1 anymore but in the programming language C which, by the middle of the 1980s was not completely new anymore, but was still one of the newer ones. And the point of that project was to make it as widely available to the research community as possible. Between the middle of the 1980s and 1990s (the implementation of the first version started in 1987) we worked on that software, making it available shortly after development began. We also made it available by providing summer schools (1987 to 1992, 1994 and 1997) which at the height of the development brought something like 100 people together for 2 weeks, to show how you could handle historical sources based on that type of software.

The only problem was that it was heavily limited in time (as such funded research still is). So, the actual development grant for the software that was developed ran for about 3 years only, with a fourth year glued on. And afterwards, to develop the software further, we had to look for research projects which would allow us to develop it in the context of content-driven research. There have been quite a few of these, one of which, for example, involved some early work on making the content of archives of the former concentration camp at Auschwitz available (*Sicherung und verbesserte Erschließung der Quellen im Archiv des Staatlichen Museums Auschwitz-Birkenau*[4]) but the scope was really very different. This is chronologically probably wrong now because it's a bit earlier, but at some stage we also did work on the comparison of the shape of medieval pottery, which has relatively few commonalities with documents at Auschwitz, but simply also has some data structures which can be supported if you have software which operates at the right level of generalisation.

JN When you look back at the ways that the computer was used in these projects, what were your disappointments …?

MT Actually, there were a couple of disappointments in the way interaction went. This, of course, is still one of the big problems of interdisciplinary work: if at some stage you are interested in developing a software product, not because you personally want to see the results, but because you want to test out some formal idea of what you can do to information, at some stage you cross the invisible line between History and Computer Science. After some time I simply got interested in the problems of formalising Historical Studies just because I was interested in these problems and not because I wanted to implement a specific study. And at this stage, as is usually the case in interdisciplinary projects between Computer Scientists and Humanists, there very frequently started the misunderstanding that when somebody from the formal part of the world wants to test something they think that they should provide a system which people can use later on in their own projects. And it is very frequently the case that people developing software get into the habit of doing it just once more themselves, to spare the time needed for the people who are interested in

[4] See: http://www.hki.uni-koeln.de/kleio/old.website/auschw/auschw.htm

the content to learn how to do that for the tools that might already be available. That is, from a Computer Science point of view, if you have developed a solution, you have developed the solution, and you would be very happy if other people apply it. From a Humanist's point of view, if a Computer Scientist develops the solution, you usually expect him or her to apply it for sufficiently long that you get some results that you can interpret. That was definitely a kind of disappointment.

But the more serious disappointment, which I still think is something which has damaged parts of the Humanities, is that in the 1990s there was a move away from working with formalised results. And I have a strong suspicion that that simply relates to the fact that if you want to study a phenomenon formally – I do not say quantitatively because my own work had moved far away from quantification by the late 1980s – computers have the obnoxious habit of telling you time and time again that your data may contain errors, while what may actually be going on is that your data contains something that does not fit your hypothesis. So, it's a long and pains-taking process. However, it is much, much faster, and much less frustrating to go into an archive and find a document with a human appeal and publish it and add a clever interpretation to it. Historical research has certainly fallen into what I con-sider a trap by getting away from doing the types of research that are harder to do.

One has to say that there was, of course, a very serious change in the 1990s with the advent of the ability to handle images and use web services, which in my opin-ion are still not completely understood. Well, still cooperating with that Austrian Institute where I had my first contract in 1976, we entered image processing, which is digitisation, image enhancement, pattern recognition in 1988 or 1989, working on Unix workstations, and built up quite some image handling capabilities, and that's the software I'm referring to.

Now, when we did that I was, at a very early stage, interested in the possibilities of making sources widely available for interpretation. So, at the conference of the ALLC and the ACH in Siegen in [1990] we presented a workstation with the kind of software I'm talking about, which showed, among other things, a very, very early version of this image processing software. And, at the same time, we were very inter-ested in what you could do with digitised documents. Around then we started a proj-ect which for me had an extremely interesting result. We got a research grant in the middle of the 1990s which allowed us to digitise a substantial amount of manuscripts, something like 60,000 pages or 70,000 pages, and make them available over the internet (see Aumann et al. 1999). This was really early and, though it is childish, I still remember with some amusement sitting on a panel beside a representative of the Library of Congress in Washington who unveiled, with great pathos, the first version of the George Washington papers. I had immediately afterwards the possibility to point out that the not so widely known city of Duderstadt in lower Saxony had online about twice as many pages of fairly obscure material from the fifteenth century! But this is just to say that we were very early with that. The strange thing I discovered was that we worked under two assumptions in that project. Firstly, that what made the applications of computers particularly interesting was that you could read some of the documents demonstrably better on the screen than in the original due to image enhancement and various other things. Secondly, we assumed that if you offered such material as digitised manuscripts on a large scale, you should look in parallel at possibilities to provide editorial techniques together with it (see Aumann et al. 1999). So, while digitisation was the main point of the project, we had a separate section where we implemented the possibility of handling manuscript variants in a way that is more meaningful than how it is typically done.

What in hindsight might have been a mistake, I'm not quite sure, was that we accompanied that project with an attempt to connect very, very closely with the user community. So, in the 3 years of the project we had a public presentation every 12 months and discussed the results achieved so far. And during these 3 years, where to a degree we followed up the feedback from the user community, we discovered that they found the possibilities for image enhancement, and various other things, interesting, but what people really got excited about was the possibility of having very great amounts of source material available on the internet, and conceptually having a couple of hundred thousand pages available at their fingertips (though in reality it was only 70,000 at that stage). So, we actually dropped all the analytical ideas we had in favour of improving access to the material.

I find it quite significant when I look at the development of digital editions in general to discover a very strange phenomenon. In the middle of the 1990s digital editions were usually connected to CD-based systems, which had a couple of very nice features that probably haven't been surpassed by most of the other systems we have nowadays. Then great amounts of data became available on the internet. At the same time, you notice that the interest in digital editions actually dropped because those people who were interested in applying technical innovation to the Humanities mainly became caught by the same trap we might have been caught by, that is that the sheer exuberance of access drowned out the analytical possibilities which might be there. This is strange in some ways and I really wonder how long it will take for a couple of things to be addressed. It is quite obvious at the moment, and I wrote papers which discussed this already in the 1990s, that there is actually not very much point in ever finishing an edition in the Humanities because howsoever good the edition is, you can be absolutely sure that beyond a certain intensity of usage the users will try to go back to the manuscripts. Still, for some strange reason people think of editorial processes as ending at a given stage, for which there are simply no technical reasons any more. I mean, if you were to concentrate on digital editions, not as tools for presenting a final result of a working process, but as an intermediate stage which could be taken up again at any stage, we would actually use the medium much more according to its characteristics. I really wonder how long it will take until what I consider the simple technical and artisan-like implications of the printed medium will be dropped in favour of adopting the possibilities that the new media create.

JN It's astonishing to see how slow this process is and to think that we're still trapped in this almost incunabular-like stage. I've kept you for the best part of an hour so I'm going to ask two more questions if that's ok? So, when you left Max Planck did you go straight to the University of Cologne?

MT No, already during my last years at Max Planck in Göttingen, I had a parallel appointment in Bergen, Norway. There I had something highly unusual, a kind of part-time professorship that's a Norwegian mechanism by which you can connect people who you want to have in your department for shorter periods of time to a university. They can be from industry or, for example, from other countries. I did a bit of teaching in History that was connected to digital methods and I was then asked to move fully to the University of Bergen to direct the merger of three independent research units there, which covered the whole scope from editorial Philology right through to Museum Information Systems. So that was a fairly large unit which, when it had been merged, was something like a 30-person infrastructure for IT usage in the Humanities in the University of Bergen. Originally I definitely had understood this to be a long-term assignment. But I have to admit that it had one shortcoming: while I endorsed this task very much it was also clear that by that step I had converted from somebody doing active research into a research manager, which had its own rewards. But when Cologne then offered a Professorship for Computer Science for the Humanities, where I had the possibility to build up my own study programs and also attract funding for projects that I could get involved in personally, rather than only managing them, this had so much attraction that I went south again, ending up instead on the Rhine at Cologne.

JN Just to close, what were the main differences between the Max Planck and the university in terms of the access to resources and the social structures that you had around you?

MT Well, that's totally different, I mean, at Max Planck I had absolutely no contact with students, originally. But on the other hand, I may hold a few records for side-teaching assignments when working at a research institute. I think I collected teaching assignments at more than a dozen universities during my years at Max Planck. I was also heavily involved in summer schools. This was not necessarily a very good qualification for taking over a regular Professorship because it meant that I had mainly encountered students who were more than normally interested in their field and particularly interested in applying new methods. Without wanting in any way to offend my Cologne students, going from that to a normally-motivated group of students certainly needed some adjustments.

And the other thing, of course, is that at Max Planck funds were considerably more easily available than at a regular university, though I have to say that in a sense I think I can call myself extremely successful at inviting third party funding for research while being in Cologne. That may have brought me away from my original purposes because out of creating historical databases it was very simple to drift into digital libraries, particularly because it was easier to get funding for digital libraries than it was for historical databases, and out of digital libraries it was particularly easy to drift off into digital preservation because that was relatively simple to fund. And that may have brought me further from my original analytical interests than I ever wanted.

References

Aumann, S., Ebeling, H. H., Fricke, H. R., Hoheisel, P., Rehbein, M., & Thaller, M. (1999). From digital archive to digital edition. *Historical Social Research, 24*, 101–145.

Bowles, E. A. (Ed.). (1967). *Computers in humanistic research*. Englewood Cliffs: Prentice-Hall.

Hymes, D. (Ed.). (1965). *The use of computers in anthropology*. The Hague: Mouton.

Laslett, P., & Wall, R. (1972). *Household and family in past times* (1st ed.). Cambridge: Cambridge University Press.

Liu, A. (2012). Where is cultural criticism in the Digital Humanities? In M. K. Gold (Ed.), *Debates in the digital humanities* (pp. 490–509). Minnesota: University of Minnesota Press.

n.A. (1972). *La Demographie Médiévale. Sources et Methodés.* Actes du Congrè de l'Association des Historiens Médiévistes de l'Enseignment Public (Nice, 15–16 mai 1970) (= Annales de la faculté des lettres et sciences humanines de Nice, 17). Paris: Les belles lettres.

Popper, K. R. (1957). *The poverty of historicism*. London: Routledge & Paul.

Prosner, M. (2015). The radical potential of the digital humanities: The most challenging computing problem is the interrogation of power. *LSE the impact blog*. Available at http://blogs.lse. ac.uk/impactofsocialsciences/2015/08/12/the-radical-unrealized-potential-of-digital-humanities/ Accessed 16 Aug 2015.

Schmid, K. (1978). Zum interdisziplinären Ansatz, zur Durchführung und zum Anliegen des Fuldaprojekts. In K. Schmid (Ed.), *Die Klostergemeinschaft von Fulda im früheren Mittelalter* (= Münstersche Mittelalter-Schriften 8, 1). München, pp. 11–36.

Thaller, M. (1975). *Studien zum europäischen Amerikabild: Darstellung und Beurteilung der Politik und inneren Entwicklung der Vereinigten Staaten von Amerika in Grossbritannien, Deutschland und Österreich im Vergleich zwischen 1840 und 1941*. Graz.

Thaller, M. (1987a). Clio – ein datenbankorientiertes system für die historischen Wissenschaften : Fortschreibungsbericht. *Historical Social Research, 12*(1), 88–91.

Thaller, M. (1987b). Methods and techniques of historical computation. In P. Denley & D. Hopkin (Eds.), *History and computing*. Manchester: Manchester University Press.

Thaller, M. (1988). Gibt es eine fachspezifische Datenverarbeitung in den historischen Wissenschaften? Quellenbanktechniken in der Geschichtswissenschaft. In J. Schneider & H. Kaufhold (Eds.), *Geschichtswissenschaft und elektronische Datenverarbeitung*. Wiesbaden: F. Steiner Verlag.

Thaller, M. (1991). The historical workstation project. *Computers and the Humanities, 25*(2–3), 149–162.

Wrigley, T. (1973). *Identifying people in the past*. London: Arnold.

Open Access This chapter is distributed under the terms of the Creative Commons Attribution-Noncommercial 2.5 License (http://creativecommons.org/licenses/by-nc/2.5/) which permits any noncommercial use, distribution, and reproduction in any medium, provided the original author(s) and source are credited.

The images or other third party material in this chapter are included in the work's Creative Commons license, unless indicated otherwise in the credit line; if such material is not included in the work's Creative Commons license and the respective action is not permitted by statutory regulation, users will need to obtain permission from the license holder to duplicate, adapt or reproduce the material.

Chapter 14
Getting Computers into Humanists' Thinking: John Bradley and Julianne Nyhan

Abstract This interview took place in Bradley's office in Drury Lane, King's College London on 9 September 2014 around 11:30. Bradley was provided with the interview questions in advance. He recalls that his interest in computing started in the early 1960s. As computer time was not then available to him he sometimes wrote out in longhand the FORTRAN code he was beginning to learn from books. One of his earliest encounters with Humanities Computing was the concordance to Diodorus Siculus that he programmed in the late 1970s. The printed concordance that resulted filled the back of a station wagon. The burgeoning Humanities Computing community in Toronto at that time collaborated both with the University of Toronto Computer Services Department (where Bradley was based) and the Centre for Computing in the Humanities, founded by Ian Lancashire. Aware of the small but significant interest in text analysis that existed in Toronto at that time and pondering the implications of the shift from batch to interactive computing he began work as a developer of *Text Analysis Computing Tools* (TACT). He also recalls his later work on *Pliny*, a personal note management system, and how it was at least partly undertaken in response to the lack of engagement with computational text analysis he noted among Humanists. In addition to other themes, he reflects at various points during the interview on models of partnership between Academic and Technical experts.

Biography

John Bradley was born in 1950 in Bracebridge, Ontario, Canada. He completed a Bachelor of Mathematics degree at the University of Waterloo, Canada in 1974 and a Bachelor of Music at Wilfrid Laurier University, Canada in 1977. Between 1977 and 1997 he held various positions in the Computer Centre at the University of Toronto and was lead developer of the influential TACT. In 1997 he joined what is now known as the Department of Digital Humanities, King's College London and was eventually moved from a non-academic post to the academic post of Senior

© The Author(s) 2016
J. Nyhan, A. Flinn, *Computation and the Humanities*, Springer Series on
Cultural Computing, DOI 10.1007/978-3-319-20170-2_14

Lecturer in 2011. His work on *Pliny*, a personal note management system, was awarded a Mellon Award for Technology Collaboration (MATC) prize in 2008.

Interview

Julianne Nyhan [JN] My first question is about your earliest memories of encountering the computer or computing technology?

John Bradley [JB] I thought I was going to be involved in computing from what was, for me, pretty darn early days actually. In the early 1960s, when I was in my early teens, I was already buying the few books on computing that were available to people like me. I started off with an interest in circuitry. So my earliest books about computing had little diagrams with transistors connecting together to make OR and AND gates. At one point I found a book about FORTRAN in what was then called 'programmed learning' style.[1] I was absolutely captivated by it; I was absolutely fascinated. I remember reading it on the bus on the 100 mile trip going from Toronto to my home, which was in Gravenhurst Ontario. I was absolutely deeply engrossed. I became so excited that I started writing code on a piece of paper because there was no possibility (this was in the early 1960s) for someone like me to have access to a computer. Relatively early on, let's say about 1965 or so, I was sent by my high school to the University of Waterloo, which was very active in the early days of Computer Science. Computer Science was part of their Mathematics Faculty and so I got my hands on these large machines, like the 1000 other students who were sent to do some programming on cards. I was just over the top and desperately excited. I knew I wanted to go to the University of Waterloo and, at that time, I was quite convinced that that was going make my career. I began to fantasise about computing, even at that time. I remember walking home one night in the dead of winter, cold, cold, cold, and thinking about personal computing. I had this vision of a little suitcase-like box that the computer would be. You'd open it up and the screen would be there and I was thinking at the time about animation on it. I had absolutely no idea how it would be done – in almost every level I had no conception of it. But I was excited about the potential for that kind of thing.

JN What was it about FORTRAN that excited you so much?

JB Now that's an interesting question. I've stayed interested in programming as an expression of my interest in computing. So, I think the ability to make the machine run to a certain extent independently of me, you know, the automaton side of it,

---

[1] Programmed learning is an 'educational technique characterized by self-paced, self-administered instruction presented in logical sequence and with much repetition of concept' see http://www.britannica.com/topic/programmed-learning.

must have been what really interested me. I wasn't that interested in the type of mathematical problems that it was traditionally being applied to: FORTRAN is a programming language for doing mathematical calculations. And, in the end, I wasn't actually that interested in Math, but I was definitely interested in the automaton nature of it.

JN Did you go on to take formal training?

JB Yes I did. I did what was classified as a Bachelor of Mathematics degree at Waterloo but it was really in Computer Science. This was still in the days of the great big mainframe. You'd walk into the faculty building and the first thing you saw was this lowered floor and this big IBM 360 mainframe sitting down there, with less computer power that what you have on your mobile phone today. But this monster machine was clearly a centre for how Waterloo thought of themselves in this field. I did an undergraduate degree and I expected to go on to do a Masters and perhaps a PhD. I was accepted onto the Masters programme in Computer Science at the University of Toronto. But suddenly there's a change and I decided I was going to do music instead. So, I went to a small music school and did an undergraduate degree. These 2 degrees didn't really fit well together. I didn't do any more education because, I think, I didn't know what to do at that point.

JN And how did you encounter Humanities Computing?

JB I was in Waterloo's Co-op programme which alternated terms with work experience. You had to get a job for 4 months and then you studied for 4 months, and so on. It lasted for 5 years (ordinarily it was a 4 year degree but it included this extra time for work experience). I started off working for Ontario's Department of Highways, but after a few terms of that I decided to switch and I went to the University of Toronto to work. In the end, my computing degree was the route by which I got the permanent job. So, my first contact with the Humanities Computing community was in the late-ish 1970s. I was, by then, working at the University of Toronto in their Computer Services Department, the UTCS it was called.

My boss said "we have someone who's interested in generating a concordance". The text was by Diodorus Siculus. They had tried to set up the Oxford Concordance Programme (OCP; see Hockey interview, Chap. 6). I'm sure it would have done a perfectly good job but for some reason or other they couldn't make it run adequately. It couldn't handle the amount of material. So they asked if I could just write something to do the job. So I did and it ran. I remember the occasion. It ran all day on the machine, it was time shared, so other people had to run their tasks at the same time. They had to dedicate a printer to this Key Word in Context (KWIC) concordance and they got so many boxes of paper that they filled up the back of a station wagon. Because they didn't ever want to run it again it was printed on paper with carbon copies attached, so you got two copies. They had this big machine to pull the paper all apart, so it was really an industrial-strength type of computing.

JN What year was that roughly?

JB Probably the very late 1970s. I called the software Concordance Generating System (COGS)[2] and it went on to do a number of similar jobs for other texts at the University of Toronto. That was the point that I became interested in this. I became involved in the Text Support Team because this was the time when the personal use of computers was starting (initially as time sharing applications and mainly on the big mainframes. This is still before there was any real availability for personal computers to do anything very serious). The department was therefore interested in time sharing rather than personal word processing. My group was given the job of preparing training for that and supporting people who were taking it up. It was called the Text Group. I could also do other stuff apart from just focusing on teaching people to type paragraphs and get them to appear properly on paper. Clearly there were faculty there who were interested in this [e.g. COGS] being provided, so it made some sense to continue it.

JN Do you have a sense of how many there were of those faculty ?

JB I don't think there was a vast number, probably six or seven. The University of Toronto is a large operation, but this was a tiny, tiny number. An important one was Ian Lancashire who you've probably had mentioned to you before, and I think Ian's really important for DH in Canada. Among the English-speaking people (Quebec is also important and completely separate) many have had some connection with Ian at one time or another. I never worked for Ian. I was always in the computer centre. He managed to get an operation called the Centre for Computing in the Humanities (CCH) started (see, for example, Gouglas et al. 2013). He convinced IBM Canada to provide some funding in support of this and convinced the faculty to support it, which was quite an achievement in those days. So, he was one person and he became quite interested in teaching it to his students and we worked together to package up things like COGS, and so on, for students to explore.

I was never really a Humanist you see. My music degree did give me some insight into the types of issues that were going on in the Humanities, but at this time I was very interested, as I think many people were, in the interactive potential of computing, I'd been trained in a batch world, where there was virtually no interaction of any kind; yet, there's no other way to think about computing nowadays! But I became very interested in what interaction would mean and in what software to support that would be like. And so the natural application for me was really the text analysis work that I had done. Ian was also quite keen on this; by this point people like Willard [McCarty] were around at Toronto as well. And there was a group of people, mainly in the French Department, Russell Wooldridge comes to mind and

---

[2] Bradley did not publish on this software. An outline description of a later version of it (COGS-3) is available: http://www.tapor.ca/?id=416. However, Bradley remarks that it never ran on DEC machines.

Ed Heinemann, both of them quite interested in text, and what we now think of as text analysis approaches.

There were other people too whose names I can't remember at the moment. So there was a small group of people and there was some opportunity and the university made it possible for me to work in this area at that time. At a later point it became obvious that my department, the computer centre, began to think of themselves just as the provider of email services and cables and it became much more difficult to work in this way. But this was still a time when the work was thought of as a bit of a partnership between Computer Central Services and the academic.

JN You must also have encountered Humanities people who weren't using computers in their work but who were watching what was going on. Do you have a sense of what their views may have been of such developments?

JB There were several different groups, of course. At the beginning of this time no one used computers for word processing because the idea didn't yet really exist. When it came along it took a long time for people in the Humanities, in particular, to see why they should even be interested in word processing. I mean, you wrote something up on a piece of paper and you gave it to your secretary who typed it up. So why in the world would you want to do it yourself? That was part of an understandable position. In those days you could hardly imagine computing having any useful role in the day-to-day life of an academic, even for word processing. Email, of course, was still years in the future. So there was that group and they gradually began to understand the virtue of word processing. I remember the early days and people sitting in front of the computer. I was head of the Word Group and so we did courses on things like WordPerfect and, in time, Windows-oriented software. I remember people coming in and looking at the mouse and picking it up and pointing it at the screen and clicking the button, thinking that's how they interact with the mouse. They had no conception of any of this sort of stuff. So there was that group.

There was also the group of people who had a natural resistance to the whole approach that text analysis represented. I think that's still an important issue today because many scholars find the text analysis approach deeply uncomfortable. I've often heard it labelled as a New Criticism approach. That's a damning comment. They also say that "we just don't think that way about our text anymore, we don't see a place for that type of work". So there was that resistance as well. As I said, I think that's understandable and it has continued even up until now.

Most academics then, and still today, just have a rather benign indifference to it. They use technology all the time: they use word processing, email and the web but they don't really think of it as having much to do with what they're actually doing in their research. Sure, the web is terrific, they can get at material that otherwise would have been a real struggle to get to see. And email is terrific, you can contact someone quickly and easily and get their comments. Word processing is terrific but all that doesn't really matter to what they're doing. Whereas with text analysis, it is a more fundamental disturbance of how you look and think about the text you're working with and I think most people just don't see it as relevant to what they're trying to do.

JN Did you feel that you were very much working at the cutting edge? Or how did you view your work?

JB Well I was becoming aware of this. I mean, I wasn't an academic and I've only recently actually been given an academic contract here at King's. For almost all of my professional life I've not been an academic. So it took me a long time to grow into thinking in those terms at all.

JN You're now a Senior Lecturer, right?

JB Yes, I am now Senior Lecturer. I'll probably die a Senior Lecturer because I'm getting up towards retirement. Before that, of course, I was more and more academic-like in the way I was thinking. King's and the Department made it possible for me to begin to put myself in those things. But in those days I don't think I was thinking in those terms particularly. Regarding COGS, for example, I didn't think of it so much as cutting edge as just a job that we could do. I guess I was interested in being on the edge of what was being thought about in terms of interactive computing, but I didn't think of myself as writing papers about it and publishing them in an academic journal. That was far from what I saw myself doing in those days. So I wrote things and had fun and tried out ideas there.

I started to work on the TACT system in the mid-1980s. For me, TACT (Bradley 1989) was as much an interest in exploring what it meant for a piece of software to be interactive because I already had COGS and I played around with OCP. I looked at some other pieces of software like that. I knew roughly what their parameters were, what they did and how they understood text, but none of them were interactive. I thought, "well, what happens if you make it interactive? How does that world change?" TACT was, more from my point of view, some thinking about the interactive side of it, what it meant for you to have the stuff on your own personal machine and to see things happen on the screen as you typed. That was mainly where my interest lay. I was thinking of myself then as maybe cutting edge, to use your expression, because I knew that there were other pieces of software around that were doing it. There was, for instance, WordCruncher[3] from Brigham Young University. To be frank, I thought I could do something more interesting from an interactive point of view. I thought I could make the interaction more sophisticated and the connections between things more so that people could exploit the interactive nature rather more than what they had done. Of course they were first and I was second so it was a little

---

[3] Wordcruncher is a 'long-standing text indexing, retrieval and analysis program offered by Brigham Young University. Its functions include tagging, contextual searching, collocation and analytical reporting, and its development has been active since the 1980s.' See: http://www.tapor.ca/?id=216.

easier to re-think it, perhaps. I was thinking about the new-ness of this for sure at that point.

It was a challenge, in a way, because the computers in those days were so tiny. It's hard for us to imagine nowadays. TACT was written for an original DOS-based IBM PC, my first box to come out of this partnership that Ian Lancashire had negotiated. Ian had provided me with my first personal computer because the computer centre didn't think I needed one in particular! So he provided me with one and I got involved very early.

I purchased the Turbo Pascal programming language and I was forced to explore writing software in it because there was no more professional language available to people like me. Anyway, that was easily available on these tiny machines with 640 K memory, that's probably 10,000th the size of the memory available on a modern computer, probably substantially less than what you have on your phone. Everything had to be squeezed into that. There was no disk in the first place and then when disks first came out 20 MBs was a huge disk. I got one of those with great pride.

I mean we can now be, as programmers, quite profligate with memory. There's always something there, you can load more data into memory and keep it there and play around with it without worrying. That was certainly not the case with this machine. I had to work very hard to figure out how to squeeze as much out of it as I could.

JN Has that increase in memory meant that programming can be less of a puzzle?

JB I think there's been several developments that have made programming more practical, such as Moore's Law, the simple increase in power of the machine. I'm not quite sure I can bring Moore's Law properly to mind at the moment but I think it was mainly around computing speed but in addition it had some impact on memory and disk space. All these things have grown 1,000s-fold from these early personal computer days. And they have liberated you from having to fuss so much about the machine at that level.

JN So did you feel that you were free to explore ideas even though you were doing things like developing COGS, for example, for somebody with a particular purpose? What was that interplay between doing service work, to an extent, and the intellectual task of building text analysis software?

JB We had quite an enlightened management for many years at Computing Services. I said that eventually it was squeezed out and I would have thought it became difficult to manage. By the 1990s it became more difficult to do such work. To a certain extent, the vice-President of the university in charge of computing made a deliberate decision that work like TACT was no longer work that the computer centre was supposed to do. And so that was deeply discouraged and I had very little involvement in TACT in those later years.

But even then, if I may say, that was the time referred to in Geoffrey Rockwell's interview (Rockwell et al. 2012) when we used to push our chairs together and explore our ideas around text analysis. He came to us from Philosophy, he really was a Humanist. We did that partly in our lunch hour, so working conditions were not entirely free. But we also were in a position to think very freely about the training that we were offering to faculty at the University of Toronto. We developed a HyperCard[4] course and that, as a service, gave us the freedom to think out of the box about what we were doing. My unit by that point became what was called the Centre for Academic Technology (CAT). This was a really grand name for what was a relatively modest operation but the name gave us the opportunity to think very freely because academic technology, what was that? It could be almost anything and we had a great deal of freedom then. I don't think we did a lot that interested our Science people because they had already launched off from academic technology on their own and they didn't need us particularly. But we were doing interesting things, I think, within the Humanities and with CCH, to some degree informally, to develop the agenda there.

JN So would it be fair to say that you felt a good deal of intellectual freedom?

JB Yes, I think I did at that time; it gradually was taken away. And it's probably the reason why eventually I left and took up my position at King's. Once again in this department, it was not quite the same, but there were similar elements of freedom here. So yeah, I think Toronto had a good environment then, partly between the CCH but UTCS also had an openness to that type of thinking for a time. So it was a good time to be engaged in the DH and I think part of the reason why Toronto became important was this possibility to work, from the perspective of our bosses, a little bit outside the box.

JN How did you encounter the Humanities Computing conference community?

JB The first conference that everyone thinks of these days is Toronto, the first joint conference between the ACH and the ALLC (see Hockey et al. 1991). CCH was the centre of it. I mean this again was Ian Lancashire's hard work to sell the idea that it should be in Toronto. It was a really exciting and interesting event. We had a substantial crowd and really interesting people came to speak.

But I had had some conference experience before that. As I said, before that I wasn't really thinking of myself as an academic. I was sent to the service-oriented conferences that IBM ran every year for a few years, but I didn't say anything at them for some time. Eventually it became evident that we had things to say. But my first experience of a more academic conference was in South Carolina, 1987, and it was part of what was called the International Conference on Computing in the Humanities (ICCH; see Oakman 1987). I vaguely remember that Ian Lancashire

---

[4] Hypercard was a powerful hypermedia system that preceded the World Wide Web and was bundled with Apple Macs sold after 1987 see Barnet (2013) p. xxiv and http://hypercard.org/.

suggested that I go and speak about my thinking about TACT, this was before TACT really emerged. I remember giving a paper on that at the conference.[5]

I don't think I gave a paper at the Toronto conference but I did run workshops on TACT. That was quite an experience. 100 people came to a couple of workshops, you'd look way out and down into the distance and you could see people sitting right at the back playing around with their computers. It may not have been 100 but it seemed like a vast number of people to me at the time. I was a little overawed by the interest in it. And after that, starting with the Oxford conference in 1992 (see Hockey and Ide 1996), I began to go regularly and give my own papers. Shortly thereafter Geoffrey Rockwell and I did some joint papers at the Paris conference in 1994. We gave several papers there on topics ranging as far as visualisation (see, for example, Bradley and Rockwell 1994). So my conference involvement began probably then and I think I began to get to know people within the conference community more at the Paris conference than in Toronto because I ...

JN Did you form an impression of the community, say at that Toronto one, did you find it changing as time went on?

JB The Toronto one was really an exciting experience. Everyone was really fired up about it. I mean, Ted Nelson was not invited but he came. He was an enormously influential and important figure in personal computing and Hypertext (see, for example, Barnet 2013). He was a key thinker in those days and he heard of the conference in Toronto and just came on his own and they found a slot for him to talk and the room was packed with people. So there was that type of excitement that I don't think I have ever seen at any of the other conferences, even though I think they were really good events. But we obviously felt that we were really into something quite extraordinary.

Of course, the DH conferences were academic, so academics, or people who wanted to act academically were there. They were talking about the potential impact of technology on scholarship. They weren't all academics, it wasn't a pure academic field and still isn't today. The DH is an interesting mix of people, some academic, and some rather less so, because the agenda that's being worked on is not a purely academic one, I think. The other conferences I would go to really were service-oriented, it was the computer centres going and talking about how to run your IBM mainframe better or that kind of thing. Occasionally there would be an interesting talk. I remember I went to one by Douglas Engelbart who came and spoke about his work on Augment (see Engelbart 1962). This would have been way back, the mid-1970s I guess. So his main splash was in the very late 1960s (see Doug Engelbart Institute n.d.) but he was still working on this and still had an extraordinary set of ideas. He came and talked, and I was desperately excited. I went to his talk, it kept me awake at night I was so excited by what he was talking about. So the service conferences were not just about optimising the running of your IBM 360, but that was really what most people came for. Whereas the academic conference had much

---

[5] It has not been possible to establish the title of that paper.

more of this type of excitement around new ideas and sometimes radically different ways of thinking about what computing may be doing.

JN Would you agree with this observation that one often hears about the community being friendly and welcoming?

JB I've always found it so. I don't know why that is exactly. I've occasionally seen evidence of professional jealousies, and so on, in the community. I know a few places where that's an issue, but it certainly hasn't, in my opinion, dominated the business. I think to a certain extent, maybe less so in the last couple of years, we were all evangelists. We were out there selling this idea and in the same way as when someone comes up and knocks on your door from one of these cults, they're going to be friendly. I think there was some of that in what was going on! But that's only a part of the story. For many people there was less at stake. For the more senior people it could be fun, it was obviously a side track to their main research aims where they continued to develop their careers. They would give a paper but it wasn't necessarily on their main research (or a primary conference in their field where it was not necessarily so much fun to go and talk about their work on e.g. a particular writer to those in their community of people who were also studying that topic.) The DH was not like that and so you could be much more relaxed and it didn't affect your career so much if in the end it didn't amount to so much. So senior people could do that and there were a good number of people there who were like that. It's hard to explain why junior people were also, in my experience, very friendly. It's always been a very friendly group.

JN And what of people who especially influenced you?

JB Well, because I was a developer I didn't have the same sort of stream of influence. Ian Lancashire was an important influence for me in terms of how he make things possible at Toronto in the way that he did. Of the well-known names, Susan Hockey and her writings were influential for me to a certain extent. I also met someone called Paul Bratley. I think he's disappeared out of the community, but he was important at the University of Montreal and an important player in some early thinking around text analysis. He was French, so he was working in French, with French texts and so on and some of his writings were important to me. I was gradually beginning to track research in interactive and personal computing and some of the important people there were important to me. But I didn't know them personally, I mean I was far too small fry to meet any of them. But nonetheless, well, Engelbart's an example. When Steve Jobs left Apple the first time and set up his own company and created the NeXT computing company, Toronto managed to get (they didn't pay for it) a free NeXT and it was plopped down in the computer centre, near my office. I got the chance to play with it and I got desperately excited about the way in which software development was thought of on the NeXT. So that was influential to my thinking at the time too and I don't know if that's quite the type of influence you're thinking of but it's what it was nonetheless.

But it wasn't so much direct person to person contact as it might have been if I had been more of a conventional academic and thought of myself as a substantial player in the field, the way that academics with careers do. Certainly that's very much a part of how we're groomed to think of ourselves these days here in King's. You're nothing if you're not up there with the big names, so it seems. But I certainly didn't have that view of myself at the time. However, I was starting to read fairly broadly, the journals that I was collecting go back a long way. I was a fairly avid reader of them all along and so I was at least aware of what the big names in the field were doing.

JN Great stuff. Would you say a little bit about Pliny?

JB Sure, thank you for asking because I don't think Pliny has had that much impact. I started off in the text analysis world and I thought I would be continuing to develop in that world. But when I started to talk to academics about TACT, I remember going and talking to some Sociologists at the University of Toronto, it became very evident that the whole text analysis agenda was just not what they were doing or interested in. Many academics were in a similar position. They became interested in computing and in thinking about how the computer might help them with their scholarly work in the Humanities. However, they'd look at the text analysis stuff and they'd say "it's not a tool for me". I rarely talked to them but when I did it seemed that there was a fundamental disconnect between what they were doing with their materials and what TACT or other tools of its kind did. I think I can speak more broadly and say that's still true today.

So, this would have been the mid-1990s, and I began to think. Because I was an evangelist too, I was keen on getting computers into humanists thinking. What could I do that would actually be relevant to what they do? I faffed around with this for a long time because it was difficult to find out what Humanists actually did. Even today there's not a nice neat description, partly because I think it's in the nature of the Humanities that so many different approaches are possible. But even in these early days I began thinking about note taking and reading as key activities. This starts to appear in my own writings so I guess I was thinking about it around the early 1990s. I was invited to a few conferences on text analysis. That was when I had started to change my thinking; and my papers, I think, were big disappointments to them because I wasn't talking about text analysis anymore. I'd already begun to shift in the direction of thinking about what traditional scholarship was like and how computing could help it.

Pliny was meant to be a response to this. It was about note taking, it was about juggling your notes once you'd taken them to help you develop a richer understanding of the material and to help you formulate concepts. I like to think of it as Engelbartian software. Engelbart had a quite sophisticated understanding of how computing would support intellectual work as a tool that became almost invisible. The main work would still be done in your own head, it was still you, the person using the machine and doing the work that was the main driver. The machine just helped you do it better and more efficiently. And this was a key idea of his for computing. He wasn't so interested in splashy new visualisation systems, not that he resented that but he didn't think that was the way forward. And Pliny was meant to be (notice the tense) a tool that works that way. I'm holding the notes I printed from Pliny for our talk today. My thinking was about taking notes as you read, juggling the notes until new ideas emerge, and then the process of codifying and organising that until you have enough to write a paper or do something with it. Pliny was meant to fit in that sort of world. It had a bit of a splash at the beginning, and I was delighted when the Mellon Foundation provided me with some funding to continue to support it. That was an acknowledgement that there was something interesting in it. But there's obviously something wrong with it too because it didn't get much attention in my view. I think it's largely disappeared out of people's thinking. But I still work away at it. The paper I'm currently working on is trying to figure out what Pliny has to say on the connection between scholarship and the semantic web. I tend to explore the building of things inside the Pliny framework to help me understand these questions better.

JN But it is a perennial problem of DH, isn't it? These beautiful artefacts are built but then they tend to have a relatively limited take up outside of the community, and sometimes even within the community. And we don't seem to be coming so much closer to solving that really, do we?

JB No, we haven't. I mean you can certainly track papers back to the 1960s where people are saying, "oh it's going to transform scholarship!" and it never has. I think it's darn hard to get people's attention. I think of how long it took for people to understand the virtue of word processing within the Humanities! I know because I was there and watching how long it took people to come around to the idea. It took 15 to 20 years or so.

Well, we've had even longer than that with our rather traditional DH thinking about the place of tools and it just hasn't had the impact. I think it's partly misdirected and although perhaps the path of Pliny is also misdirected I think it would be really useful for us to think more broadly about what the right direction might be. Do we still want to be an evangelical kind of community where we still think we have something? Is computing important? The digital world is important in a more fundamental way to what the Humanities programme is. Right now, the big push is big data and the various funding bodies have funded big data a couple of times now,[6] I think we're now on the third round of it being funded. I have no objection, I think that some interesting work is being done, but I also think that it's just going to be a niche. It has to be a niche activity for most Humanists. Why these funding bodies can't try something else, as another big new thing and fund some exploratory work in other areas too, I haven't quite understood.

---

[6] See, for example, the multilateral 'Digging into data challenge' http://diggingintodata.org/.

JN So you mentioned when you were a teenager that you had this fascination with automaton as a theme. Do you think that's been a theme that you have traced in your work?

JB That's an interesting question. Automation or algorithmic thinking was very much a part of the text analysis work that I did because, you know, you develop a new approach to having a machine transform some material. It's almost batch-like. You give the text to the computer, it does something to it and some new insight hopefully comes out as a result of it. But with modern computing you don't have that sense of your interaction with your machine. When you turn on your laptop it feels much more like Engelbart's perspective on the thing, where you don't really notice what the machine is doing and you keep it on rather a short leash. As you type it does things but after you stop typing it stops doing things. This batch idea is rather foreign to how much computing is now thought of and I think I've moved there now too. The interactive interest that I had in the early days – I think the interactive side of things has continued to interest me more than anything – it was non-automaton-like. Instead, it's much more the machine as some type of partner to your own interests. I've been much more interested in that and I think that interest started way back in the early days of word processing. So no, the automaton side of things, it's not an interest for me. I think robotics, for example, is fascinating but it's not something I've taken up very much.

JN Something I also wondered about is why you wanted to be an evangelist for the use of this machine in the Humanities? What was it that you saw?

JB Well, I'm not a natural evangelist. I could never possibly go up and knock on people's doors and I find the equivalent of that in the academic world very difficult. But of course, I've always had work that had this element in it. In the early days in the computer centre we were promoting the idea of using the machine in new places where it hadn't been used before. From the earliest days it was a brand new thing that had to find its place and is still working its way through society. To a certain extent, I'm more comfortable with trying to say new things in papers and I'm happy enough to give formal presentations if I have a script and I've prepared it. Knocking on people's door though is not a natural thing for me, but it should be. I think it's still very much a part of where the DH community is and therefore where I am, to a certain extent.

JN And what was it about the computer that made you think "I want this to be accepted, I want to help it to be accepted, I want to build some of the foundational software for this discipline"?

JB Well, perhaps it's as difficult to tell you why I decided computing was my thing as it would be for a violinist to tell you why a violin was their thing: it just caught the interest somehow. I mean I was older than most violinists start playing the violin. This just happened in my early teens but I was still vulnerable to this, if that's the right word. I simply discovered my thing and I don't think I've ever really found a way of putting it into words. I mean, I mentioned automation, the thing you picked up. Well, even now that was a spur of the moment thought about what it was that appealed to me. So I got into computing just because it fascinated me and, no more than a violinist can tell you why it's the violin and not the oboe, or not working outside of music altogether, I think that's part of what happened to me.

The Humanities side of it was also serendipitous. I guess I was never such a wonderful mathematician but it was obvious for me to go into the mathematical side and therefore into the scientific side of computing. I might have managed reasonably well in the right Computer Science programme. I was quite into it but I never really got that into it beyond my undergraduate degree. So who knows what would have happened or not? The Humanities happened by accident, to a certain extent, but even then in the earliest days, as I said, we were already interested in exploring the potential of bringing the machine into that world. At Toronto we had, with the CCH and so on, a framework for exploring this and for trying things out. We really were explorers; we thought of ourselves as explorers there, we really were. You had Ian Lancashire, you had Willard McCarty, you had Geoffrey Rockwell involved, you had several really interesting people at the time and all sorts of interesting students too. It was quite an exciting business, as it was when I came here. I mean the aim of the Centre for Computing in the Humanities (now the Department of Digital Humanities (DDH) at King's in the beginning was to promote computing in the Humanities so I just had to be working in this area.

JN Did you ever feel that working with computers was a disadvantage or held you back in some form or other? Did you ever have, let's say, negative experiences as a result of choosing this area?

JB Well, sure, there have been some negative experiences. I think the answer to that question is related to how career-oriented you are. "Were you held back in your career?" is usually what the question means. I was struck by Willard McCarty's (2014) comments at the opening of his Busa award presentation where he said he never really thought of it in terms of a career, things just happened. He moved because opportunities turned up and I think I was more like that actually. I never really thought in a career-oriented way. I certainly never, for most of my time working in the university world, thought of myself as an academic. And so, it's probably true that trying to find my place as a non-academic in our field, which has a strong academic component, was sometimes a problem. You know it was very easy for people who weren't interested to dismiss the types of things that I could offer "that's just not relevant to the type of great work that I'm doing". And you'd see that sometimes.

JN Are you referring to fellow DH people or mainstream Humanities?

JB I don't know what DH people think; I've never had the feeling from them. Within the Department of Digital Humanities at King's we've certainly had a few

projects where clearly our supposed partners were not interested or engaged in significantly in re-thinking what they are doing because of what the computer enabled.
They just clearly were not, but that was pretty rare among the people we worked
with. Harold Short, of course, was very much interested in trying to find a way to
develop a field that had an academic or a research agenda, but wasn't always run in
the conventional academic fashion. The department started off trying to find ways
to operate outside of the academic mainstream but connected with it too and I think
it's been a real struggle. And we're now becoming normalised. The moment at
which it became possible for me to become an academic was the moment when that
vision began to obviously disappear because I could have continued doing most of
what I do without being on an academic contract too. I mean, I've done it for years
after all. But the College wanted us to be official, nowadays it's the academics and
the non-academics. That wasn't so clearly the case when I was first here.

JN Do you think it's a missed opportunity?

JB I think that it shuts off certain types of discourse and certain types of possibilities. The piece I wrote for Harold's Festschrift tries to describe how I thought CCH
was operating under Harold's direction, how I thought non-academics like me were
operating and the possibilities that existed for their intellectual development and
how universities had to find some way of respecting and fostering intellectual work
that wasn't conventionally academic. I think Harold was exploring that in how he
ran King's CCH (see Bradley 2011). But that's no longer possible to do.

JN No, I suppose, not with the REF[7] and …

JB Exactly. I filed for the RAE[8] as a developer last time but I wouldn't have been
able to this time. So, there you are!

JN The final question from my side is about the participation of women in the field,
your impression of how many women there have been or how well represented
women have been and how that might have changed.

JB It's so obvious that academia in general has missed their potential for so long. I
don't think we've got it completely solved, even within our Department. Although I
think there's still old white guys all over the place, many of our newer academic
people are younger for one thing, that's bound to help, and I think we're much more
gender balanced now, thank goodness. Long overdue!

---

[7] The Research Evaluation Framework (REF) is the 'system for assessing the quality of research in
UK higher education institutions' see http://www.ref.ac.uk/.

[8] The Research Assessment Exercise (RAE) was the precursor of the REF. It was introduced in
1986 as 'an explicit and formalised assessment process of the quality of research'. See http://www.
rae.ac.uk/aboutus/history.asp.

JN Are there any points that I didn't bring up that you wanted to mention from your notes?

JB We didn't say a lot about the change when I came here and what a different sort of world it was.

JN It would be good if you would touch on that if you don't mind?

JB Sure. My post here was originally part of the computer centre. Harold Short's team was still part of the computer centre in those days at King's. Originally, my post was partly for the School of Law and partly for the Humanities School. It was very much a techie post, you know, setting up technology to serve the academic interests of Humanists and the academics in the Law School.

So I was much involved in building websites in the early days and there was not much scope for my own particular interests; but, Harold had a broader vision. He just had to take positions as they were. So it became evident that the way forward for me was to connect into the various types of project work that were going on. Much of that work had a quite different technical agenda to what I'd worked on up until then. The earliest project I became significantly involved in was the Prosopography of the Byzantine Empire,[9] which was already well-developed by the time I came to King's. It was being created on a mainframe and it was using relational databases for data storage. The design was already essentially finished and there was a change of technology shortly after I came but I was not significantly involved in that.

What I was involved in for that project was thinking about how to publish the results. You had a very "user unfriendly" interaction environment, non-web-based for the database and it clearly wasn't practical to publish the material that way. And so my original work was to think about how you could publish this. It became evident to me that you could take all the data and create a vast number of fixed web-pages. A vast number for those days (they all fit on a CD now) but we managed to squeeze them all on to a CD and we took the data from the database and transformed them into a bunch of tightly interconnected webpages. And that's how the thing was published in the end, so my contribution was primarily thinking about that.[10] From there I became clearly involved as the developer for the technical side of these various projects, so from there it was a relatively short step to think about the Clergy of the Church of England (CCEd)[11] project and eventually the Prosopography of Anglo Saxon England (PASE) project.[12] I became also involved partly when the design work was already done around the CRSBI (Romanesque Sculpture) project and CVMA (Corpus Vitrearum Medii Aevi), the Stained Glass project.[13] I was involved

---

[9] See http://blog.pbw.cch.kcl.ac.uk/.

[10] For a description of the PBE work referred to here see: http://www.pbe.kcl.ac.uk.

[11] See http://theclergydatabase.org.uk/.

[12] See http://www.pase.ac.uk/index.html.

[13] See http://www.cvma.ac.uk/index.html.

in them technically in the early days and so my work was centred around web publishing and web application development. In those days it was very much a collaborative venture and my role was in developing the frameworks in which this stuff could be published. When I was first here I was keen on exploring the potential for Linux and so I was given a new desktop machine to work on, which was my official work machine. But the old one was still there, so I turned it into a Linux machine and set up a Linux web server on it and explored all that. I think I got Harold to see the potential of that because we really didn't have a place for looking at that sort of technology at the time. I thought I might be able to continue to work on TACT because I was still interested in TACT, but it became very obvious that, for a complicated set of reasons, some of them political, that was not going to be possible. So those sort of interests came back to me as personal interests later on as I gradually found that I had some liberty to explore them. But my early work was all heavily web application development really.

JN And what about the differences in the work cultures?

JB By the time I had left Toronto I had been given the responsibility of managing the media centre. So, I was responsible for the people who rolled the trolleys around and set up the overhead projectors in the rooms. This was deeply uninteresting to me. My job had been gradually dripping away into the management direction. The UTCS senior management couldn't figure out what I was actually good at and this was their best effort. So coming here was an enormous liberation. I wouldn't have come if my work in Toronto had not been continuing as it had. I was not interested in management and it was very obvious I was not going to be a manager and that's been confirmed over the years since.

I saw the post at KCL over the internet. Willard McCarty had come the year before and I was deeply envious of his having left Toronto with, at that time, its lack of vision about what the potential of computing was. To come to a place where there was obviously potential and real interest in Humanities Computing … And I was obviously interested in that, at least from the text analysis perspective. I mean, I was really keen to get back to that and I thought I was going to when I came here first, and although it didn't turn out to be in my work here, this other work was really interesting too, as it turned out. So I felt enormously liberated and I was enormously thankful that I got the opportunity to do it. I applied to the post and Harold Short found a way of making it possible. I mean it was quite a thing, if you think about it. To hire someone from across the ocean for what was a non-academic junior post was quite extraordinary, I think!

JN And so you didn't look back since?

JB No, I've never regretted it. I mean Toronto had many good things and I'm not by any means denigrating it as an academic institution or anything like that. But for me personally, it didn't know what to do at that time. I think it's part of the North American culture problem that there's the academics who the place is for and the non-academics who are just there to serve them and that's the only vision that there is. And I think we're going that way here in the UK too, to some extent. There was the loss of that third classification for posts, 'academic-related' about 10 years ago and its continuing still today. But at that time, when I came here that was not yet in place. King's didn't have such a clear-headed view of who was an academic and who wasn't, so I really was privileged to come here, I have no doubt about that.

References

Barnet, B. (2013). *Memory machines: The evolution of Hypertext*. London/New York: Anthem Press.

Bradley, J. (1989). *TACT user's guide: Version 1.1*. Toronto: University of Toronto.

Bradley, J. (2011). No job for techies: Technical contributions to research in the Digital Humanities. In M. Deegan & W. McCarty (Eds.), *Collaborative research in the digital humanities* (pp. 11–26). Surrey/Burlington: Ashgate Publishing.

Bradley, J., & Rockwell, G. (1994). *What scientific visualization teaches us about text analysis*. In ALLC/ACH conference. Paris Sorbonne.

Doug Engelbart Institute. (n.d.). *Doug's 1968 demo*. Doug Engelbart Institute. Available at: http://www.dougengelbart.org/firsts/dougs-1968-demo.html. Accessed 22 July 2015.

Engelbart, D. C. (1962). *Augmenting human intellect: A conceptual framework*. Menlo Park: Stanford Research Institute. Available at: http://www.dougengelbart.org/pubs/papers/scanned/Doug_Engelbart-AugmentingHumanIntellect.pdf.

Gouglas, S. et al. (2013). Before the beginning: The formation of Humanities Computing as a discipline in Canada. *Digital Studies / Le champ numérique, 3*(1). Available at: http://www.digitalstudies.org/ojs/index.php/digital_studies/article/view/214.

Hockey, S. M., & Ide, N. (Eds.). (1996). *Research in Humanities Computing: Selected papers from the 1992 ALLC/ACH conference, Christ church, Oxford, April 1992*. Oxford: Clarendon Press.

Hockey, S. M., Ide, N., & Lancashire, I. (1991). *Selected papers from the ALLC/ACH conference, Toronto, June 1989*. Oxford: Clarendon Press.

McCarty, W. (2014). Getting there from here: Remembering the future of Digital Humanities (Roberto Busa Award lecture 2013). *Literary and Linguistic Computing, 29*(3), 283–306.

Oakman, R. (Ed.). (1987). *Proceedings of the eighth international conference on computers and the humanities*. Dordrecht: Kluwer.

Rockwell, G. et al. (2012). Trading stories: An oral history conversation between Geoffrey Rockwell and Julianne Nyhan. *Digital Humanities Quarterly, 6*(3). Available at: http://www.digitalhumanities.org/dhq/vol/6/3/000135/000135.html. Accessed 10 Mar 2015.

Open Access This chapter is distributed under the terms of the Creative Commons Attribution-Noncommercial 2.5 License (http://creativecommons.org/licenses/by-nc/2.5/) which permits any noncommercial use, distribution, and reproduction in any medium, provided the original author(s) and source are credited.

The images or other third party material in this chapter are included in the work's Creative Commons license, unless indicated otherwise in the credit line; if such material is not included in the work's Creative Commons license and the respective action is not permitted by statutory regulation, users will need to obtain permission from the license holder to duplicate, adapt or reproduce the material.

Chapter 15
Moderate Expectations, Tolerable Disappointments: Claus Huitfeldt and Julianne Nyhan

Abstract This interview was conducted on 11 July at the 2014 Digital Humanities Conference, Lausanne, Switzerland. Huitfeldt recounts that he first encountered computing at the beginning of the 1980s via the Institute of Continental Shelf Research when he was a Philosophy student at the University of Trondheim. However, it was in connection with a Humanities project on the writings of Wittgenstein that he learned to programme. When that project closed he worked as a computing consultant in the Norwegian Computing Center for the Humanities and in 1990 he established a new project called the 'Wittgenstein Archives', which aimed to prepare and publish a machine-readable version of Wittgenstein's *Nachlass*. Here he discusses the context in which he began working on the encoding scheme (A Multi-Element Code System) that he developed for that project. The influence of MECS went beyond the Wittgenstein Archives. According to Ore (2014) 'when XML itself was under development, the idea of well-formed documents (as different from documents valid according to a DTD or schema) was taken into XML from MECS'. In addition to discussing matters like the trajectory of DH research and his early encounters with the conference community he also discusses some of the fundamental issues that interest him like the role of technology in relation to the written word and the lack of engagement of the Philosophy community with such questions. Ultimately he concludes that he does not view DH as a discipline, but rather as a reconfiguration of the academic landscape as a result of the convergence of tools and methods within and between the Humanities and other disciplines.

Biography

Claus Huitfeldt was born in Norway in 1957. He is Associate Professor of Philosophy and Vice Dean for Education and Internationalisation at the University of Bergen. He graduated from the University of Trondheim with a dissertation on transcendental arguments in 1984. From 1985 to 1989 he worked at the Norwegian Computing Center for the Humanities, in 1990 he became Director of the Wittgenstein Archives at the University of Bergen and held various other roles at the University before becoming Associate Professor in 1994. In addition to his work on

© The Author(s) 2016
J. Nyhan, A. Flinn, *Computation and the Humanities*, Springer Series on Cultural Computing, DOI 10.1007/978-3-319-20170-2_15

Wittgenstein sources he has published widely on text encoding, text technology and textual scholarship.

Interview

JN What is your earliest memory, in any context, of encountering computing or computing technology?

CH I remember that very well, that was in the very early 1980s, '80 or '81, perhaps. I was a Philosophy student at the University of Trondheim, Norway and across the corridor was the Institute of Continental Shelf Research. They had computer terminals that were accessible to all students, thus also to us. Not many students of Humanities were very interested, but since it was across the corridor and I had learned from somewhere that you could use these things as typewriters, I sat down by a terminal and somebody came along and taught me how to use it. It was a DEC [Digital Equipment Corporation] machine with the VAX/VMS operating system which had a very good text editor. So I learned to use that. It had formatting commands in the old-fashioned way, where if you wanted to add some formatting to your document you put a line-break, a full-stop, and a code into it. For example, if you wanted to italicise a word, it was a line break, a full stop, an 'i', the word; then new line etc. I also learned to use macros, and had my first experience of writing a log-in script which contained the command 'log out', so that I was logged out immediately as soon as I logged on! Very useful experience. That was my first experience with computers.

JN And how did you encounter the use of computers in Philosophy then? How did you start having ideas about the use of computing in this context?

CH Well, first of all I wrote my dissertation with computers, but that was not really computation in Philosophy. My first encounter was when I was hired to work on a project called the Norwegian Wittgenstein Project, which was a co-operation between the Philosophy Departments at the (then four) universities of Norway. They had acquired a microfilm copy of Wittgenstein's writings. Finding things on a microfilm is difficult, so they got the idea that they should index entries to the microfilm by keywords. It turned out to be so hard for them to agree on keywords that they realised, "we might as well try and transcribe the parts we're interested in". And I was hired to transcribe Wittgenstein's writings. At that time the transcription was done on a typewriter, and then it was OCR-read off site somewhere. But gradually, since I had learned to use text processing, we typed it directly into the machine, which was wonderful.

JN It's astonishing to think about those iterations that one almost takes for granted! What would have been your first encounter with the conference community we see here? How did you first encounter that wider picture?

CH Later I was fortunate to get the job as the leader of the Norwegian Wittgenstein project. They had already started using some kind of text encoding and had written software for doing things with the stuff. It wasn't finished, so I had to learn programming languages. So I learned to program, and with good help from colleagues at the Norwegian Computing Center for the Humanities, I managed to get into the matter.

JN Did you take formal training?

CH No formal training.

JN And how did you go about the process of learning programming?

CH Well, by then I had moved to Bergen, and the project was situated in the Norwegian Computing Center for the Humanities, which had been established already in 1972 in Bergen (see Ore 2014). And they had a staff of people who were trained in applying computing to Humanities, for example. I never had any formal training but I was introduced to it by a colleague and then started trying to do things. In general I found that it was easy to learn these things if you knew exactly what you wanted to do. So, if you take formal training with many other students, you learn general stuff and you learn some specifics, but it's not targeted directly to your own needs. I was very clear about exactly what I wanted to do. I wanted to parse this encoding, I wanted to check errors, I wanted to be able to index and to do retrieval and all these things. I think it was the best way, back then at least, to learn programming.

JN So I guess now might be a good time to ask about the people who particularly influenced you, and how and why. And that can be from any of the academic fields.

CH In the beginning, that would be hard to say as so many people were involved. But the Director of the computing center, Lars H. Hauge, gave me the self-confidence I needed. Lars G. Johnsen (now at the National Library in Oslo), Espen S. Ore (now at the University of Oslo) and Øystein Reigem (now at Uni Computing, Bergen) were particularly helpful in introducing me to programming.

Later in the 1980s, I got in touch with the Text Encoding Initiative, and started to take part in its working group meetings and conferences. There were lots of people I learned from there. Although it's hard to mention any one in particular at that time, encounters and discussions with people like Michael-Sperberg McQueen (see Chap. 12), Dino Buzzetti, Ellie Myllonas, Julia Flanders, Allen Renear, Manfred Thaller (see Chap. 13), Susan Hockey (see Chap. 6), David Durand, Steve DeRose, Peter

Robinson and Lou Burnard are some of the names that stand out as particularly helpful.

It was also through the Text Encoding Initiative that I got to know Michael Sperberg-McQueen, with whom I have had a close cooperation ever since, later to be joined by Yves Marcoux from the University of Montreal.

JN And what about the Wittgenstein project? At what point did you move away from that?

CH Much later. This first project was closed because of lack of clarity about copyright and some other matters. So then I had to earn my living as a computing consultant of sorts at the Norwegian Centre for Computing in the Humanities. There I did all sorts of things such as travelling around the world and preaching the holy gospel of optical storage media, which many people thought to be the future of computing etc. That turned out not to be the case, but anyhow. At the same time I was unhappy about the fate of the Norwegian Wittgenstein Project that I had been working on because we had, after all, produced a lot of material and because of the situation with copyright etc, not only could we not continue the work, we were not even allowed to give access to the work to anyone else. I thought it was just too bad. So I worked very hard on establishing a new project, called the Wittgenstein Archives at the University of Bergen.[1] That project started in 1990, based on an understanding with the Wittgenstein Trustees

Wittgenstein had assigned the copyright to his writings to colleagues in Philosophy in England and Finland. We had an agreement with them, and the agreement allowed us to produce what was called a machine-readable version of the Wittgenstein *Nachlass*,[2] and to publish it in electronic form, but very clearly not to produce anything in book form. And then we got support from the University of Bergen and worked on that for 10 years. We spent exactly 10 years transcribing and finishing all the 20,000 pages of Wittgenstein's *Nachlass* and published them with Oxford University Press.[3]

JN Why was it that the *Nachlass* couldn't be published as a book but could be published online? What was the thinking there?

CH It was made very clear that we did not have the right to a book publication, partly because there was another project going on towards that aim, and partly

---

[1] See: http://wab.uib.no/1990-99/

[2] A *Nachlass* is a collection of papers such as correspondence, unpublished manuscripts etc. that remain after a scholar's death and that can form the basis of an archive.

[3] 'In cooperation with Oxford University Press, the Wittgenstein Archives published the entire *Nachlass* in four volumes as *Wittgenstein's Nachlass. The Bergen Electronic Edition*. Each volume contains two CD-ROMs, one with facsimiles and one with retrieval software and updated info-bases of the corresponding transcriptions' see: http://wab.uib.no/1990-99/. A text only version of the edition is available here: http://www.nlx.com/collections/124

because we did not want it. Personally, I didn't think that a book edition was a good idea anyhow, so I was not unhappy about that. But it was a lot of work because, you know, this was 1990, the World Wide Web did not exist and SGML had just been established as an ISO standard a few years before. The Text Encoding Initiative (TEI) had just begun working and there were no published TEI guidelines. We, or I, decided not to use SGML for a number of reasons. So I decided on a code system or markup language (A Multi-Element Code System (MECS)) especially for this (see Huitfeldt 1994), which meant that I had to develop all the software and this was a lot of work. You had to do everything, from programming to markup design and …

JN Was it chiefly the overlapping hierarchies[4] issue that led you to reject SGML or were there other factors also?

CH That was one factor. Another factor was very simply a trivial factor, namely that no software that I knew of at that time existed for doing the things that we wanted to do with the transcriptions that we produced. SGML was a very complex system, much more complex than XML (which of course, didn't exist at all at that time). So it had to do with overlapping hierarchies and that kind of thing but it also had to do with the concern that I felt that developing software for SGML would be much more difficult than developing software for a system that I had designed myself and, you know, that I could adapt so I had it all in my own control, so to speak. That was also a reason. I think if I had started such a project today I would not have done it that way, I would have probably have used XML, but it was a very different situation. So we spent 10 years on this and then we published the entire collected works on CD at Oxford University Press. And I thought, by then, that this has been a very interesting and wonderful time. I was thankful that I had had the chance to do this work. But 15 years with Wittgenstein – it was time to do something else!

But the Wittgenstein Archive still exists, which is a little bit paradoxical, you might say. The whole reason for doing this work was to make the writings accessible so it would not be necessary for scholars to travel to see the originals in Cambridge, in the Austrian National Library and there are a couple of manuscripts in Canada as well, and now it is accessible electronically. But still people keep going to Bergen. I think it's simply because it has become a centre for Wittgenstein research and people travel there to see people, other people.

---

[4] Metamarkup languages like XML and SGML represent document structures using a tree-model that is hierarchical and requires properly nested structures. This can cause problems when XML and SGML is used to make texts that contain overlapping hierarchies machine readable, for example, when a paragraph spans a page break or enjambment in a poem. The MECS language used a non-SGML notation and permitted overlapping hierarchies (see Sperberg-McQueen and Huitfeldt 2004). An overview of present day XML- and non-XML-based 'workarounds' are set out in Chapter 20 of TEI P5 (TEI Consortium 2007).

Also I should say, if we had done this today, well even then, we wanted to make the source material freely available on the internet. But it was out of the question because the copyright holders did not want to let that happen. Because of the contract restraints it is still not possible although parts of the *Nachlass* is now available on the web.[5]

JN And did Wittgenstein himself leave those instructions about copyright?

CH No, he left no real instructions. He said in his will that he gave the copyright of all his unpublished manuscripts to the four people mentioned to publish and dispose of as they think fit. That was 1951.

JN Did MECS require a huge investment of your time?

CH It was a huge investment of my time, yes.

JN How was this funded and justified within the project? Were you quite free to use your time as you saw fit?

CH Yes, I was given a very free hand and that's one of the reasons why I'm thankful. I mean it was a lot of work to establish the project, lots of formalities and all that, but once it got started I was given a very free hand. That was very good.

JN So when you then moved on from the Wittgenstein project did you go straight to a professorship?

CH I became an Associate Professor of the Department of Philosophy in 1994 but, of course, I didn't really start working in a normal position in the Department until this project was finished in 2000. Actually, that's not true, for a couple of years after that I was Acting Director of the Humanities Computing Center in Bergen and that's when I decided that it was too much. That was fun too, lots of fun, but I had come to an age where I realised that if I continued with management work that I could never go back to do research. So I had to make a choice. In 2002 I picked up the position that I held at the Department of Philosophy since 1994. Since then I have been teaching Philosophy and been fortunate enough to be able to also teach Humanities Computing in Bergen.

JN What about the perceptions of other scholars and fellow Philosophers who weren't using computing or computers in their research? Could you reflect a bit on the types of reception that your work received from the broader community?

CH Within Philosophy, both locally, and as far as I could tell, globally, the application of computing to Philosophy was largely regarded with some scepticism.

---

[5] See http://tinyurl.com/p7frdhp

Sometimes you could encounter some hostility. But that was also at the time when there was a lot of talk about artificial intelligence in connection with computing (and I was not doing that kind of thing, of course). But Wittgenstein scholars regarded it with positive anticipation, at least those who wanted to have access to the material. There was a certain scepticism towards whether an electronic edition could ever substitute a real, critical publication in book form, but apart from that there was no problem.

JN How did you find the transition to the associate professor role?

CH Well I found that quite stimulating because, as I said, I had been so focused on the Wittgenstein edition for so many years that it was nice to be able to do something different and it was also very good for me to do Philosophy properly again. And there was some interest from students and other colleagues in trying to integrate this. My interest – even after having worked with Wittgenstein for such a long time – was not primarily Wittgenstein's Philosophy, it was the philosophical problems that could arise from aspects of the work that we were doing. I was interested in the problems of trying to represent a document in another form; the semantics of the whole operation; the kinds of cognitive processes that are involved and the criteria for judging etc; and the role of technology in relation to the written word. These were issues that interested me a lot, so we organised some seminars along those lines and that was quite interesting.

JN So when I do these interviews, people often reflect to me about their first engagement with the conference community and the type of society that they found there. Would you talk about that?

CH Yes, I was very struck by the fact that philosophers, with exceptions, but in general, were so completely unconcerned about the status of the text as an object of study. And, of course, text is not the object of study in Philosophy, but what is it? Whatever it is it is transmitted through text. I mean Philosophy is a discipline which is performed almost entirely in language: you talk, you listen, you read, you write. That's what you do as a philosopher. And then when faced with the fact that what they had been working with for years (a published edition of Wittgenstein's writings) had a problematic status in relation to what Wittgenstein actually wrote, that it had been heavily edited, that editors had selected passages and suppressed others etc, that was something that was completely unknown to them. And it seemed to me that it didn't concern most people and that there really was little interest. So that struck me as very paradoxical.

But then I found that this has to do with philosophical traditions too, mainly the English/American Analytic Philosophy which, to a large extent, is a systematic, problem-oriented discipline. The attitude is that the author is not of interest, it's the problems. If what Wittgenstein wrote was in some details different from what is actually being published, well, we can look at it and see if it gives us some new and interesting philosophical ideas. But what we are working on is the basis of the published texts, that's an independent object. Whereas the continental, especially the German tradition, historically had a lot of editorial works. So that made me aware of things I hadn't known. That was useful. That is the role of text technology in Philosophy itself.

But apart from that it's been one of my hobby horses or concerns. I still find it very puzzling that the research communities who one would expect to have the highest expertise about ways of working with texts have almost no role to play in the development of modern text technology. So, one of my hobby horses has always been that we as Humanities scholars should not sit there at the end of the production line being passive recipients of tools like text analysis or text editors and things like that. But it doesn't seem to have changed much, I mean, of course, Humanities scholars develop their own tools for doing their own research. But I don't know that there are many or any commercially successful products in which experts from the field of Philology have had any leading hand in designing the basic representational structures, so that still puzzles me.

JN I also wanted to ask about the nature of the community that you encountered. People often say to me that the Humanities Computing community tended to be very welcoming and very open (some have said excessively so), in contrast with their home discipline, which could be characterised by territorial behaviour at conferences and so on. Would you agree or disagree? What is your opinion on that?

CH I haven't thought so much about that but yes, I think it's true. I mean the project that I worked on for so many years (the Wittgenstein Archives) wasn't there primarily as a result of the connected pressure from the Department of Philosophy, so to speak. It came into being because there were a few enthusiasts and some of them were very good at manoeuvring in the university. Yes, so I guess I have the same experience, you might say, but it's never really struck me as a problem, in part because I have never really been able to relate to the idea of DH or Humanities Computing as some kind of discipline. I mean, it's natural, in a way, to give practical help if you are using the same tools in your work. Perhaps also because DH has not been so established academically there is little of the kind of competition that you find within the established disciplines. You know, if you have a good idea about something then you'd better write it up, lock it up in your drawers and don't mention it until you've got it published. I'm sure there's very little of that in this community.

JN So, it's fair to say that you don't see DH as a discipline but as a sort of convergence of interesting tools? In your time in the field, have you seen that change or go through different cycles of development?

CH Yes, and through the years there has been an ongoing and endless discussion about DH, its status and identity and all that. You know, that's not in a way so surprising because there is always also the endless debate of what the Humanities are and the crisis of the Humanities etc. When you've been around for a while you get used to that. The crisis cannot be a crisis because it's been going on for at least the 30 years that I have been in the Humanities. But at the same time, in the last few years there seems to be a larger emphasis not so much on the tools and methods, but on studies of ethical aspects and the consequences for society and culture of the introduction of new technology. I'm a little bit worried about that because, I mean, again it gives the Humanities a role in relation to technology as servants or as users. Very often, as soon as there is a question of involving Humanities in some kind of non-core Humanities activity we are set to look at the cultural consequences and the ethical aspects. Of course, as Humanists we can do that but we can do much more, we can contribute to the development of the technology itself and be there in the process of deciding what useful aims to work for etc are. I think that's going in the wrong direction now. That worries me a little bit.

JN The final question is about any disappointments you might have about the limitations of computing, either in relation to Wittgenstein or Philosophy in general, I guess, or your area of interest?

CH Disappointments? No, I don't really think so because I have never had such high expectations. I mean, you used computers to collect data, to analyse data, to massage them in various ways. We have never, or at least I have never had high hopes in terms of computer-supported philosophical analysis. What would that be? No! So I'm fortunate, not too high expectations and no disappointments!

References

Huitfeldt, C. (1994). Multi-dimensional texts in a one-dimensional medium. *Computers and the Humanities, 28*(4–5), 235–241.

Ore, E. (2014). Some thoughts on Digital Humanities in Norway. *H-Soz-Kult*. Available at http://www.hsozkult.de/debate/id/diskussionen-2442. Accessed 24 July 2015.

Sperberg-McQueen, M. & Huitfeldt. C. (2004). GODDAG: A data structure for overlapping hierarchies. In P. King, & E. V. Munson (Eds.), *Digital documents: Systems and principles* (pp. 139–160). Berlin/Heidelberg: Springer. http://link.springer.com/chapter/10.1007/978-3-540-39916-2_12

TEI Consortium. (2007). *Guidelines for electronic text encoding and interchange: TEI P5*. Chicago/Oxford: Text Encoding Initiative. http://www.tei-c.org/release/doc/tei-p5-doc/en/html/index.html

Open Access This chapter is distributed under the terms of the Creative Commons Attribution-Noncommercial 2.5 License (http://creativecommons.org/licenses/by-nc/2.5/) which permits any noncommercial use, distribution, and reproduction in any medium, provided the original author(s) and source are credited.

The images or other third party material in this chapter are included in the work's Creative Commons license, unless indicated otherwise in the credit line; if such material is not included in the work's Creative Commons license and the respective action is not permitted by statutory regulation, users will need to obtain permission from the license holder to duplicate, adapt or reproduce the material.

Chapter 16
So, Into the Chopper It Went: Gabriel Egan and Julianne Nyhan

Abstract This interview took place at the AHRC-organised Digital Transformations Moot held in London, UK on 19 November 2012. In it Egan recalls his earliest encounters with computing when he was a schoolboy along with some memories of how computers were represented in science fiction novels, TV programmes and advertising. His first job, at the age of 17, was as a Mainframe Computer Operator. He continued to work in this sector throughout the 1980s but by the end of the decade he recognised that such roles would inevitably disappear. In 1990 he returned to university where he completed a BA, MA and PhD over the next 7 years. He recalls his shock upon returning to university as he realised how little use was then made of computers in English Studies. Nevertheless, he bought a relatively cheap, second-hand Sinclair Z88 and took all his notes on it. Later he also digitised his library of 3000 books, destroying their hard copy versions in the process. The interview contains a host of reflections about the differences that computing techniques and resources have made to Shakespeare Studies over the past years, along with insightful observations about the contributions and limitations of DH. In this interview Egan describes himself as a 'would be Digital Humanist'; indeed, it is the landscape that he describes from this vantage point that makes his interview so interesting and useful.

Biography

Gabriel Egan was born in 1965 in London. He is Professor of Shakespeare Studies at De Monfort University, Leicester, UK. He researches and teaches on Shakespeare, theatre history from 1,500 to 1,700, book printing and publishing from 1,500 to 1,700 and critical theory (especially Marxism and ecocriticism). He has been Director of the Centre for Textual Studies since 2012. He also serves on various external committees, for example, he has chaired the Joint Information Systems Committee (JISC) Historic Books Advisory Board since 2011. This group serves to guide development of JISC's new digital archive of 300,000 books published in England up to 1,800. He is Principal Investigator of the 2-year project "Shakespearean London Theatres (ShaLT)" which is a collaboration with the Victoria & Albert Museum and has made available a large collection of digital materials including an

© The Author(s) 2016
J. Nyhan, A. Flinn, *Computation and the Humanities*, Springer Series on
Cultural Computing, DOI 10.1007/978-3-319-20170-2_16

interactive map of early modern London, a smartphone app and a hour of documentary film, collectively called Shakespearean London Theatres. In 2014 he was awarded a National Teaching Fellowships by the Higher Education Academy in recognition of excellence in teaching and learning. His recent publications include *Green Shakespeare: from Ecopolitics to Ecocriticism* (Egan 2006), *The Struggle for Shakespeare's Text: Twentieth-Century Editorial Theory and Practice* (Egan 2013) and he is a General Editor of the New Oxford Shakespeare Complete Works that will appear in 2016.

Interview

JN I want to begin by asking you about your earliest memory of encountering computer technology

GE My very earliest memory is from sometime in the 1970s and computers were in films and on television. I'm the youngest of eight children and my elder siblings were mostly technologically mad and excited by computers especially. There were three boys older than me in my family. That's where I *saw* computers.

The first actual hands-on encounter was when I took Computer Science, as it used to be, when there were still O-levels[1] in the late 1970s. We had a Teletype machine with an acoustic coupler and a modem. You would call up the local polytechnic and when you got the connect tone you put the handset into this fur-lined box, which connected the Teletype to the mainframe. You would write your programs in BASIC and this was an interactive service. Before that it had all been batch-wise. That is, you wrote your program on a form and it was mailed to the computer centre at the polytechnic. It was run and you were sent the results as a paper printout. So it was a new leap forward to have Teletype as an interactive service and I used that throughout my O-level.

And then, my O-level Physics teacher at school got hold of an Acorn System 1, a micro-processor kit, and he and his A-level students[2] had to build the kit. They lost interest once they built it and it worked and it switched on. I wanted to do the programming and I learnt assembly language programing from the handbook that came with this little £80 kit. It was a single 6502 microprocessor with a full 1 k of RAM and I taught myself programming that way.

Then I went through the usual 1980s route of having a Sinclair Spectrum and Commodore 64 computer. I left school at 16 and did a TOPS (Training Opportunities Scheme) training course, which was a way of getting commercial training for young

---

[1] O-levels were examinations taken by children in the United Kingdom (except Scotland) between the ages of 14 and 16. They were later replaced by GCSE examinations.

[2] A-level is the school leaving examination taken by children in the United Kingdom (except Scotland).

people in the early 1980s. I took a TOPS course in Computer Operating, so I ended up at the age of 17 as a Mainframe Computer Operator, which in those days really was about staying up all night and changing the tapes whenever the machine wanted a new tape at 3:30 am. Someone had to be there to put the correct tape up on the machine or to put the right deck of punch cards in to the hopper. It was still clunky punch cards, huge disc packs and exchangeable discs. The discs were old fashioned. You see them in the films, they look like a big washing machine: someone lifts the lid, puts a disc pack in, closes the lid down, and that's another 70 MB of storage the machine's got.

So I worked as a Mainframe Computer Operator from 1982 to 1988 and by the end of the decade I could see this job disappearing. It was very clear that microprocessors were going to be taking over from mainframe operations. Large rooms full of servers that don't need much physical attention were taking over the old-fashioned mainframes that had exchangeable discs and tapes. I tried to get into helpdesk operations, into the more customer-orientated side of the work, but by the late 1980s I figured I'd actually chosen the wrong career all together. So, I went back to school and got my A-levels, and then just carried on with a BA, MA, PhD and didn't stop for 9 years. Luckily I was funded all the way through, and came out, at the age of 32 with a PhD. But for all that time I was interested in computer applications for the work I was doing on literary texts.

JN: I thought it was interesting that you mentioned depictions of computers in the 1970s in films and literature. Can you reflect on that a little?

GE The philosophical side of it was things like HAL in Kubrick's Space Odyssey, the whole question about machines becoming intelligent and then disobedient because they were intelligent. I remember that sort of recurring theme of some dystopian and science fiction films. Yeah, computers in Star Trek, computers in that sort of vaguely science fiction stuff appealed to me as a child, as it did to my elder brothers and sisters. That's how I got into to it. My family had a large science fiction collection of books in the house.

JN: What about depictions of computers in the general media at the time, did they also have a sort of dystopian and foreboding element? Or was it all revolutionary …

GE: I'm trying to remember actually. You'd get the occasional piece on the TV program Nationwide, some talk about the newest computer installation somewhere. It would be something like, you know, all the traffic lights now in Reading are controlled by this new computer centre and there'd be a picture of a room full of white boxes with flashing lights and people very smartly dressed.

In fact, I showed some slides on this to a group recently that got a huge laugh out of it. I was showing them adverts from the 1970s for why you should buy the new Honeywell or the new ICL computer. There was a picture of a new computer room, beautifully clean and white, with very smartly dressed people, usually women, who would be moving between the machines and doing the work. And then I cut to an actual picture that I'd taken of the computer room that I worked in, which, of course, was extremely dirty and full of very scruffy people. It was overcrowded – in the advert the room was large and had white spaces between the boxes. There was the central processor here and 10 ft away was the disc drive, and it was all spacious and clean and white, it looked like a Scandinavian home. But cut to the computer rooms I worked in, which were basements, overcrowded with monitors and lots and lots of scraps of paper and dirt and boxes of pizza, and there's a large disjunction between the public perception of a computer room and the reality. I found this out quite early in my first job at the age of 17.

JN So your PhD, then, was English Literature?

GE Yes, I did a BA. I'd started but failed at A-levels aged 16–17, so at 23 I went back and got my A-levels in English Literature and History, did a BA in English Literature and an MA in Shakespeare Studies and a PhD in Shakespeare Studies.

JN Was it immediately obvious to you to apply computing to Shakespeare Studies?

GE As soon as I started to do my A-levels I thought "this is ridiculous". I remember sitting there, I had some Chaucer homework so I needed to have open a dictionary, a guide to Middle English and my book. I had three books open on the bed and was trying to keep my place in all three of them. I remember thinking "this should be computerized, I should be able to look up these words." I was used to interrogating databases for work and it seemed the Humanities were miles, decades, behind. There was faffing around with all these books.

So I very quickly got computerized: I mean I did my BA entirely on a computer. By which I mean I took no paper notes of any kind whatsoever. I had a thing called a Sinclair Z88. It's a thing about the size of an A4 sheet of paper, with a little six line display at the top and a rubber QWERTY keyboard and it ran for day on 4 double AA batteries. I could take notes on it and at the end of the day (you plug it in through a standard serial port) you could squirt the entire text down to your PC. So I sat in my lectures with this thing called a Z88.

JN What date was this roughly?

GE 1990. I remember people saying "ooh he is very rich because he's got a laptop". But I got this thing second-hand for £50 and it was just for taking a day's worth of notes. When I worked on books I found other people would annotate the margins of the books and I never did that. I'd have the book open, I'd take notes and I'd type into the computer. I still have those notes, I mean I still have everything I ever did for my BA in the early 1990s, because I kept no paper. I was paperless from the start. Well, the only paper I had was books. Back then, you still had to have the books. But I kept none of my own files on paper.

What I found about 7 or 8 years ago was that I could actually transfer all my existing books to computer as well. So I digitised all of my several thousand books and destroyed them in the process, but that was okay. So it was possible, even then, to do all your BA all electronically.

I found exams were part of my assessment requirements for the BA, and I did the first year exams writing by hand. But I do actually have a hand injury and I really can't write for very long. I had done very well in my essays but I did very poorly in the 3 hour exam and I asked if in future I could do my exam on a computer because of this disability. The university agreed and my grades shot up. I had no advantage – there wasn't even a spell check or anything. It was just a basic text editor. So it wasn't that I started Humanities and then applied the digital to it. They started simultaneously for me and I didn't think it was feasible to do a degree if it couldn't all be computerized.

I think I've had a phobia against paper right from the start. It's a diabolically bad medium for storing human knowledge in my view and I say that as a book historian. I'm used to that technological revolution, the Gutenberg revolution, and our revolution. The bit in-between doesn't much interest me.

JN How, what was it that caused you to destroy the books when you were digitising them? Did you use the sheet feeder?

GE Yeah, the fast way to do it is to cut the spine off so you got a bundle of loose leaves and then put them through a sheet feeding scanner. I did try cutting a few spines myself and I still do. If I get a new book I just cut the spine off using an office guillotine, the old fashioned kind with the big arm that comes down (not those silly roller ones, they don't work) you need a big, powerful one. But for doing the 3000 books I found a local printing shop that had an electrically powered guillotine and they would machine the spines off for me for 50p a go. So, I would bring them a box of 100 and they'd return them to me neatly wrapped up as a bundle of loose leaves and then into the sheet feeding scanner they went.

JN And do you feel no attachment or sentimentality for the materiality of the book or the book as artistic object?

GE Well I didn't have any rare books. So no, these were just functional. I have had one or two tricky cases. For example, I've got a copy of the Norton facsimile of the First Folio of Shakespeare (Hinman 1968). Its only 1968 but the copy I've got I was given by my PhD supervisor, Stanley Wells.[3] It was the one he used when he was making the Oxford Shakespeare edition of 1986, which was a big-deal edition (he was the main Editor; see Wells et al. 1986). I felt a little bad chopping it up. But I thought "I want this thing, I need it, and I want to have it with me! I want to have it everywhere I go". So, into the chopper it went.

---

[3] 'Born in 1930, Stanley Wells is a renowned authority on Shakespeare and other writers of his time'. See http://literature.britishcouncil.org/stanley-wells

I haven't done that with anything sixteenth or seventeenth century; but, I think, on principle, I would be obliged to. I think our fetish for paper is terribly harmful.

JN Do you feel any fetish for the digital? Would you be just as willing to take the digitised forms and put them into, I don't know, whatever comes next? Is the medium irrelevant to you?

GE Yes! Yes that's important, thank you, medium is irrelevant. I think Martin McLuhan's had a lot to answer for with such old nonsense about the medium being the message. We read for the content mainly. And I say this as I actually teach students how to print on a sixteenth century hand press. The medium does shape but you've always got to remember that it's not about the medium. The printers of Shakespeare's time didn't want to impose themselves upon the works. When they did their jobs to the best of their ability they disappeared from the picture. You don't feel you're reading a book when it's working properly. I think Book History is taking a detour into an intellectual dead-end where people think that the making of a book is somehow a collaborative act involving not only the author but the scribe and the compositor and the publisher and everyone else. I think, ideally, when that system works properly, everyone gets out of the way of the author essentially.

What we really want is a totally transparent medium. Digital is much better for that than paper. Right now, I'm looking at a piece of paper on the table. That's great if your eyesight can accommodate that size, but I might need to have it three times the size, and in digital I can just select the size of the type and I think that's very important. Or I may need to hear it, in digital I can just listen to the text being read. So, I've got a bit of a bee in my bonnet about the limitations of the printed book. People always say "ooh, it's a wonderful technology, the printed book, you know, it doesn't need any power". And you realize, it's not a technology. The Egyptians had it down once they'd got away from the scroll and turned to the codex. We've moved on since then.

JN Were you unusual among your contemporaries (your fellow students or those who were teaching you)?

GE You mean into digital stuff?

JN Yes, to the extent that you were.

GE: Yeah, yeah. When I was an undergraduate sitting in my first lecture, in 1990 with a Z88, I remember thinking "in 5 years' time they'll all be doing this". And to my horror, in 5 years' time they weren't all doing this. In fact, even now, it is not common to go to a lecture hall, in my area at least, English Studies, and find students using laptops. They will be sitting there, with their phones in their hands, they may be updating their Facebook status or texting each other, but they are not using computers as a tool for their learning very much. Which really surprised me, because

I figured I was 5 years ahead of the curve. But I was 20 years ahead. Compared to my contemporaries, yeah, I used computers much more than anybody else.

Some made it quite clear they felt they resented the intrusion of computers into English Studies, some people still do actually, there is still a bit of that about. But I was just ahead of my fellow students and doing things like going into the library to find out what digital resources they had. My fellow students didn't know that in 1989 the *Oxford English Dictionary* (OED) was published for the first time on CD-ROM, so you could search for words by their meaning, which is the first time you could ever do that. Or that you could find indexes of the contents of journal articles that were available as databases, actually on CD-ROMS back then. So yeah, I was ahead of my fellow students just for that reason.

I had a friend called Peter White when I was doing my Master's degree in Stratford-Upon-Avon. White had bought with him his printed concordance to Shakespeare. I had my digital text of, well, the Oxford edition digitised and my big desktop computer. We got into big debate, in front of other people, about the relative merits of the printed concordance and the computer version. He said he could beat me in any search for given words (where does the word 'blue' come within five words of 'box' in Shakespeare?) and he raced me. We had a formally adjudicated race, him with the Bartlett concordance and me with my computer. We had to find 10 or 20 things in Shakespeare and come back immediately by saying "that's Julius line one, act 2, scene X". He won. He was very proud of having won but I pointed out to him that this machine I'm sitting here with will be twice as fast next year, and twice as fast again the year after. So, you know, pretty soon I'm going to beat you at this, and obviously the future is that these machines are going to get much, much faster and the printed book isn't.

The irony is actually Peter then went on to be ProQuest's person in charge of EEBO (Early English Books online).[4] He became a digital convert a few years after that. I claim some credit for opening his eyes to the power of the computer in Humanities studies.

JN You mentioned those who felt that computing had no place in English Studies or the Humanities. Will you reflect further on this and also think about how that may have changed over the time?

GE Well, the first person who put it in to words for me actually was my wife, who I met about 20 years ago. She said that when she was doing her undergraduate degree in English at Queen's University Belfast she noted with disappointment that one by one, in different lecturer's and tutor's offices, the computer would appear on the desk. Basically, there had been a desk and papers and a typewriter and suddenly this new device started to appear, in the late 1980s early 1990s. Since then she has

---

[4] EEBO contains 'more than 125,000 titles listed in Pollard & Redgrave's *Short-Title Catalogue (1475–1640)* and Wing's *Short-Title Catalogue (1641–1700)* and their revised editions, as well as the *Thomason Tracts (1640–1661)* collection and the *Early English Books Tract Supplement*'. See http://eebo.chadwyck.com/home

herself become an academic expert in the use of computers in Literary Studies and finds others' Ludditism as annoying as I do.

I think it's largely because of people's abilities. People go into English Studies because they find particular things interesting and other things either not interesting or intimidating. People in English Studies do not tend to be into technology. By and large, they seem to be quite vocal about not being very good with computers and usually they say they're not very good with numbers. Those things tend to go together; they tend to think of computers as rather soulless beasts. This has all changed in the last, 15 years, 10 years I think, really. But back in the early 1990s, of course, most computers didn't have graphical user interfaces. They had a command line and green dots of phosphor. They were forbidding, formidable looking beasts; they weren't the very cuddly, round-edged devices we have now. They looked like they should be in a science fiction film and doing something super-technical in Engineering. They didn't look like artsy things; they didn't look like something a poet would want to engage with.

JN Even if it's almost funny, in a way, because a command line is text-based so you would think that a poet would somehow like all the words?

GE Well, I'd say that's it, isn't it? People don't seem to know that they are largely text-based, but they are indeed. Computer languages are languages. Although, I learnt, as I say, machine code programming, which was 0s and 1s, although the short cut was you didn't have to put in 0s and 1s, you'd use hexadecimals (base 16), but you were still putting in numbers. But, yes, by the 1990s we could have text-based machines. And that was the interesting thing to me: these machines could store the very material that I worked on. You could have the poem in there, and what is more, the thing that really grabbed me was I could have all my notes. I was aware there was virtually no chance I could memorise everything I was learning as an undergraduate or a graduate student. I knew if it sat in a cabinet somewhere it would never really get used. There was no way anybody could build a reasonable concordance to my notes, so the point of computerizing everything was that everything I'd ever thought was recoverable by me. And so the classic situation is, you know, you've read a book in which someone says something about Heidegger and hammers, and you know they occurred in the same sentence but you can't find it. Well, I knew I could search my own notes and find those two words collocating. So, it is as a prostheses, that I was most interested in these computers. I never understood this feeling that they were unpoetical because they were an aid to intelligence and I knew that I needed every aid I could get.

JN Why do you think that has changed over the last 15 years?

GE Regarding the anxiety about the machines? A lot of it is to do with Graphical User Interfaces, they just don't look quite as forbidding as they used to. They have got, I suppose, easier to use. It's also because they've become unavoidable in other areas of life, so people have just got used to the fact that a computer is just a machine

you have to engage with. You really can't go shopping or use the library these days
… and libraries are an important one, actually. Once the library catalogues forced
everyone to start using some aspect of computers I think the artsier people thought
"I'm not too bad at this. I'm able to use a keyboard and enter a search and get something meaningful back".

   In English Studies I think it's the digitisation of the library catalogue that has
been the big help. And the other thing is that all the machines just got nicer to use. I
remember, when I was an undergraduate, I often used to go to Senate House, in
Malet Street, in London, to use the library. I actually saw a very old scholar who was
trying to key in an enquiry in to the library catalogue and had obviously no training
at all and was told just to go and use it. He knew the thing that he wanted to search
for, and he said to me "I can see how to get those letters in, they're written on the
keys, but how do I get the space in between?" I said "well that long bar across the
bottom, that's the space bar." He had literally never used a keyboard, he'd obviously
given anything he wanted to publish to a secretary to type up and he actually had to
be told what the spacebar was. But once he was told he said "there's nothing written
on it, it makes sense that it's a blank. I see, thank you very much." And off he went
and I'm thinking "wow, imagine getting to the end of your career and encountering
the keyboard for the first time!" That's something you have to use or no-one's going
to do things for you. He also pointed out to me, which I thought was quite an
insightful thing, that the letters on the screen do not match those on the keyboard. I
said "yes they do", he replied "look". He pressed an upper case 'A' on the keyboard
and said "that's a lower case a on the screen". I said "oh you're right!" We've written
on the keyboard itself all the upper case letters but you have to hold the shift key
down to get those. The ones that appear on the screen aren't the same letter 'a' at all,
it's a totally different letter shape.

JN I never noticed that.

GE No… I hadn't until he'd pointed it out.

JN This question may be difficult for you to answer because you were already fully
proficient in computing and programing, but if you had wanted to take, say, a programming language during any stage of your BA, MA, or PhD, within the English
departments you were in, would that have been possible?

GE It would have been for me, only in so much as I would've known to go outside
the English department to get that training. But I was a little older as a student
because I spent 7 years straight after school working in computers. So I had that
advantage that I felt more entitled to go straight into some part of the university and
say "look I'm an English student but I'd like to learn about something else, what can
you do for me?" So I just had that slightly older person's confidence about presenting a lack in myself. And I did actually, there were actually things I needed to learn
about. I took training courses in the library, as a student, so that did happen.

JN So what about your first encounter with a Humanities Computing stroke DH project.

GE Well, there were resources I was starting to use, like the Modern Languages Association International Bibliography (MLA 2015), which were quite hard to access 10 to 15 years ago. So you have to go to the library – where they're usually only expecting researchers to want to know about these things – and say "look I know the MLA IB is available digitally, how can I get to it?" You'd have to get some librarian interested in your case and they'd show you. So do you mean engagement in that way? As a user? Or do you mean in development?

JN Yes, we could start thinking about your more hands on and research work with Computing in the Humanities and DH, that sort of an area, when did that begin? When did you encounter that?

GE I haven't yet very much encountered that and what I mean by that is, I'm still largely in the lone scholar model. I find the resources I want and I use them on my own. I haven't done a big DH research project that is specifically digital. What I mean is I've done collaborative research projects that had a digital component, but we weren't really inventing anything or doing anything new. So I haven't yet reached … I got some plans for a few.

JN One might ask how much of DH has really invented something new. I mean, for the most part, a huge amount of the work is applied concepts and technologies, isn't it?

GE Yes

JN Or at least, that would be definitely my view.

GE Well, my way into these things is to always try to be the expert speaking to those who are trying to do the project. For example, I mentioned Peter White from EEBO. Once EEBO became widely established across universities, I sort of made myself available to them and asked, if they were having events, would they be interested in having someone who is a very heavy user of the resource? So, I ended up on a few committees, that's been my way in. I advise quite a few bodies on what the scholar needs. In fact, on the university website that I run at De Monfort University, which is the Centre for Textual Studies,[5] I describe myself as a 'would-be Digital Humanist'.[6] I don't think I've done it yet. I haven't actually come up with anything. I've advised groups, I've advised various libraries on their digitisation projects, I advise the AHRC on how to evaluate the attempts to do certain things. So, if some-

---

[5] See: http://cts.dmu.ac.uk/
[6] See: http://cts.dmu.ac.uk/members + affiliates/index.html

one says I'm going to digitise this body of work, I help evaluate the technical side, but I haven't done my own project.

JN So, for that reason, you wouldn't necessarily see yourself as a Digital Humanist. Do you believe that a Digital Humanist must make …

GE [Laughter] – good one! Do they have to make? I've had that question before and yes! When I grow up I wanna be Ray Siemens (see Siemens et al. 2012)! Ray finished his PhD in 1997, same as me. We were in contact all the time and I watched Ray's career shoot up. He got made Professor very, very quickly, by his brilliance, by his knowledge, but, in particular, he gets things made, he gets things done. So, I think there is a perception that you have got to get something made.

That's interesting because it bares directly on my work at the moment, I'm Director of the Centre for Textual Studies at De Montfort University. I've taken over the centre after about 10 years of its existence and its main work in the past has been making stuff: "let's make an edition of Chaucer, of Virginia Woolfe's so and so". The creation of new editions has been perceived to be what Textual Studies is. A lot of what I do with computers is to analyse and to study, to say "look how we can use computers to address this particular research question". And the answer takes the form of something that is just a standard research answer, which comes out as a research paper, or maybe a book. What I do is about textual analysis rather than creation. So, I don't know, I would leave it to other people to decide whether a Digital Humanist has to create stuff, but I haven't created any stuff. And I still have a slight inferiority complex when I say Gabriel Egan is a would-be Digital Humanist cos he hasn't done that yet. You're not going to call that one? You're not going to say "YES Digital Humanists have to create stuff?"

JN I don't think they do, personally. I think that exactly the kind of work that you do is as important as the pure making. I suppose it is because I'm based in UCL's Information Studies Department that I believe the ability to communicate and understand needs and to translate between the domains is a crucial part of DH. I see that as DH too.

GE I think if it can't be done other than by digital means and it's in the Humanities, then its DH. Let me give you an example of that when I used to work at the Globe Theatre in London. At the Globe it was commonly said, by all sorts of people, that theatre had changed a lot in 400 years. It was said that in Shakespeare's time people talked about going to hear a play whereas we talk about going to see a play. I started there in 2000 and I thought is that actually true? I mean, can we actually just count how often they, in all their different writings from the period, used the different expressions 'hear a play', 'heard a play', 'hearing a play', 'hears a play' versus 'sees a play' 'seeing a play' 'saw a play', 'seeing a play' ?

So I went counting, just using Literature Online actually. I needed all the variant parts of speech amidst all the various possible verb-subject constructions, and I just did the counting. It took me a couple of weeks using Literature Online and it turned out that 92 % of the time they would say "going to see a play", exactly like us. They did not say what everyone said they said, which was they would have preferred to go 'hear a play'. They do exactly what we do, 'we're gonna go and see a play tonight', or 'I saw a play yesterday'. Actually, Shakespeare was the odd man out, Shakespeare spoke predominantly about hearing a play. So, what's happened is we've taken his locution as our norm for the period even though he is, in fact, quite anomalous, he's in that 8 % minority.

That was only possible because of Literature Online being available and search-able (this was before EEBO was searchable because of TCP). So I published that piece of work (Egan 2001) that couldn't be done, other than digitally. I think as a project it would have taken possibly a lifetime to do it on paper.

Personally, I always think that it can be a limitation of DH if people only focus on the making and they never actually go beyond it. I mean, the TEI is wonderful as it is, yet how many projects do you know out there who really used those TEI-encoded editions to answer a research question? There's a lot of moribund projects as well, things that were made for which no-one actually had a question that needed an answer.

JN So could you reflect on one or two more of those earlier DH encounters or projects say the committees that you advised on or the other early work that you did in that area?

GE I'm trying to think of them, the recent ones are more in my head. What's the sort of advice that I gave? I was on the JISC e-books project.[7] When the E-Books working group started I was, I think, one of only two academics on it. This is maybe 7 years ago when journal articles had gone digital, by and large. But no-one could see what monographs would do and whether they ought to go digital. So the e-book committee was about looking into that and the only thing I was able to do really, my only expertise was simply I was a Humanist who was ahead of the curve, as it were, because I'd gone digital with everything as soon as possible.

People would say things like "oh! of course nobody wants to read a book, all of a book on the screen". I'd say "I've been doing so for 15 years. In fact, I haven't read a book not on the screen for the last 10 years." Or, they would say "no-one wants a Shakespeare play on the screen". Actually, this reminds me of back in the early 1990s, for my MA in Shakespeare Studies I wanted to read one of Ben Jonson's plays like *Bartholomew Fair*. I found that the Oxford Text Archive[8] had a copy, but I had to ask the person who was curating the copy if I could have it. It was some-body called Hugh Craig (see Chap. 3), who I now know through the University of

---

[7] See JISC e-books http://jiscebooks.org/ and the national e-books observatory project that ran from 2007–2010 http://observatory.jiscebooks.org/

[8] 'The University of Oxford Text Archive develops, collects, catalogues and preserves electronic literary and linguistic resources for use in Higher Education, in research, teaching and learning'. See: http://ota.ox.ac.uk/

Newcastle, Australia. I emailed him, and he said what "do you want it for?" I said "well, I want to read it". And I think he thought I was kidding! I wanted to see the electronic text because I wanted to read the play. I didn't want to have to go into the library and have to get a book. I wanted to see it on the screen. And then I also knew that if I could have it that way I could search it or if I want to quote it I just copy and paste and it's quoted and accurate. It astounded him that this was an MA student that was asking for an electronic text because he wanted to read the thing!

Through committee work it is usually me saying, "no, actually, don't accept that it is impossible to read for 12 hours a day on a computer". What I do now is project onto the wall and I don't look at the glowing screen. It's much easier on the middle-aged eye ball. But you asked me to reflect, sorry, on the early committee work. I didn't get into the advising stuff until quite recently. I've been a Shakespeare Scholar, I worked at the Globe theatre, and I got a job at Loughborough University. Digital has always been how I'd do it. But I haven't had that much engagement with many other people, except for the last 5 or 7 years.

JN Yes, but that is great. Did you ever feel that your engagement with the digital hindered you? Or was it ever something that others may have looked upon and questioned to some extent?

GE You get a bit of sniggering, and yeah, some colleagues at Loughborough then and now hand you something and say "Oh no, don't give him that bit of paper, no no, he won't like that, and you've given him paper!" It has not really hindered me. In working practices, once or twice I've thought "actually is this the very fastest way?" For some things it's probably just quicker to thumb things through. Or particularly when you're working with multiple documents, someone will say "look, I'd like to have one copy on paper in front of me and then I'll do my notes on the screen". They claim there's a speed advantage to having a paper copy of something and I have sometimes pondered "am I doing this the fastest way"? But then I say, well, even if I'm not, 99 % of the time I'm doing it the fastest way, and I can't be bothered to carry that bit of paper with me. I want to be able to do this work wherever I am. Because then you don't have anything to worry about during your travels. These people who plan to go away and have to think about what paper to carry around with them … I don't understand. I know that I have a bunch of things that I have to do and they're all in my laptop. And as long as I'm with my laptop I can do them. When I'm in Amsterdam next week, I have those proofs to read, they're in there, I have an article to write, and it's all in there. That freedom from the constraint of carrying stuff is a large part of it. Ok, maybe one percent of the time I'm actually not working in the very fastest way and it would be quicker to print something out. And because of the way memory works, you know how sometimes, when you're looking through a book you can remember where on the page what you want is? You don't know why you know this, but you know it's near the top of the page and so you can flick back through. There are times when that medium seems to have a slight edge. But they are so few and far between that I ignore them.

JN What about your engagement with the conference community around Humanities Computing/Digital resources in the Humanities/DH. The nomenclature is so varied that I'm hesitant about using a particular term in case I then block out other ones.

GE I'm stuck because I don't go to that many DH conferences because I'm really, really intent on not getting distracted from my main thing, which is Shakespeare and in my case, at the moment, Textual Studies or what's been done with the early editions of Shakespeare. The DH conferences tend to include a very wide range of subject disciplines. I don't know enough about any of them to really gain a lot from it. I still find that I mainly learn stuff from Shakespeare conferences and tend to concentrate on those.

I've actually been reading papers for the big DH conference and before that it was called the LLC. Since it changed its name to DH I've read papers for them every year. It is great because the scoring system is all done online, but I've never actually been.

Really, in a conference, I want to learn stuff about my subject and it's a very specific kind of knowledge that I want to get. I go to the Shakespeare Association of America meeting and I know there's half a dozen people who, if I go to their paper and take good notes, I'll be a year ahead of publication. I'll know what they're going to say a year before they publish it. And that's why I go. And it really does thrill me and I think, you know, "that's a brilliant idea" and because I was in that room I'll cite it a year ahead of time in my own work and build on it.

JN And do you notice more and more digital work coming into those conferences?

GE There is a bit. There is very little in Shakespeare Studies, well under 5 %; 10 % maximum papers will be on a matter specifically digital. The Renaissance Society of America has a digital strand every year. I went to one and ran a session with a huge figure from DH and another huge figure in our subject of early printing and technology. But only one other person actually turned up to listen. It's like, I used to be in a band and you do some gigs where there are more of you on the stage than there are in the audience and that was the situation. And I was thinking "my god!" The power in this room but there's only one person getting any benefit from it. The conference was in Venice, so there's no great hardship, I didn't feel hard done by. Wow! Most Renaissance scholars are not interested in this subject. Most Shakespearians aren't interested in it.

There is a certain amount of backlash at the moment and muttering – this is towards the back of the hall, where I often sit, where there's usually a power socket to plug your laptop in – you hear a kind of scoffing when someone says "look the big thing emerging in Shakespeare Studies is counting stuff in Shakespeare. Counting different kinds of words, counting how often his book will be printed, counting the length of his plays compared to other people's plays, all sorts of things you can count with a computer". I do frequently hear from the back "oh … the accountants have taken over Shakespeare Studies". It's no longer – I'm going back to that question about the poetical versus the engineering approach – the Arts versus the Sciences. You get – and I think it is just an anxiety of one's own limitations – people talking about how this is bad scholarship, it's just counting stuff and it's not sufficiently sensitive, so you get a lot more prejudices. So I'm saying that there is a small group of digital work going on in my area of Shakespeare Studies, and English Studies in general, but it's still very marginal and is meeting a lot of resistance.

JN That's really interesting, because the next question I was going to ask was about those who don't use computing in their research and their sense of DH research.

GE Some of them will say "Oh… it's all very interesting, it's all very well but I'm not interested in that kind of work." There is a significant number who are just panicked and terrified because they never thought they were very good with computers and they don't understand the papers they're reading.

One problem is there's a bunch of stuff that's being published about … I'll give you a concrete case. We know pretty much the core of the Shakespeare cannon, we know what he wrote, the collected plays edition was published after his death and these are the plays of Shakespeare, all 36 of them. But there's a few other plays that are probably Shakespeare or partly by Shakespeare. And there's work being done to explore that boundary, did he, perhaps, write one scene in this other play? Or when that play was expanded upon for a revival, did he write the editions? For example Thomas Kyds' play the *Spanish Tragedy* got expanded at some point in its life and the latest thinking is that Shakespeare wrote the editions to that. You've got these extra 500 lines, to make the revised version of the *Spanish Tragedy*.

I go and listen to papers about this and the papers are highly technical. You need to understand the statistics being used to talk about the significance of certain phrases occurring in Shakespeare and in these unknown author chunks, and not occurring elsewhere. So you can say "look at this word that every so often occurs next to this word in Shakespeare's known works and in these editions of *the Spanish Tragedy* but do not occur in all these other peoples' work". You can hear peoples' minds switching off – Shakespearians aren't generally very good with the Maths or the technology. So there is a definite reaction against this sort of research. One response is "that's all very well but none of my concern". Another is a kind of panicked rejection because people find it very difficult. Another is a kind of rather cynical response that the digitisation of the Humanities is part of a wider government and business-led instrumentalisation of the Humanities that is trying to drag us out of our academic work or into something that might have some commercial or wider societal impact. In other words, it's not a neutral or beneficial technology, its actually trying to find out what's exploitable about the Humanities. So they see it as being the nasty intrusion of business into Humanities.

I think those fears are all unfounded and quite mistaken, but they're definitely there. The reason I think those fears are mistaken is that Humanists were at the forefront of the last technological revolution that mattered, which was the printing press. Humanists were right there. Thomas More and Erasmus understood the printing press, understood what it would do for textuality and the printing presses were aligned with this great movement of sixteenth century Humanism. So, for me it's happening again and Humanists need to be at the forefront of technology in the twenty-first century. I'm an old fashioned Marxist, it's the march of progress, technological progess driving social change in a good way. I mean, I've got quite a simple model of progress which is the sort of quaintly old fashioned left-wing idea that the world's getting better! And this is part of the process, I mean you factor in all the negative aspects as well.

Your lovely digital machine is made by some near slave child worker in China or Taiwan, but factoring that in, that technology is, I think, ultimately liberating. The inherent quality of technology is that it liberates and therefore there is such a thing as human progress. Isn't that old fashioned of me? I happen to think it's true but that might just be a leap of faith.

JN Ok, can you reflect on some of the key changes that you have seen in the digital resources that have been developed for your area?

GE In my area, EEBO is a huge deal. Anybody who works for a university can have pictures of all the books published up to the Civil War, and then with Eighteenth Century Collections Online (ECCO), right up to 1800.[9] That is utterly transformatory and levels the playing field between universities and between the researchers and everyone else. Students can get access to early books that they couldn't before. I can now teach using early printed text, I'm about to give a lecture at De Montfort on Christopher Marlowe's poem Hero and Leander, and I quote in the lecture solely from the first edition of 1598. It is perfectly usable and I think the students should see how this poem was first confronted by its readers. I mean, ok, it's only a digitisation of a microfilm, it's not the book itself, but they can see what it looked like to its early readers. That's very important to me. So EEBO and ECCO is a big deal.

Before that Literature Online[10] was a huge deal. We could essentially give everyone all the poetry, prose and plays and they could search them as well. The students could search and, say, research students could come up with their own questions. A friend of mine from Sheffield Hallam University called Matt Steggle told me that he

---

[9] 'Consisting of every significant English-language and foreign-language title printed in the United Kingdom during the eighteenth century, along with thousands of important works from the Americas, *Eighteenth Century Collections Online* was the most ambitious single scholarly digitization project ever undertaken' is the description of ECCO given on its website. See http://gdc. gale.com/products/eighteenth-century-collections-online/. More recently, ECCO-TCP has come about to make the texts contained in the collection machine readable. See http://www.textcreation-partnership.org/tcp-ecco/

[10] Literature online states that it is "a fully integrated service that combines the texts of over 355,000 literary works with a vast library of key criticism and reference resources". See http://literature. proquest.com.libproxy.ucl.ac.uk/infoCentre/contents.jsp;jsessionid=5566C77B702B87B036EF1 198996D7C10

did his entire PhD on questions about how Aristotle figures in early modern writing: what is said about Aristotle, how do they think about him? So just finding references to Aristotle was a huge project for him. Now, with these resources someone could just pull up all the occasions when Aristotle is mentioned in early print. So EEBO, ECCO and Literature Online, totally changed the whole subject and enabled work to proceed on certain particular things at a much faster rate. There were a bunch of things I couldn't have done without Literature Online such as that paper 'hearing a play, heard a play, saw a play' that I mentioned.

OED, being online and digital, was a huge transformation. There's not much beyond that, the subject specific ones haven't made a big difference. Shakespeare Quartos Archive,[11] I regret to say, hasn't made much difference. This is a digitisation of all the early quarto printings of Shakespeare at the British Library, the Bodleian, the Folger in Washington DC, [the National Library of Scotland] and the Huntington Library in California. Although I've got plans for a project which involves those images, it hasn't had a great transformatory effect, yet.

JN You already mentioned text analysis applications like stylometry and authorship attribution in relation to Shakespeare. Are there any other techniques that you think have started to be taken up by English Studies?

GE Yes, certain kinds of stylometric stuff is starting to be and it's leading to a big debate. Before I move on, I just wanted to mention what we haven't talked about, namely digital procedures that affect scholarship. Now we have free software, like Zotero, which is great.[12] When I first started doing this with students they had to use EndNote, an awful bit of software. The point is, managing a database of your own references is something I teach research students to do. It transformed my work. I didn't actually buy bibliographical database software. I wanted to do exactly what I wanted to do, so I programmed my own one. Still the availability of these things makes a lot of difference to scholarship and a big difference to how fast people work.

Back to stylometry etc., those techniques tend to be a bit closed, black-box-type things. In Shakespeare Studies people are looking at tools that will analyse language. They will take a page and categorise each word in it into, say, 100 different categories and say "look! How interesting" or "look how the profile for this comedy is very different from the profile for this tragedy. You know, tragedies have much more words about night time and dark things whereas comedies have lots of words about lightness and happiness etc."

The tools are not open, that is one of my bugbears. People are publishing work saying "here is what our tool does" and they don't tell you how the categories work, they don't give you the algorithm and they don't show you the method, which is very dangerous, I think. We all got our fingers burnt with this about 16 years ago

---

[11] See: http://www.quartos.org/info/about.html

[12] Zotero is 'is a free, easy-to-use tool to help you collect, organize, cite, and share your research sources'. See https://www.zotero.org/

when a guy called Donald Foster at Vassar College had a new tool he called SHAXICON, which was doing those kind of analysis of Shakespeare's writing. He could tell you who'd written what, "that isn't by Shakespeare because it doesn't have his profile". He never actually said how his profile was worked out, he never gave me the algorithm, never gave me the categories and he always promised the thing was going to be published any day now on the internet. He had huge articles, he had papers in world-class Shakespeare journals (see, for example, Foster 1996), and major newspapers claiming that a computer had solved certain mysteries of authorship but he never published the actual method, how it worked. He still hasn't, 16 years later.[13]

So what I'm saying as well is that there's digital work going on but of a very low quality, not because it's inherently necessarily wrong but because we can't check it. That makes it low quality. If I can't validate your results because I haven't got access to your database or your algorithm then as far as I'm concerned that isn't scholarship, its vanity publishing.

JN It is amazing, it seems almost like an aspect of digital literacy that is being missed.

GE Exactly, yes. It precedes that digital age actually, really my field is quite allergic to all kinds of technical approaches. When I was doing my PhD, I was working on attempts to reconstruct the Globe Theatre, including the one that was being built in London in the mid-1990s. One of the great books that was part of that project was by John Orrell (1983), in which he analysed a contemporary picture of the Globe. From the picture, because of the way the picture was made, with a very precise instrument, he was able to work out the size of the building it was showing. He reconstructed the entire construction of this picture with a thing called a topographical glass, a sort of surveyor's instrument. When you got to page 80 of his book about this, it was suddenly all equations, 7 and a half pages of trigonometry, it was A-Level trigonometry, which I didn't have but I wasn't just going to let this go and not check this.

So, first of all I went to one of my tutors and said, "you reviewed this book, didn't you?", "oh yes", "what did you do when you got to page 80 when it's all Maths?" He said, "I just kept turning the pages until it wasn't Maths anymore." He didn't check it. I asked everyone I knew who had read the book and who was a theatre historian. No one had actually checked the maths, which astounded me because they then built this thing on the basis of this calculation, which none of them had actually verified was correct. Luckily, my sister is a maths teacher at A-Level, so she had to teach me the trigonometry, Actually in an appendix to my PhD thesis I take the same measurements and by a totally different trigonometrical method see if I come up with the same result or not as a validation of his method. It took me ages, but I did it, and I remember thinking, "wow these people in my subject just take things on

---

[13] See Egan's work on SHAXICAN, a series of Perl scripts 'that do the sorts of things Donald Foster's SHAXICON database is designed to do' http://gabrielegan.com/shaxican/index.htm

trust, they don't actually check for themselves that the numbers add up or that the equations are valid and sometimes they're not, it's quite extraordinary!"

JN You used the metaphor of the prosthesis in connection with the computer. How has that metaphor changed or has it changed in those intervening years?

GE It's just got lighter; I can just carry the thing now. It's still this amazing device that's got all my knowledge in it and it's searchable. So it's the same thing, just smaller and lighter and lasts for longer without a power supply, they are the only advantages! Funnily enough, I don't see the new technologies of mobile devices being of any use here; in fact, I'm quite against them. The last thing we needed in the software industry is fragmentation. There's a great advantage in everyone having the same machine, so you have one piece of software that runs on everyone's machine. It was bad enough when it was PC versus Mac and 8 % of the market was Mac so software writers had to write another version for the Mac but then to have another one for the Android operating system and another one for iOS – I think is a very backwards step.

So we've recently seen a real backward step in the power to use the computer prosthetically because the market is fragmenting into four different markets. Apps can't do anything for us. The smartphones have one advantage over everything else, they know where you are on the surface of the earth and they know which way you are facing because they have a compass built in, sometimes that matters. I don't yet have a smart phone, I haven't yet found the need for it. I've got to be careful though because at some point everyone says, you know, you're finally getting old when you don't want to have young person's technology and don't even understand why they want it!

JN Ok, well I think that was absolutely fascinating, thank you very much.

References

Egan, G. (2001). Hearing or seeing a play? Evidence of early modern theatrical terminology. *Ben Jonson Journal, 8*, 327–347.

Egan, G. (2006). *Green Shakespeare: From ecopolitics to ecocriticism*. London/New York: Routledge.

Egan, G. (2013). *The struggle for Shakespeare's text: Twentieth-century editorial theory and practice*. Cambridge: Cambridge University Press.

Foster, D. (1996). *A funeral elegy*: W[illiam] S[hakespeare]'s 'best-speaking witnesses'. *Publications of the Modern Language Association of America, 111* (1996), 1080–1105.

Hinman, C. J. K. (1968). *The Norton facsimile. The first folio of Shakespeare. Prepared by Charlton Hinman*. New York: W. W. Norton & Co.

MLA. (2015). MLA international bibliography | modern language association. Available at: https://www.mla.org/Publications/MLA-International-Bibliography. Accessed 2 Nov 2015.

Orrell, J. (1983). *The quest for Shakespeare's globe*. Cambridge/New York: Cambridge University Press.

Siemens, R., et al. (2012). Video-gaming, paradise lost and TCP/IP: An oral history conversation between Ray Siemens and Anne Welsh. *Digital Humanities Quarterly, 6*(3). Available at: http://www.digitalhumanities.org/dhq/vol/6/3/000131/000131.html. Accessed 2 Nov 2015.

Wells, S., et al. (Eds.). (1986). *William Shakespeare: The complete works.* Oxford: Clarendon Press.

Open Access This chapter is distributed under the terms of the Creative Commons Attribution-Noncommercial 2.5 License (http://creativecommons.org/licenses/by-nc/2.5/) which permits any noncommercial use, distribution, and reproduction in any medium, provided the original author(s) and source are credited.

The images or other third party material in this chapter are included in the work's Creative Commons license, unless indicated otherwise in the credit line; if such material is not included in the work's Creative Commons license and the respective action is not permitted by statutory regulation, users will need to obtain permission from the license holder to duplicate, adapt or reproduce the material.

Chapter 17
Revolutionaries and Underdogs

Abstract Taking the work of Passerini (1979) and Portelli (1981) as a theoretical backdrop, this chapter will describe, contextualise and interpret a narrative (or 'story') that was recalled in a number, but not all, of the oral history interviews. This narrative concerns interviewees' experiences of having been ignored, undermined or marginalised by the mainstream academic community. For the purposes of discussion we will refer to this as the 'motif of the underdog'. We will complement this analysis of the oral history interviews by looking to the scholarly literature of the field and examining a theme that often occurs there, namely DH's supposedly revolutionary status (referred to below as the 'motif of the revolutionary'). Our analysis will raise the question of how DH managed to move from the margins towards the mainstream while continuing to portray itself as both underdog and revolutionary? Drawing on literature from social psychology, the history of disciplinarity and the wider backdrop of oral history, we will argue that the motifs discussed here can better be understood in terms of their function rather than their internal coherence.

Introduction

> *But what is really important is that memory is not a passive depository of facts, but an active process of creation of meanings. Thus, the specific utility of oral sources for the historian lies, not so much in their ability to preserve the past, as in the very damages wrought by memory. These changes reveal the narrator's effort to make sense of the past and to give a form to their lives, and set the interview and the narrative in their historical context* (Portelli 2006, pp. 37–8)

This book utilises oral history as an approach to meaning making which is not focused on what happened in the past (or at least not only what happened in the past). Rather, we utilise it in the manner suggested by Portelli (above) as a collaborative process by which the narrator and interviewer combine in the present to make sense of the past and their lives and experiences. The use of oral history methodologies (both in interviews and their subsequent interpretation) towards the production of histories of DH offers the tantalising possibility of revealing hidden histories and filling archival gaps with individual narratives. Furthermore, by taking the interviews together as a group that is, in turn, a subset of the more broad and loose DH community, they can be used to identify and analyse the shared narratives,

© The Author(s) 2016
J. Nyhan, A. Flinn, *Computation and the Humanities*, Springer Series on
Cultural Computing, DOI 10.1007/978-3-319-20170-2_17

silences and misrememberings, community motifs and foundation myths that are essential to the binding of a community. Shared narratives and ways of understanding can be both inclusive and exclusive and help to determine a community's relationship with the present and future as much as with the past. The identification of narrative tropes and motifs, the importance of story-telling, and the interaction and interplay between individual memories and collective myths and stories are all, as this final chapter will argue, essential components in this process (Abrams 2010). Ever since the publication of *Myths We Live By* (Samuels and Thompson 1990), and indeed before that under the influence of Passerini (1979) and Portelli (1981), oral history has been recognised as a valuable tool for exploring individual and collective narratives and stories, how they give meaning to the past in the present and how they can play a powerful function in articulating shared identity. We argue below that this seems especially true of an academic community such as DH which perceives itself to be misunderstood and the recipient of hostility and antagonism but is, nevertheless, in the process of establishing itself in the academic mainstream.

Narratives and stories can salve the complexities and tribulations of daily life. They allow us to imagine alternative lives, to encounter novel situations and to engage, however indirectly, with creative and imagined communities far beyond our immediate social settings. Stories can play important roles in professional life too; indeed, many academic disciplines tell stories about their creation and development and identify with various labels. These can offer a coherent and stable narrative about where a discipline perceives it has come from, what it believes it is doing and why it has taken the shape and course that it has. This serves an important purpose given the inherently 'changing nature of knowledge domains over time' (Becher 1989, p. 21) and the social contexts in which such knowledge is created, shaped and transmitted. Indeed, Weingart and Stehr also emphasise the social dimension, writing that disciplines are:

> intellectual but also social structures, organizations made up of human beings with vested interests based on time investments, acquired reputations, and established social networks that shape and bias their views on the relative importance of their knowledge ... Disciplines are diffuse types of social organization for the production of particular types of knowledge (cited by Trowler et al. 2012, p. 7–8)

Within such conditions, Taylor, who looked at the role of 'heroic myths' in the discipline of Geography, has argued that their function is to create an 'overall purpose and cohesion to the very obvious disparate researches of members of the geography community' (Taylor 1976, p. 131).

Considering the nature of DH, which is very much characterised by such 'disparate researches', it is plausible to expect that stories should play an important cohesive function for it too. However, the stories that Digital Humanists tell about their discipline, and the labels that they apply to it have received little critical analysis (with the exception of McCarty who has critiqued the applicability of established metaphors like 'Tree' and 'Turf' to DH and argued for others such as 'archipelago' and 'Phoenician trader', as outlined in Chap. 1).

Taking the work of Passerini (1979) and Portelli (1981) as a theoretical backdrop, this chapter will describe, contextualise and interpret a narrative (or 'story') that was recalled in a number, but not all, of the oral history interviews. This narrative concerns interviewees' experiences of having been ignored, undermined or marginalised by the mainstream academic community. For the purposes of discussion, we refer to this as the 'motif of the underdog'. We will complement this analysis of the oral history interviews by looking to the scholarly literature of the field and examining a narrative that often occurs there, namely DH's supposedly revolutionary status (referred to below as the 'motif of the revolutionary').

Though we will explore some fundamental contradictions that cross cut the motifs of the revolutionary and underdog our aim is not to invalidate or ridicule them or the significance of their telling. Indeed, it is possible to be both an underdog and a revolutionary – many, if not most revolutionaries are by definition in the minority and spend much of their time being pursued by hostile forces. For much of this time they might act as a vanguard for change but their inability to influence or affect that change would have them characterised as underdogs. Our analysis will raise the question of how DH managed to move from the margins towards the mainstream while continuing to portray itself as both underdog and revolutionary? Drawing on literature from social psychology, the history of disciplinarity and the wider backdrop of oral history, we will argue that the motifs discussed here can be better understood in terms of their function rather than their internal coherence.

The Motif of the Underdog

Interview Perspectives

One of the most evocative memories recalled during the oral history interviews is what we refer to as the motif of the underdog. It refers to interviewees' recollections of how they or their research was ignored, ridiculed, or, more rarely, blocked by the mainstream academic community. Space will not allow all references to this motif to be included here; rather, an exemplary selection that also goes beyond the interviews included in this book is presented.

Geoffrey Rockwell discussed at length the opposition he encountered c.1994 when he developed and set up early courses in Humanities Computing in Canada, for example, the 'Combined Honors in Multimedia and Another Subject program' at McMaster University. He recalled, in particular, the opposition he faced when presenting the details of such courses to Faculty Council for approval:

> In the early years, taking courses through, you would hit Faculty Council and … people would get up and go, you know, "I don't understand why we are running computing classes, this is like 'Pencils in the Humanities.'" … I distinctly got the feeling that there was a class of people for whom this was seen as a Trojan horse. The Humanities were under attack, people felt that back then and … now the Humanities were not even the Humanities! (Rockwell 2012)

He also recalled the opposition he encountered over hiring decisions and at various committee meetings:

> A second type of response was "you guys are intellectually lightweight." I can remember one way that that manifested itself was through hiring. Because we were not a department until 2005, whenever we hired a tenure track Prof .... there was the question of whether or not the department that they would naturally fit in would host [them]. [A]nd Chairs, especially English, would inevitably tell me that, you know, "you may think this guy is interesting because he can programme, but I gotta tell you, intellectually he's a lightweight." ... The third type of argument that we got ... was just blatant sarcasm and ignorance. ... I think there was a class of older Profs who just literally felt: "I'm too old to understand this" and, you know, sometimes that could mean that they'd be quite supportive – "I'm too old to understand this, I was before the computer generation, you know, I wish I could know about this and I respect your knowledge but I don't get it at all." So that's a positive spin on it, but there were also people going "I don't understand it, it must be bullshit," you know, "[t]his isn't the good old stuff; we used to do Philology." (Ibid)

A hint of the 'intellectually lightweight' refrain is also detectable in the interview with Nitti (see Chap. 9) who recalled how a colleague gibed that he had been given his tenured position only because he was able to attract grant money.

In his interview, McCarty recalled that 'the coolness of the reception is what I felt from the people that weren't using computers' (McCarty et al. 2012). Indeed, this coolness seems to have contributed to his founding of the online, international seminar Humanist which has been running since 1987. Of its founding, McCarty wrote 'Humanist was initially founded for those who worked in computing support and who encountered, among other things, a 'lack of proper academic recognition" (1992, p. 209).

Towards the use of computing in Philosophy more generally, Huitfeld (see Chap. 15) recalled that an attitude of 'scepticism' and 'even sometimes ... hostility' was to be found. However, he portrays the Wittgenstein scholars as pragmatic and reasonably open to such developments such was their desire to access the material. He also commented 'there was a certain scepticism towards whether an electronic edition could ever substitute a real, connected publication in book form, but apart from that there was no problem'. This comment implies that it was the more pedestrian (at least conceptually) uses of computing that were acceptable to the wider discipline. This issue is also touched on by Bradley (see Chap. 14) who recalls how most academics routinely used email, the web and word processing in their research (that is, tools that have not emerged from the DH community). The resistance he encountered mostly pertained to potentially disruptive uses of computing in research: 'there was also the group of people who had a natural resistance to the whole approach that text analysis represented. Text analysis is a more fundamental disturbance of how you look and think about the text you're working with and I think most people just don't see it as relevant to what they're trying to do'. Within the context of electronic publishing, Unsworth recalled that his decision, as a junior faulty member, to set up a peer reviewed journal raised some eyebrows, and all the more so because it was published electronically (Unsworth et al. 2012).

Others recalled stronger opposition. Thaller (see Chap. 13) said that some historians viewed computing as an affront to the methodological basis of their discipline or 'as a kind of vulneration against the principles established by Ranke'. Yet, he emphasises that their primary objection was to the use of quantitative methods in history and the computer was, in turn, rejected as a facilitator of this. Harris (see Chap. 8) recalled that while undertaking her PhD in the 1970s 'one of the graduate advisers swore that I was trying to destroy literature by using the computer'. Both Harris and Sperberg-McQueen raised the issue of employment. Harris recalls that when she was finishing her PhD 'in this oddball field' she was initially unable to secure an academic job. She went directly from working as a bar tender to teaching in a Computer Science department.

Perhaps the most poignant recollection is that of Sperberg-McQueen (see Chap. 12), who described his mounting disappointment and dismay at his unsuccessful academic job search. He recalls that the regret he felt over the loss of an academic career afflicted him on a daily basis for many years after finishing his PhD. He communicated the deep sense of loss that he felt by recalling a conversation with his wife where he asked her 'if someone loses their leg do you expect them to forget that they ever had a left foot?' Though not captured in the transcript, the emotion in Sperberg-McQueen's voice whilst recalling these events is notable on the audio recording. Careful to emphasise that 'causality … is probably a far step' he recalls how 'I always thought that in later years [the tutor who had warned him off computing in the Humanities] must have told his students the same thing and pointed to me as an awful example: "he's never gotten a job in Philology", as indeed was the case'.

Interviewees did not all interpret the scepticism they encountered negatively. Some, such as Craig (see Chap. 3), discussed how (albeit from the perspective of one who had secured a tenured post) such scepticism could be beneficial because it offered a 'very good sort of proving ground'. Nevertheless, he regretted not having persuaded more colleagues to take up such work and said that many feel that the time it takes to learn such techniques is not outweighed by the quality of the results they can facilitate.

Notwithstanding the discussion above, it is important to note that feelings of marginalisation were not universally experienced. While discussing the advisor who warned him off computing, Sperberg-McQueen also recalled the advisor who had set him to work on computerising the bibliography of the Elder Edda, thus evoking the range of attitudes to the role of computing in the Humanities that existed. Hockey (see Chap. 6), Ott (see Chap. 4) and Nitti (see Chap. 9) stated that they had encountered little hostility. Hockey and Ott believed this was due to the positions they held where part of their job was to support those interested in using computing in Humanities research. Nitti, Short and Hockey also recalled how they benefitted from collaborations with well-known, mainstream Humanities scholars and Hockey speculated that many of those working in DH benefitted from such alliances (this may well be the case and it is interesting that it is rarely discussed in the interviews we have carried out).

Most significantly, Rockwell carefully points out that the resistance that he encountered (discussed above) ceased:

In fact, one of the things that strikes me the most is how quickly it changed from something I had to fight to explain … It seemed like overnight there was no longer a battle, it was just accepted (2012).

These are issues that we will return to below.

Cross-Referencing the Evidence

Before moving on it is important to address the context in which the motif of the underdog tended to be recalled. In many cases it was raised in response to a particular question asked of all interviewees, namely 'what about scholars who were not using computers in their research – do you have some sense of what their views were of Humanities Computing?' Therefore, it might be argued that this motif may not arise with the same frequency were this particular question not asked. This may be so. Indeed, in contrast with documentary research a hallmark of oral history is the active participation of the researcher in the creation of the resource. As Portelli put it: 'The content of oral sources … depends largely on what the interviewer puts into it in terms of questions, dialogue, and personal relationships' (2006, p. 39). Far from being an unmediated, autobiographical account of the past 'as it was', the dialogic nature of oral history is multi-layered. It includes 'a conversation in real time between the interviewer and the narrator and [also] what we might call external discourses or culture' (Abrams 2010, p. 19).

Nevertheless, it is important to state that there is no evidence to suggest that the motif of the underdog is a fiction that came into being in response to this question. Rather it was a narrative (or 'myth to live by') that circulated about the community and formed part of shared DH 'discourses and culture'. This can be demonstrated with reference to the wider literature of the field where the theme is variously and independently mentioned. For example, as cited in Chap. 1, in his retrospective on the occasion of the quarter century anniversary of the journal CHum, Raben discussed the peripheral nature of the field and how its publications were often not accepted by conventional journals (1991, p. 341). Brink evoked the cold-shouldering referred to above when he wrote that despite years of work 'here we still are, looked at as somehow slightly suspect, slightly irrelevant to the core activity of humanities research' (1990, p. 105). That employment prospects could be hampered by computing was blogged about by Rockwell. Referring to conditions that had been prevalent during an earlier stage of his career he asked 'How many times were we warned not to do computing or not to put it on our CV if we wanted to be taken seriously as humanists?' (Rockwell 2011). Various references to the 'odd ball' nature of the subject referred to above can also be found, for example, Spiro uses the term 'misfits' (2012) to refer to its practitioners.

We find an echo of the 'intellectually lightweight' charge in Kaltenbrunner's study of a COST-funded, international and collaborative project that aimed to build a digital resource based upon an existing digital database. Senior scholars working on the project deemed the digitally-mediated work to essentially be non-scholarly (though they had engaged with it in a superficial way only) and delegated the development of this aspect of the project to graduate students and research assistants because their time was allegedly 'not as valuable' (2015, p. 219). Various articles have also addressed the low take up of DH methodologies and outputs by mainstream Humanities (see, for example, Olsen 1993; Juola 2008; Prescott 2012a). That this has become less true in recent times is suggested by a 2014 survey of four institutions in the USA that revealed that 'nearly 50 % of respondents reported not just making use of digital tools and collections, but also creating them' (Maron and Pickle 2014, p. 5).

Questioning the Motif

For all the references to the motif of the underdog discussed above its consistency can be questioned in various ways. Firstly and most obviously is that the motif is often recalled by those who occupied, or went on to occupy, senior academic positions such as professor. Appointment and promotion boards tend to comprise senior staff representatives of all faculties in a university and not just representatives from a candidate's immediate faculty. The fact that such boards approved senior appointments in the area of DH can be construed as evidence that such marginalisation was not as systemic as might be assumed (which is not to say that it did not happen). It also suggests a temporal dimension, and the possibility that ambivalence was stronger in the earlier period and eventually receded to a point where academic appointments and promotions where approved. Further interviews must be carried out with those who worked in the field at a later stage before such a claim can definitively be made. However, in general we have noted that the motif of the underdog does occur less frequently in oral history interviews with younger members of the field (see, for example, Siemens et al. 2012). So too, in the interviews included in this book the very many forms of support and assistance that individuals received, not only from the mainstream Humanities but also from the commercial and other sectors are in evidence.

Secondly, as argued in Chap. 1, DH has (in terms of 'institutional hallmarks' such as the founding of centres and teaching programmes, the appointment of faculty and other tenured positions and the expansion of the community) been undergoing a process of moving from the margins towards the mainstream. This process has not followed a steady upward trajectory and individual experiences of it may vary depending on one's geographical location, institution, position or disciplinary interest (cf., for example, Gold 2012). Yet, on the whole, the subject has been growing in strength and vitality. In this context, the frequent mention of the myth of the underdog in oral history interviews is especially interesting because in light of more recent developments other narratives are also available to interviewees, for example, the (albeit rather trite) narrative of 'triumph over adversity'. Perhaps it is not surprising that interviewees should recall painful memories more readily than pleasant ones. Viewed from this angle we may interpret the motif as one that grants an insight into interviewees' individual experiences and narratives of personal struggle and sacrifice that triumphal stories of the forward march of DH do not accommodate.

It is interesting that few references to the word revolutionary are to be found in the oral history interviews. Thaller was one of the few to mention it, noting that 'the people at [DH] conferences considered themselves, well, if not as a group of elite, at least as a group of revolutionaries who grumbled against the conservative people trying to keep away from their inter-disciplinary work, which at that time was rather innovative in many humanities disciplines'. While the motif of the underdog often occurs in the oral history interviews it is the arguably corresponding motif of the revolutionary that often occurs in the field's scholarly literature, as set out below. Before exploring what we argue to be the deeper interconnections between these motifs an analysis of relevant literature that uses the term 'revolutionary' is presented.

Revolutionaries

A review of the main DH journals (namely *Literary and Linguistic Computing*; *Digital Humanities Quarterly*; and CHum) shows that 'revolution' is a term that preoccupies the field. In the discussion below we focus mostly on scholarly articles that contain the term 'revolution' and its associated forms. Space has not allowed us to follow up what appear to be related terms or movements, for example, hacktivism or more indirect allusions to revolution.

References to many revolutions occur in the literature, for example, the 'computer revolution', the 'information revolution', the 'communication revolution', the 'quantum revolution', the 'technological revolution', the 'ebook revolution', the 'revolution in human-computer interaction', the 'community revolution', the 'metadata revolution', the 'printing industry revolution', the 'digital revolution', the 'mobile revolution' and even the 'cost-effectiveness revolution'. They are invoked in various ways. Despite the destructive import that the term revolution often has, in DH literature it frequently functions to provide some overarching background and structure to the otherwise disparate activities of the field. An example of this is when an external revolution is referenced to provide a contextual and predictive framework for the potential contributions of DH. For example, notwithstanding that 'the first generation of digital classics has seen relatively superficial methods to address the problems of print culture', Crane et al argue that 'cyberinfrastructure' for digital classics may prove transformational. In support of this, an analogy between movable type and cyberinfrastructure is set out in order to imply a kind of equivalence between them:

> Rarely, if ever, can we predict the full implications of relatively modest technological change. Gutenberg did not think that, in using movable type to print a Latin bible, he was creating a technology to make translations of the bible ubiquitous, enable new forms of Christian worship and facilitate revolutionary change (Crane et al. 2009)

Such comparisons can serve to provide a relatively new discipline such as DH with a genealogy that connects it with a distinguished past in addition to foretelling an auspicious future: 'these new technologies will have a major role to play because they are the culmination of the revolution that started with the invention of printing' (Schneider and Bennion 1982, p. 35)

The relationship of DH to such revolutions is variously construed. Sometimes, the revolution is seen as external to the field but capable of transforming its ways of working. Bolton, for example, wrote that the 'October Revolution', which saw the arrival of the IBM personal computer, redressed some of the 'strange couplings' that came about in a time when Humanities Computing was bound to the mainframe and Computer Scientist (1991, p. 431). Some portray DH as a bridge to the digital revolution: 'Academics wishing to join the 'digital revolution' may have an introduction to the field of Digital Humanities through the discipline of textual markup' (Terras et al. 2009, p. 298). Others view the revolution as a potential threat. A proposal for teaching computers in the liberal arts curriculum warns: 'we can ill afford to sit back as spectators while the computer revolution takes its course' (Cramer and Taylor 1973, p. 418). Indeed, McCarty has addressed the fear of computing that can be noticed in the professional literature of DH and the Humanities more generally (2013).

The revolution is also described as something that is (or should be) happening within DH. For example, various of its methods are described as 'revolutionary' (Robinson and Taylor 1998). Milic wrote of how his

mildly revolutionary [doctoral] proposal was received with an absolute lack of sympathy, the notion of a dissertation in English ornamented with statistics, charts, tables and complex linguistic jargon and formulas (as it supposedly would be) being anathema to the conservative senior professors of that period (1982, p. 19).

Sometimes individual scholars are portrayed as revolutionaries. Burton wrote how Busa had 'revolutionized the fields of concordance-making and of computer applications'(Burton 1981, p. 4). Sands characterises Meserole as one who would become a 'prominent figure in the vanguard of this new revolution' (Sands 1967, p. 113).

Sometimes the field as a whole is characterised as having revolutionary intent: 'So, when does the Humanities Computing Revolution Start?' asks Brink who proceeds to lament its continuing peripheral position (1990, p. 105). Clubb advises DH to avoid repeating the mistakes of other disciplines 'in their own revolution' (Anon 1971, p. 61) Bosak's closing talk to TEI 10 mapped out the communities role in the 'revolution' (1999).

Considering the above it is surprising that explanations of and consensus on what the revolution will entail are difficult to find in the main DH journals (and one notices a parallel here with ongoing debates about how DH is to be defined). An exception is the work of Berry who discusses the DH revolution in terms of a Kuhnian paradigm shift (Porsdam 2013). More often, however, the nature and scope of the 'revolution' must be inferred.

In a number of discussions the use of the term revolution evokes the determined overthrow of existing approaches and the drawing of lines between the traditional and emergent. Regarding authorship attribution, for example, it is argued that the work of

Mosteller and Wallace 'combined with the late twentieth-century revolution in computing, inaugurated a new era for "non-traditional" statistically based studies of authorship' (Holmes et al. 2001, p. 315). For others the revolution is happening in epistemology
(Beacham and Denard 2003). Discussing analytical modelling (a methodology that is
fundamental to DH), McCarty argues: 'It's great and revolutionary success for the
humanities is to force the epistemological question—how is it that we know what we
somehow know—and to give us an instrument for exploring it' (2008, p. 256).

It is not only research problems that are in range. The revolution can result in
new genres of computer-mediated conversations (Potter 1996). It can also be about
professional processes, as in Ott's discussion (1979) of preparing classical editions,
where he states that he believes the revolution will result in editors being able to
access areas that were otherwise blocked to them, such as typesetting. Discussing
'instructional materials' DeBloois warns that 'Old structures must yield to the pressure of the technology revolution' (1984, p. 192). Prescott does not use the term
revolutionary but draws approvingly on Badmington's desire to see 'the destruction
of this cold, grey building. I wish for the dissolution of the departments that lie
within its walls. I wish, finally, that from the rubble would arise the Posthumanities'
(Prescott 2012b). Spiro does not use the word either but the title of her article certainly evokes it: '"This Is Why We Fight": Defining the Values of the Digital
Humanities' (2012). The Digital Humanities manifesto 2.0 situates the activities of
DH within the aims of the Humanities yet it frames its 'inaugural role' as being both
distinct from and a challenge to the ways that Humanities is now done. It asserts that
'the [DH] revolution promotes a fundamental reshaping of the research and teaching landscape' (Presner et al. 2009, p. 8) and also contrasts 'our [i.e. DH's] response'
with 'the traditionalists response' (Idem, p. 6). Of the manifesto, Fish wrote '[t]he
rhetoric of these statements (which could easily be multiplied) is not one of reform,
but of revolution' (2012).

However, a certain contradiction in such uses of the term can occasionally be
detected. The technologies used in the DH revolution may be 'the culmination of
the revolution that started with the invention of printing' (Schneider and Bennion
1982), yet in some formulations it is the medium and culture of print technology
that is to be challenged. For example, discussing hypermedia, Bolton argues that
'the idea of a snapshot, fixing the state of a discipline in time through the medium
of print, is one of the things that hypermedia are rapidly revolutionizing out of existence' (1996, p. 81). Other understandings of 'revolutionary' are apparent too,
Jessop for example, equates it with something that is 'lacking in rigorous scholarly
value' (Jessop 2008, p. 281).

In addition to the apparent disagreement about the results of the revolution a
number of articles also disagree with or critique its appropriateness as an aim. The
problematic nature of such 'revolutionary' rhetoric for the perception of the field is
occasionally discussed (see, for example, Goldfield 1993). Some argue that
revolution is not an appropriate goal (Byerly 1978) and that the computer may offer
other important possibilities that are not necessarily revolutionary, like new creative
affordances (Beatie 1967). Others believe that in any case the computer is 'unlikely
to spread into those areas of history in which investigators lack or reject the habit of

putting part of their work into quantitative form, [and] the prospects that the computer will revolutionize historical analysis as a whole in the near future are slight indeed' (Tilly 1973, p. 327). Others remark on the various expected revolutions that didn't come off (see, for example, Lawrence et al. 1986, p. 121; Byerly 1978). Indeed, a degree of frustration with the unimaginative use that some scholars (Raben 1991) and some students (Ess 2000) have made of the fruits of the computer revolution is also to be encountered.

Neither is the timing of the revolution agreed upon. For Potter (1991), Smith (1994, p. 316) and Prather and Elliott (1988) it remains very much a subjunctive and contingent upon other factors. The latter, for example, argue that the revolution that has taken place in Computer Science methodology '… could have had a dramatic effect on the way we look at the musical encoding process' (p. 137). As McCarty wrote:

> It may seem with all the activity we are witnessing, so much we cannot see it all, that the long-awaited revolution has begun … But actually it's been proclaimed before—e.g. by literary critic Stephen Parrish at the first conference in the field in 1964—but then 'postponed owing to technical difficulties' (Mahoney 2011: 56). The truth is that the great cognitive revolution for us has not begun even once. (2014, p. 292)

In summary, the term 'revolution' and associated forms occur frequently in the literature of the field but detailed discussions of what it might require or achieve, and how this might shape the research agenda of the field are difficult to find. Furthermore, there is not a consensus that an appropriate aim for the field is to foment revolution or even on whether the revolution is ongoing or still in planning.

Two interrelated questions arise from this summary: what influenced the take up of the term revolutionary in the field of DH and why does it continue to be used in what is often such an imprecise way?

Origins of the Term Revolutionary

Space will not allow a detailed exploration of the issues that helped to give rise to the field's preoccupation with the term 'revolution'; instead, we here outline two of many possible influences before going on to discuss in detail the context lent by the oral history interviews. The most obvious is, of course, the wider context of technology and computing which so frequently promises and is analysed in terms of revolutionary changes. As Mahoney remarked, '… [C]omputers and computing … have always been surrounded by hype (it was – and may still be – the only way to sell them)' (2005, p. 120). Relevant too must be influential developments and debates in wider academia such as the publication of Kuhn's highly influential *The Structure of Scientific Revolutions* (published in 1962, with subsequent editions appearing in 1969 and 2012). This book argued against Whiggish or Positivist interpretations of the History of Science, which view it as a process of constant progress. It argues that periods of normal Science, when Scientists share a common paradigm (or shared opinions and practices about a field's theories, methods, problems and achievements) are broken by sporadic revolutions that interrupt such periods of normal Science and push it forward.

The interviews we have carried out suggest a further way of examining and contextualising the revolutionary rhetoric of DH. At first glance, the role of underdog and revolutionary may seem rather removed from one another but as commented earlier, the view of revolutionaries as vanguardist minorities bring these motifs together. As with the motif of the underdog, certain tensions can be noted once the surface of the motif of the revolutionary is scratched.

The more obvious way that the metaphor is inadequate is in its sketchy definition. As we have seen above, despite many references to DH's revolutionary nature or potential there is little agreement about the form the revolution should take or what exactly is to be transformed. Furthermore, the metaphor has a number of unfortunate historical associations. As history shows, revolutionaries can, in time, become oppressors. Did Digital Humanists consider themselves immune from such processes? This is an issue that we will return to below. Also, as argued elsewhere (Nyhan 2016), it is notable that despite the revolutionary claims of some individuals, the transactions of the inaugural year of Humanist (1987) indicate that acceptance from the mainstream Humanities, or the Academy more generally, was a dominant concern of DH. In summary, then, the question arises of why such a problematic and ill-defined metaphor was used so often in the writings of the field?

Whilst noting the previously discussed irony of oral history practitioners often also adopting the motifs of underdogs and revolutionaries bent on transforming history and systems of knowledge production more generally, we will now argue that oral history opens the possibility of interpreting these motifs in a less literal way by considering them not in terms of their veracity but rather in terms of their potential function and symbolism for the group that wielded them. Above we asked how DH was able to move from the margins to the mainstream while espousing a narrative of both underdog and revolutionary. We will now argue that this process can be better understood when such motifs are not viewed as literally true (or necessarily internally coherent) but instead viewed as powerful labels, or shared expressions of identity, around which DH proceeded to rally and bind itself.

Narratives and Groups

As discussed in Chap. 1, not only are definitions of the term discipline contested but the question of whether DH can best be categorised as a discipline, an interdiscipline, a community of practice, and so on, continues to be debated. So too, for a good deal of the period under discussion, Humanities Computing was in the process of becoming more established and then 'transforming' into DH. For such reasons, we thought it important to consider the motifs discussed here in more universal terms by drawing on the social psychology concept of group processes. Indeed, the literature on group processes provides an intriguing framework to explore some of the dynamics that may be at stake.

According to Brown 'a group exists when two or more people define themselves as members of it and when its existence is recognized by at least one other' (2001, p. 3). He examines a number of elementary processes of groups, the first being 'changes in self-concept': 'our social identity – our sense of who we are and what we are worth – is ultimately bound up with our group memberships' (Idem, p. 28). Considered in this context one possible way of interpreting the interplay of the motifs of the underdog and revolutionary becomes clear. It must have been painful and disquieting to have one's academic competence (and, to some extent, social identity) questioned at the individual and group level in the way that a number of interviewees recalled. One wonders whether the motif of the revolutionary might (also) have been developed and evoked as a shield and form of redress against such attacks? Given the prevalence of the motif it is also plausible to argue that it functioned as a kind of 'common goal' (or 'task interdependence' (see Idem 37–40)) around which the group could organise itself. As mentioned by McCarty (see Chap. 3), the exact nature of the contribution that computing has made to the Humanities is not agreed upon. Perhaps the aim of securing (albeit rather vague) revolutionary changes can be seen as providing a common cause for the group to rally around while undertaking a deeper analysis of the changes the discipline might ultimately herald. This brings an added dimension to the criticism of the use of this motif by some in the group: failure to attain the expected revolutionary changes could conceivably have the effect of undermining the very rationale of the group's existence.

The second elementary process that Brown discusses is that of 'initiation into the group', a ritual that tends to take place especially in 'established or formal groups and organizations' (Idem, p. 30). Such initiations can vary widely and range from a positive experience where certain benefits are conferred on new member (like financial and other employee benefits that some organisations give new members) to 'a distinctly unpleasant (not to say painful) experience in which the newcomer is mocked, embarrassed or even physically assaulted' (Idem, p. 30–31). From the literature that Brown cites it seems that such initiation ceremonies are invariably conducted by existing members of a given group. Thus, the motif of the underdog cannot be seen as an initiation ceremony because all interviewees report that the resistance they encountered emanated from outside the field of DH. Yet, given the regularity with which the motif is recalled, one wonders whether it may have taken on a form that was akin to that of a 'right of passage' in that one marker of becoming a Digital Humanist was the endurance of such vicissitudes?

In this regard it is notable that the motif of the underdog can be traced from what is commonly held to be the 'foundation myth' of DH. This is based on Busa's recollection of how he met with Thomas J. Watson, Sr, CEO of IBM and convinced him to fund his *Index Thomisticus* project for what would turn out to be the next 30 years:

I knew, the day I was to meet Thomas J. Watson, Sr., that he had on his desk a report which said that IBM machines could never do what I wanted. I had seen in the waiting room a small poster imprinted with the words: "The difficult we do right away; the impossible takes a little longer," (IBM always loved slogans). I took it with me into Mr. Watson's office. Sitting in front of him and sensing the tremendous power of his mind, I was inspired to say: "It is not right to say 'no' before you have tried." I took out the poster and showed him his own slogan. He agreed that IBM would cooperate with my project until it was completed "provided that you do not change IBM into International Busa Machines." I had already informed him that, because my superiors had given me time, encouragement, their blessings and much holy water, but unfortunately no money, I could recompense IBM in any way except financially. That was providential! (Busa 1980, p. 84)

In the extract above, Watson can be read as symbolising the power and success of IBM as he sits behind his desk, slightly aloof, one imagines. Busa, a Jesuit priest, of all things, ventures into the hive of capitalism and ambition (as Jones wrote, 'Priest walks into CEO's office: it sounds like the beginning of a joke' (cited in Jones forthcoming)). Though Busa emphasises his canniness with his observation that 'IBM always loved slogans', the attention he draws to the waiting room, and the small poster that he acquired there, serve to underline the asymmetrical power relations that he implies to be at play. Although Busa describes how he emerged victorious due to his wit and the grace of his god, he again emphasises his underdog status by describing how his order could not provide the funds that were so essential to the project (and that only IBM could bestow). In this regard, Jones' finding that the meeting between them was not even recorded in Watson's formal datebook is all the more telling (Ibid).

That negative 'initiation' experiences can be used to the advantage of a group is suggested by Arson and Mills who drew on the theory of Cognitive Dissonance to argue that 'the more severe the initiation, the more attractive the group would appear [to the initiate]' (cited in Brown 2001, p. 32). One wonders whether the frequent recalling and citing of the motif of the underdog evokes a similar process as interviewees use it not only to underscore what they perceive to the attractiveness of the group but also to underline their resilience in embracing insults and reutilising them as a mechanism for fostering cohesion?

Space has not allowed us to consider other related questions about the relationship of the individual to the group or about the intergroup relationship between DH and the wider Humanities. For now, we will point out that as groups also define themselves through a process of differentiation (see Crozier 2001 for a discussion of this in academic disciplines) the motifs discussed here serve an important function in differentiating DH from the mainstream Humanities, thus reinforcing DH's status as a group and as a functioning, supportive community.

Conclusion

Above we asked how DH has been able to move from the margins to the mainstream while portraying itself as at once a group of underdogs and revolutionaries. We have argued that this process can better be understood when such motifs are interpreted on a utilitarian rather than literal level. In this reading, the motifs of the revolutionary and underdog are not only self-sustaining and interdependent, they also play important social functions in the way that they have contributed to DH's sense of purpose and unity. This seems all the more important in an area such as DH which is especially characterised by the 'disparate researches' of its members. Thus, we propose that the motifs of the underdog and revolutionary have played an important role in the development of DH as a discipline and in its movement from the margins towards the mainstream.

Notwithstanding this, we believe that DH must now reflect on the centrality that such motifs continue to be given when retelling its history and to ask whether new motifs are needed as the discipline moves forward. Three arguments can be put forward in support of this claim. The first is the disquiet of some of its members at the way the field continues to trade in outmoded and inaccurate metaphors. As Rockwell put it: 'What concerns me … is that within digital humanities we are still trading stories, we're still acting as if we're the underdog and we're not' (2011). Thus, there is a discord between how the field portrays its situation and the realities of that situation. Our second and third arguments are framed in terms of the complications that we hold to arise from this.

Above we demonstrated that the revolutionary motif occurs often in the literature of the field but that it is poorly defined. Our second argument is that the motif is also an inadequate means of communicating the aims of the discipline to other researchers and members of the public. This is evidenced by the way that DH is portrayed (or sometimes vilified in the mainstream media). Since 2012, a rush of essays and opinion pieces have appeared in publications like, inter alia, the *New Republic* (Kirsch 2014), the *Los Angeles Review of Books* (Marche 2012), the *New York Times* (Leroi 2015) and *Inside Higher Ed* (Straumsheim 2014). These essays are mostly written by non-specialists in the area of DH and the publications they appear in have far greater readerships than the typical academic journal. In them the field's revolutionary intent is often emphasised and accorded a degree of destructive import that it does not usually have in the DH literature. Kirsch, for example, argues that DH poses an existential threat to Humanities and that its revolutionary rhetoric has an 'undertone of menace, the threat of historical illegitimacy and obsolescence' (2014).

He goes on to argue that the parity that DH accords to building, tool-making and images, on one side, and thinking and writing, on the other, is a threat to the Humanities:

> In this vision, the very idea of language as the basis of a humane education—even of human identity—seems to give way to a post- or pre-verbal discourse of pictures and objects. Digital humanities becomes another name for the obsequies of humanism (ibid).

The reaction often made to such essays by the DH community is that their writers do not seem to understand DH or what it aims to do. This is a reasonable response. However, the more important question of how and why such egregious misunderstandings and misrepresentations arise seems to go unasked. Numerous texts have appeared that seek to define DH (see, for example, Terras et al. 2013). Yet, while Kirsch and others have failed to grasp the basics of what the field does they certainly have not failed to grasp its supposedly revolutionary nature. As it continues to move from the margins towards the mainstream DH must pay more careful attention to how it is communicated to the public and to those outside of its immediate frame of reference. A crucial prerequisite of such a development is a critical analysis of the usefulness of the revolutionary rhetoric that it often uses to describe and project itself.

The third argument that we will put forward also pertains to the future of the field. Above we argued that the motif of the revolutionary offered DH a way of discovering its *raison d'etre* and a means of coalescing around a common goal (if even to reject that goal, as we have seen in some of the articles cited above). Yet, looking at the scholarly areas that DH has been criticised for not engaging with, one wonders whether the motif of the revolutionary has paradoxically proven to be one that shut down truly radical thinking? After all, if one is assured of their revolutionary status what need is there to reflect critically on the agenda and research trajectory of the discipline? We might go further and say that in such circumstances it is not even necessary for a "revolutionary" discipline to articulate what makes it revolutionary. As discussed in Chap. 1, the field has been convincingly criticised for its paucity of engagement with issues that are at the heart of the unfolding encounter between human and machine, for example, cultural criticism, gender issues, postcolonialism and posthumanism (and, we would add, emerging modes and structures of knowledge production and digital epistemology). Though some progress in relation to such lacunae can be noted of late, we propose that responding to such 'grand challenges' will involve not only new research agenda but a wider reflection on the ways that the field perceives and projects itself, and how this may be advance or stifle its progress. The shaking off of its revolutionary mantle may well be important in this regard.

In conclusion, then, as DH becomes more institutionalised and mainstream, we ask whether it can and should maintain its revolutionary and radical discourse about its origins? Whereas once such rhetoric may have fostered 'an overall purpose and cohesion' (Taylor 1976) we ask whether it is still performing such a service today? Does creating a sense of purpose and cohesion have the same importance and weight that it once did? Indeed, could the means of achieving this have also served to circumscribe the intellectual agenda of the field? We believe that it is important that the community pays closer and more critical attention to the stories, metaphors and labels that it uses to describe itself and to the impact this has not only on how those outside DH perceive it but also on how DH understands its frame of reference. Is it time to become more aware of the stories that are told and to ask whether new stories and foundation myths and, most of all, new and more critical histories of DH are needed? We propose that in this way a better understanding of the history of computing in the Humanities has the potential to contribute to conversations that are as relevant to the present and the future as they are to the past.

References

Abrams, L. (2010). *Oral history theory*. Abingdon: Routledge.
Anon. (1971). Abstracts and brief notices. *Computers and the Humanities, 6*(1), 59–64.
Beacham, R., & Denard, H. (2003). The Pompey project: Digital research and virtual reconstruction of Rome's first theatre. *Computers and the Humanities, 37*(1), 129–139.

Beatie, B. A. (1967). Computer study of medieval German poetry: A conference report. *Computers and the Humanities, 2*(2), 65–70.

Becher, T. (1989). *Academic tribes and territories: Intellectual enquiry and the cultures of disciplines.* Milton Keynes/Bristol: Open University Press.

Bolton, W. (1991). Opinion. *Computers and the Humanities, 25*(6), 431–432.

Bosak, J. (1999). XML ubiquity and the scholarly community. *Computers and the Humanities, 33*(1–2), 199–206.

Brink, D. (1990). Input…output. *Computers and the Humanities, 24*(1–2), 105–106.

Brown, R. (2001). *Group processes* (2nd ed.). Oxford/Malden: Wiley-Blackwell.

Burton, D. M. (1981). Automated concordances and word indexes: The fifties. *Computers and the Humanities, 15*(1), 1–14.

Busa, R. (1980). The annals of humanities computing: The index thomisticus. *Computers and the Humanities, 14*(2), 83–90.

Byerly, G. A. (1978). CAI in college English. *Computers and the Humanities, 12*(3), 281–285.

Cramer, H., & Taylor, I. (1973). Computer language: An innovation in the liberal arts curriculum. *Computers and the Humanities, 7*(6), 417–418.

Crane, G., Seales, B., & Terras, M. (2009). Cyberinfrastructure for classical philology. *Digital Humanities Quarterly, 3*(1). Available at: http://www.digitalhumanities.org/dhq/vol/003/1/000023/000023.html. Accessed 4 Mar 2016.

Crozier, M. (2001). A problematic discipline: The identity of Australian political studies. *Australian Journal of Political Science, 36*(1), 22.

DeBloois, M. (1984). Designing instructional materials for the humanities: Is there a role for interactive videodisc technology? *Computers and the Humanities, 18*(3–4), 189–193.

Ess, C. (2000). Wag the dog? Online conferencing and teaching. *Computers and the Humanities, 34*(3), 297–309.

Fish, S. (2012). The digital humanities and the transcending of mortality. *Opinionator, the New York Times.* Available at: http://opinionator.blogs.nytimes.com/2012/01/09/the-digital-humanities-and-the-transcending-of-mortality/. Accessed 9 Feb 2014.

Gold, M. K. (2012). Whose revolution? Towards a more equitable digital humanities. *The Lapland Chronicles.* Available at: http://mkgold.net/blog/2012/01/10/whose-revolution-toward-a-more--equitable-digital-humanities/. Accessed 7 July 2012.

Goldfield, J. D. (1993). An argument for single-author and similar studies using quantitative methods: Is there safety in numbers? *Computers and the Humanities, 27*(5–6), 365–374.

Holmes, D. I., Robertson, M., & Paez, R. (2001). Stephen Crane and the New-York tribune: A case study in traditional and non-traditional authorship attribution. *Computers and the Humanities, 35*(3), 315–331.

Jessop, M. (2008). Digital visualization as a scholarly activity. *Literary and Linguistic Computing, 23*(3), 281–293.

Juola, P. (2008). Killer applications in digital humanities. *Literary and Linguistic Computing, 23*(1), 73–83.

Kaltenbrunner, W. (2015). Scholarly labour and digital collaboration in literary studies. *Social Epistemology, 29*(2), 207–233.

Kirsch, A. (2014). Technology is taking over English departments. *The New Republic.* Available at http://www.newrepublic.com/article/117428/limits-digital-humanities-adam-kirsch. Accessed 3 May 2014.

Lawrence, J. S., et al. (1986). Software reviews. *Computers and the Humanities, 20*(2), 111–145.

Leroi, A. M. (2015). Digitizing the humanities. *The New York Times.* Available at: http://www.nytimes.com/2015/02/14/opinion/digitizing-the-humanities.html. Accessed 6 Mar 2015.

Mahoney, M. S. (2005). The histories of computing(s). *Interdisciplinary Science Reviews, 30*(2), 119–135.

Mahoney, M. S. (2011). In H. Thomas (Ed.), *Histories of computing.* Cambridge, MA: Harvard University Press.

Marche, S. (2012). Literature is not data: Against digital humanities. In *Los Angeles review of books*. Available at: http://lareviewofbooks.org/essay/literature-is-not-data-against-digital-humanities/. Accessed 9 Feb 2014.

Maron, N. L., & Pickle, S. (2014). *Sustaining the digital humanities. Host institution support beyond the start-up phase*. Ithaka S + R. Available at: http://sr.ithaka.org/sites/default/files/SR_Supporting_Digital_Humanities_20140618f.pdf. Accessed 11 Feb 2015.

McCarty, W. (2008). What's going on? *Literary and Linguistic Computing, 23*(3), 253–261.

McCarty, W. (2013). What does Turing have to do with Busa? In F. Mambrini, M. Passarotti, & C. Sporleder (Eds), *Proceedings of the third workshop on annotation of corpora for research in the humanities (ACRH-3)*. The third workshop on Annotation of Corpora for Research in the Humanities (ACRH-3). The institute of information and communication technologies, Bulgarian Academy of Sciences, pp. 1–14. Available at: http://www.mccarty.org.uk/essays/McCarty,%20Turing%20and%20Busa.pdf. Accessed 1 Jan 2016.

McCarty, W. (2014). Getting there from here. Remembering the future of digital humanities (Roberto Busa Award lecture 2013). *Literary and Linguistic Computing, 29*(3), 283–306.

McCarty, W., et al. (2012). Questioning, asking and enduring curiosity: An oral history conversation between Julianne Nyhan and Willard McCarty. *Digital Humanities Quarterly, 6*(3). Available at: http://www.digitalhumanities.org/dhq/vol/6/3/000134/000134.html. Accessed 11 Nov 2015.

Milic, L. T. (1982). The annals of computing: Stylistics. *Computers and the Humanities, 16*(1), 19–24.

Nyhan, J. (2016). In search of identities in the digital humanities: the early history of humanist. In J. Molloy (Ed.), *Social media archaeology and poetics*. Cambridge, MA: MIT Press.

Olsen, M. (1993). Signs, symbols and discourses: A new direction for computer-aided literature studies. *Computers and the Humanities, 27*(5–6), 309–314.

Ott, W. (1979). A text processing system for the preparation of critical editions. *Computers and the Humanities, 13*(1), 29–35.

Porsdam, H. (2013). Digital humanities: On finding the proper balance between qualitative and quantitative ways of doing research in the humanities. *Digital Humanities Quarterly, 7*(3). Available at: http://www.digitalhumanities.org/dhq/vol/7/3/000167/000167.html. Accessed 4 Mar 2016.

Passerini, L. (1979). Work, ideology and consensus under Italian fascism. *History Workshop, 8*, 82–108.

Portelli, A. (1981). The peculiarities of oral history. *History Workshop, 12*, 96–107.

Portelli, A. (2006). What makes oral history different? In A. Thomson (Ed.), *The oral history reader*. London: Routledge.

Potter, R. G. (1991). Statistical analysis of literature: A retrospective on computers and the humanities, 1966–1990. *Computers and the Humanities, 25*(6), 401–429.

Potter, R. G. (1996). What computers are good for in the literature classroom. *Computers and the Humanities, 30*(2), 181–190.

Prather, R. E., & Elliott, R. S. (1988). SML: A structured musical language. *Computers and the Humanities, 22*(2), 137–151.

Prescott, A. (2012a). Consumers, creators or commentators? Problems of audience and mission in the digital humanities. *Arts and Humanities in Higher Education, 11*(1–2), 61–75.

Prescott, A. (2012b). Making the digital human: Anxieties, possibilities, challenges. *Digital Riffs*. Available at: http://digitalriffs.blogspot.co.uk/2012/07/making-digital-human-anxieties.html. Accessed 31 Oct 2012.

Presner, T., et al. (2009). *The digital humanities manifesto 2.0*. Available at: http://www.humanitiesblast.com/manifesto/Manifesto_V2.pdf. Accessed 1 Dec 2011.

Raben, J. (1991). Humanities computing 25 years later. *Computers and the Humanities, 25*(6), 341–350.

Robinson, P., & Taylor, K. (1998). Publishing an electronic textual edition: The case of the wife of Bath's prologue on CD-ROM. *Computers and the Humanities, 32*(4), 271–284.

Rockwell, G. (2011). Inclusion in the digital humanities. *Philosophi.ca*. Available at: http://www. philosophi.ca/pmwiki.php/Main/InclusionInTheDigitalHumanities. Accessed 20 Jan 2011.

Rockwell, G. (2012). Trading stories: An oral history conversation between Geoffrey Rockwell and Julianne Nyhan. *Digital Humanities Quarterly, 6*(3). Available at http://www.digitalhumanities.org/dhq/vol/6/3/000135/000135.html. Accessed 10 Mar 2015.

Samuel, R., & Thompson, P. (Eds.). (1990). *The myths we live by*. London: Routledge.

Sands, A. E. (1967). MLA, ERIC, and the future. *Computers and the Humanities, 1*(4), 113–122.

Schneider, E. W., & Bennion, J. L. (1982). The McKay institute videodisc project: Rationale, history, and goals. *Computers and the Humanities, 16*(1), 35–37.

Siemens, R., et al. (2012). Video-gaming, paradise lost and TCP/IP: An oral history conversation between Ray Siemens and Anne Welsh. *Digital Humanities Quarterly, 6*(3). Available at: http://www.digitalhumanities.org/dhq/vol/6/3/000131/000131.html. Accessed 2 Nov 2015.

Smith, M. (1994). Technical reviews. *Computers and the Humanities, 28*(4–5), 311–316.

Spiro, L. (2012). "This is why we fight": Defining the values of digital humanities. In M. K. Gold (Ed.), *Debates in the digital humanities* (pp. 16–35). Minneapolis: University of Minnesota Press.

Straumsheim, C. (2014). *Digital humanities bubble*. Inside Higher Ed. Available at: https://www. insidehighered.com/news/2014/05/08/digital-humanities-wont-save-humanities-digital-humanists-say#sthash.8ixV4wNi.dpbs. Accessed 8 Mar 2015.

Taylor, P. J. (1976). An interpretation of the quantification debate in British geography. *Transactions of the Institute of British Geographers, 1*(2), 129–142.

Terras, M., den Branden, R. V., & Vanhoutte, E. (2009). Teaching TEI: The need for TEI by example. *Literary and Linguistic Computing, 24*(3), 297–306.

Terras, M., Nyhan, J., & Vanhoutte, E. (Eds.). (2013). *Defining digital humanities: A reader*. Surrey/Burlington: Ashgate Publishing.

Tilly, C. (1973). Computers in historical analysis. *Computers and the Humanities, 7*(6), 323–335.

Unsworth, J., et al. (2012). Postmodern culture and more: An oral history conversation between John Unsworth and Anne Welsh. *Digital Humanities Quarterly, 6*(3). Available at: http://www. digitalhumanities.org/dhq/vol/6/3/000132/000132.html. Accessed 4 Mar 2016.

Trowler, P., Saunders, M., & Bamber, V. (Eds.). (2012). *Tribes and territories in the 21st century: Rethinking the significance of disciplines in higher education*. London: Routledge.

Open Access This chapter is distributed under the terms of the Creative Commons Attribution-Noncommercial 2.5 License (http://creativecommons.org/licenses/by-nc/2.5/) which permits any noncommercial use, distribution, and reproduction in any medium, provided the original author(s) and source are credited.

The images or other third party material in this chapter are included in the work's Creative Commons license, unless indicated otherwise in the credit line; if such material is not included in the work's Creative Commons license and the respective action is not permitted by statutory regulation, users will need to obtain permission from the license holder to duplicate, adapt or reproduce the material.

Chapter 18
Conclusion

Abstract In this concluding chapter we explore some of the ways that the oral history interviews included in this book can be 'read'. We give particular attention to an approach to the interviews that we find intriguing and productive: how they reinforce, extend or problematize current scholarship on the history of DH, or the history of computing more generally. A case in point is the nature of the relationship that existed between DH and the wider computing industry, especially from the 1950s–1970s. We argue that the interviews included here, and the oral history methodology that underpins them, help to recover a more nuanced picture of the origins and history of DH (and computing in the Humanities more generally). They grant insights into the social, cultural, intellectual and creative processes that shaped the field's uptake and development and address how such processes were sometimes aided and sometimes hindered by external circumstances. They also provide new insights into the role of individual agency in the way they address some of the experiences and motivations of individuals who contributed to the development of this field. Such experiences are otherwise very difficult, if not impossible, to investigate using the extant professional literature. In this way, we believe that this book pushes forward the current boundaries of scholarship on the history of DH.

The interviews included here provide new information about, and reflections on, the history of DH. They include insights into the social, cultural, intellectual and creative processes that shaped its uptake and development and address how such processes were sometimes aided and sometimes hindered by external circumstances. They also provide new insights into the role of individual agency in the way they address some of the experiences and motivations of individuals who contributed to the development of this field. Such experiences are otherwise very difficult, if not impossible, to investigate using the extant professional literature. Thus, the interviews included here and the oral history methodology adopted help to recover a more nuanced picture of the origins and history of computing in the Humanities and allow questions related to this to be further explored. In this way, we believe that this book pushes forward the current boundaries of scholarship on the history of DH.

© The Author(s) 2016
J. Nyhan, A. Flinn, *Computation and the Humanities*, Springer Series on
Cultural Computing, DOI 10.1007/978-3-319-20170-2_18

It is possible to 'read' these interviews in many ways. Each individual interview may be read in an immersive way. They may also be read non-consecutively and dipped in and out of in a more thematically-driven fashion (of course, the print format is somewhat limiting in this regard but the common core of questions that each interview is built around will aid the reader in this, to some extent). They may be read for what they contain or equally for what they do not contain. By reading them in conjunction with their audio recordings they may be read as much at the level of narrative as meta-narrative (for example, in terms of the interaction between interviewer and interviewee, or taken as a group, between the individual and the academic discipline as a community that shared stories and ways of sense-making). In turn, they may be interpreted according to any number of analytical frameworks drawn from areas such as literature, linguistics or psychology. Indeed, a further book that will take up the analysis and interpretation of all the interviews we have conducted is planned.

Another approach to the interviews that we find particularly intriguing and productive is to read them in terms of how they reinforce, extend or problematize current scholarship on the history of DH, or the history of computing more generally. A case in point is the nature of the relationship that existed between DH and the wider computing industry, especially from the 1950s to 1970s. Aspects of this relationship are brought out in the extant secondary literature. For example, it is often mentioned that Roberto Busa benefitted from the funding and technical expertise of IBM for almost 30 years. Jones (forthcoming) has done much to illuminate the nature of their relationship during its first 10 years, from 1949 to 1959. It is also known that John W. Ellison received the technical support of Remington Rand to complete his concordance to the Bible which was published in 1957. In Chap. 1, we mentioned how many early DH conferences were sponsored by IBM and Vanhoutte has also written how:

> The first monographs about computers in the humanities, however, came from the computer industry. In 1971, IBM published a series of application manuals on computing in the Humanities: *Introduction to Computers in the Humanities … Literary Data Processing …* and *Computers in Anthropology and Archaeology*. Almost a decade later, and after thirty years of computing in the humanities, supporters on both sides of the Atlantic were treated to two textbooks on the topic which appeared in the same week in January 1980 (2013, p. 130).

The interviews published here have provided new information on another aspect of this relationship, namely the training that a number of Digital Humanities scholars received from or in the computer industry. This training was formal in the sense that they took formal courses or informal in the sense that it was possible for them to acquire their computing knowledge partly as a result of the conditions that they encountered when working with such companies. For example, regarding the interviews contained in this book, in the mid-1960s, Harris (see Chap. 8) was initially trained in computing by IBM at the Jet Propulsion Lab (JPL) in Pasadena, California. Rutimann (see Chap. 11) also took training courses with IBM at the end of the 1960s. Around the same time Malloy (see Chap. 7) took training in FORTRAN in the Ball Brothers Research Corporation, where she then worked. Hockey recalled that she learned FORTRAN in the 1970s at the Atlas Computer Laboratory (which was not a commercial business but was set up by the British government to support the educational sector) partly through self-instruction and partly through attending what seem to have been informal tutorials and asking her colleagues for assistance.

Relevant also are the wider opportunities that were opened to interviewees as a result of their connections with the computer industry. For example, Ott (see Chap. 4) mentions how his initial connection with Bonifatius Fischer in the late 1960s came about through Dr Hübner of IBM (who had earlier worked in the Classics Department in Tübingen before he went to IBM). As Nitti explains in his interview (see Chap. 9), he did not take training from industry but was deeply inspired by the computer hardware shows that he attended. The partnerships that he forged there allowed him to apply bespoke technologies that would otherwise have been unavailable to him to use in his lexicographical research.

To the best of our knowledge, this aspect of the wider connections that existed between the emerging field of DH (especially at the earlier Humanities Computing stage) and the wider computing industry has not received sustained attention in the literature on the history of DH. Indeed, it is often assumed that those working at an earlier stage simply would not have had access to training in computing because Computer Science as a formal discipline was not established until c.1965. The interviews that we have so far conducted show that this is an oversimplification in that it focuses on the university context only and DH researchers were clearly able to gain access to training via other routes. Thus, it seems reasonable to suggest that the nature of the relationship that existed with the wider computing industry deserves more attention. Mahoney's research on the formation of the fields of theoretical computer science and software engineering argues that "people engaged in new enterprises bring their histories to the task, often different histories reflecting their different backgrounds and training" (2005, p. 120). In the context of the history of DH, the interviews included in this book suggest that we should look further than the immediate context of the Humanities and the University in order to more fully understand such backgrounds and training.

Reference

Mahoney, M. S. (2005, June 1). The histories of computing(s). *Interdisciplinary Science Reviews, 30*(2), 119–135. doi:10.1179/030801805X25927.

Open Access This chapter is distributed under the terms of the Creative Commons Attribution-Noncommercial 2.5 License (http://creativecommons.org/licenses/by-nc/2.5/) which permits any noncommercial use, distribution, and reproduction in any medium, provided the original author(s) and source are credited.

The images or other third party material in this chapter are included in the work's Creative Commons license, unless indicated otherwise in the credit line; if such material is not included in the work's Creative Commons license and the respective action is not permitted by statutory regulation, users will need to obtain permission from the license holder to duplicate, adapt or reproduce the material.

Index

© The Author(s) 2016
J. Nyhan, A. Flinn, *Computation and the Humanities*, Springer Series on
Cultural Computing, DOI 10.1007/978-3-319-20170-2

Printed in the United States
by Bookmasters

Printed in the United States
By Bookmasters